Ana
June 2016

Flawe

Flawed Logics

Strategic Nuclear Arms Control from Truman to Obama

JAMES H. LEBOVIC

The Johns Hopkins University Press
Baltimore

Printed in the United States of America on acid-free paper
2 4 6 8 9 7 5 3 1

The Johns Hopkins University Press
2715 North Charles Street
Baltimore, Maryland 21218-4363
www.press.jhu.edu

Library of Congress Cataloging-in-Publication Data
Lebovic, James H.
Flawed logics : strategic nuclear arms control from
Truman to Obama / James H. Lebovic.
pages cm
Includes bibliographical references and index.
ISBN 978-1-4214-1102-6 (pbk. : alk. paper)
ISBN 978-1-4214-1103-3 (electronic)
ISBN 1-4214-1102-4 (pbk. : alk. paper)
ISBN 1-4214-1103-2 (electronic)
1. Nuclear arms control—United States—History—20th century.
2. Presidents—United States. 3. Arms control—Decision making.
4. United States—Defenses. 5. United States—Military policy. I. Title.
JZ5687.L44 2013
327.1'7470973—dc23 2013004822

A catalog record for this book is available from the British Library.

The Johns Hopkins University Press uses environmentally friendly book materials, including recycled text paper that is composed of at least 30 percent post-consumer waste, whenever possible.

To Holly

CONTENTS

PREFACE

In this book I offer a critical intellectual history of bilateral nuclear arms negotiations from the Truman through Obama administrations. I argue that realists are correct to insist that states propose or accept the terms of treaties based on assessments of relative advantage. I also establish, however, that U.S. policymakers accepted vulnerabilities under strategic nuclear arms treaties that were not easily offset and rejected terms that promised benefits, at limited cost and risk. I attribute these anomalous findings to prevailing beliefs about the "security threat" and, more directly, to constructs and measures that U.S. policymakers employed to understand and solve arms control policy problems. In this, I recognize that assumptions about Russian (Soviet) goals dictated the points of reference in the arms control debate: these assumptions were a driving, dividing, and (largely) unyielding force in arms control. But they were evaluated from a distance—and poorly informed U.S. policy—throughout the Cold War and post–Cold War periods.

I assume that the U.S. experience in nuclear arms control has much to say about the general challenges for arms control—that nuclear arms control is not an exception to the rules of a security dilemma. Although nuclear weapons are peculiarly destructive and were largely the monopoly of two major powers in a rivalry of unprecedented global proportions, they are, for those very reasons, plausibly the exception that proves the rule. By merit of their "exceptional" standing, these weapons were subject to more scrutiny and debate—in academia, think tanks, and government—than any other weapon of the post–World War II era. That severe maladies in thinking about the purposes and consequences of using these weapons still exist suggests that the book's conclusions rest soundly on a "hard" or "unlikely" case. These intellectual shortcomings are plausibly more prevalent and severe, then, when the stakes for the participants (indeed, for humanity) are lower.

The book is structured around five central periods: (1) the Truman through Eisenhower years, which are examined together to disclose the central features of the initial U.S. forays into arms control; (2) the Kennedy years, which, while small in number, produced the first major U.S. nuclear arms control achievement (the 1963 Limited Test Ban Treaty); (3) the Johnson through Carter years, which bookend the negotiating of pivotal agreements pertaining to arms control (the Strategic Arms Limitation Talks (SALT) I, Antiballistic Missile (ABM), and SALT II treaties); (4) the Reagan years, which saw a pullback from past treaties and negotiating practices and eventually produced the Intermediate-Range Nuclear Forces (INF) Treaty, with its important precedents in arms control; and (5) the George H. W. Bush through Obama years, which produced four major treaties focused on arms reduction—the Strategic Arms Reduction Treaty (START) I, START II, the Strategic Offensive Reduction Treaty (SORT), and New START—and the U.S. withdrawal from another, the ABM Treaty.

To assist my purposes, I adopt several useful practices. First, in chapters 2 through 5, I examine the strategic environment of a period and U.S. doctrinal responses. I then assess U.S. relative advantages and disadvantages under the terms of each of the major arms control treaties, as viewed by competing sets of U.S. policymakers. I conclude each chapter by presenting conflicting views of Russian goals that drove policy in a period, the domestic politics that led some assumptions about these goals to prevail over others, and an analysis of the logic by which arms control positions were forged and tied to these assumptions. I argue that domestic politics and prevailing beliefs, no less than the international-threat environment, shaped the treaty terms that U.S. policymakers accepted and rejected.

Second, to reinforce the centrality of ideas, I give "numbers" only tertiary treatment. As a rule, they are introduced only as necessary to detail the basic terms of an arms control treaty and then, typically in a small number of introductory paragraphs. I seek, therefore, to establish that—pretensions aside—judgments about treaty terms were far more sensitive to the underlying assumptions of the protagonists about the size and value of the numbers than to the fact of "balances" or "imbalances." I discuss these assumptions as they pertain to each of the various treaties in light of the principles "peace through strength" and "trust but verify." I argue that, in each instance, U.S. policymakers differed in their conceptions of "strength" and willingness to "trust" the Russians, though most policymakers denied that they relied, at all, upon trust.

Third, I emphasize the "big debates" over U.S. nuclear strategies that undergirded U.S. thinking about Cold War–era arms control. By juxtaposing "hawkish" and "dovish" positions on the purposes and uses of nuclear weapons, I seek to convey schools of thought, as propounded by the most thoughtful proponents of a given position. One useful consequence of offering these "collective" viewpoints is establishing that the same arguments and concerns surfaced repeatedly in the U.S. policy debate, whatever the specific issue at hand. (Indeed, the same individuals—Henry Kissinger, Paul Nitze, Henry Jackson, Richard Perle, James Schlesinger, Edward Teller, Walter Slocombe, and Paul Warnke among them—were active participants in treaty negotiations and ensuing ratification debates over multiple decades.) Admittedly, this practice risks implying that policy participants tended, in general, to hold firm, extensive, and uniform beliefs about the costs and benefits of a treaty. For our purposes, the net benefits of fostering that implication exceed the costs inasmuch as viewpoints did tend to polarize around fundamental beliefs and assumptions. To avoid creating artificial logical inconsistencies, however, by combining the thoughts of different people, qualifiers are added to highlight divisions within a given school of thought. Thus, I observe, for example, that hawks held divergent views. Some U.S. policymakers borrowed from war-fighting principles when arguing that the United States required military options for bargaining with the Soviet Union and for weakening it, should deterrence fail. Others believed that the United States should acquire the means to fight and prevail in a nuclear war with the Soviet Union. Whereas the former generally saw the Soviets as opportunistic, conflicted, and capable of miscalculating and stumbling into war, the latter invariably viewed the Soviet Union as expansionist, aggressive, unyielding, striving for dominance, and accepting of violence. For an excellent discussion of these positions, see Seay (1989).

Fourth, I make no claim that the logic or illogic of arms control translates into success or failure, in terms of gaining the upper hand, at the bargaining table. The U.S. record of accomplishment here was certainly mixed. Apparent "failures" include the Harry Truman administration's efforts to internationalize control of nuclear weapons and the Dwight Eisenhower administration's Atoms for Peace, Open Skies, and test ban proposals. Apparent "successes" include the Limited Test Ban Treaty in the John F. Kennedy administration, the SALT I Treaty of the Richard Nixon administration, the INF Treaty of the Ronald Reagan administration (not technically a "strategic arms" pact but intimately connected to strategic nuclear negotiations and weaponry), START I of the George H. W. Bush administration, SORT in the George W. Bush administration, and New START in the Barack Obama administration. Outcomes between success and failure also spanned the decades: the Reagan, George H. W. Bush, and William Clinton administrations fought the constraints of the ABM Treaty, which had been negotiated in the Nixon administration; the Carter administration—encountering overwhelming opposition—pulled the SALT II Treaty from Senate consideration; and the Clinton administration could not obtain Senate approval of the Russian Parliament's terms for accepting START II. But, as we shall see, negotiating success and failure say little about the viability of the ideas that drove U.S. arms control policies.

Finally, I rely in great part on public documents and the "public debate," although I draw also from declassified sources and the abundant secondary literature on presidential decision-making in arms control. I assume that public pronouncements, no less than private utterances, discussions, and confidences (as gleaned from diaries, memos, and meeting transcripts), provide important evidence of the thinking behind arms control policies. Obviously, participants have political motives to distort or hide their "true" positions when addressing a broad public audience, and these reasons (and their potential impact on the documentary record) must be noted. But public statements, as in the give and take of congressional testimony, provide participants an opportunity to articulate, develop, and refine their views.

I do not pretend to offer the last word on the subject. My basic conclusions are likely insensitive to the arrival of new documentary material (or dramatic revelations), however, for they rest on striking patterns across time, issue, and political ideology.

I have been working on this book, at some level, for many decades. The reason, I would like to pretend, is that I could do no less, living with the bomb as a child of the Cold War. The truth is that I was consumed early in life by the politics of the period—a time in which dueling partisans, with the ardor of true believers, vented prescriptions to save humanity from nuclear obliteration. It is the politics—and the pretense—of that period that inspired me finally to write this book. My hope is that it will show that, despite enormous attention to an all-important problem, the best and the brightest of multiple generations, convinced of their logic and rectitude, were still able to rely on dubious arguments. The book is written, then, as a plea for humility and civility as we continue to cope with vexing problems in difficult times. We survived the Cold War and the policymakers and intellectuals who fought it at home; maybe that was mostly due to good fortune.

In its long journey to completion, the book has benefited from the contributions of friends and colleagues who have encouraged me, supported me, or argued with me along the way, all of which made this a stronger work. It benefited more directly from comments on conference papers that I received from the initial chapter drafts written during my sabbatical leave in the 2009–10 academic year. For those useful remarks I thank the various participants in panels at the annual meetings of the American Political Science Association in Washington, D.C., (where I presented chapter 2) and the International Studies Association in Montreal and San Diego (where I presented parts of chapters 1 and 4, respectively). I owe a special debt of gratitude to panel discussants Michael Desch, Charles Glaser, and James Wirtz. I also express my appreciation to Todd Sechser and other members of the Department of Politics, University of Virginia, for inviting me to give a talk on arms control and for the useful feedback that I received (on parts of chapter 4). Appreciation is due, as well, to Elizabeth Saunders, from up the hall, who generously agreed to include arms control among the issues on the weekly agenda of the Department of Political Science's Vietnam Study Group, of which we remain the only members—and to various other colleagues at the George Washington University who made a point or offered a fact, here and there, that found its way into this book. I am indebted to the anonymous reader from the Johns Hopkins University Press for providing useful criticism; Martin Schneider, who copyedited the manuscript with great care and attention to detail; and especially to Greg Koblentz, who responded to my request for comments on the manuscript in fourteen thoughtful, single-spaced pages. For those comments, I hope that I am eternally grateful. I also thank Suzanne Flinchbaugh, my editor at the Johns Hopkins University Press, for believing in this project, providing useful advice on framing my argument, and carrying the manuscript through the publication process.

I reserve my greatest expression of gratitude for my wife, Holly, to whom this book is dedicated. If we ever had reason to discuss arms control, she, too, would surely have believed in the book. But, as always, she gave me her support.

Flawed Logics

Introduction

Arms Control and the Power of Belief

The logic—or, rather, the illogic—of the U.S. approach to strategic nuclear arms control is featured in this book, which is written with a hint of irony. In negotiating the control of strategic nuclear weapons, U.S. officials weighed the numbers carefully to get a better deal, to split differences to close a deal, and to create offsets to sweeten a deal. Given the stakes, they could do no less: these weapons can travel intercontinental distances, from land, air, or sea, to destroy entire cities. But their sense of security derived not from objective readings of the *numbers;* instead it drew on underlying *beliefs* about U.S. benefits and costs under the proposed or accepted terms of an agreement. These beliefs provided a deficient understanding of whether, how, and when various arms control treaties with Russia worked to the U.S. advantage or disadvantage. Consequently, the terms of these treaties were never as good as U.S. proponents claimed—or as bad as opponents feared.[1]

By the 1960s, a major problem was that U.S. policymakers gave too little thought, in turn, to whether, how, and when Russia (given its goals) might be inclined to use nuclear weapons. Their thinking produced a perverse paradox: U.S. policymakers divided ideologically—as hawks and doves—on their assumptions about Russian goals yet ignored these same assumptions in developing their arguments. They concentrated, instead, on operational matters—preserving force structures (the U.S. triad of air, land, and sea capabilities), various balances and imbalances (which favored the United States or Russia), and "loopholes" in treaties for cheating—that were consequential only because of those assumptions.

The logic of arms control suffered, accordingly, from two main deficiencies. First, it was incomplete: advocates for and against various treaty provisions took vague positions on key specifics or left basic questions unanswered. Whereas hawkish analysts highlighted unfavorable "imbalances" in numerical aggregates and in various types of weapons in various locations, their reasoning centered far more on the fact of an imbalance than on the actual utility of the weapons that were involved. They failed to ask, what benefits do the Soviets derive from the alleged advantages, and how will the Soviets realize or capitalize on them? It was one thing to claim that the Soviets could employ their silo-killing, land-based missiles in a disarming strike on U.S. land-based missiles; it was quite another to establish that the United States—given its formidable surviving assets (on the land, in the sea, and in the air)—had to address an underlying asymmetry in U.S. and Soviet land-based missile capabilities. Second, the logic was inconsistent: advocates supported or opposed treaty terms by employing contradictory arguments. For example, critics derided the 1972 Strategic Arms Limitation Talks (SALT) I Treaty for weakening the U.S. competitive position while conceding that the Soviets were in the stronger position without a treaty. Likewise, policymakers made their case for removing U.S. intermediate-range missiles in Europe under the "zero-zero" formula of the 1987 Intermediate-Range Nuclear Forces (INF) Treaty without reconciling it with the logic—of extending deterrence to Europe—that was used to justify placing missiles there in the first place.

In consequence, neither Cold War nor post–Cold War policymakers could validly claim that the United States was actually better off with one set of treaty provisions than another—or that arms control "successes" and "failures" were all that they seemed. The United States made arms control concessions that could actually have compromised U.S. interests, and it failed, at times, to seize opportunities by making necessary concessions to achieve a useful agreement. These deficiencies in logic—on all sides of the policy debate—impugn realist assertions that states, trapped by a security dilemma, scale their arsenals to meet certain relative-capability standards.

The Security Dilemma: A Questionable Basis for Policy

The realist "security dilemma" has long shaped our understanding of why states arm and spurn disarmament even when conditions appear ripe for an international agreement that would limit or reduce national arsenals. The appeal of the logic stems largely from its compelling simplicity: in an anarchic international system, states must provide for their own security by attending first and foremost to their relative capabilities, that is, they must boost their capabilities to thwart the improvements of others (Jervis 1978). Because any gains for one state effectively amount to losses for another and because offensive and defensive weapons are indistinguishable, states must vigilantly monitor and anticipate the acquisitions of other states, err on the high side as a precaution when evaluating threat, and seek redress by procuring, deploying, and employing appropriate weaponry. In its extreme form, the dilemma has states focused entirely on the capabilities, not the intentions, of others: intentions can change quickly and dramatically, are opaque to outside parties, and are easy to disguise to lull opponents into complacency.

Although material factors—the "relative capabilities" of realist analyses—can contribute greatly to the beliefs of key U.S. policymakers about threats and the means to counter them, these beliefs form and stand apart from material capabilities and acquire prominence over others through domestic (including intragovernmental) politics. Thus, realists have a case that U.S. policymakers sought, through nuclear arms negotiations, to protect and extend U.S. prerogatives and to limit U.S. exposure to Russian cheating. Realist explanations suffer, however, when they fail to answer two critical sets of questions.

First, what makes another state's capabilities a threat? Realists are certainly correct that capabilities garner attention and facilitate action in international politics. But they must also recognize that states "play favorites" in international politics. After all, the United States never cared about maintaining a margin of nuclear superiority over British or French nuclear forces; indeed, when the Cold War ended, it downgraded the threat from a Russian nuclear force that remained perfectly capable of annihilating the United States. They must also acknowledge that a "hostile" state's capabilities are a threat only to states that lack offsetting capabilities, when the fact of "offsetting" capabilities is open to dispute. Was it necessary, then, for the United States to achieve equivalence with Soviet forces in earlier decades when a lesser U.S. force could still destroy much of the Soviet military and civilian infrastructure in a retaliatory attack? Conversely, given worst-case arguments that the Soviets might attack the United States to realize some advantage from striking first, should the United States have settled for equivalence? If U.S. policymakers really believed their public claims that the Soviets might attack without provocation, should not the United States have sought superiority to counter Soviet attack capabilities, perhaps even have struck first?

Second, how much assurance do states require, before accepting a treaty, that others will abide by it? Was the United States prudent, then, to sign treaties with the Soviets without knowing whether they would comply with them—indeed, without the capability for knowing, with certainty, whether they were complying with them? At first glance, the answer appears to be no. But arms control skeptics should not have the last word on the subject. After all, an imperfect treaty might still enhance U.S. security: compliance is never knowable with absolute certainty, is more important for some treaty provisions than others, and can dampen an arms competition, even if partial or incomplete.

These issues of power and transparency are controversial. Academics defend or contest the staunch realist view that states must offset the capabilities of others and avoid formal restrictions that would allow others to cheat. Likewise, policymakers do battle over the assertions that the United States should (1) seek "peace through strength"; and (2) "trust but verify" that others are complying with treaties. These assertions—touted by their backers (most prominently, President Ronald Reagan) as "good common sense"—leave far too much unsaid, which is indeed reason enough to doubt their validity.

"Peace through Strength"

"Peace through strength" articulates the paradoxical deterrence logic that guided U.S. nuclear weapons strategies and deployment from the beginning: simply expressed, if you want peace, prepare for war.[2] But this logic skirts essential questions: What constitutes "strength"? Could the United States obtain deterrence benefits from a level of capability that was sufficient only to punish the Soviets for their transgressions? If so, what kind of punishment would it take to produce the desirable effect? If not, what capabilities would be required to convince the Soviets to forgo a conventional or nuclear attack because it would end in a Soviet military "defeat"? As will become clear, these questions were unanswerable in a vacuum. Adequate responses required an appreciation of Soviet goals and accompanying cost tolerance.

The question of how much capability is enough has long bedeviled realists, who often draw different conclusions from the same set of assumptions. So-called offensive realists suggest that states must seek "superiority" as a hedge against risk (Mearsheimer 2001); so-called defensive realists maintain that states might settle for a capability that is "sufficient" to deter aggression even if it is insufficient to defeat an opponent in a traditional sense (Glaser 1997). The two groups divide primarily in their assumptions about whether intentions feature into assessments of threat. Accordingly, defensive realists recognize that a party can effectively signal its benign intent to others, for example by demobilizing its forces to invite re-mobilizing costs, scaling its forces for "sufficiency" rather than superiority, or increasing its exposure to the costs of war. Still, such "costly signals" make it difficult—not impossible—for the party to resort to war or to seize the offensive if it has hostile intent. An irony of a costly signal is that any signal that is strong enough to grab an adversary's attention might be strong enough to render the signaler vulnerable, preventing it from sending a convincing signal in the first place.[3]

To understand how, when, and why states cooperate and conflict with others requires a shift in focus from the material (including the mechanics of signals) to the ideational. In this book I accordingly assert that U.S. capabilities to address nuclear threats have always hinged on beliefs about when, where, and how nuclear weapons are likely to be effective. It has depended, then, on assumptions about the adversary's intent—and related beliefs about the adversary's strategies, cost acceptance, and cost-benefit calculations (before and during a nuclear conflict)—that were never duly examined.

"Trust but Verify"

"Trust but verify" appears to rest on unassailable logic for dealing with adversaries: trust only as far as you can see. The main problem with the logic stems from the word *trust*. If it means essentially that only "seeing is believing"—that trust requires knowing with certainty—trust does nothing to move negotiating parties toward agreement. To say, then, that the United States would have trusted a transparent Soviet Union is to admit backhandedly that it was not trustworthy and thus that the United States had to monitor Soviet behavior and could not accept any agreement that would permit the Soviets to cheat. In sum, it is to concede that there is "little room for trust among states" (Mearsheimer 2001: 32).

But verifying compliance with arms control treaties requires some element of trust, understood as a belief that the other party will not act as it is capable.[4] So defined, trust—like verification—is an essential part of any arms control agreement: the verification of arms control treaties "is a *judgment based on information* provided by various technical monitoring systems and based on a *guess of the intentions and trustworthiness* of the other side" (Oelrich 1990, emphasis in original). This book argues, then, that the capability to verify Russian compliance with a treaty was never absolute and always required an element of trust that the Russians valued the legal benefits of a treaty and would not undermine it. Indeed, I argue that trust permeated all aspects of the U.S.-Russia relationship: the harsh reality of the nuclear era was, in fact, that Russia could always act to the fullest extent of its capabilities to inflict unacceptable damage upon the United States. Even hawks trusted, albeit in varying degrees and respects, that Soviet leaders shared the aversions of U.S. leaders to the potential consequences of a nuclear exchange and would not attack the United States at the first opportunity. Even the hawkish-leaning Reagan administration did not simply defer to worst-case assumptions and plan dutifully around Soviet capabilities.[5] Hawks and doves disagreed over the costs and risks that Soviet leaders would willingly incur to achieve their goals, not over whether these leaders were actually trustworthy.

How Beliefs Affect Assessments of Strength and Vulnerability

It might well be, then, that realist efforts to reconcile the material and ideational have stretched realism to its breaking point, rendering it a nonfalsifiable theory that is all things to all theorists (Vasquez 1997). The intent here is not to enter that minefield, which would only distract from the thesis of this book. Contrariwise, I take the view—as a point of departure—that the security dilemma centers on physical capabilities, calculations of relative advantage, and potential uncertainty about them. I also argue, however, that U.S. bargaining positions were grounded (to their detriment) in beliefs about the capability balance—its favorableness, stability, and robustness. These beliefs informed assessments of the net benefits of adhering to the proposed or accepted terms of an arms control treaty. Although these beliefs drew heavily on judgments about adversary intent, "inequalities," "loopholes," and alleged openings to cheating typically dominated assessments of the U.S.-Soviet strategic nuclear balance, compromising their logical integrity.

The argument that policymakers are overly indebted to key referents is not new. Social scientists from various disciplines have noted that people anchor their thinking in salient indicators. Organizational theorists observe that individuals employ immediate goals as surrogates for more abstract ones, perhaps from a (rational) desire to establish clear and observable criteria for assessing organizational performance (March and Simon 1993; Steinbruner 1974). One effect of this decisional tendency is that policy centers on performance outputs that are tied only tenuously to policy success: in Vietnam, the U.S. military read progress into a high enemy "body count" based on problematic assumptions, including that the United States would eventually reach a crossover point when the enemy would die faster than it could obtain new recruits. Another effect is that policy centers on inputs rather than outputs: for example, the U.S. military measured "success" in the Vietnam War with the numbers of aircraft sorties that were flown and bomb tonnages dropped, not with measures that were tied directly to whether the United States was actually winning or losing the war. For similar reasons, organization planners and engineers focus on the performance and promise of a technology—that is, how technology *could* perform given its tantalizing potential—apart from its practical uses and fit with organizational missions—that is, how it *should* perform given actual benefits and costs (Gelber

1974; Lapp 1970; Lebovic 1996). The U.S. development of multiple independently targetable reentry vehicles (MIRVs)—for striking dispersed nuclear targets with a single missile—stemmed in part from the allure of a technology that "was too good to pass up."[6]

Cognitive psychologists offer more complete explanations, however, for the subordination of abstract ideas to concrete ones in policymaking: as psychological beings, policymakers reduce abstractions—"threats," "national security," the "balance of power," and so on—to their specifics, particulars, and tangible features. Their thinking can suffer accordingly.

First, people view superordinate concepts in light of "basic-level concepts" (Rosch et al. 1976). We grasp the concept of "dog" and "cat" earlier in life—and more easily, given the visual and auditory cues—than we do the concept of "mammal" or "animal." Similarly, we grasp the specific notion of "equality" between opposing forces more easily than a force "balance" or "equivalence" in which the characteristics of one force offset unlike characteristics of another. That two arsenals are the same in quantities and qualities is more readily apparent than that they are comparable in some aggregate sense.

Second, people give content to ideas by using exemplars (Brosius and Bathelt 1994). When we think about birds, we tend to think of robins and sparrows, not ostriches and penguins.[7] We thus imagine them flying, twirping and tweeting, or pecking for seeds and worms in a yard, not covering large areas quickly on foot or rocketing through the water. Our thinking belies our conscious acknowledgment that "bird" is actually an inclusive category and that these variants have equal standing as birds by definition. When Cold War–era analysts spoke about nuclear war in terms of "war-fighting," then, they appear to have been drawn to its familiar conventional form with tanks engaging tanks and so on in decisive combat that was confined to a largely uninhabited battlefield. In consequence, they resisted the notion that in a nuclear war, the civilian-military target distinction would erode due to the dual function of these targets, their geographical overlap, and their vulnerability to the secondary and tertiary effects of a nuclear strike. Thus, war-fighters constructed scenarios in which the Soviets attacked U.S. nuclear targets while leaving U.S. cities untouched, either to defeat the United States outright or to press it to surrender by threatening to attack those cities.

Third, people draw their ideas from salient and familiar referents rather than acquire holistic understandings of policy problems (Kahneman and Tversky 1979; Levy 1997). The effects of these referents were visible, for example, when U.S. policymakers associated nuclear "instability" with the narrow Soviet advantage in a force-on-force matchup between U.S. and Soviet land-based missiles;

equated a U.S. "assured-destruction" capability (discussed in chapter 3) with the (fairly arbitrary) level of damage that U.S. forces of the 1960s could inflict on the Soviet industrial and population base; and judged the Soviet incentive to violate an arms control treaty by its technological openings to cheating, not from the actual benefits and costs to the Soviet Union of cheating. The effects of these referents were apparent, as well, when U.S. policymakers and analysts predicted Soviet nuclear acquisitions from U.S. technological experience or potentials (as revealed through U.S. R&D) or when U.S. policymakers used U.S.-Soviet (relative) capability assessments to form judgments about Soviet goals. For example, many U.S. policymakers and analysts took the rapid Soviet closing of the nuclear capability gap and alleged Soviet nuclear superiority—especially in land-based missiles—as convincing evidence of Soviet malevolence. Such interpretations downplayed the logical possibility that the Soviets were seeking to offset anticipated U.S. capability advances in order to achieve a margin of superiority as a hedge against U.S. capability improvements, to build a force that could survive a U.S. first strike, or to reinforce the fact of U.S.-Soviet nuclear parity to build Soviet global stature (Podvig 2008: 137; Wohlforth 1993: 191). Narrow interpretations were similarly offered in response to the Soviet defense burden (military spending over GDP). The U.S. Defense Intelligence Agency (DIA) maintained that the high Soviet defense burden signified a strong Soviet commitment to defense and capacity to claim national resources. The accompanying danger was that, despite its economic disadvantages, the Soviet Union had chosen to compete with the United States. The DIA thereby defied the Central Intelligence Agency (CIA) position attributing the high defense burden to Soviet inefficiency (Berkowitz and Richelson 1995: 38–39). The cognitive appeal of these referents is undiminished by their political usefulness for "selling" a given position. Just as President Reagan employed the "zero-zero" formula (banning U.S. and Soviet intermediate-range missiles in Europe)—because its simplicity and equanimity commanded attention—to broaden support for asymmetric Soviet reductions, hard-line arms control critics referenced large and compelling margins of Soviet advantage to galvanize opposition to various treaties.

Preoccupied with the operational at the expense of assumptions about Soviet intent, U.S. policymakers insufficiently developed their logic, which bore the effects in incompleteness and inconsistency. U.S. policymakers failed to ask the key questions—when and why would Russia use its nuclear weapons?—when the answers would determine the actual favorableness of treaty terms, not any reading of the numbers in a vacuum. Thus, seemingly compelling arguments, both for and against a treaty, withered under scrutiny.

CHAPTER ONE

Initial U.S. Nuclear Arms Control Initiatives

The Truman through Eisenhower Years

The political and strategic assumptions of U.S. policymakers who pursue or resist arms control determine its fate. In the early postwar years, a policy consensus was lacking, however, over the implications of the nuclear revolution—indeed, even over whether it was a "revolution" that required a rethinking of U.S. national security goals or strategies. The Truman administration struggled with a basic question: to further its security, should the United States retain possession of nuclear weapons? Its eventual affirmative answer went unchallenged in successive administrations: in fact, the Eisenhower administration greatly increased U.S. dependence on nuclear weapons even as it pursued several control initiatives.

In the first fifteen years of the nuclear era, U.S. behavior appears appropriate under a security dilemma: the United States sought favorable treaty terms and rejected others when (Soviet) compliance with them would prove difficult to monitor. So the U.S.-Soviet negotiations of the period appear to constitute "hard cases" for establishing that ideas actually contributed to treaty outcomes. But looks are deceiving. In the negotiations, U.S. policymakers offered terms that only appeared to play to the U.S. advantage and rejected others that only appeared to advantage the Soviets. By failing to explore the full conditions under which U.S. gains and losses would occur, U.S. policymakers impeded agreements that might have served U.S. interests and, had the Soviets accepted U.S. negotiating terms, exposed the United States to risk.

The Truman Administration

It is fair to say that Truman had mixed feelings about the bomb. As vice president, he had been kept in the dark about the bomb program; upon Franklin Roosevelt's death, he inherited the bomb under trying conditions and without relevant experiences to guide its use. The end of World War II left him torn between wanting to ban these weapons through international control and harnessing them to deter aggression and reduce the threat of war. As Broscious surmises, "Truman envisaged nuclear weapons as the gateway to Armageddon," but "he reluctantly granted that under certain, unspecified conditions, they might have to be used despite their promise of destruction" (1999: 20). Indeed, for Truman, maintaining U.S. control of nuclear weapons and increasing the size of the U.S. nuclear stockpile were necessary until a satisfactory system of international controls was in place and the default option should these controls prove infeasible. Although this conflict in thinking was echoed in divisions among Truman's advisors, the administration's position on nuclear weapons and arms control evolved in three successive phases. The first of these covered the last months of World War II when the United States chose to drop nuclear bombs on two Japanese cities; the second centered on U.S. attempts to bring nuclear weapons and technology under international control; and the third covered the U.S. retreat from international control and push for a nuclear advantage.

World War II: Nuclear Weapons in War-Fighting, Preemption, and Compellence

That nuclear weapons were initially seen by policymakers as "exceptional" is conveyed by the resources, urgency, and secrecy invested in the Manhattan Project to develop the bomb. Many dozens of scientists involved with the project surely viewed the bomb in these terms and launched a rearguard effort to dissuade the president from using it against Japan after the defeat of Nazi Germany. With the potential atomic threat from Germany now neutralized, they expressed concern that using these weapons would produce catastrophic damage and undermine efforts to bring the bomb under international control.[1] Their reasoning did not prevail. The bomb was made to serve existing military strategy without having inspired much debate at the highest levels of U.S. policymaking.[2] But the bomb's alleged wartime uses and the early logical tension and controversy foreshadowed the Cold War–era nuclear debate. It would center on war-fighting, preemption, and compellence.

Paramount among the weapon's recognized uses was *fighting wars*. In the decades to follow, the idea that a nuclear war could be fought to weaken the enemy—by targeting its urban or military infrastructure—was controversial. The eventual fear was that the weapon's indiscriminate destructiveness would invite an indiscriminate adversary response. But U.S. policymakers showed little trepidation about using the bomb for military and psychological advantage against a non-nuclear Japan. In their view, the bomb had been developed to be used; indeed, the Interim Committee was tasked to advise Truman on how to employ the bomb, not whether to do so (Holloway 1994: 122). It fulfilled its mission by proposing a course that would maximize the terror value of the new weapon. It recommended dropping the bomb as soon as possible on a military target without warning so as to increase the psychological impact and minimize risks should the bomb not deliver as promised. More important to U.S. officials than whether innocents would die in a nuclear attack was whether the bomb would actually work. That the bomb might not go off was a decisive argument against demonstrating the bomb's destructiveness to Japanese officials to convince them to surrender. As Secretary of Defense Henry Stimson later described the thinking, "Nothing would have been more damaging to our effort to obtain surrender than a warning or a demonstration followed by a dud—and this was a real possibility" (Stimson 1947). If the bomb did go off, questions were raised nonetheless about whether a demonstration, minus the actual destruction, would maximize the bomb's impact (Dower 2010: 233). The United States could reap the greatest reward from the small number of nuclear weapons in the U.S. inventory by hitting a "dual target, that is, a military installation or war plant surrounded by or adjacent to homes or other buildings most susceptible to damage."[3] For the Interim Committee, the latter virtues made a target "most desirable" for producing the "greatest psychological effect." The committee expressed little concern about inflicting civilian casualties. In its judgment, "we should not concentrate on a civilian area" but "should seek to make a profound psychological impression on as many of the inhabitants as possible."[4]

The point here is simple: U.S. policymakers regarded the atomic bomb as a weapon of mass destruction that had the virtue of being very visible. Hiroshima and Nagasaki were selected as nuclear targets because their annihilation would create palpable damage for having largely escaped prior U.S. bombing, would impose direct military and industrial costs upon Japan, and would have psychological multiplier effects by taking the lives of civilian workers, their co-located families, and a sizable share of the inhabitants of these cities. After years of fighting a global war that had inflicted over four hundred thousand U.S. troop deaths and sixty million fatalities worldwide, U.S. policymakers hardly fixated on limiting damage. If anything, they had become desensitized to death, and their desire was to inflict damage—"collateral" and otherwise—to deplete enemy capabilities and resolve. Indeed, the Allies had taken to bombing populated areas in a manner that was designed to increase the civilian toll. With U.S. aircraft relying overwhelmingly on incendiary devices, military leaders selected specific urban targets in the final phases of the U.S. war effort because of their "congestion and combustibility"—and because they were "still standing." U.S. planners targeted Japan's war-making capabilities, which were defined loosely to include virtually any and all targets—transportation hubs, industries, the workforce, and the populace that provided direct and indirect support to the government (Dower 2010: 165, 185, 225). In the prelude to the nuclear attacks on Hiroshima and Nagasaki, sixty-four other Japanese cities were subject to U.S. saturation bombing, inflicting fatalities in excess of the numbers produced in the atomic bombings (Dower 2010: xxii). In one twenty-four-hour period in March 1945, around 100,000 civilians were killed in the firebombing of Tokyo alone. Thus, the unhesitating use of the atomic bomb in a densely populated area was entirely in line with previous Allied tactics (Tannenwald 2007: 79). A weapon that could kill indiscriminately with efficiency offered hope of bringing a speedy end to the war (thus avoiding a costly offensive against the main Japanese islands that could take the lives of tens, if not hundreds, of thousands of U.S. soldiers).

The bombing of Japanese cities engendered intense scholarly debate over whether it was necessary to achieve U.S. war aims—whether Japan was on the verge of surrender and whether the first, let alone the second, bomb was required to bring peace. The debate centered in part on whether the Soviet Union was actually the (indirect) target of the atomic bombing.

If so, the question arose as to whether nuclear weapons were employed effectively as instruments of preemption. The debate over preemptive uses of nuclear weapons was still to come and would have a very different focus. In the postwar period, attention focused on whether the United States should launch a preemptive attack—a potentially disarming strike against the Soviet Union as it was preparing or commencing an attack—in the hope of acquiring a meaningful advantage. Such thinking followed early U.S. flirtation with a strategy of preventive war—disarming strikes against the Soviet Union before it acquired the capability to retaliate. As we shall see, both policies were highly controversial in U.S. policy circles—though, given the inevitability of war in preemptive scenarios, the latter more than the former.[5] In 1945, neither U.S. atomic bomb strikes was preemptive, as strictly understood. But these attacks arguably were meant to preempt Soviet intervention in Asia.[6] Although Roosevelt and Churchill had sought to obtain Stalin's support for the war in Asia and had acceded to his terms at Yalta to gain his participation, Truman viewed Soviet actions in Eastern Europe with grave concern (Holloway 1994: 123). With an atomic bomb in hand, Truman might well have concluded that he need not incur additional territorial and population losses to Communism to defeat Japan. Buoyed by word of the successful U.S.

atomic bomb test at the Trinity site in the New Mexico desert, he coyly presented the news to Stalin at the Potsdam Conference (Holloway 1994: 116–117).

The case that the bomb was meant to preempt Soviet intervention is strengthened by the seeming inevitability of Japan's defeat. The Japanese navy was in ruins, U.S. forces were closing the ring around Japan's main islands and subjecting them to unrelenting attack, Soviet intervention was immediately forthcoming and would surely press Japan further to concede, and the United States was apparently willing to allow the emperor to remain as Japan's titular leader, which would become Japan's sole negotiating demand (Bernstein 1995: 240–241; Craig and Radchenko 2008: 88). Even if the Hiroshima bombing was required to force Japan's surrender, the rapid pace of the atomic bombing—with little time between the two attacks for a Japanese diplomatic response—suggests quick U.S. action to thwart Soviet territorial gains. But the case is hardly open and shut: the quick pace of attacks is far from conclusive evidence of the U.S. leadership's anti-Soviet intent. For one thing, overwhelming an opponent makes sense from a psychological perspective. If the future is really on the attacker's side, why would it merely demonstrate its strength—attack, pause, and negotiate—rather than continue to fight? Even absent a psychological rationale, the Truman administration had good reason to assume the worst and continue the onslaught: Japan had not capitulated previously despite the enormous destruction that it had suffered from air attacks. Indeed, the administration appears to have been surprised by Japan's quick surrender, virtually on U.S. terms. Moral considerations aside, it is not hard, then, to understand why the attack occurred, why the United States was preparing a third bomb for use within days of the Nagasaki attack, or why that attack was followed by devastating U.S. bomber runs intended to destroy Japan's oil refining capability and, with a force of over a thousand aircraft, to send a final message to Tokyo (Dower 2010: 280). Clearly, preempting Soviet intervention was a potential bonus of a U.S. nuclear strike—rarely does a single goal motivate behavior—but such a bonus does not appear to have been decisive in U.S. thinking (Bernstein 1991: 169–170; 1995: 246). Ending a bloody war before it would take additional U.S. lives and justifying the resources invested in procuring the bomb, when it could have saved U.S. lives, were sufficient reasons for U.S. policymakers to act (Bernstein 1975: 50–52; 1995: 236). It is telling that U.S. public opinion polls reveal strong popular support, at the time, for pressing Japan to surrender unconditionally and, later, for having used the bomb to force Japan's capitulation. Given contemporary U.S. sentiment over three generations removed from the passions of that war, the strong supportive sentiment is unsurprising: whereas 85 percent of Americans voiced approval of the atomic bombing immediately thereafter, 57 percent of Americans still endorsed the bombing as its sixty-year anniversary approached (Moore 2005).[7]

Another question that follows is whether the United States sought, through the "symbolic" demolition of two Japanese cities, to send the Soviets the powerful message that they had better comply with U.S. postwar plans. Secretary of State James Byrnes is frequently mentioned as a powerful administration advocate of an assertive U.S. global role backed by nuclear weapons. Indeed, Byrnes did not want the Soviets to know about the bomb until it had been used against Japan "in order to maximize its shock value and, hence, its leverage in dealing with an increasingly difficult Soviet ally." His position brought him into conflict with Henry Stimson, who worried that such furtiveness would provoke the Soviets and endanger postwar cooperation (Broscious 1999: 24).[8] Even Stimson remarked, however, that the bomb helped give the United States significant leverage—a "royal straight flush"—for handling the Soviet Union (Holloway 1994: 122).

The coercive use of nuclear weapons has inspired scholars to study compellence as a distinct form of influence (see Freedman 2004: 109–112; Lebovic 2007: 22–24). Whereas deterrence involves causing a party *not to act* by threatening to impose costs, compellence involves inducing a party *to act* by threatening punishment. The distinction is not merely semantic. There is little dispute in U.S. policy circles over whether the United States (or any other state) can employ nuclear weapons for deterrence—specifically, to prevent other states from acting in an undesirable fashion—but there is substantial controversy over whether these weapons can serve compellence purposes—that is, inducing other states to back down, withdraw, or renounce gains out of fear of the consequences of defying U.S. demands.[9] The details of this debate are unnecessary here, for the point is that some U.S. policymakers might have believed initially, whether rightly or wrongly, that these weapons—which had, after all, compelled Japan to surrender—could make the Soviets comply in their subsequent dealings with the West.

How much credence should we accord to claims that the Soviets were the symbolic targets of the Hiroshima and Nagasaki attacks? Perhaps less than the thinking of prominent Truman advisers seems to warrant. Casual statements by U.S. leaders about future uses of nuclear weapons should not overshadow the shared understanding—so clear and widespread that it required no articulation—that the United States must defeat Japan through all available means. U.S. leaders were focused on defeating a Japanese enemy that was keeping the United States at war and, until defeated, would continue to impose a heavy toll on U.S. troops. Moreover, these statements should not overshadow Truman's reluctance to rely on nuclear force for coercive purposes. His support for the Hiroshima attack might actually have stemmed from his false belief that the bomb would be employed, in some limited fashion, against a military target, and he eventually chose not to use a third nuclear weapon against Japan, to avoid additional civilian carnage.[10] His nuclear aversions helped shape U.S. nuclear policy in the war's aftermath.

Postwar Efforts to Internationalize Nuclear Weapons

That U.S. policymakers were open to sharing control of atomic weapons stems from their reputedly special dangers. Once the bomb spread to other countries, the United States might have to choose between a destructive nuclear war with the new nuclear states or concede critical ground to them to avoid a nuclear exchange. Well aware of these dangers, the administration launched the first major U.S. nuclear arms control initiative—meant to ban the bomb and transfer nuclear knowledge and technology to international control. Under the U.S. plan, nuclear weapons would be owned by no single state, and nuclear energy would be placed in the public domain, to be controlled by everyone. The Truman administration appears to have concluded that the United States was more secure in a world where no state possessed nuclear weapons than in a world where the United States and other states possessed them.

The U.S. blueprint for international control was developed and articulated in the high-level *Report on the International Control of Atomic Energy*, issued in 1946. It became known as the Acheson-Lilienthal (or Lilienthal) Plan.[11] Under the plan, an international organization, the Atomic Development Authority, would own all fissile material and distribute it to nations for their peaceful use. When Bernard Baruch was appointed by President Truman to head the U.S. delegation to the United Nations that would negotiate international control, he accepted the basics of the Lilienthal report and added strong enforcement provisions.[12] Whereas the initial report had sidestepped the matter of enforcement, the Baruch plan—as it was known—called for delivering " 'immediate and certain' penalties" to punish any country that violated the agreement. On nuclear matters, no state would have the right of veto granted the Permanent Members of the Security Council under the UN Charter.

In some respects, the Lilienthal report was implicitly crafted around thinking about a security dilemma. These origins were apparent in its underwriting sense that, absent an agreement, states would seek nuclear weapons to protect against rivals. Indeed, nuclear weapons would presumably exacerbate the security dilemma given the advantages that go to the offense—specifically the "devastating effect" of atomic bombs as a "surprise weapon" ("secretly developed and used without warning"), should states unexpectedly acquire nuclear weapons. In this unregulated environment, states must constantly protect themselves against the potential transgressions of others: "Fear of such surprise violation of pledged word will surely break down any confidence in the pledged word or rival countries developing atomic energy if the treaty obligations and good faith of the nations are the only assurances upon which to rely." Put more strongly, "there is no prospect of security against atomic warfare in a system of international agreements to outlaw such weapons controlled only by a system which relies on inspection and similar police-like methods."

But by drawing on the logic of a security dilemma, the report also offered the prospect of international stability under international control. Its key assumption, in this regard, was that states were disinclined to cheat because the defense would become dominant—for three reasons. First, the United States would not relinquish control to the international authority until measures to verify compliance with the plan were in place. Under the plan, the United States would slowly turn over its nuclear knowledge, materials, and bombs to the international agency while inspection procedures were established to verify that other states were not hedging their bets (by retaining nuclear capabilities) or seeking a unilateral advantage (by developing nuclear weapons in secret). So, absent critical safeguards to ensure its security, the United States would retain its enormous edge over potential competitors in nuclear knowledge and materials. Second, offenders would encounter severe challenges in a race to develop a nuclear weapon. With international controls restricting access to technology, stockpiles, and knowledge, states need not fear surreptitious military applications: effective controls could separate military from civilian nuclear technology, knowledge, and materials; disperse the nuclear infrastructure globally to reduce incentives to "preempt"; and ensure that the most dangerous facilities were located in more secure parts of the world. The time required for offenders to realize military benefits from defection would thereby allow others to employ their own nuclear knowledge, materials, and infrastructure to offset any gains that offenders could achieve from breaking (or sneaking) out from the treaty. Third, defenders would benefit because "offensive" action would be apparent: violators would send clear and unambiguous signals of having violated the agreement. The mining and refining of uranium ore and the construction of primary reactors for making plutonium or separation plants for extracting it—the exclusive preserve of an international agency—would send "red light" signals of a country's bad intent. The signs were made more visible by the presumed enormity of the required breakout effort and the assorted violations that would occur as violators climbed the many interrelated steps to produce atomic weapons: the "total effort needed to carry through from the mine to the bomb, a surreptitious program of atomic armament on a scale sufficient to make it a threat or to make it a temptation to evasion, is so vast, and the number of separate difficult undertakings so great, and the special character of many of these undertakings so hard to conceal, that the fact of this effort should be impossible to hide." Fearing less, now, for their security, states could secure the peaceful fruits of nuclear technology. Indeed, through cooperation to benefit all, these would grow in absolute terms.

In sum, the Lilienthal report suggests that states can override the security dilemma by manipulating conditions that are recognized in realist theory. With international control of nuclear materials and knowledge, the report promised a world in which offensive violations were impaired, because (1) offenders would encounter immense challenges producing and assembling the materials necessary to construct a functioning nuclear weapon; and (2) defenders would possess adequate warning time and capabilities to detect and thwart the offenders before they threatened the interests of law-abiding states. But the lengthy report also impugns the conclusion of defense dominance by adopting specious or contradictory assumptions. These assumptions, and their deficiencies, are as follows.

First, the report assumes that security fears will subside under international controls. Yet it suggests just the opposite when it acknowledges that (1) security fears might increase when, for reasons of efficiency, rising demand for nuclear energy leads to decentralized controls; (2) the worldwide distribution of uranium stockpiles is determined by nature, not security considerations; (3) "dangerous" reactors (with threatening byproducts)—located on national soil—are essential for producing the materials to fuel "safe" reactors (owned by national or private entities); and (4) national and private research into nuclear energy will flourish under international control. The report's assumptions about abating fears are challenged, then, if states can play on these conditions to acquire relevant technology surreptitiously, maintain stockpiles of prohibited fissile materials, or acquire "dangerous" nuclear knowledge. Indeed, a justification for these fears resides in the report's arguments—in favor of international control—"that every stage in the activity, leading from raw materials to weapon, needs some sort of control, and that this must be exercised on all of the various paths that may lead from one to the other." A robust system of controls exists presumably when inefficiencies permit the relaxing of controls at some stages because the barriers to acquiring requisite knowledge, technology, or resources are sufficient at others.

Second, the report assumes that the offense is significantly impaired under international control. Yet the assumption of a defensive advantage is hard to sustain knowing that the offending state (1) was the first to act by seizing uranium facilities, processing plants, and so on; (2) might act only after capitalizing on knowledge gained through participating in the nuclear-control agency; and (3) could time its breach to obtain a lead over opponents. The report provides no compelling reason to assume that the monopoly of knowledge enjoyed by the international authority worked to the defense's advantage. Nor does the report provide reason to suspect that security against defection lies in the sheer number of law-abiding states. The report notes that "the real protection" against the unauthorized state seizure of international facilities "will lie in the fact that if any nation seizes the plants or the stockpiles that are situated in its territory, other nations will have similar facilities and materials situated within their own borders so that the act of seizure need not place them at a disadvantage." But in such a "self-help" system, it is reasonable to ask whether states will pool their resources (rather than "defect") or, for that matter, whether a collective effort would necessarily give these states a competitive edge. Consequently, the offense might well have retained the advantage under the plan, leaving all states insecure under the arrangement.

Third, the report assumes that an international inspection agency could operate effectively in a state-centric world. Indeed, it downplays state power vis-à-vis nonstate entities when it suggests that a community of international scientists and technical experts can be trusted to make sound decisions concerning nuclear energy in the interest of humankind. It assumes, then, that states will not try to undermine scientific or bureaucratic professionalism to obtain nuclear secrets and technology, whether by playing on the national loyalties of industry personnel, exploiting personal vulnerabilities or vendettas, offering lucrative payoffs to scientists and technocrats, or planting agents in the international agency. This optimism is belied, however, by the report's concession that an inspection agency would operate from a severe disadvantage in a state-centric system and for that reason had to acquire "affirmative powers and functions" beyond its powers of "inspection and supervision." The report concludes that inspectors could not hope to compete with national offenders, that is, to operate effectively in the face of hindrance by national bodies, nor to recruit at an advantage for skilled personnel, as long as nuclear knowledge and skills remained decentralized. In consequence, the report begs the question of whether that monopoly is possible to construct and maintain and whether the international body can compete successfully with potential transgressors even with ostensible controls.

Finally, the report assumes that states will do the "right" thing by forgoing nuclear temptations and blocking nuclear offenders. It thereby defers to a fairly idealistic vision of international politics, at odds with the assessments of hard-headed realists. For that matter, by placing enforcement out of range of a veto, the Baruch plan borrowed from the principles of "collective security" that had failed to stop German and Japanese expansionism, which led to World War II, and that UN designers had pointedly rejected in crafting a Security Council in which each of the five major powers, as Permanent Members, had a right of veto. Whereas collective security assumes that all right-thinking states will recognize a threat to the peace for what it is and act accordingly—that states either stand with or against the community—the design of the UN Security Council speaks instead to moral ambiguity (see Claude 1984). It defers to the realities of power in the international system, accepts the inevitability of rival state interests, and acknowledges the dangers of embroiling international institutions in major power disputes. In the world in which the UN Charter was intended to apply, would states choose to go it alone, by reason of security or avarice, and obtain nuclear weapons despite existing prohibitions? Moreover, would states, when left to their own devices (per the Lilienthal report) collectively counter an offender?

Notwithstanding the questionable assumptions within the plan, the negotiating history of the U.S. proposal for international control followed the script of a security dilemma. Although the United States was apparently willing—under some strict conditions—to "surrender" its nuclear capability to international control,[13] it was unwilling to sacrifice its nuclear prerogatives, short of a world in which U.S. interests were secure. Simply put, the United States wanted to maintain its nuclear monopoly until international controls were in place to prevent others from acquiring atomic weapons. From its perspective, the United States could not afford to cede control over its nuclear weapons, technology, and facilities to an international body until the Soviet Union had irrevocably done so.[14] For the U.S. plan to work, then, the Soviet Union would have to accept U.S. nuclear dominance and forgo the bomb. The Soviet Union had reason to suspect, though, that the plan was a ploy meant to disarm the Soviet Union while allowing the United States to retain its nuclear monopoly. After all, under the Lilienthal Plan, the United States could continue to manufacture nuclear weapons until security conditions improved. In the words of the report, the timing of U.S. decisions about these weapons "will involve considerations of the highest policy affecting our security" and "must be made . . . in the light of all the facts of the world situation."

The Soviet response to the Baruch plan was issued within days of the plan's unveiling. The Soviets seized the moral high ground by arguing that, if the United States were serious about disarming, it would simply disarm—that the ball was essentially in the U.S. court. As the world's only nuclear power, the United States carried the burden—and alone possessed the means—of delivering a world free of nuclear weapons. For that matter, the Soviet Union would not sacrifice its own prerogatives, and it was unwilling to accept intrusive inspections on its national territory as part of a deal (Seaborg 1981: 5). In its view, the U.S. proposal was a thinly veiled effort to institutionalize—and thereby freeze—the status quo (Craig and Radchenko 2008: 101–105; Gordin 2009: 53; Holloway 1994: 161–164).[15] The Soviets countered, then, by turning the U.S. proposal on its head: they emphasized that nuclear abolition was essential and had to precede international control. Thus, the Soviets proposed outlawing the production and use of nuclear weapons, followed shortly thereafter by their destruction. But they left enforcement up to individual governments and sought to subordinate the Atomic Development Authority to the UN Security Council—and a Soviet veto.

With their fundamental positions in conflict, the two sides reached an impasse. Outwardly, the United States and the Soviet Union might have created the appearance that haggling and accusations had undermined the good will that was required to rid the world of nuclear weapons. But the challenges for arms control ran deeper than a missed opportunity. The United States had nuclear weapons, the Soviet Union did not, and the United States—with a grave fear of Soviet objectives—intended to keep it that way. Questions nevertheless remain. Why was Truman apparently optimistic that his plan would succeed, and why was the plan crafted around nonrealist precepts that, had the Soviets accepted the plan, might have placed U.S. security at risk? Maybe realists are correct that the international system will eventually "correct" ill-founded notions when policymakers are slow to recognize the appropriate course of action. But Truman's flirtation with international control does make one wonder why the world's most powerful state—in sole possession of the world's most powerful weapon—would not have seized the moment and moved quickly and unabashedly, instead, to try and establish the largest possible margin of U.S. superiority.

The Retreat into Unilateralism: The Origins of Nuclear Superiority

The bomb's properties and their strategic implications were cause for disagreement among U.S. policy officials and—for Truman—a source of deep ambivalence. The dominant view was that, with the bomb, the world had entered a new era. This was implied in frequent reference to the bomb as an "absolute," "revolutionary," or "terror" weapon—or a weapon of "last resort" or "mass destruction." U.S. policymakers recognized accordingly that the bomb could either profoundly hurt or else profoundly help U.S. security. It threatened U.S. security as the technology proliferated to hostile states, but it could also deter potential aggressors and increase U.S. preparedness for war should it occur. But U.S. policymakers (and analysts) could not agree over whether, how, or when these weapons might serve U.S. national security.[16]

Air power advocates were among those who believed that nuclear weapons, by augmenting conventional capabilities, would greatly increase U.S. military efficiency and effectiveness. Accordingly, the Air Force planned, in war, to take maximum advantage of its scarce nuclear stockpile by using it in a massive strike on Soviet urban-industrial targets. It assumed that exclusive military targeting was not a viable alternative given the geographical dispersion of military targets, deficient U.S. reconnaissance capabilities, and formidable Soviet air defenses (Lebovic 1990: 96). Yet even these plans did not resolve the issue of whether nuclear weapons had revolutionized warfare. After all, the Air Force touted the effectiveness of strategic bombing in general: its belief that nuclear weapons would prevail in war was tied more generally to the service "ideology" that the air offensive (conventional or nuclear) would be decisive. Doubters and detractors could wonder, then, if the Air Force had simply appended the bomb to preexisting service war plans and had actually come to terms with the political and military consequences of possessing and employing nuclear weapons given the small size of the U.S. nuclear arsenal, deficiencies in U.S. delivery capability, and evidence that the effects of bombing during World War II were less than decisive (Lebovic 1990: 32; Quester 1970: 1–7).

With the U.S. retreat from international control, the bomb's exceptional properties were reason for the United States to strive for superiority in a nuclear arms competition. Once U.S. policymakers had concluded that conflict with the Soviet Union would be profound and long-lasting, it seemed obvious to them that the United States must build up its arsenal and ensure its preeminence. In this competitive environment, the U.S. decision to proceed with the "super," as the hydrogen bomb (or H-bomb) was then called, was a virtual nondecision: the United States could not allow the Soviets a monopoly stake in this quantum leap in nuclear destructive power, with weapons bearing explosive yields ranging from the tens of kilotons (a thousand metric tons of TNT) to the tens of megatons (a million metric tons of TNT).[17] That internal advocates for the hydrogen bomb did not insist that the increasing explosive potential per weapon was necessary militarily is telling: according to them, available fission weapons could cover the existing target set, composed then of soft urban-industrial targets. Instead, the Joint Chiefs of Staff recommended the acquisition of the super as a "logical extension of existing weapons programs that neither offered great advantages nor posed new dangers" (Rosenberg 1979: 83). Its psychological standing (that is, its coercive or symbolic value)—as a weapon of now even greater mass destruction—convinced U.S. officials that they could not allow (and the U.S. public would not tolerate) the Soviet Union alone to possess them. Even the proposal of an H-bomb test ban was a political nonstarter for the Truman administration (Bernstein 1989: 158).

Truman's behavior and ambivalence toward these weapons left considerable doubt, nonetheless, about whether they would be used in combat. Despite sending strong nuclear signals to the Soviet Union during the 1948 Berlin crisis—by flying U.S. B-29 bombers to England[18]—the bombers were incapable, contrary to appearances at the time, of carrying nuclear weapons (Young 2007: 124–125). Truman considered employing nuclear weapons during the Korean War but rejected that option in large part because of the likely human cost. In fact, Truman took measures to ensure that atomic weapons were kept out of the military's hands, placing the nuclear stockpile and nuclear production facilities under the (civilian) control of the U.S. Atomic Energy Commission (AEC). Overall, Truman set the bar high for the employment of nuclear weapons. He rejected specific proposals to use nuclear weapons to defeat the Soviets in times of war or to prevent a dangerous Soviet nuclear buildup—and failed even to specify the general conditions under which nuclear weapons might be used (Paul 2009: 42–45). Formal deliberations of the President's National Security Council "provided no guidance on when and how the atomic bomb would be used, and left the decision to use the bomb, and the burden of moral responsibility, where it had always been, with the President alone" (Rosenberg 1983: 14).

Ultimately, the Truman administration did not come close to determining whether and how these weapons might contribute to U.S. military security. Following the logic of a security dilemma, U.S. policymakers were unwilling to concede their advantage to the Soviets in a key—perhaps decisive—weapon and sought to obtain the largest possible edge over the Soviets in an all-out nuclear competition. But they were poorly positioned to scale the U.S. arsenal to serve U.S. security needs without a better understanding of relative advantage as it pertained to these weapons.

The Eisenhower Administration

The Eisenhower administration's approach to nuclear arms is commonly associated with a doctrine of "massive retaliation." As articulated publicly, the doctrine supposed that the United States could play to its comparative advantage by choosing the place, means, and time to respond to a Communist attack. Presumably, the place for the response was the Soviet Union, the center of Communist global power: U.S. policymakers tied the doctrine to a monolithic view of the enemy. The means for the U.S. response was the superior U.S. nuclear force, which could deny the adversary the capability to wage war. The timing was possibly immediate, to prevent the adversary from realizing gains on the ground or from obtaining any advantage from striking first. The doctrine does accurately characterize the administration's policies in certain respects (as we shall see), but massive retaliation, as posited, emerged from campaign rhetoric and early administration efforts to develop a strategic stance (Wells 1981). Thus, it clearly overstated the administration's ongoing willingness to use nuclear weapons, invoke nuclear threats to serve U.S. policies, and preserve U.S. nuclear prerogatives. It is no surprise, then, that the administration's rhetoric and conduct has sparked intense scholarly debate. Was Eisenhower an ardent Cold Warrior who had little serious interest in arms control or a closet champion of arms control?

Eisenhower's thinking about the bomb revealed signs of the conflict that had afflicted his predecessor. He was sobered, it seems, by classified film of the first U.S. H-bomb test, which showed an entire island disappearing into the Pacific Ocean (Greene 2003: 161). At various points during his two terms in office, he sought to push arms control measures that he hoped would reduce the U.S. and Soviet nuclear stockpiles, lower political tension, and ameliorate the temptation for either superpower to launch a first strike against the other. Indeed, his reluctant pursuit of arms control was attributable, in part, to opposition from his own advisors. His initiatives faced strong resistance, from the military; at first, from Secretary of State John Foster Dulles, who was renowned for his relatively uncharitable view of the Soviet Union; from the Atomic Energy Commission; and from its commissioner, Lewis Strauss, who maintained a strong personal relationship with Eisenhower. Strauss used his position to control the flow of technical opinion to the president and to express to him the grave suspiciousness of Soviet intent—indeed, disdain for the communist "dupes" in the scientific community who sought to bind the United States to a test ban treaty (Greene 2007: 5). Strauss claims to have voiced contempt to the president in 1958 for a proposed test moratorium by stating, "I felt about Communism as I did about sin—that there was no compromise with it, and that the arms race between good and evil had been going on for centuries and that there would never be an end to it."[19] In fact, Eisenhower became more open to limiting U.S. arms once he broadened his advisory circle (Divine 1978: 209–212; Greene 2007: 6).[20] His thinking also appears to have evolved over time. He seems to have become increasingly pessimistic about the outcome for the United States of a nuclear conflict: Eisenhower, who once equated nuclear weapons with "bullets," later dismissed talk of nuclear war as "preposterous" (May 1999: 5).[21]

Eisenhower's qualms extended into the specifics of nuclear target selection. He pressed the military to rule out the targeting of population centers per se—that is, targeting because they were populated areas instead of the (many other) military reasons that they could be hit. As the size and capabilities of the U.S. nuclear arsenal increased, Eisenhower railed against the excesses of U.S. nuclear war planning: in his view, the proliferation of targets and their redundant targeting reflected a military penchant to focus on what it *could* do given current or desired U.S. capabilities rather than what it *should* do given actual combat needs (Rosenberg 1983: 40, 55). After all, he noted, military officials had once touted the capabilities of the relatively small nuclear force that he had inherited from Truman. In his view, the United States could defeat the Soviet Union with attacks on various urban-industrial targets and did not require the enormous capability that the military had acquired toward that end (Rosenberg 1983: 55).

Yet Eisenhower had strong reasons to suspect Soviet motives and to prepare accordingly. The frightening rapidity with which the Soviets had acquired fission and then fusion weapons instilled fears—throughout the United States—that the Soviets were closing the nuclear gap: they tested an atomic bomb in 1949, four years after the first U.S. atomic bomb test, and a hydrogen bomb in 1953, less than a year after the first U.S. H-bomb test. One of the consequences was inflation of the Soviet threat within the U.S. government. In the wake of the 1949 test, the U.S. military tended to overestimate Soviet atomic capabilities (Rosenberg 1979: 84–85)—as did U.S. intelligence in the years thereafter, judging from authoritative U.S. National Intelligence Estimates (NIEs).[22] In these assessments, overestimation is clearly evident in the exaggerated reaction to the Soviet threat. These threats reflected U.S. intelligence community concerns about strong Soviet military production capabilities, (deceptive) public displays of Soviet military hardware, bold claims by Soviet leaders, assorted evidence that the Soviets were rapidly acquiring bombers and missiles, and a lack of hard evidence of Soviet capabilities. The NIEs of the mid-1950s offered inflated assessments of the capabilities of the bomber force that the Soviets would soon obtain. Fears of a "bomber gap" subsided by 1957, reflected in that year's NIE in downward projections in the size of the Soviet bomber force, with mounting evidence that Soviet aircraft were less capable, and aerial photographs revealing fewer Soviet aircraft, than had been supposed (Prados 1986: 46–48). The ironic result was U.S. concerns about another gap, caused by the Soviet investment of resources in missiles (Prados 1986: 81). Fears of the imminent deployment of thousands of Soviet missiles rose dramatically in 1957, when the Soviets test-launched an ICBM and placed Sputnik into orbit (Licklider 1970: 603); the concern was that these missiles could preemptively hit the U.S. bomber force. At the time, the United States relied on a relatively small number of bomber bases and a deficient early warning system and could not get large numbers of bombers airborne, then, to prevent their destruction once warning was received of an attack. Concerns about the "missile gap" abated only when Soviet (SS-6) missiles were not viewed in suspect locations (near railroad links) and testing halts after test failures indicated that missile deployment was well behind schedule (Prados 1986: 75–95).

Given the Soviet threat, Eisenhower looked to nuclear weapons to solve U.S. strategic problems. The combined Soviet nuclear and conventional threat convinced him that the United States needed to increase its dependence on nuclear weapons—which offered "more bang for the buck"—to help control the high costs of maintaining a peacetime military establishment. Accordingly, the administration expanded the size and versatility of the U.S. nuclear force to cover a vast Soviet target set, and it integrated tactical nuclear with conventional weapons for the defense of Europe. It refused overall to observe an "arbitrary" distinction between conventional and nuclear weapons (or between conventional and nuclear war): nuclear weapons, like other weapons, would be employed in war to "win" (Trachtenberg 1988/89: 37).

For Eisenhower, no less than for the military, nuclear weapons were usable instruments of war. He backed military plans to employ the initially small U.S. nuclear arsenal to hit Soviet urban-industrial areas in the event of war, and he did not press the military to deemphasize urban-industrial targeting as the U.S. stockpile grew,[23] given the inefficiencies of locating, identifying, and striking purely military targets. He was not a champion of a "minimum deterrence" strategy that required a force scaled to impose unacceptable costs on the Soviet Union. Instead, he supported military plans to deliver a "single massive blow" against the Soviet Union in war (Rosenberg 1983: 63). Under U.S. war plans, U.S. aircraft would deliver their full payloads against the Soviets without hesitation or restraint: the military beat back efforts to impose a "no-cities" strategy (Rosenberg 1983: 35, 38) and retained preemption as a potential option to guarantee the effectiveness of a U.S. strike. A full U.S. strike under the 1960 Single Integrated Operational Plan (SIOP) called for hitting over a thousand targets in the Soviet Union, China, and allied countries (without distinction) with over three times that many nuclear weapons. In all, at least 130 cities were targeted for destruction, perhaps many times over: given redundant capabilities and requirements, a city the size of Nagasaki was to be hit with three nuclear weapons, with individual yields roughly four times larger than those that leveled that city. Casualties were expected, under the plan, to reach somewhere between a third to half a billion people (McKinzie et al. 2001: 6).[24] Eisenhower was greatly troubled by the excesses of the plan—"the sheer number of targets, the redundant targeting, and the enormous overkill"—but ultimately he acquiesced to them (McKinzie et al. 2001: 6).[25] When Eisenhower left office, the U.S. nuclear arsenal was almost twenty times larger—at around 18,000 warheads—than it was at the end of Truman's term.

Compared to Truman, Eisenhower was apparently less hesitant to use nuclear weapons against third parties (Paul 2009: 50–62). During the Korean War, Eisenhower (and his advisors) seriously considered employing nuclear weapons against North Korean and Chinese targets and might well have done so had the 1953 armistice talks failed. That Eisenhower chose ultimately not to employ these weapons despite a push from within his administration—most notably from the Joint Chiefs of Staff—does not mean that he opposed using nuclear weapons per se (Tannenwald 2007: 146–147). At the time, the policy debate centered on whether good targets existed for such weapons in Korea, whether the use of any weapon against China would expand the conflict, and whether these weapons might not perform as advertised, which could undermine deterrence around the world.[26] Although Eisenhower also rejected a preventive war with the Soviet Union—destroying it before it could harm the United States—this restraint spoke less to his basic disinclination to use nuclear weapons and more to his concerns about the military and economic consequences for the United States of inviting a devastating nuclear war (Trachtenberg 1988/89) and his deeply held belief—in his view, his American belief—that an unprovoked surprise attack was wrong.

In sum, Eisenhower struggled to reconcile his competing nuclear predilections. He accepted the principle of disarmament as a noble goal but seemed comfortable, throughout his term, with the existing balance between U.S. and Soviet nuclear forces. He rejected U.S. superiority as a sustainable U.S. objective (Smith 1981: 23) but envisioned that nuclear weapons would be employed in a war with the Soviet Union; assessed U.S. security in light of the edge that the United States maintained over the Soviets in rapid nuclear delivery capability; and refused to countenance treaties that might give the Soviet Union an advantage. Insights into his thinking can be derived by examining his three arms control initiatives—the Atoms for Peace, Open Skies, and test ban proposals.

Atoms for Peace

Eisenhower's first major proposal—Atoms for Peace—was delivered at the end of 1953 in a speech to the United Nations General Assembly. In the speech, the president called on the nuclear-armed countries "to the extent permitted by elementary prudence . . . to begin now and continue to make joint contributions from their stockpiles of normal uranium and fissionable materials to an international atomic energy agency" that would answer to the United Nations. Scientific and technical experts would secure the stockpile and make the atomic energy available to the people of the world to "serve the peaceful pursuits of mankind."[27] In Eisenhower's view, the proposal had the "great virtue that it can be undertaken without the irritations and mutual suspicions incident to any attempt to set up a completely acceptable system of world-wide inspection and control." He assumed that "initial and early contributions to this plan would be small in quantity" but that contributions would grow as the parties came to appreciate the limited costs and major benefits of participating. The proposal led eventually (in 1957) to the formation of the International Atomic Energy Agency (IAEA) under the UN umbrella; its reception was disappointing, however, given its underlying ambition—to reduce the fissile material in national stockpiles by gradually turning it over to international control, to harness nuclear energy for civilian *over* military purposes, and to contribute, ultimately, to global peace, development, and stability.

For Eisenhower, the proposal promised bountiful blessings. A realist might concur: the system—as envisioned—would not weaken the U.S. position relative to the Soviet Union given the preexisting size of the U.S. stockpile. To the contrary, as Eisenhower actually recognized, it would increasingly benefit the United States as stockpiles were reduced.[28] Accordingly, he seems at some level to have appreciated the relativist logic of the security dilemma that militated against Soviet participation in the program. Courtesy of its initially smaller stockpile, the Soviet Union could not contribute a matching share without hurting itself militarily and actually depleting its stockpile before the United States had fully contributed its own. The logical problem, however, is that Eisenhower also appears to have believed that his approach could and would facilitate disarmament, to the benefit of all parties. It would do so by sidestepping the contentious inspection issue that had bedeviled prior negotiations: it would not require active monitoring of holdings or facilities and would shift the focus to the receipt of nuclear materials by the international agency.[29] The program's advantage was that states could not hide their noncooperation: they could not pretend to comply with the treaty by withholding or hiding evidence of noncompliance. Instead, states had to take positive, visible steps to establish their treaty abidance and peaceful intent. States would be motivated to participate, then, to preserve and enhance their good reputations within the international community and to help spur a spiral of giving that would increase the security of all participants. By gradually transferring their stockpiles to the international organization, with no amount so deleterious to security that it would raise concerns that others are "cheating" by withholding contributions, each side would come to accept the positive motives of other nuclear stakeholders to create a more stable political and military environment.[30]

Not surprisingly, then, the proposal suggests, in various other respects, that Eisenhower and his advisors had not fully worked through (or accepted) the logic of relative advantage. The inconsistencies of the proposal are apparent in multiple respects.

First, the proposal did not actually surmount challenges of monitoring and verification. Without knowing the actual size of an adversary's material stockpile, a party could never be sure if it was conceding too much capability to international control and hurting its standing relative to an opponent. A country's concerns about the deteriorating balance would increase, not decrease, as the country's capabilities were diminishing in size. Simple math shows that a country can achieve a greater advantage relative to another when the latter has a smaller capability. Indeed, the stronger country—by holding back even small amounts of capability, in the spirit of matching the weaker's contribution in general—can sizably increase its relative advantage when the weaker country's capability is small. Even if the size of existing stockpiles were known, the proposal was nonetheless encumbered by a lack of transparency. As U.S. government experts appreciated, the effectiveness of the proposal hinged ultimately on the willingness—or, unwillingness, as it turned out—of states to accept far-reaching safeguards to prevent the production of additional fissile materials (Sokolski 2001: 30–31).

Second, the proposal focused on transferring fissile *materials* when the United States and the Soviet Union would retain a substantial number of nuclear *weapons*. Thus, the competition to obtain or maintain relative advantages in nuclear weapons could fuel a demand for fissile material. It could be diverted, without detection, in sufficient quantities to build a fairly large number of nuclear weapons.[31]

Third, the proposal implicitly exaggerated the independence of civilian and nuclear applications of atomic energy. Indeed, the Soviet leadership believed (correctly) that the distinction between civilian and military nuclear power amounted to a false dichotomy—that the dissemination of nuclear energy plants would actually increase the risk of nuclear proliferation (Hewlett and Holl 1989: 221; Holloway 1994: 350).[32] Thus, by participating in the program—and perhaps disarming—a state might reduce its own security.

Fourth, the proposal focused on the "vertical" (accumulation) problem that was posed by the growing size of the U.S. and Soviet arsenals in fission-based weapons, not the "horizontal" (proliferation) challenge from those weapons, should other states acquire them, much less the vertical problem that stemmed from the U.S. and Soviet pursuit of fusion-based weapons. At best, this focus appears ill conceived, knowing that the United States and the Soviet Union would soon shift to hydrogen bombs that offered a blast measured in megatons.[33] The parties would therefore have a greater incentive to build more weapons of greater destructiveness.

Finally, the proposal revealed no recognition of the undesirable effects should the benevolent spiral lead to actual reductions in the size of the U.S. or Soviet nuclear arsenals. These negative effects derive in part from the stability challenge that is inherent in small arsenals. A small arsenal creates a tempting target for a numerically superior force, making war more "thinkable" (for the attacker)—and therefore more likely.[34] It can also fuel an arms race if each of the parties—and the various third parties—know that they can quickly obtain a relative advantage by acquiring a small number of weapons.

Certainly, Eisenhower appreciated the U.S. strategic and nonstrategic benefits under the plan but less so the potential costs. Missing from the historical record is evidence that U.S. leaders understood that the proposal might actually accelerate proliferation, place the United States at a strategic disadvantage, decrease nuclear stability, fail to overcome the cheating problem, or channel resources toward the construction of ever more dangerous weapons. Indeed, Eisenhower was not fully cognizant of the plan's major failing: if it actually worked to the U.S. relative advantage, it presented the Soviets with a losing proposition that they would have to reject. So the Soviets responded by challenging the U.S. commitment to arms control and by calling, instead, for an outright ban on nuclear weapons (Wenger 1997: 97).

Open Skies

In mid-1955, Eisenhower presented his Open Skies proposal at the Geneva Summit, which included the United States, Soviet Union, Britain, and France. Unlike Atoms for Peace, the proposal did not call for disarmament directly; instead, it addressed the problem of deception and uncertainty by proposing an increase in military transparency. Under the proposal, the United States and the Soviet Union would open their airspace to overflight of their military infrastructure and exchange blueprints and supportive information on the facilities. Like all of Eisenhower's proposals, Open Skies also had a political purpose: Eisenhower hoped that Open Skies would produce greater transparency, political openness, and trust and ultimately further the cause of disarmament and peace. This would occur because Open Skies could detect advance signals of preparedness for war—thereby limiting the danger of surprise attack—and because each side could accurately assess its opponent's military preparedness and need not rely on "worst-case" thinking to hedge against risk (Greene 2003: 169). Despite its apparent equanimity, the proposal was shaped by considerations of comparative advantage. In various respects, Eisenhower and the Soviets understood—at some level—that it advantaged the United States.

First, the proposal implied that information that facilitated peaceful relations had no military value. But by providing information about the location and operation of Soviet military facilities, the Soviets were effectively abetting U.S. war planning and inviting a preemptive attack. Information about these military facilities (and the unimportance of others) would only increase the effectiveness of a U.S. attack and therefore had to figure into calculations of relative capability and advantage (Holloway 1994: 342).[35] Consequently, the Soviet Union had to consider whether, by opening itself up to inspection, it was giving up more of military value than it was receiving.

Second, the proposal assumed, in principle, that all of the participants would benefit equally. But U.S. policymakers recognized that, owing to the open U.S. society and the closed Soviet political system, the Soviet Union had a far better sense of U.S. military facilities and preparations than the United States had of Soviet capabilities in return. Therefore, increased openness was bound to benefit the United States more than the Soviet Union. Regardless, the proposal would have required the Soviet Union to make a revolutionary concession—opening its national territory to inspection. The Soviets were hypersensitive to their own vulnerabilities—which would become visible through the release of information—and the potential for espionage should the United States have access (even at a distance) to Soviet facilities. They were also hypersensitive to the relaxing of any and all sovereign controls, which could loosen the Soviet grip on domestic power. In this case, they had good reason, for in Eisenhower's mind, Open Skies was linked to open societies (Marquardt 2007: 83). Information revealed or questions raised from aerial inspection could give U.S. leaders leverage to chastise the Soviet Union for its opaqueness, either in the hope of pushing the Soviets to release more information or delegitimizing their political system, at home and abroad. Unsurprisingly, the Soviets viewed the U.S. initiative as an intrusion on Soviet sovereignty, a thinly veiled justification for espionage, and a threat to Soviet military standing should Open Skies expose Soviet weaknesses (Holloway 1994: 342).

Presuming, however, that the Eisenhower administration would have bettered the U.S. military position gets us only so far. In a hostile environment of charges and countercharges, the U.S. prospects for maintaining or improving U.S. relative advantage—whether through competition or arms control—could have been damaged. Certainly, Eisenhower and his advisors understood this and might have thought that they could balance the demands of pursuing U.S. unilateral interests and the requirements of maintaining U.S.-Soviet cooperation. But their proposal shows little regard for an important negative treaty impact: information that can reassure an adversary can also provoke it (Finel and Lord 1999). If a party is inclined to assume the worst, its fears could actually be reinforced by the receipt of incomplete or ambiguous information about the other's behavior. The information could suggest, for example, that the party had underestimated the other's strength or that the other had engaged in willful deception and now cannot be trusted. That Open Skies did not require a party to share the impugning evidence could lead to further distrust:[36] the accused could not then refute allegations or allay suspicions about its behavior. In consequence, Soviet leaders argued—maybe correctly—that Open Skies would increase tension, not reduce it (Marquardt 2007: 85).

Even if the proposal worked to the U.S. relative advantage, did Eisenhower fully appreciate that? That Eisenhower thought that the Soviets might accept the Open Skies proposal is arguably evidence, in itself, that he did not fully comprehend U.S. relative advantages and disadvantages under the plan. After all, no one in the administration thought that the Soviets were nice or naive. The Soviets would not allow that: once again, they chastised the United States for its insincere commitment to disarmament (Greene 2003: 170; Hewlett and Holl 1989: 335).

A Test Ban

A test ban was perhaps the most vexing arms control issue for the Eisenhower administration. Frustration grew as the two sides moved closer to an agreement but could not surmount a major hurdle.

The Eisenhower administration was well aware of the growing global outcry against the damaging biological and environmental effects of nuclear testing.

These effects were highlighted early by some serious mishaps. The most infamous of these occurred in 1954 in the Bikini Atoll. Eighty miles from Ground Zero, a fifteen-megaton hydrogen bomb (the explosive equivalent of one thousand Hiroshima bombs) irradiated Japanese fishermen onboard the *Lucky Dragon*. With twice the anticipated yield, the bomb spewed radioactive debris over five thousand square miles—contaminating sea life and showering the fisherman (and unsuspecting islanders) with lethal ash (Greene 2003: 165; Hewlett and Holl 1989: 271, 277; Kaysen 1999: 96). Persisting criticism from concerned citizens, nongovernmental organizations, church leaders, antiwar activists, and various neutral governments about the effects of testing raised concerns about the global costs and risks of the nuclear arms race. Still, the Eisenhower administration was slow to embrace a test ban. Advisory opinion (especially from the JCS and the AEC) around the president was stacked strongly against initiatives that would constrain U.S. options and leave the United States vulnerable to Soviet deceit. Early support for a test ban from a pivotal Eisenhower advisor—Secretary of State Dulles—cooled considerably when he realized that a test ban proposal would not necessarily produce a U.S. propaganda coup. He feared (correctly) that the Soviets would respond with a far-reaching proposal for a comprehensive test ban that was unverifiable and hence unacceptable to the United States (Greene 2003: 166). Eisenhower conceded later that he had grave doubts, in those years, about whether the Soviets wanted "true agreement" and that he saw test ban negotiations as a way to score political points at Soviet expense. Consequently, the administration promoted arms control proposals that were unacceptable to the Soviet Union in order to expose its unwillingness to negotiate seriously.[37] The administration also paired its test ban proposals with a push for general disarmament to ensure that U.S. advantages would not erode under a treaty.

Eisenhower faced growing pressure from a domestic public concerned (at times, panicked) by revelations of environmental contamination from atmospheric tests, with scares related to poisoned food products, U.S. children with higher-than-normal levels of radiation in their bodies, fallout drifting unexpectedly over populated areas, and radiation hovering in the upper atmosphere. In fact, in the 1956 presidential campaign Eisenhower's opponent, Adlai Stevenson, called for a test ban.[38] The administration managed to deflect the challenge by portraying the proposal as symptomatic of Stevenson's weakness on defense—a charge that was strengthened by the unfortunate Soviet endorsement of Stevenson's recommendation (Oliver 1998: 5). But electoral politics belied Eisenhower's evolving stance on the issue (Greene 2007: 87–111). By the start of his second term, Eisenhower had reportedly become quite concerned about the fallout problem and the public reaction to it.[39] He no longer dismissed a test ban outright as a Soviet propaganda tool and viewed it, instead, as a useful step toward disarmament—over military objections that a test ban would endanger U.S. security (Divine 1978: 143, 231). Eisenhower's philosophical transition was reflected in, and aided by, the widening of his policy circle to include prominent scientists and arms control advocates—including his science advisor and disarmament advisor (Harold Stassen, dubbed the "Secretary of Peace"). It was furthered, too, by the supportive counsel of Secretary of State Dulles, who had become somewhat of a convert to the cause (Firestone 1999: 70–71; Hewlett and Holl 1989: 384; Seaborg 1981: 10).[40] Still, discord within the administration and Eisenhower's own tendency to defer to his trusted policy advisors—and reluctance to weigh in on technical matters (Jacobson 1964: 98)—left the administration unable to move boldly in arms control: "At no point did the Western side, with Eisenhower as American president, table a draft treaty in Geneva; under Kennedy a full treaty was tabled fewer than three months after the new president took office" (Firestone 1999: 71).

Notwithstanding the pressure to reach agreement, negotiations on a test ban dragged on for years in various forums, punctuated by spasmodic nuclear testing. The result was to dash hopes of a compromise that would overcome the impasse. In the summer of 1957, the United States announced a test suspension, conditional on progress toward a control system and a halt to weapons production. Later in the summer, it announced, however, that the deadlock in negotiations had left the United States no choice but to resume nuclear testing (Divine 1978: 153). The result was fifty-five bomb tests that year (by the Soviet Union, Britain, and the United States), a two-thirds increase over the previous year (SIPRI 2007: 555–557). In 1958, following a Soviet-announced March 31 moratorium on testing, the United States called for a moratorium to begin on October 31. Yet, again, such gestures could not hide the parties' serious nuclear ambitions. The United States accelerated its underground and atmospheric testing as the deadline approached; in turn, the Soviet Union commenced testing on the last day of September, exploded over a dozen high-yield devices in the atmosphere, and continued testing into November (Divine 1978: 233–239). Although the moratorium soon took hold, the year brought the largest number of nuclear explosions to date, with 116 by the three nuclear powers, nearly 40 percent of the number recorded since the Trinity test (SIPRI 2007: 555–557).

Despite the provocative testing, both sides appeared to prefer an agreement. But neither side wanted one badly enough to compromise its basic positions. The United States wanted a test ban that was tied to U.S.-Soviet disarmament—specifically, a cutoff in the production of fissile material (perceived to favor the larger U.S. arsenal)[41]—and a comprehensive test ban with compliance monitored through intrusive onsite inspections. In a departure, the Soviet Union wanted the testing issue separated from disarmament; it also wanted a comprehensive test ban without inspections. To the Soviets, the need for comprehensiveness outweighed concerns for verification: an onsite inspection regime was a matter for political leaders to decide, not a technical issue to be settled by science.[42] Anyway, from the Soviet standpoint, the United States already had adequate verification capabilities to monitor compliance with the agreement.[43] To be sure, U.S. concerns that the Soviets would cheat without onsite inspections were not misplaced. Although experts believed uniformly that underground tests at low yields posed the biggest verification challenge and that detecting some low-yield tests and distinguishing them from earthquakes required onsite inspections, they disagreed over the sensitivity and specificity with which the United States could monitor Soviet compliance with a comprehensive test ban.[44]

In the end, Eisenhower refused to accept the unverifiable test ban that the Soviets were seeking and held to the position that adequate inspection was "essential both to avoid the risks of Soviet transgressions inherent in a comprehensive test ban treaty and to achieve the goal of a first step towards ending the arms race" (Pharo 2000: 581). That position doomed comprehensive test ban negotiations in his administration (as well as the next).[45] As always, the assumption was that the United States alone might adhere to the agreement: Eisenhower and his advisors agreed that the United States "historically labors under the disadvantage in all its treaties of intending to fulfill these agreements, whereas other nations may not."[46] U.S. officials voiced concerns, then, that the United States would concede critical strategic advantages under a test ban treaty. Admiral Arthur Radford—the JCS chairman—spoke for many when he exclaimed, to Eisenhower's dismay, "We cannot trust the Russians on this or anything. The Communists have broken their word with every country with which they ever had an agreement" (quoted in Divine 1978: 144). These sentiments were echoed by Thomas D. White, the Air Force chief of staff, in his bold assertion that the Soviets would only be interested in a test ban on which they could cheat (Divine 1978: 248–249). The military was joined, in opposition, by influential civilian experts, such as physicist Edward Teller (the "father" of the H-bomb), who insisted that the Soviets could gain a significant edge through cheating. Indeed, AEC Chairman Strauss argued that Soviet cheating on a test ban could produce technological breakthroughs that could induce the Soviets to attack (Divine 1978: 208). In the unlikelihood that the Soviets adhered to the letter of the treaty, dissenters believed that the Soviets could still use the treaty to advantage. With a test ban, the United States would see its assets wither, as skilled personnel sought greener pastures, whereas the Soviets could keep their laboratories together "by simple fiat" (Hewlett and Holl 1989: 386). Having cloaked their breakout preparations behind the treaty, the Soviets would presumably wait until the time was right and then restart testing with a vengeance.

By the middle of 1958, the Eisenhower administration was willing to separate a test ban from disarmament—albeit en route to disarmament—to meet Soviet objections (Divine 1978: 146–147). Accordingly, the United States proposed a ten-month test suspension to arrange a halt to nuclear weapons production and detail an inspection regime. The Soviets countered by proposing a longer moratorium without committing concretely to inspections or accepting a halt to weapons production (Divine 1978: 153–155). The negotiations continued. In April 1959, the United States sought to meet Soviet objections to a less-than-complete ban on nuclear testing by proposing a ban on atmospheric tests as an interim measure toward a comprehensive ban (Kaysen 1999: 100). Although this proposal would become the basis for the Kennedy-era agreement, the Soviets would not budge at the time from their objection to anything less than a complete ban. Thus, the parties modified their positions, just not enough to reach agreement.

With an absence of progress, the United States announced that it would not be restricted by its declared moratorium when it expired at the end of the year. In return, the Soviet Union indicated that should the United States resume testing, it might answer in kind (Seaborg 1981: 21). In early 1960, the positions of the two sides inched closer: with verification in mind, the United States proposed a ban on testing in the atmosphere, under water, or in outer space (up to a verifiable height) or above an underground threshold of 4.75 on the Richter scale with various quotas proposed for onsite inspections. Although Eisenhower had decided to accept the Soviet-imposed condition—an underground test moratorium—the parties had yet to negotiate its length or the number of permissible inspections (Kaysen 1999: 100; Seaborg 1981: 22–23)—or, for that matter, the control and function of those inspections (Seaborg 1981: 191).

Progress then stalled. U.S.-Soviet cooperation plummeted in May 1960 with the downing of a U-2 spy plane over the Soviet Union—once the Soviets presented indisputable evidence of the plane and its mission in a manner that was meant to embarrass the United States. That incident precipitated the collapse of the Four-Power Summit in Paris and any hope of acting on Eisenhower's proposal.[47] Talks continued in Geneva, to no avail: Soviet leaders seemed content to put U.S.-Soviet relations on hold until the Kennedy inaugural (Kaysen 1999: 100).

In all, the United States and the Soviet Union failed to come to terms due to Soviet objections to onsite monitoring and strong U.S. concerns that the Soviets would cheat on any treaty if they could get away with it. But from the standpoint of relative advantage, was the United States ultimately better off *with* a treaty that allowed the Soviets to cheat to the limits of U.S. monitoring capabilities or *without* a treaty and thus full and open competition? A deliberative answer eluded the Eisenhower administration. Instead, by presenting the Soviets with a deal breaker (in the form of a demand for onsite inspections), the United States rejected the potential benefits of an outright testing ban that excluded the verification provisions. These benefits included (1) ending tests that were polluting the atmosphere; (2) restricting illicit Soviet tests to those that would evade U.S. detection; and (3) slowing the rate of Soviet nuclear progress to preserve the U.S. edge over a longer time period.

Assessment of Arms Control in the Early Years

The Truman administration's response to the nuclear challenge was a bold initiative—international control of nuclear technology. Although the United States sought, under the proposal, to protect its nuclear assets until a system that could verify the compliance of other states was in place, the proposal could very well have jeopardized U.S. security (at some point) by placing U.S. competitors in sole possession of nuclear capabilities. Once the initiative was off the table, U.S. arms control proposals were never again as grand in their vision, though the Eisenhower administration generated a variety of arms control initiatives that failed to produce agreements.

The Eisenhower administration's Atoms for Peace proposal held the potential, in theory, to deliver international control of fissile materials through their gradual relinquishment to an international agency. At the very least, the initiative promised to reduce the consequences of war indirectly by lowering the amount of fissile material in the world for nuclear weapons. Still, the system lacked mechanisms to achieve transparency and sanction noncompliant behavior, falsely presumed that civilian were separable from military nuclear-technology applications, failed to address the emerging challenge from thermonuclear weapons, and might well have yielded an unstable and potentially dangerous outcome had the proposal actually led to a reduction in national fissile material stockpiles and nuclear armament levels.

The administration's Open Skies proposal offered a potentially useful step toward transparency that could conceivably have reduced U.S.-Soviet competition. Indeed, the proposal contained the basics of the verification system—permitting visual inspection from above—that would become a critical part of the Strategic Arms Limitation Talks treaties and subsequent nuclear arms reduction agreements. But the proposal could not overcome a profound political asymmetry that was bound to weigh decisively in Soviet thinking about concomitant relative advantages and disadvantages (and should then have featured in U.S. thinking about the relative benefits and costs of the plan). Whereas the Soviets viewed U.S. plans for transparency as an inappropriate and illegitimate intrusion into Soviet affairs,[48] U.S. policymakers required increased Soviet transparency to reverse an unfavorable informational balance—the relative difficulty of keeping secrets in the open U.S. society. Even had the Soviets accepted the proposal, it hinged on the risky "bet" that increasing the information flow would facilitate cooperation. The plan would have allowed the parties to acquire information that could assist military targeting or inform a propaganda campaign in which the parties sought to score political points at the other's expense. Regardless, the information that was available under the plan might have fed mutual suspicions and worsened U.S.-Soviet tension given preexisting antagonisms.

Finally, the administration's comprehensive test ban proposals could well have put a damper on arms competition, constrained (if not ended) U.S. and Soviet nuclear testing, and curtailed the atmospheric tests that threatened the environment and its inhabitants. Test ban negotiations dragged on for years and remained deadlocked, however, on the issue of verification throughout Eisenhower's presidency.[49] Ultimately, test ban negotiations floundered in the Eisenhower administration because it was loath to accept a resolution—despite its plausible benefits—that allowed the Soviets to improve their position, in any measure, through cheating.

In sum, the failures at arms control in these early years were hardly unexpected given the realist logic that informs thinking about a security dilemma. Simply put, the United States wanted to retain its nuclear advantage while the Soviet Union sought to reverse it. Thus, each party tried to codify rules that would work to its own advantage. Yet the early Cold War experience warrants some consideration of the thinking and optimism behind various U.S. arms control proposals. Otherwise, it is difficult to explain the prolonged and dedicated U.S. involvement in the negotiations, the repeated disappointment at Soviet "perfidy" and unwillingness to accept U.S. terms, and the specific terms that the United States offered and rejected.

Put differently, missing from the realist account is an appreciation that U.S. policymakers (1) did not fully comprehend U.S. relative advantages (and disadvantages) under various U.S. arms control proposals; and (2) could not comprehend the net benefits of the proposals merely by acquiring "information" and resolving uncertainty about Soviet capabilities. The fact is that calculations of relative advantage in U.S. arms control positions owed fundamentally to pessimistic assumptions about Soviet goals as well as to fairly simple standards of symmetry and reciprocity. This proved to be fatal to comprehensive test ban negotiations in the Eisenhower administration. In these negotiations, the administration rejected the principles (1) that U.S. non-nuclear advantages (for instance, in delivery capability) dwarfed potential Soviet gains through cheating; (2) that absolute benefits from a halt to atmospheric tests offset the U.S. relative costs from Soviet cheating in underground tests; and (3) that the United States would gain from a porous test ban that would only reduce the rate of Soviet nuclear progress. All of these principles deserved serious consideration and won adherents in the Kennedy administration to follow (though the last two lacked the backing to convince the administration to accept Soviet terms for a comprehensive test ban).

It is possible that even a limited test ban treaty, first proposed by Eisenhower, could not have been negotiated and ratified in his administration if the Soviets had been warm on the idea. Certainly, a ban was plausibly in reach of the administration because Eisenhower (1) wanted to halt the arms race and viewed a test ban as an important political step toward that end; (2) recognized that the United States and the Soviet Union were at an impasse on the critical issue of onsite inspections for verifying compliance with a comprehensive test ban; (3) had been willing to accept an atmospheric test moratorium despite significant pressure from within his administration to resume testing; (4) chafed under his dependence on conflicting scientific and technical opinion on verifying a ban; (5) received support from the Defense Department and the AEC for an atmospheric test ban (that would allow the United States to continue underground tests); and (6) could count, eventually, on his personal prestige, popularity, Republican credentials, and backing from pivotal Democrats to get a treaty through the U.S. Senate (on these factors, see Greene 2007). Yet militating in the U.S. government at the time against such a treaty were (1) substantial antipathy among U.S. military and civilian officials toward any deal that might impede the U.S. development of new technologies or constrain the growth of the U.S. nuclear stockpile; (2) strong adherence to the (war-fighting) position that U.S. gains were Soviet losses (and vice versa); (3) concerns that the Soviets had overtaken the United

States through accelerated nuclear testing and were advantaged in large-yield atmospheric tests; (4) fears that the United States could not adequately monitor Soviet tests in the upper atmosphere and other environments (which were excepted, therefore, from Eisenhower's limited test ban proposal); and (5) support within the administration for pursuing "peaceful" nuclear explosions.[50] Also weighing against a treaty was the administration's strong desire for a comprehensive test ban that required onsite inspections. For Eisenhower, these inspections held the promise of increasing U.S. access to the closed Soviet system, building U.S.-Soviet cooperation through active participation, and creating a facilitative environment for nuclear disarmament. Thus, "the limited treaty concluded by the Kennedy administration failed to serve many of the purposes for which Eisenhower originally pursued a test ban" (Greene 2007: 261). (Even Eisenhower's proposal for an atmospheric test ban was intended as an interim measure on the path to a comprehensive treaty.) Had a test ban proposal that was acceptable to the Soviets worked its way through the U.S. policy process, opposing Senate voices might have outshouted treaty proponents in the absence of a strong and united administration push to support the treaty. It is worth mentioning in this regard that Eisenhower again sought the counsel of hawkish advisors before deciding to support the Kennedy-negotiated limited test ban treaty with some reservations (Greene 2007: 247–262). Presumably, championing his own limited test ban initiative and navigating the political minefields in Congress and in his own administration would have required that he fully embrace a limited test ban. Given the risks and his desire for a comprehensive treaty, would he have done so?

So, in the final analysis, how well does attention to "strength" and "verification" characterize U.S. thinking about strategic arms control in the first nuclear decades? In some respects, quite well. U.S. policymakers appeared to champion U.S. strength through their consistent efforts to maintain or extend U.S. nuclear dominance, but only at a price. Truman's major arms control proposal (the Lilienthal plan) could have created conditions that benefited treaty violators; Eisenhower's Atoms for Peace proposal would have invited nuclear proliferation through the spread of (civilian) nuclear technology, could have increased nuclear instability (and stimulated rearmament) had it led to smaller U.S. and Soviet arsenals, and would not have stemmed the emerging competition in thermonuclear weapons; Eisenhower's Open Skies proposals could have fed instability and distrust (and led ultimately to a closing of the skies) to place the United States at a net disadvantage. In turn, U.S. policymakers appeared to champion the principle of verification by resisting any treaty that would permit Soviet gains through cheating. Still, the verification procedures under the Lilienthal plan and Atoms for

Peace were unlikely to preclude significant illicit activities and therefore were unlikely to instill confidence among the parties that cheaters would not prosper. Other proposals might well have placed the United States in a net unfavorable position. Eisenhower's insistence on a verifiable test ban treaty precluded the negotiating of a comprehensive treaty with less stringent verification requirements, which might have benefited the United States simply by constraining Soviet testing.

Early Success at Arms Control

The Kennedy Administration and the Limited Test Ban Treaty

Notwithstanding Eisenhower's multifaceted efforts, major success in arms control was not realized until the Kennedy administration, when it signed and ratified the Limited Test Ban Treaty ("Treaty Banning Nuclear Weapon Tests in the Atmosphere, in Outer Space and Under Water"). This accomplishment owed to a shift in the Soviet negotiating position but also to the administration's optimism over U.S. nuclear advantages with an agreement and trust that shared U.S.-Soviet objectives would induce the parties to adhere to the agreement.

Backdrop to the Agreement

The Kennedy administration sought to narrow the distance between the U.S. and Soviet positions. So it went back and forth with the Soviets on various specifics that included the number of permissible detection stations, the annual quota for inspections, and the duration of the test moratorium. Any hope that the negotiations might produce a treaty was dashed dramatically on August 31, 1961, when the Soviets broke the moratorium with a ferocious series of atmospheric tests—fifty-nine, by year's end (SIPRI 2007: 555–557)—and the United States answered with tests of its own. Although negotiations continued, the United States was now unwilling to accept Soviet terms that had bridged the divide in the past. When, in early 1962, the Soviets offered a ban on testing in the atmosphere, under water, and in outer space as well as a moratorium on testing under the ground pending an agreement on control mechanisms, the United States held its ground. Given recent history, a Soviet moratorium offer appeared an empty concession (Oliver 1998: 130; Seaborg 1981: 121–122). When the United States answered with two proposals—one for a partial test ban (allowing underground testing) and the other for a comprehensive test ban that made some headway in addressing Soviet objections—the Soviets, in turn, were dismissive (on these early negotiations, see Kaysen 1999: 101–106).

Despite the feverish testing (which appeared no less than a mock nuclear exchange) and the fits and starts of diplomacy, the treaty that eluded Eisenhower was eventually finalized under Kennedy. The political impasse was broken in the wake of the Cuban Missile Crisis when the Soviet Union accepted a ban on testing in three environments, short of a ban on all nuclear testing. The result was a treaty prohibiting tests of nuclear weapons in the atmosphere, outer space, or under water, including seas, lakes, and waterways within a country's territory, as well as tests through surrogates. Underground tests were permitted under the treaty, but only if the fallout was contained within the testing nation's borders. The treaty contained no provisions—supernational or otherwise—for an intrusive inspection regime: the parties were left to monitor compliance through "national technical means," as it is known in the arms control literature. Per the convention, the treaty allowed a party to withdraw, with three months' notice, if it believed that its national security was jeopardized by events related to the treaty.

The Kennedy administration's success in negotiating the treaty is plausibly attributable to several factors that are drawn from realist and nonrealist analyses. Yet many of these factors exhibit limited variance across these administrations and cannot explain the Kennedy administration's success. These (nonexplanatory) factors are as follows.

First, the treaty did not result from fundamental breakthroughs in the science of monitoring. Doubts remained—at least in some quarters—over the openness to detection of tests conducted in the upper atmosphere, inland seas, and outer space. Moreover, some underground tests could still evade detection and identification. Although this meant that the United States would not sign a comprehensive test ban treaty that did not permit onsite inspections, it also meant that the United States was not induced to accept a limited test ban agreement by the greater certainty with which it could track Soviet activities in the sole environment in which tests were allowed.

Second, the treaty did not result from a fundamental realization that the United States could "make do" with less nuclear capability and could therefore allow the Soviets to reap potential advantages from cheating or from unexpected breakthroughs in the underground test environment. Through the Kennedy years, the United States remained dependent on the many thousands of nuclear weapons that were incorporated into U.S. war plans. Even U.S. efforts to rework the SIOP for conducting a nuclear war—to give the U.S. nuclear options short of an all-out nuclear offensive—still had the United States employing nuclear weapons in quantities that stretched the notion of a limited nuclear engagement. The SIOP that the Kennedy administration inherited (SIOP-62) appears to have given the United States little to no real flexibility: under each of its various options, the United States "simply launched all available strategic forces against the 'optimum-mix' of military and urban-industrial targets throughout the Sino-Soviet bloc" (Sagan 1987: 37).[1] The revised SIOP (63) contained a spectrum of major attack options, from striking Soviet nuclear targets, at the low end, to an all-out attack—with the option of withholding attacks from certain categories of targets, like cities (Ball 1982/83: 34; Ball and Toth 1990: 66–68). Still, all these options involved attacks of massive proportions (Ball 1982/83: 34). Although the Kennedy administration ostensibly pursued a "flexible response" strategy, which increased U.S. non-nuclear options, it did not rule out using tactical or strategic nuclear forces against Warsaw Pact countries. Indeed, documentary evidence reveals that Kennedy and his secretary of defense, Robert McNamara, "did not spend much time or effort on creating strategic nuclear options that were more flexible in any meaningful way, and had far more in common with the Eisenhower administration than anyone would have guessed" (Gavin 2012: 4). Both the Eisenhower and Kennedy administrations would likely have employed nuclear weapons massively and indiscriminately against enemy targets if it had been deemed necessary to turn the tide in war.

Third, the treaty was not a response to unanticipated deleterious changes in the U.S.-Soviet nuclear balance. In both administrations, U.S. policymakers assumed that the United States held a significant—but declining—edge in nuclear capability over the Soviet Union. Eisenhower-era policymakers recognized after the Sputnik launch in 1957 that the Soviets would inevitability acquire the capability to deliver nuclear weapons by missile over intercontinental ranges. By 1960, the Soviets had in fact fielded the world's first ICBM in the SS-6; by 1961, it was capable of delivering a three-megaton warhead to distances as great as 7,500 miles. Although only a handful of these missiles entered service, they were joined by the SS-7 missile in 1961, which, unlike the SS-6, could be fueled in a matter of hours and would eventually be sheltered in underground silos. By the mid-1960s, the Soviets had placed almost two hundred SS-7s in operation, with a smaller number of SS-8s and SS-9s.[2]

Fourth, the treaty did not arise due to favorable shifts in the domestic or governmental political environment. Both administrations had to contend with exaggerated threats of impending Soviet force improvements within the U.S. government. Into the 1960s, U.S. intelligence—though acknowledging its prior overestimates—continued to inflate the Soviet threat with predictions that the

Soviets would soon deploy hundreds of second-generation (SS-7 and SS-8) missiles (U.S. DI 1989: 5). For its part, the JCS was among those pressuring the administration to resume nuclear testing even before the Soviets violated the test moratorium in 1961 (Firestone 1999: 77). Although the public lent some support to the causes of peace and an end to radioactive contamination from atmospheric tests, it also voiced deep distrust for the Soviet Union. Even the strong public support, in the late 1950s, for a test ban and moratorium proved short-lived. With deteriorating U.S.-Soviet relations, moratorium opinion turned negative and remained so in Kennedy's first year in office. By midyear, only around a quarter of the public opposed a U.S. resumption in nuclear testing; toward the year's end, after the flagrant Soviet breach of the moratorium, around half of those polled wanted the U.S. to resume atmospheric testing (Terchek 1970: 115, 119).

So the origins of success lie elsewhere. A test ban treaty became possible in the Kennedy administration because the negotiating focus had narrowed (to three environments where verification was less problematic): for the first time, the Soviets were open to a less-than-complete ban on testing. It became possible, too, because a U.S. policy consensus had emerged—indeed, been forged—around the beliefs that the United States held a strategic advantage, the United States would benefit strategically and otherwise under the agreement, the United States and the Soviet Union were reaching the point where there would be no winners (only losers) in a nuclear war, and the Soviet Union would likely hold up its end and adhere to the treaty.

Relative Advantage under a Test Ban

U.S. negotiators circumscribed the critical challenge to verifying compliance in underground testing by banning tests in the three less problematic environments. The solution did not mollify critics: they argued that the United States was severely disadvantaged should the Soviet Union exploit or violate the terms of the agreement. Treaty proponents won the debate with arguments that might now appear uncontroversial—maybe irrefutable. But the case for ratifying a limited test ban treaty was hardly open-and-shut at the time, given the reputedly high stakes: "the test-ban issue went to the heart of the ambivalence in the American approach to the Soviet Union, for while it promised to lessen the chances of nuclear war it also raised dark anxieties about the dangers of negotiating with the communists" (Firestone 1999: 68). The Kennedy administration drew on its substantial political capital and acumen to get the treaty through the Senate. Even the 81–19 vote for ratification followed fairly contentious Foreign Relations Committee hearings, which nonetheless resulted in a positive recommendation, with one dissenting vote; longer hearings of the Armed Services Committee's Defense Preparedness Investigating Subcommittee, which recommended overwhelmingly against ratification; and fierce opposition from prominent experts. Testifying to the strength of resistance is that skeptical claims would reemerge—as winning arguments—in subsequent ratification debates.

Individual treaty opponents and skeptics did not always embrace the assumptions and arguments of many who shared their respective dispositions toward the treaty. Yet the beliefs of treaty supporters, like the views of treaty opponents, are sufficiently complementary that they are useful to present and discuss (here, as elsewhere) as a coherent viewpoint and, then, to pit the views of treaty "proponents" against those of "skeptics." Indeed, positions on the treaty split substantially on the question of whether the United States was advantaged or disadvantaged if the Soviets (1) abided by the treaty; or (2) cheated on its terms.

Evaluating Strength

Critics assailed the agreement for allegedly having been written to the Soviet advantage. They argued that the treaty would restrict U.S. action in an environment (the atmosphere) where the Soviet Union was ahead and permit Soviet activity in the environment (under the ground) where the Soviet Union was currently behind. They feared that the treaty would lock in a permanent U.S. disadvantage and allow the Soviet Union—at a minimum—to close the gap.

Critics were correct to note that the Soviet Union was the main perpetrator of atmospheric tests, both in number and magnitude. Atmospheric tests were required to test the multi-megaton weapons that the Soviets favored: underground tests were limited to yields in the hundreds of kilotons. Critics worried that the Soviets had gained critical knowledge of these powerful weapons' properties and potentials to offset the limited accuracy and number of Soviet systems. They had a point: one big explosion—far off target—could still destroy a (soft) target. Critics also recognized that atmospheric tests could provide useful knowledge about the performance of systems in their environment of use. By revealing information about radar blackout from a nuclear explosion, the disabling effects of electromagnetic pulse on communication, radar, and various electronic systems, and the fratricidal effect of one (friendly) warhead on another, a party was better positioned to assess the hardness of military facilities (command centers, missile silos, and so forth) to nuclear blast and to address various issues necessary for designing and developing effective nuclear-armed, antiballistic missile systems. The relevant effects could not be fully recreated under the ground, under water, or in outer space, nor could they be portrayed adequately in the laboratory. For critics, it was unprecedented and wrongheaded to deploy systems that had never been tested under battlefield conditions. All systems reveal unanticipated limitations through operational tests that require reengineering, but an antimissile system would now reveal its limits only in an actual nuclear conflict. Consequently, there would no opportunity to learn from experience and to rework the technology to improve its performance.

Critics actually worried that the Soviets sought a test ban to secure a lasting nuclear advantage. In their view, the Soviets had accepted a ban only after having acquired invaluable knowledge through accelerated atmospheric testing. In essence, critics charged that the Soviets had duped the United States into signing a test ban treaty: in failing, instead, to keep pace with Soviet advances—for that matter, by not pursuing superiority by capitalizing on abundant U.S. economic and technological assets—the United States was effectively settling for inferiority (Seaborg 1981: 277).

Treaty proponents ultimately prevailed in the debate. At the core of their arguments was an opposing conception of comparative advantage that decidedly favored the United States. Their arguments echoed in the testimony of prominent policymakers and policy experts before the Senate. The proponents argued as follows.

First, they argued that, despite reputed Soviet military advantages, the United States had offsetting military strengths. On defense, the United States could compensate for large Soviet explosions by dispersing U.S. nuclear targets, burying command and control facilities, and relying on mobile, airborne command posts (U.S. Senate 1963: 101). On offense, the United States could inflict far more damage with multiple smaller warheads than it could with a lower number of high-yield explosions: a 100-megaton weapon was impractical to deliver by missile and would require delivery by slower-moving aircraft that were presumably vulnerable to air defenses and the collateral effects of the weapon itself (U.S. Senate 1963: 101). In fact, the United States had repeatedly rejected the high-yield route in favor of pursuing numerical superiority in weapons with high yield-to-weight ratios. Multiple warheads allowed for redundant targeting in order to compensate for weapons that failed to explode or clear enemy defenses. Indeed, against soft urban targets, such smaller-yield weapons were not disadvantaged per se, for they could inflict devastating levels of destruction with the assuredness provided by their reliability, numbers, and accuracy. Compared to the Soviets, the United States had more deliverable capability; had an advantage in mobility, dispersion, propellents, and range; and had correctly stressed accuracy over size (given the greater sensitivity of hard-target destruction to accuracy than yield).[3]

The United States could capitalize, then, on its triad of forces, on alert, to offset any Soviet knowledge acquired through testing (see U.S. Senate 1963: 98). On this point, U.S. officials stressed that the major constraint in force performance was not nuclear technology; instead, it was the delivery capabilities that were unrestricted by the test ban treaty.

Therefore, in their view, the United States was not conceding its advantage under the treaty, it was building on it. U.S. quantitative and qualitative superiority in offensive arms meant that the Soviet Union would remain vulnerable: it could not engage in atmospheric tests to develop the defensive weapons that could neutralize the U.S. advantage. Indeed, even underground testing seemed unlikely to produce major breakthroughs (Seaborg 1981: 142). Treaty proponents turned the skeptics' logic on its head: the United States could continue to compete in its area of strength, while the Soviets had to compete in an area—nuclear weapons technology—that was constrained by a test treaty and unlikely to produce big dividends. Proponents could embrace U.S. "nuclear superiority" and proclaim their determination to retain it (U.S. Senate 1963: 98).

Second, U.S. policymakers argued that underground testing itself played to U.S. advantages and offset U.S. disadvantages. From their perspective, this test environment was peculiarly suited to U.S. weapons: the Soviets could not test their large megaton warheads under the ground, and the United States could not easily test its weapons in the atmosphere (with or without legal constraints) given opposition within the open U.S. society (U.S. Senate 1963: 532). In consequence, the Soviet Union—not the United States—had accepted unfavorable rules of competition. These rules were stacked further against the Soviets because underground testing was an acquired skill—and costly and difficult to boot. As Kennedy himself noted, underground tests allowed the United States to draw on its abundant resources, technological prowess, and experience in that specific test environment (U.S. Senate 1963: 3). For these reasons and others, McNamara maintained that, by shifting to underground tests, the United States could "at least retard Soviet progress and thereby prolong the duration of [U.S.] technological superiority," though he conceded that unlimited testing under the ground would most likely produce U.S.-Soviet parity (U.S. Senate 1963: 105).[4] To improve the U.S. competitive position, the administration promised to launch a robust and sustained underground testing program.

Third, U.S. policymakers argued further that any potential disadvantage in the "testing balance" (my coinage) had to be evaluated in the context of shared uncertainty. McNamara insisted that the limits imposed on U.S. testing were mitigated by unknowns—pertaining to hardened missile site vulnerability, the accuracy of missiles, and so on—that disadvantaged both sides and perhaps the Soviet Union more than the United States. Indeed, he suggested that the United States could work around these problems, presumably to retain the U.S. edge. In his words, "By theoretical analysis of presently available data, we believe we can adequately predict effects over the range of yields and altitudes in which we are most interested. We will be able to design around the remaining uncertainties" (U.S. Senate 1963: 103).

Fourth, proponents argued that the United States maintained the capability to render any Soviet advantage inconsequential. The United States could deliver, under all contingencies, a retaliatory blow against the Soviet Union that would saturate its defenses and assuredly destroy it. As McNamara put it, "Regardless of the design of any Soviet ABM system, in view of the warhead improvements we can make under the treaty, of the massive U.S. force available to saturate their defenses, and of the array of penetration aids which are being developed and will continue to be developed and improved, by underground testing where necessary, the U.S. will continue to have the capability, and most importantly, the Soviets will know that we will continue to have the capability—to penetrate and to devastate the Soviet Union if a retaliatory blow is required." By outlining the basic logic of emerging Assured Destruction doctrine (as discussed in chapter 3), he suggested that Soviet advantages in testing were meaningful only under the unlikely condition that the resulting knowledge would deny the United States the capability to destroy the Soviet Union in response to its transgressions.

Finally, proponents pointed to safeguards within the treaty. At U.S. insistence, an explicit right of withdrawal was written into the treaty. Although the Soviets, arguing that state sovereignty provided the inherent basis for treaty abrogation, fought a thereby "redundant" withdrawal provision, U.S. negotiators sought to make explicit that the U.S. commitment was reversible: the United States was bound to the treaty only as long as it served U.S. interests.

Trust and Verification

The potential for cheating on a comprehensive test ban confounded U.S.-Soviet negotiations and prevented the two sides from forging an agreement. Unsurprisingly, potential Soviet cheating was the most contentious issue in the U.S. ratification debate over a partial test ban treaty. The consensus on the U.S. side was, of course, that the United States would abide by the agreement, but treaty skeptics worried that the Soviets would cheat. Even treaty supporters recognized that the Soviets could obtain some benefits by violating the treaty's letter or spirit.

Skeptics had long feared that the Soviets would cheat on underground tests by disguising them as natural events, limiting their yield to avoid detection, or exploding bombs in caverns to muzzle the blast. They now trumpeted the Soviet capability to avoid detection by testing nuclear weapons in large inland lakes, in the upper atmosphere, and deep in outer space, for example, behind lead shielding or on the other side of the sun. But it was not just clear violations of the treaty that worried the skeptics. They expressed concern about terms in the agreement that the Soviets could interpret to advantage. Questions were raised, for instance, about the definition of an "underground" test—whether the Soviet Union could claim that it was conforming to the treaty by "putting a few shovelfuls of dirt over a nuclear device," to quote Secretary of State Dean Rusk's rhetorical response (U.S. Senate 1963: 44). Their bigger concern was that secret Soviet preparations to resume atmospheric tests—under the cover of the treaty—would give the Soviets a significant advantage over the United States with the resumption of testing. Even McNamara implied that a planned breakout could give the Soviets as much as a year's jump on the United States in weapon development tests.[5] The Soviet lead would only increase if the United States lost its capabilities to test in the interim: U.S. policymakers conceded, in fact, that the prior test moratorium had left the U.S. underprepared to respond when the Soviets renewed their testing. Over the next sixty days, the Soviets exploded fifty devices in the atmosphere; after restarting tests on September 15, the United States conducted twenty tests (all under the ground) over a six-month period (Seaborg 1981: 90).

Whether the Soviets brazenly cheated or prepared to break out from the treaty, skeptics worried that, absent ironclad verification mechanisms, an asymmetric flow of information would advantage the Soviet Union. Given the open U.S. society and closed Soviet political system, the Soviets could obtain useful information about U.S. plans in the public domain—newspapers, congressional testimony, and statements from U.S. experts and political leaders; conversely, the United States had to rely on sketchy, contradictory, and unreliable information about the Soviet Union, obtained indirectly and surreptitiously.[6] But the question that proponents asked in return was whether the Soviet Union could obtain a significant advantage from violating the treaty or preparing to withdraw from it. The answers were a matter of assumption, as treaty proponents implied in their various retorts to the skeptics.

First, treaty advocates argued that perfect detection was unnecessary to yield net U.S. benefits under the treaty. The United States needed only to ensure, through the agreement, that the Soviets could not conduct illegal tests in sufficient quantities and qualities to jeopardize U.S. security. U.S. policymakers recognized that passive monitoring of seismic sensors was no substitute for the active collection of radioactive evidence at suspect test sites and that even onsite monitoring of a comprehensive test ban would not prevent the Soviets from continuing to conduct illicit tests. For them, the point of inspections was not to catch all illicit testing; instead, it was to raise the probability of detecting an illicit test (Seaborg 1981: 44). Because the detection probability would increase, all other things being equal, with the ambitiousness of the Soviet test program, that is, with the number and size of Soviet tests, the paradox of monitoring was that greater threats of illicit testing allowed for reduced sensitivity in their detection and identification. Thus, by increasing the probability of detection, the U.S. could prevent violations that would, in McNamara's words, "shift the military balance of power" (U.S. Senate 1963: 141).

Second, advocates stressed that U.S. nuclear superiority and Soviet technological challenges countered any potential Soviet advantage from outright cheating or withdrawing from the agreement. For instance, any knowledge that the Soviets would acquire from atmospheric tests on nuclear weapons effects could not offset significant Soviet impediments to acquiring the technology needed to detect and track incoming warheads, discriminate them from decoys, and target warheads successfully.

Third, treaty advocates stressed that cheating was simply cost-ineffective for the Soviet Union. The risks of detection were high, the costs of devising undetectable tests were prohibitive, and the usefulness of the information acquired from such tests was limited. Treaty advocates maintained accordingly that the United States was favored by another paradox of testing: the testing modes that could reveal the most useful information to the Soviets were the least open to cheating. Sure, the Soviets could theoretically escape detection by testing a nuclear weapon many millions of miles from the earth—for instance, to determine the effects of radiation—but with only a limited payoff. Tests in outer space could not reveal the effects of electromagnetic pulse or the vulnerability of hardened sites to surface blasts. Also weighing against that approach was the huge expenditure in resources, the preparation involved, and the non-negligible risk of discovery. The risk of detection might actually force the Soviets to test only small-yield weapons that could be tested under the ground perfectly legally at far less expense. Thus, proponents maintained that secrecy and fear of discovery exact an onerous penalty for cheating and would still not allow the cheater to resolve the formidable technological issues that might shift the nuclear balance. In consequence, despite cheating, the Soviets would end up in the same place—extrapolating from test data and relying on computer simulations, with large margins of uncertainty.

Fourth, U.S. policymakers stressed—once again—that the United States could simply withdraw from a treaty that the Soviets had willfully violated. For that very reason, the United States could feel secure that the Soviets would adhere to the agreement: they had to realize that a transparent pretext or obvious violation would constitute a justification for leaving the treaty. Presumably, the Soviets thought enough of the benefits under the treaty to sign it in the first place, so they would not run the risk of undermining it.

The Power of Belief in U.S.-Soviet Arms Control in the Kennedy Administration

The Kennedy administration negotiated and ratified an important treaty. Success in that regard owed to the administration's fairly benign assumptions about Soviet intent, adroit political handling of the test ban issue, and an appreciation of the U.S. relative advantages under a partial test ban.

Soviet Objectives

Across the political spectrum, attitudes toward a test ban treaty drew from diverging assumptions about Soviet goals. Whereas proponents stressed the harmony between U.S. and Soviet goals, skeptics claimed that these goals were fundamentally in conflict. Skeptics assumed the worst of the Soviets and voiced suspicions of any and all treaty openings that might allow the Soviets to cheat. They argued as follows.

First, skeptics insisted that a lesson of history is that the Soviets cannot be trusted. In their view, the factual record demonstrated an enduring Soviet pattern of deceit and disregard for treaty obligations and commitments. Soviet offenses included the invasion of Manchuria in 1929, the very year that the Soviet Union ratified the Kellogg-Briand Pact (banning war as an instrument of national policy) and broken promises made to Soviet allies about elections and self-determination in areas under Soviet control. Hard to ignore was the recent Soviet placement of nuclear-armed missiles in Cuba under a veil of secrecy and deception. To quote Senator Bourke B. Hickenlooper of the Senate Foreign Relations Committee while grilling the secretary of state, "I believe that we have it on the highest authority that just before the October incident in Cuba on the missiles, or shortly before that, the spokesmen for the Kremlin said that there were no missiles in Cuba and flatly denied that there were missiles in Cuba and, in fact, openly and flagrantly lied to the President of the United States and to this country about the situation in Cuba shortly before the proof became incontrovertible" (U.S. Senate 1963: 76). Given Soviet perfidy, the United States had to fear that Soviet cooperation was at best an anomaly and at worst a ruse. Accordingly, skeptics warned consistently of the (false) "euphoria" that might follow treaty ratification (a danger that even proponents acknowledged).

Second, skeptics found in Soviet negotiating terms reason to assume that the Soviets would cheat. Especially egregious for them was the longstanding Soviet resistance to onsite inspections that could ensure compliance with a comprehensive test ban agreement. That a treaty should provide adequate means to monitor and verify compliance was so obvious and noncontroversial to skeptics that they could not conceive of a party objecting unless it had something to hide and had no intention of adhering to the agreement. In general, skeptics read treaty provisions that might allow cheating as having been written by the Soviets for that purpose. This included treaty language with benign origins. Skeptics worried, for instance, that a passage that banned "other explosions" (meant to prevent military tests in the guise of testing "peaceful" devices) could prevent the United States from employing nuclear weapons in self-defense (Seaborg 1981: 274).

Third, skeptics read malevolence into the Soviet style of testing. To them, Soviet tests were more than just a disproportionate response to U.S. behavior; they revealed a Soviet ruthlessness in pursuit of military capability that could only be attributed to Soviet aggressiveness. From 1961 to 1963, the Soviets conducted 135 atmospheric tests—over three times the number that the United States conducted (SIPRI 2007: 555–557). Of concern, too, was the unfathomable magnitude of these tests. As one treaty critic put it, "In their two test series [the Soviets] conducted more tests above one megaton than the U.S. had made in its entire history" (MacBride 1967: 27). The Soviet testing of a 58-megaton device—which provided the technological basis for a 100-megaton bomb—grabbed their attention (Kaysen 1999: 103).

Fourth, skeptics tied Soviet negotiating tactics to a grand military strategy. The implicating regularities included Soviet nuclear tests after the Soviets had proposed or accepted a test moratorium, Soviet moratorium offers upon the completion of a Soviet test series or in anticipation of a U.S. series, the Soviet rejection of treaty proposals despite U.S. flexibility in negotiations, and so forth. For skeptics, the purpose was transparent: the Soviet Union wanted to test its weapons freely while constraining the U.S. test program.[7] That the strategy supposedly "worked" could only strengthen the skeptical conviction that the Soviets sought military gains by pretending to cooperate.

That skeptics were reading Soviet proclivities—untrustworthiness, an inclination to cheat, malevolence, and purposiveness—into discerned behavior patterns, rather than testing their assumptions against the evidence, is apparent from alternative inferences that could easily have been drawn from the evidence.

Counter to their interpretation, Soviet negotiating and testing behavior was not unusually self-interested. The United States proposed moratoriums after it, too, had completed its test series (Seaborg 1981: 14);[8] the Soviets tested two nuclear devices after October 1958, not having accepted a U.S.-proposed moratorium, but soon stopped testing for almost three years (Seaborg 1981: 14–15); all the parties engaged in significant testing before the moratorium (with the United States apparently conducting more tests). Similarly, Soviet testing seems less menacing, despite its raw intensity, when the U.S. test-program is examined in historical perspective: by 1963, the United States and the Soviet Union had conducted a roughly equal number of atmospheric and underwater nuclear tests—215 and 221 tests, respectively. Although the United States conducted only 43 such tests from the breakdown of the moratorium in 1961 through 1963, compared to 136 such tests for the Soviet Union, the United States conducted 110 underground tests in those years, compared to 2 tests for the Soviets (SIPRI 2007: 555–557). In general, treaty skeptics gave little thought to alternative interpretations of Soviet behavior. For example, they failed to ask whether the Soviets had good reason to fear that the United States would use inspections as a cover for espionage—opportunities that were discussed by U.S. policymakers—or that increasing transparency would weaken the Soviet political system. Likewise, they seemed unconcerned with how the Soviets might view U.S. behavior. Did the Soviets have reason to suspect that the United States wanted to write a treaty to the U.S. advantage, for example, when it sought to permit tests of small-yield explosions (below a given detection threshold) that would favor the testing of U.S. devices, with their high yield-to-weight ratios? Indeed, the Soviets had challenged the United States for pushing inspection demands that lacked grounding in science and for linking a test ban to disarmament and a cutoff in fissile material production that would, in their view, lock in Soviet inferiority (Seaborg 1981: 9, 41).

Although worrisome Soviet goals weighed heavily on the minds of skeptics when they argued against the treaty, proponents claimed that Soviet goals—and U.S. trust in them—were irrelevant to the agreement. McNamara repeatedly insisted that it was in the U.S. and Soviet best interest to accept and respect the terms of the treaty. Similarly, Rusk insisted that the United States had rejected "trust" and "faith" as a basis of agreement by refusing to accept Soviet terms for a comprehensive test ban treaty (U.S. Senate 1963: 27). Yet trust did play some part in the negotiations. The United States took calculated risks during the negotiations by suspending testing (and reducing U.S. preparedness for testing): it thereby expected—that is, trusted—that the Soviets would reciprocate. As important, U.S. policymakers were willing to accept a limited test ban treaty that they conceded presented non-negligible risks should the Soviets violate the terms in letter or in spirit. They accepted explicitly that the Soviets could achieve gains by violating the treaty—and implicitly that these gains were potentially sufficient to motivate the Soviets to undermine the treaty. In sum, they conceded that, by becoming a treaty party, the United States might render itself vulnerable to Soviet misbehavior. Still, they trusted that the Soviets would hold up their end. In various specific ways, treaty proponents revealed their indebtedness to a benign conception of Soviet intent.

First, treaty proponents assumed that the United States and the Soviet Union shared an interest, quoting the treaty's preamble, "to put an end to the contamination of man's environment by radioactive substances." The global consequences of such contamination had been the consistent focus of test ban proponents throughout the prior decade and was an undeniable cost of continuing to allow atmospheric testing.

Second, treaty proponents assumed that the United States and the Soviet Union shared an interest in preventing nuclear proliferation (Wenger and Gerber 1999: 460). Kennedy was greatly concerned about the proliferation threat—he might even have believed it was the only reason for a test ban—and hoped that a ban on testing would impose political and practical barriers that would keep nuclear weapons technology from spreading (Seaborg 1981: 188).[9] This is not to say that the Kennedy administration was optimistic that a test ban would curtail proliferation. The administration had insisted on the explicit right to withdraw from the treaty, anticipating that China would engage in testing, and actively considered (non-nuclear) preventive attacks on China's nuclear program assuming that it could not otherwise be stopped (Burr and Richelson 2000/01). Nevertheless, administration officials expressed varying degrees of optimism that a test ban treaty would help the cause of nonproliferation—due to Soviet backing—for example, by strengthening the Soviet hand in dealings with China.

Third, treaty proponents assumed that the Soviets shared the U.S. interest in limiting military competition and expanding cooperation. As one observer surmised, "Kennedy shaped a broad policy framework of conciliation with the Soviet Union within which the [limited test ban] was a logical, supporting element" (Neidle 1988: 195). Indeed, Kennedy promoted the test ban agreement as a first step in building trust between the United States and the Soviet Union. Thus, he instructed the military chiefs to consider the political, not just the military, implications of ratifying (or not ratifying) the test ban treaty when evaluating its benefits and costs (Seaborg 1981: 271). He obviously thought that the political implications weighed toward ratification.

For the administration, concern about the impact of U.S. behavior on trust was not cheap talk: U.S. policymakers took concrete—politically difficult—steps to reassure the Soviet Union about U.S. intentions. For instance, Kennedy's response to the Soviet moratorium breach of August 1961 was crafted to send a tough message to a U.S. domestic and official Soviet audience, but it was also designed to avoid one-upmanship. Although Kennedy was visibly disturbed that the United States had no quick and powerful tests with which to answer,[10] he chose not to respond to the first two Soviet tests in kind; delayed a decision on atmospheric testing despite formidable pressure from the laboratories, the military, civilians in the Defense Department, the AEC, and conservative critics (Firestone 1999: 78; Kaysen 1999: 104); and insisted that U.S. tests have practical payoffs—that they "provide information of substantial importance to the national defense"—and then end sooner rather than later (Seaborg 1981: 116–117). Thus, in April 1962, the United States conducted its first atmospheric test since 1958. These tests were not intended to confront the Soviets on their own terms; instead, they were designed around U.S. concerns that the Soviets had gained ground in the battle for technical knowledge and that the global perception that the United States had lost ground to the Soviets could undermine U.S. alliances (Wenger and Gerber 1999: 467–468). Thirty-nine U.S. tests were to follow, involving dozens of devices dropped from aircraft, but the collective yield of U.S. tests amounted to around 10 percent of the 200-megaton yield of Soviet tests in the fall of 1961—that is, a bit more than a third of the yield of the single Soviet test of a 58-megaton device in October of that year (Seaborg 1981: 151–152).

For that matter, the administration implied strongly that, in Soviet calculations, shared interests outweighed considerations of comparative advantage. For instance, by arguing that the U.S. lead in nuclear technology would decline less rapidly with an underground test ban treaty—and less rapidly, still, with a (verifiable) comprehensive test ban treaty—McNamara suggested that the Soviet Union would (1) compete vigorously in permissible test environments; and (2) benefit most with the least test constraints. If so, why would the Soviets sign any test ban treaty, assuming that McNamara was correct that the Soviets were not looking for an opportunity to cheat? The inescapable conclusion is that the Soviets were lured by the treaty's potential nonmilitary benefits.

Thus, both sides in the debate calculated the treaty's military benefits, costs, and risks with reference to ostensible Soviet goals. Senate proponents overwhelmingly emphasized the nonsecurity benefits of the treaty—shared by both parties—when pushing for its ratification on the Senate floor (Terchek 1970: 164). Conversely, skeptics assumed that the Soviet Union would seek licit and illicit gains under the treaty because its goals justified incurring high costs and taking great risks to secure an advantage.

The Politics of Arms Control

Success at negotiating and ratifying a limited test ban was not the apolitical result of optimism triumphing over pessimism. The quick consummation of the treaty, once negotiations commenced in earnest in 1963, and the treaty's subsequent ratification by the U.S. Senate had everything to do with the changing international political environment and the administration's dedicated pursuit and adroit selling of the treaty. Ultimately, the treaty became hard even for skeptics to oppose. Yet a positive outcome was by no means preordained.

The evidence is persuasive that the Cuban Missile Crisis—which placed U.S. and Soviet leaders at the helm of a dangerous military confrontation—was a critical turning point in negotiations. The evidence includes the hope for arms control expressed in the U.S.-Soviet exchanges that ended the crisis (Neidle 1988: 177), the softening of previously intractable positions after the crisis, the short (twelve-day) period required to negotiate the treaty,[11] the delinking of a test ban from political issues that had previously confounded the negotiations,[12] and the increase in Kennedy's political standing after the U.S. confrontation with the Soviets in the Caribbean. Still, an arms agreement was hardly a foregone conclusion. Both parties continued to test their nuclear weapons and to hold to established terms for an agreement. Much of the credit for the successful negotiation of the treaty goes to Kennedy for devoting considerable attention and resources to the issue. Indeed, he sat in on interagency meetings and monitored the daily progress of negotiations (Firestone 1999: 78; Neidler 1988: 195). With arms control options exhausted, the treaty became his singular focus—and maybe even his last hope—of helping to end the nuclear arms race. The president also deserves credit for his eloquent appeal to the Soviet leadership. The negotiating atmosphere improved considerably after the much-heralded June 1963 commencement address at American University in which Kennedy acknowledged Soviet suffering in conflict and security fears in a broad appeal to "our mutual abhorrence of war." Accordingly, he promoted a "treaty to outlaw nuclear tests" as one in "a series of concrete actions and effective agreements which are in the interest of all concerned" on the road to a "genuine peace"—as he put it, "the kind of peace that makes life on earth worth living, and the kind that enables men and nations to grow, and to hope, and to build a better life for their children." His Soviet counterpart, Nikita Khrushchev, apparently took the appeal to heart (Seaborg 1981: 218).

Of course, securing a treaty was only part of the battle: a Senate ratification battle loomed. That the path through the Senate was fairly smooth owes again to Kennedy's political acumen. Kennedy oversaw the negotiating of the treaty with an eye to Senate ratification, articulated his vision to the U.S. public, and helped orchestrate the public relations and legislative lobbying campaigns (Firestone 1999: 89–91). The Kennedy administration had pushed, in fact, to include a withdrawal provision to deflect anticipated Senate opposition to a treaty (Firestone 1999: 87). By the time the Senate took up the issue, public opinion was overwhelmingly on the president's side, which dampened Republican efforts to play politics with the issue (Firestone 1999: 91). Credit should be given, more generally, to his administration for presenting a united front to the U.S. public and Congress and a strong and consistent case in selling the treaty as well as for handling military dissent so deftly. As late as April 1963, the JCS maintained that "only through an energetic test program in all environments can the United States achieve or maintain superiority in all areas of nuclear weapons technology."[13] The administration responded to potential military opposition with artful maneuvering and assorted carrots and sticks. It excluded the JCS from the negotiations in their critical final stages, later presented the Chiefs with a fait accompli (Firestone 1999: 94), placed significant pressure on the JCS to acknowledge that the treaty was in the U.S. interest (to the point that critics voiced strong suspicions that the military had been muzzled), and extended the JCS a critical side payment: it promised that any U.S. disadvantage from restricted testing would be offset by a U.S. investment in research, monitoring technology, and underground tests and by preparations to test in the atmosphere should the Soviet renege on the treaty.

These successes en route to treaty ratification owe unquestionably to a prominent feature of the Kennedy White House—a broad advisory circle of technical and policy experts who spoke consistently to the merits of a test ban: "Apart from the military, therefore, there were within the Kennedy administration no strong, anti-test-ban dogmatists" (Firestone 1999: 79). Indeed, the advocates for a test ban included Glenn Seaborg, the new chairman of the Atomic Energy Commission—in a position that under Eisenhower had been a seat of hawkish dissent (with Lewis Strauss and later John McCone at the helm)—and William Foster, the first director of the newly created Arms Control and Disarmament Agency (a bureaucracy with a built-in bias toward arms control). Within Kennedy's circle, opinion converged around the ideas that the Soviets would not benefit overall from a nuclear exchange, that the U.S.-Soviet nuclear balance was sufficiently stable to survive breakthroughs in nuclear testing, and that Soviet leaders believed that they had more to gain from cooperating with the West than from engaging in conflict that would isolate the Soviets, distort their economy, and risk a ruinous war.

Assessing, Safeguarding, and Improving U.S. Relative Capabilities

The Kennedy administration accepted potential risks under an atmospheric test ban. That these risks were small—in an objective sense, perhaps—does not mean that they were accepted as such by many experts at the time, much less by treaty skeptics. For one thing, the treaty would constrain the United States by preventing tests of nuclear weapons in their environment of use. The United States would have to forgo tests that could assist the development of an antiballistic missile system, aid the hardening of U.S. facilities to blast effects, and generally improve the U.S. capability to act, if necessary, in a nuclear environment. U.S. policymakers were betting in part that the lost U.S. opportunities to acquire technological knowledge would be offset by depriving the Soviets of similar opportunities. For another, the nuclear balance could conceivably shift unfavorably due to secret Soviet preparations for atmospheric tests. The Kennedy administration acknowledged as much when it yielded to pressure to restart atmospheric tests to deflect perceptions of weakening U.S. nuclear might while also conducting development tests that the weapons laboratories, the AEC, and military claimed were necessary for U.S. national security (Oliver 1998: 24). Indeed, the administration conceded this implicitly, in the leadup to the limited test ban agreement, when it resisted another unpoliced moratorium with the Soviets (after they had breached the prior one) out of concern for the U.S. strategic position (Seaborg 1981: 120–121).

Although the Kennedy administration tried to build support for the treaty by claiming that the United States would retain the capability for atmospheric testing, history suggests that the administration had promised what it could not deliver. U.S. preparedness for atmospheric tests would inevitably suffer: program deficiencies that could be revealed only through tests would go unrecognized, attention would naturally shift to programs that offered immediate and tangible benefits over those that were purely precautionary, and people and skills for conducting these tests would be lost and resources for conducting these tests would be diverted. Just such a diversion had occurred before the Soviet breach of the moratorium: "Starting with fiscal year 1960, no funds had been budgeted for testing nuclear weapons, and test sites were maintained on a minimal basis" (Jacobson 1964: 99).[14] Preparedness for a renewal of atmospheric testing was likely to suffer, as well, due to domestic resistance to a restart of atmospheric testing (which was now proscribed by a treaty). The point is, then, that the United States did accept some costs and risks under the treaty to realize its cooperative benefits.

To understand why the treaty emerged requires movement beyond static calculations of relative advantage—per the security dilemma—to acknowledge that assumptions both about relative advantage and the shared objectives of the participants were essential for reaching agreement. A limited test ban was enabled because the Soviets dropped their opposition to a less-than-complete ban on testing and also because U.S. policymakers were convinced that the United States would benefit under the agreement—in part because they assumed that essential interests were shared by the parties that tempered their will to compete.

In the Kennedy administration's view, the United States was advantaged—relative to the Soviet Union—under the treaty: the United States could capitalize on its investment in underground testing and its superior economic and technological assets to compete from a favorable position in the demanding underground test environment. The administration assumed, then, that the Soviets would not leap forward in nuclear capability by building on knowledge obtained from atmospheric testing or by shifting its test program effortlessly below ground. Moreover, it assumed that the Soviets were disadvantaged in the larger military competition. The administration insisted that any immediate Soviet advantage in nuclear weaponry was neutralized by U.S. advantages, for example in delivery capability, hardware mobility, and warhead numbers. So the administration surmised that the U.S. advantage was robust and would surmount breakthroughs in knowledge from legitimate testing. It would also survive Soviet cheating, which would require a heavy Soviet financial and resource investment, bring a significant risk of discovery, and offer limited offsetting benefits (to reduce Soviet uncertainty about wartime outcomes or significantly improve Soviet nuclear capabilities).

The administration took its argument even further: not only was the United States advantaged under the treaty, it was better off with the treaty than without it. It based its conclusion on potential Soviet gains through atmospheric testing and the nonstrategic costs of such testing absent an agreement. These costs included environmental contamination, the perpetuation of the arms race, the failure to impede nuclear proliferation, and the potential for conflict should the United States and the Soviet Union infer that they could not peacefully resolve their differences. Indeed, from the administration's perspective, these shared costs had likely led Soviet leaders to conclude, as well, that they were best off foregoing illegal activities that could undermine the agreement in order to realize its many benefits.

Yet thinking about the U.S.-Soviet nuclear balance was apparently central to both sides in the U.S. test ban debate: the contending parties devoted considerably less thought, by comparison, to the goals of the Soviet Union that determined its perceived gains and losses under the treaty. Although the administration had sought to focus legislative attention on the international political implications of ratifying the treaty, the Senate Foreign Relations Committee focused around half of its attention on scientific, technological, and military aspects of the treaty, with only around a quarter of questions and answers pertaining to the international political dimensions of the agreement. Indeed, the military consequences of the treaty featured prominently in the expressed concerns of Senate skeptics. These included the Armed Services Committee members who, in soliciting testimony, "ignored the political aspects of the treaty and were virtually unconcerned about the effects of the treaty on radioactive fallout" (Terchek 1970: 150–151). Their priorities were clear from the lineup of military and scientific experts that were called as witnesses (Terchek 1970: 157). For that matter, proponents and opponents revealed their inattention to Soviet goals by addressing them with contradictory logic. Proponents claimed that the treaty would help the United States to maintain nuclear superiority even as they argued that the treaty would help stem the arms race and reduce U.S.-Soviet tension; they discounted trust as a basis for agreement but seemed confident, nonetheless, that Soviet leaders had much to gain from the agreement, that U.S. and Soviet goals converged in various respects, and that the treaty could benefit U.S.-Soviet relations; and they assumed that a comprehensive test ban might prompt Soviet cheating, when a limited test ban would not, yet implied that the Soviets could gain little in both instances from deceit. For their part, skeptics suggested that the Soviets sought a treaty to freeze in U.S. inferiority and reverse U.S. advantages in underground testing while failing to specify the exact goals that the Soviets could pursue, then, at an advantage or the reasons that the Soviets would risk these useful treaty constraints through surreptitious testing that might provoke the United States to renounce the agreement.

Still, does the final result—which includes a failure to negotiate a comprehensive test ban—also validate the logic of the security dilemma? Suggesting as much is that the limited test ban treaty permitted continuing competition. It did not prohibit testing in all environments. Nor did it prevent the United States and the Soviet Union from continuing—in fact, accelerating—their nuclear test programs: in the 1945–63 period, the United States and the Soviet Union collectively conducted an average of 30 tests a year compared to an average of 42 tests a year from 1964 through 1991 (the end of the Cold War). The critical concession—allowing underground tests—negated one of the treaty's promised benefits. Rather than dampening the U.S.-Soviet arms competition, the treaty, when tied to the upgraded commitment to research and testing, might actually have fueled it: the United States conducted 677 underground tests from 1964 to 1991, compared to 494 tests for the Soviet Union.[15] Indeed, the treaty appears to have reduced the momentum for comprehensive test constraints by allowing parties to hide their nuclear ambitions under the ground and removing a principal global grievance against nuclear tests—atmospheric contamination.[16] But would a bolder treaty have better served U.S. interests?

Various administration officials voiced their beliefs that the United States might have been better off with a comprehensive test ban without strict inspection provisions than with the more limited agreement that the United States had accepted (see, for example, Seaborg 1981: 128–129). Even Kennedy conceded that the problem of Soviet cheating on an underground test ban had been overstated (Oliver 1998: 128–129). Key members of the administration were willing to relax the demands of the prior administration—on the number of required inspections—with the hope of reaching an agreement (when neither monitoring technology nor its apparent capabilities changed substantially in the Kennedy administration). They appear to have concluded that the United States could detect and identify nuclear tests above a low-yield threshold, that continued testing was unlikely to produce scientific breakthroughs in the immediate future (that is, that the parties had already learned much of what was likely to be learned in the foreseeable future through testing), that clandestine tests—given their costs and risks—were especially unlikely to generate such breakthroughs (Seaborg 1981: 142), that the United States maintained a substantial lead in the non-nuclear technologies that drove calculations of the nuclear balance (Oliver 1998: 149), that a nuclear war would impose a significant price on all participants (with or without further testing), and that the need to fight a common proliferation threat mitigated concerns about cheating on the Soviet side. Whether because of political opposition or a failure to forge an administration consensus around these views (given the ambivalence of key officials), the administration continued to adhere to the longstanding position that onsite monitoring was necessary to ensure Soviet compliance with a comprehensive test ban treaty. In an important sense, the Soviet potential to cheat—regardless of its severity—had become a sine qua non of agreement.

It is possible, then, that with some additional Soviet flexibility, the two sides would have come to an agreement. But Kennedy officials were unwilling to stray far from the longstanding U.S. position that intrusive inspections—of some number, judged too high by the Soviets—were necessary to ensure compliance with the agreement. Thus, successful negotiations—much less a ratified treaty—were likely proscribed by the administration's unwillingness or inability to forge a domestic consensus that an unpoliced underground test ban benefited the United States with limited risk. Kennedy recognized that conceding to Soviet demands on onsite inspections would invite formidable political attacks (from the military, the AEC, weapons laboratories, and Congress) that would endanger the treaty. Treaty opponents would have argued—maybe convincingly—that the United States could ill afford a treaty that would allow Soviet gains from cheating, that would prevent the United States from achieving the superiority (via the unrestricted pursuit of technology) that was required to deter and fight Soviet transgressions (Oliver 1998: 95; Seaborg 1981: 221, 227), and that would allow the Soviets to profit from their totalitarian governance. Whereas U.S. free markets and declining interests would pull U.S. scientists and technicians away from dormant U.S. test facilities and laboratories, the Soviets could keep their operations together by edict for the next round of development tests, once U.S. capabilities were depleted (Oliver 1998: 120).

In sum, it might now appear that the changing U.S.-Soviet nuclear balance foreclosed all other options and made an atmospheric test ban—short of a comprehensive test ban—all but inevitable. From this (realist) perspective, the United States was bound to view a ban on atmospheric testing as a favorable development: it came seemingly without strategic costs (for instance, the United States could continue to test under the ground) and with significant benefits (environmental effects of testing were lessened, Soviet technology acquisition was constrained, and so on). But the problem with this hindsight view is that it makes hard, controversial choices appear almost preordained and it implies that policy battles amount to a struggle between "right-thinkers" and the naive, the politically self-interested, or the delusional. How else to explain the rigidity of the opposition if material realities were clearly pointing the direction that policy must take? The facts are, though, that treaty proponents had not fully reconciled the U.S. strategic with the shared U.S.-Soviet benefits of the treaty and that treaty critics did offer a plausible logic. Given their assumptions about Soviet goals, compromising with the Soviets actually was a bad investment that would undermine deterrence and increase U.S. costs in a nuclear war. If the Soviets were relentless and risk-prone in the pursuit of strategic advantage, the United States had no choice but to seek a comfortable margin of nuclear advantage to dissuade them from attacking and to secure a more favorable military outcome for the United States should war occur.

Conversely, it might now appear that potential Soviet cheating on a comprehensive test ban treaty, without provisions for onsite inspections, ruled out U.S. acceptance. But that was not the case if the administration's assertions held true. The stability of the U.S.-Soviet nuclear balance was arguably not jeopardized by such a treaty given the assumptions that the Kennedy administration embraced in defense of a test ban in the three environments. A comprehensive test ban—with or without the capability to verify compliance—would still have constrained Soviet testing, would have played to the U.S. advantage in delivery technology, would have forced the Soviets to concede sizable benefits if caught cheating, and would have allowed the United States to develop various capabilities to withstand a Soviet attack and to retaliate with devastating force. In point of fact, the ban on atmospheric testing—by constraining U.S. defensive efforts and so on—might have had a greater impact on the nuclear balance than an unpoliced ban on underground tests.

It is the U.S. acceptance of the limited test ban treaty, then, that makes it look inevitable—indeed, the best course—not the state of the U.S.-Soviet nuclear balance at the time the treaty was accepted and ratified. The acceptance by Eisenhower or Kennedy of a comprehensive test ban—largely on Soviet terms—would probably now make that outcome look wise and inevitable too. Logic aside, the essential battle of the period was in fact over assumptions concerning U.S. "strength"—how to measure it and whether some U.S. strengths offset various U.S. weaknesses. Whereas Kennedy administration advocates relied on preferred metrics to show that the Soviet closing of an underground testing gap would not neutralize overwhelming U.S. advantages in delivery technology, administration critics focused on alleged Soviet advances and openings in the treaty to cheating. But, unlike their critics, Kennedy officials reached their conclusions by presuming that the Soviets could be trusted to act with restraint when closing the gap and to abide by a limited test ban treaty. They surmised that the Soviets believed they were better off upholding the treaty than violating its letter or spirit.

The Era of Bilateral Nuclear Arms Limitations

The Johnson through Carter Years

The Strategic Arms Limitation Talks (SALT) treaty negotiations, which began in 1969, yielded three landmark agreements. Together, the 1972 Interim Agreement ("on Certain Measures with Respect to the Limitation of Strategic Offensive Arms," commonly termed the SALT I Treaty), the 1972 Antiballistic Missile (ABM) Treaty ("on the Limitation of Anti-Ballistic Missile Systems"), and the 1979 SALT II Treaty ("on the Limitation of Strategic Offensive Arms") imposed upward ceilings on nuclear offenses and defenses when neither were previously restricted. Yet the negotiations and subsequent Senate hearings proved contentious: the SALT I negotiations left critical issues unresolved; the SALT II disputes required seven years of arduous negotiations to overcome; and the SALT process was ultimately stymied when the Carter administration withdrew the SALT II Treaty from Senate consideration. The treaties are notable, in fact, for what they did not do. The participants settled for limitations on further acquisitions and repeatedly postponed reductions to the "next round" of negotiations. Within the treaty ceilings, the parties retained significant flexibility to arm: actual reductions in the number of weapons would occur only to offset the growth in others. Indeed, the parties could increase their numbers of new missiles (when retiring older ones) and could even develop entirely new systems—strategic bombers, land-based missiles, and submarines. Then, the allowances were generous. Under the SALT II Treaty, U.S. and Soviet nuclear arsenals were not expected to reach the ceilings until the mid-1980s, when the treaty would expire (U.S. Senate 1979c: 4).

The SALT controversies within the U.S. policy community come into focus when examining treaty specifics. These include the weapons covered, the U.S.-Soviet asymmetries permitted, the ceilings established, and the standards of verification employed by the treaties. The fundamental underpinnings of the controversies emerge, however, when examining competing sets of beliefs about U.S. relative advantages under the terms of the treaties, grounded in diverging assumptions about Soviet goals.

The Changing Strategic Nuclear Threat

Whether due to fear or political effect, Soviet nuclear capabilities in the 1950s and the early 1960s were often exaggerated—most famously, when Kennedy made the alleged Soviet missile buildup (the so-called missile gap) a presidential campaign issue. The Soviet buildup achieved very real proportions, however, in the years to follow. In 1962, the Soviets attempted to reverse the U.S. advantage quickly by placing intermediate-range missiles in Cuba, which led, of course, to the Cuban Missile Crisis. If successful, their bold move would have brought adjacent portions of the United States—and beyond—within Soviet nuclear range. The gambit failed, and the Soviets—unable to contest U.S. naval strength in the Caribbean—backed down when confronted (and offered a quid pro quo in a promise by the United States to withdraw its missiles from Turkey). But the Soviet debacle may well have inspired the massive Soviet nuclear buildup over the next decade. The Soviet Union soon exceeded the U.S. land-based missile force in sheer numbers of launchers and throw-weight (or payload capacity).

A main concern within the U.S. policy community was that the Soviet Union had made a strong commitment to heavy land-based missiles. This did not bode well for the future. During the SALT I negotiations, the Soviets possessed only single-warhead and multiple-reentry vehicle (MRV) capacities: with the latter, they could release multiple warheads from a single missile—in a set pattern (a footprint that varied with missile travel distance)—to hit multiple targets in the same general area or a single (large) target zone with multiple weapons. These capabilities presumably allowed the Soviets to offset emerging U.S. defenses or to compensate, with multiple hits, for the unreliability and inaccuracy of Soviet weapons. The fear in the U.S. policy community was, however, that the Soviets would eventually harness their enormous missile throw-weight to carry a large number of (high-yield) independently targetable warheads. These fears were realized. With the introduction of multiple independently targetable reentry vehicles (MIRVs), the Soviets improved their counterforce capabilities: they could now release numerous high-yield warheads accurately from a single missile to destroy U.S. missiles in their silos.

The increase in the number of Soviet warheads per missile, matched against multiple-warhead U.S. missiles, had a disturbing implication. In a world of single-warhead missiles—distributed equally between the parties—an attack was self-defeating: the Soviet Union would effectively disarm itself by attacking U.S. missiles. The United States would actually emerge in a stronger relative position from a one-on-one exchange because some Soviet missiles, due to their inaccuracy or unreliability, would fail to destroy their targets. All of that changed with MIRVs: now, one Soviet missile had numerous opportunities to strike U.S. missiles (in their silos) and, in destroying them, could place the United States at a severe disadvantage. If every missile on each side contained ten warheads, in a "frictionless" environment ten Soviet missiles (each armed with ten warheads) could theoretically destroy one thousand U.S. warheads (each Soviet warhead targeting one missile armed with ten warheads). The alleged danger, then, was that the Soviets would try to achieve nuclear supremacy by disarming the United States in an attack.

U.S. fears were further evoked by bothersome Soviet deployments. One major source of U.S. concern was the Soviet commitment to land-based missiles over less vulnerable air- and sea-based nuclear platforms. The United States—by placing its nuclear weapons on invulnerable submarines and aircraft (which presumably would be airborne before a Soviet attack)—sought to ensure that it could respond to any and all Soviet attacks. In contrast, the Soviet Union, by maintaining its forces on land, had supposedly conveyed little concern for platform vulnerability. This fed suspicions that the Soviets planned to strike first. A second U.S. concern was improving Soviet defenses, both active and passive. That the Soviets had sought a missile defense for Moscow made many U.S. observers wonder whether the Soviets had good reason to fear that their capital would come under (a U.S. retaliatory) attack.

Soviet defensive measures were a prominent rationale for the United States to acquire a MIRV capability, which was initially conceived as a "penetration aid" (Newhouse 1973: 75). The argument was that multiple independently targetable warheads carried by a single missile—when paired with chaff and decoy warheads to distract radar and draw fire—could exhaust and overwhelm the missile defense system that was in reach of Soviet technology. Although the Johnson administration's concerns about (and interest in) missile defense faded when it came to appreciate the overwhelming technological challenges of constructing an effective defense, U.S. interest in MIRVs persisted. U.S. military and civilian leaders came to embrace the new technology's various advantages.[1] It was a cost-effective means for greatly extending U.S. coverage of countervalue and counterforce targets, ensuring their destruction through redundant attacks, and freeing up large-megaton warheads for specific missions. It was actually the only means available for increasing U.S. force quantities when U.S. civilian leaders froze the number of U.S. land-based missiles and blocked the acquisition of a new strategic bomber (see Greenwood 1975: 37–50).

Conclusions about U.S. relative advantages and disadvantages in strategic nuclear forces were not determined by new or emerging technologies, however. Instead, they owed to diverging assumptions about a U.S.-Soviet nuclear exchange—its precipitating conditions, scope, targets, and likely outcome. Thus, the question of how much nuclear capability is enough drew conflicting responses in U.S. policy debates over appropriate nuclear doctrine.

U.S. Strategic Goals: Declaratory Doctrine

Once the Soviet Union acquired the capability to hit the United States with nuclear weapons under all conceivable conditions, U.S. policymakers sought to devise a doctrine that would lessen the chances and effects of a nuclear war. Despite the "great debates" that ensued, the practices of successive administrations were more similar than their professed doctrines suggested.

The Johnson Administration

Robert McNamara—as U.S. secretary of defense in the Kennedy administration and most of the Lyndon Johnson administration—oversaw a critical shift in U.S. nuclear declaratory doctrine. The war-fighting principles that dominated U.S. thinking about a nuclear conflict in earlier administrations were eventually subordinated under McNamara to new thinking about Assured Destruction (AD). AD soon became virtually synonymous with "deterrence" in the academic and policy communities. It supposed that the Soviets would not attack the United States if it retained the capability to destroy the Soviet Union under all conditions, including a surprise ("bolt-from-the-blue") Soviet attack. Still, for McNamara (and his successors), the doctrine was a reluctant concession to the harsh reality that neither the United States nor the Soviet Union could protect itself from the devastating effects of nuclear war or limit its scope and intensity (Burr 2005: 47; on the Kennedy years, see Ball 1980).

As we have seen, the doctrinal transition was foreshadowed early in the test ban debate of the early 1960s. But it was not automatic. McNamara looked first to war-fighting principles to address the challenge posed by increasing Soviet capabilities: under his guidance, the U.S. Defense Department initially adopted a "damage limitation" strategy to disarm the Soviet Union in the event of war. He recognized, however, that counterforce attacks on the Soviet Union would leave it with sufficient nuclear capability to threaten the United States. In this, he departed significantly from prior administrations by also pursuing a "city-avoidance" strategy. His hope was that a like-minded Soviet response—sparing U.S. cities—would forestall an all-out nuclear conflagration. McNamara acknowledged eventually that U.S. nuclear superiority gave the Soviets limited incentive to play by U.S. rules inasmuch as trading counterforce strikes would exhaust (inferior) Soviet nuclear capabilities first. The Soviets in fact rejected the notion that a nuclear war would be limited. As John Holdren surmised, "Presumably seeing in these propositions a U.S. attempt to turn its continuing superiority in nuclear forces into a usable advantage in time of conflict, the Soviets were having none of it: they insisted that any use of nuclear weapons by the superpowers against one another would inevitably become a full-scale nuclear war, resulting in overwhelming destruction" (1986: 55).

By the mid-1960s, the McNamara-led Defense Department hoped that the U.S. possession of AD capability would deter a Soviet attack. McNamara's systems analysts determined that four hundred one-megaton bombs would suffice for the task; McNamara extended the logic to require a U.S. residual force of twelve hundred "equivalent megatons,"[2] with the assumption that the United States should invest the necessary retaliatory capability in each leg of the U.S. strategic nuclear "triad"—strategic bombers, intercontinental land-based missiles in hardened silos, and submarine-launched ballistic missiles—to guard cautiously against the failure of any two (Kaplan 1982: 53). Successive DOD annual reports translated these numbers into damage assessments. The verdict: the Soviet Union could be deterred if the United States could destroy one-quarter to one-third of the Soviet population and two-thirds to three-quarters of the Soviet industrial base in a retaliatory attack.

Now, with an AD capability, the United States need not preempt in a crisis to avoid the disadvantages from striking second. It also had no need to chase Soviet armaments to claim security benefits from superiority or to avoid the security costs of inferiority. That the United States had the capability to destroy the Soviet Union assuredly—and need not do more—would inform the arms control initiatives of future administrations and give political cover to a defense secretary who was trying to control military spending.[3] Assured Destruction was undercut, nonetheless, by various flaws in its reasoning.

First, there was far less to administration calculations than met the eye. McNamara had not determined what it would actually take to deter the Soviet Union under any given contingency and thus whether the United States could afford significant cuts in the U.S. retaliatory force. His force-size requirements were derived not from studying Soviet cost tolerance but from subjecting U.S. capabilities to a cost-benefit analysis: given the density and dispersion of the Soviet population, anything more than a prescribed allotment would invite an exponential increase in U.S. costs per inflicted unit of destruction. In other words, McNamara scaled the U.S. force around the declining marginal utility of U.S. capability without considering whether the United States should pay more to acquire additional destructiveness or should reduce U.S. capabilities, instead, given their excessiveness for the task at hand. Thus, AD was conceived around a simplistic, poorly elaborated, worst-case scenario: unless the United States possessed the retaliatory capability that was then within reach of U.S. forces, the Soviet Union—tempted by a net positive return—would launch a surprise all-out attack on U.S. military assets. These conclusions held only because the Soviets would presumably strike to realize some undefined benefit from destroying a significant part of the U.S. retaliatory arsenal.

Second, the AD standard implied that a nuclear conflict was cost-prohibitive for both parties when the administration viewed a U.S.-initiated nuclear conflict with the Soviet Union as warranted under some circumstances. U.S. policy called for using nuclear weapons if necessary to defeat a Soviet conventional offensive in Europe and, for that purpose, included the option of attacking the Soviet Union preemptively (Burr 2005: 38). That policy could have provoked the Soviets, in turn, to preempt in a crisis. Whereas U.S. policymakers hoped that maintaining ambiguity about U.S. first use—exactly how and when the United States would strike—would provide deterrence benefits and preserve U.S. flexibility in action, ambiguity of this sort could have provoked the Soviets to act without restraint to avoid the prohibitive costs of being the second to strike. So the question remained: "Could U.S. AD capabilities deter a Soviet attack?"

Third, the AD standard was offered on the false pretense that the administration would forgo limits or spare military targets in a nuclear conflict. But U.S. policymakers established a continuum of major options—all devastatingly blunt—that nonetheless fell short of a spasmodic response to a Soviet attack. For that matter, all the nuclear options involved attacks on Soviet military targets (Ball 1982/83: 34). Although the United States retained the option of destroying Soviet urban industrial areas, even this damage was sought in the context of inflicting "moderate damage to 70 percent of *war-supporting industry*" (Burr 2005: 41, emphasis added). Over the next decade, actual U.S. targeting plans changed little. The United States continued to plan for second-strike counterforce attacks that might limit the lethality of subsequent Soviet nuclear strikes (Friedberg 1980: 53).

The U.S. doctrinal innovation left the Soviets unimpressed, despite the U.S. arms ceiling that was inherent in AD principles. The Soviets did not take naturally, for example, to the idea (as discussed below) that defending cities to escape the effects of a nuclear conflict would destabilize the nuclear balance (Labrie 1979: 7). They were no more enthusiastic about initiating arms control negotiations, suspecting that the U.S. call for negotiations was a ruse to derail the Soviet nuclear buildup. But the Soviets finally relented, pressed apparently by U.S. plans for a limited ABM defense (dubbed the "Sentinel"). The parties planned, then, for arms limitation talks in the fall of 1968. With the Soviet invasion of Czechoslovakia, arms control was deferred, however, until the next administration.

The Nixon and Ford Administrations

The Richard Nixon administration tried to bring its nuclear arms control (and force-employment) policies into line with U.S. doctrine. It crafted its arms control proposals ostensibly to meet two interrelated standards. The first of these was "sufficiency," which meant that, under the worst of circumstances, the United States would retain retaliatory capability in amounts that could deter the Soviets from initiating an attack. The second was "essential equivalence," which meant that the United States need not match Soviet weapons in numbers and varieties as long as the United States was not left with inferiority in the aggregate. For Nixon and his National Security Advisor, Henry Kissinger, appearances mattered when assessing relative nuclear capabilities: "Kissinger and, especially, Nixon believed nuclear weapons had powerful military and political utility beyond simple deterrence" (Gavin 2012: 111).

Notwithstanding the nod toward AD principles in the idea of sufficiency, the Nixon administration had trepidations about depending on the constricted set of nuclear options that were then available. Nixon and Kissinger were aghast, it seems, at the nuclear destructiveness that the SIOP then promised. Indeed, they believed that an option set amounting effectively to "all or nothing" could undermine deterrence, and the political utility of the U.S. nuclear force, by hurting the credibility of the U.S. threat to use nuclear weapons under some contingencies (Gavin 2012: 112). The Nixon administration sought, therefore, to expand U.S. options in light of thinking about "escalation control" (Ball 1982/83: 35). Drawing from the ideas of Thomas Schelling, U.S. policymakers assumed that the United States could tacitly negotiate with the Soviet Union in a nuclear war (Schelling 1960, 1966). The logic—which had informed the U.S. Rolling Thunder bombing campaign in Vietnam (1965–68)—was to hit some targets while holding others "hostage," that is, to squeeze the adversary but leave it with "something to lose" (Pape 1996: 179). The bargaining strategy was meant to convince the Soviets to end hostilities by upping the level of nuclear violence if necessary (and, presumably, lowering it if possible) without crossing some (ill-defined) threshold to trigger a cataclysmic Soviet response. Accordingly, the administration sought to keep weapons in reserve to attack Soviet urban industrial targets.

By the end of the Nixon administration, the military was directed to increase the variety of nuclear options that were available to U.S. leaders. The military had strong views on how a nuclear war (indeed, any war) should be fought and had heretofore resisted (or ignored) administration efforts to assess and introduce limited nuclear options into the U.S. targeting mix. It feared that the United States, by trying to limit its attacks, would lose the initiative and leave itself vulnerable to a massive Soviet counterattack. To make its case, the military pointed to the vulnerability of U.S. command and control facilities to attack; the U.S. inability to identify spent Soviet silos (as required to employ residual U.S. nuclear capabilities efficiently); the disabling effects of Soviet atmospheric bursts on U.S. electronic systems (and thus the launching of U.S. missiles); and the likelihood that the Soviets, given their military doctrine, would forsake limits in nuclear war (Burr 2005: 39, 43, 59). Even doves did not take kindly to talk of limited nuclear options. They feared that reducing the perceived consequences of a nuclear war might hasten its occurrence and that a doctrine that had the United States exchanging nuclear blows with the Soviet Union might reignite an arms race by validating the U.S. military's nuclear procurement requests. Pinched from both ends, the administration was nonetheless positioned to act. In 1974, it announced what would be known as the Schlesinger Doctrine (for Secretary of Defense James Schlesinger). The doctrine would bring a relatively dramatic revision in U.S. targeting strategy to implement the report's recommendations: attack options included "major" attack, "selected" attack (which involved small numbers of military targets), "regional" attack (which addressed threats to some geographical region), and "limited" attack (which fit somewhere between "selected" and "major") (see Burr 2005: 73). Thus, Nixon-Ford initiatives led to designating a wider variety of target sets, new emphasis in urban industrial targeting, and variations in the possible magnitude and sequence of attacks (Richelson 1986: 159; Sagan 1989: 44–48).

But U.S. policymakers nonetheless assumed that the United States lacked the capability to engage effectively in "silo trading" with the Soviet Union, given various U.S. technological limitations that included the inaccuracy of U.S. land- and sea-based missiles. They assumed, too, that the Soviets might not back down in a fight. Thus, they sought to give the United States the option of attacking Soviet "economy recovery targets" to prevent the Soviets from revitalizing their economy and reemerging as a postwar threat. These targets were generously defined so that virtually any target—soldiers who would enforce order, fertilizer plants that would boost agriculture, government officials who would provide security and services—could legitimately be hit. Moreover, their destruction was assessed by measuring blast effects and ignoring ancillary effects (such as fire): the resulting inflation of blast requirements increased the amount of damage—from all nuclear effects—that the Soviet civilian population would absorb in a nuclear conflict (Burr 2005: 43, 74).[4] The Jimmy Carter administration was left, then, to pursue nuclear options in earnest (Burr 2005: 78).

The Carter Administration

Improvements in Soviet MIRV capability widened the schism between hawks and doves within the U.S. government and the strategic policy community. The Soviet technological advances were less troubling for doves than for hawks. Doves supposed that the United States would obliterate the Soviet Union should it attack, with or without a MIRV capability. Their "dovishness" derived from their claim that existing U.S. capabilities were adequate for the retaliatory task and their belief that, given the Soviet aversion to war, the United States would not have to act upon its threat. But hawks—drawing from war-fighting assumptions—were bothered greatly by Soviet technological developments. They posited that the cold, calculating Soviet leadership would pursue its ends by taking great risks and incurring great costs. Their fears derived principally from a troubling scenario in which the Soviets launched a devastating counterforce strike on U.S. military targets that left the United States with no alternative between suicide—all-out U.S. retaliation, which would invite a reciprocal Soviet response—and surrender—a concession that U.S. declaratory doctrine was essentially a bluff. Of course, hawks were not equally pessimistic about Soviet motives and conduct. Many hawks conceded that the Soviets were sensitive to cost, were perhaps risk-averse, and might somehow stumble into a nuclear confrontation and seek a way out. But hawks agreed that U.S. leaders had to possess some range of nuclear options for confronting the Soviets in the event of war. The pessimists among them insisted that the United States had to prepare to fight a protracted nuclear war that would be "won" by the side that could achieve "escalation dominance" by intensifying a conflict horizontally or vertically; the optimists assumed that limited nuclear options (perhaps confined to military targets) might convince the Soviets to deescalate ("blink first") in a battle of resolve. For pessimists and optimists alike, the availability of U.S. options would enhance deterrence—not undermine it, dovish fears notwithstanding.

The Carter administration crafted its strategic policies with an eye to war-fighting principles and concerns. Secretary of Defense Harold Brown—the primary architect of the Carter administration's nuclear strategy—claimed that the United States would seek "essential equivalence" with the Soviet Union and rejected "sufficiency" as a basis for U.S. policy. In his view, the United States should not allow its security to hinge on the credibility of the U.S. threat to inflict unacceptable costs on the Soviets should they attack. The United States required a force that was, at the very least, equivalent to the Soviet force—in capability, effect, and appearance—and that created U.S. military options, whether striking first or second.

The U.S. "countervailing" strategy, as it was termed—codified in 1980 in Presidential Directive-59 (PD-59)—sought in nuclear war (1) to degrade and perhaps neutralize Soviet nuclear capabilities through the coordinated, accurate, and persistent targeting of Soviet forces; and (2) to capitalize on U.S. defensive improvements—for instance, a less vulnerable basing mode for the MX missile (see chapter 4) and the upgrading of U.S. command, control, communications, and intelligence (C^3I) capabilities—to survive and perform effectively in a nuclear war environment. In short, the strategy was meant to give the United States the capability to engage in a "protracted" nuclear war.[5] To its adherents, the strategy thereby offered some hope of confining nuclear destruction to military targets in the event that the Soviets sought to prosecute a war of that sort. The strategy received some support in Carter's first year in office when the military finally expanded its nuclear options beyond a massive counterforce or counterforce/countervalue attack (Friedberg 1980: 55).

SALT I: The Interim Agreement and ABM Treaty

The SALT I and ABM treaties were milestones in arms control: for the first time, the United States and the Soviet Union accepted constraints on their buildup in nuclear forces. The forging of the agreements required that the parties overcome their diverging assessments of the relative value of competing offensive weapons of varying numbers, technological quality, and deployment modes. The agreements also required that the parties reconcile their views on the relationship between offensive and defensive weaponry. The best that could be accomplished, on offense, was an interim agreement that placed upward constraints on the overall number of strategic missile launchers that the United States and the Soviet Union could possess without limiting the numbers of warheads or other strategic systems. The formal understanding was, however, that the agreement would be replaced, before its expiration, by a more encompassing treaty. Even this limited agreement on offensive systems was enabled by key U.S. concessions on missile defense that were written into the ABM Treaty.

The Interim Agreement

The SALT I Treaty was a five-year interim agreement signed by Richard Nixon and Leonid Brezhnev in May 1972 when a more complete and permanent treaty proved elusive. The agreement froze ICBMs and SLBMs at the number of launchers deployed or under construction; it also constrained missile modernization by limiting the dimensions of new launchers and restricting the replacement of light with heavy missiles. In effect, the agreement froze the Soviet advantage in the numbers of ICBM and SLBM launchers with the ostensible goal of moving toward parity, at lower deployment levels, through negotiation. The agreement placed no constraints on other weapon systems, including strategic bombers and cruise missiles (slower-moving, non-ballistic missiles carried by U.S. heavy bombers). The exclusions stemmed from the parties' preoccupation with the ballistic missile threat, U.S.-Soviet disagreement over what counts as a "strategic" weapon, a U.S. desire to compensate for the perceived imbalance in numbers of permitted missile launchers by forgoing restrictions on other weapons, and the challenges and political sensitivity of incorporating these other weapons into a "balance." Most sensitive of these were U.S. forward-based weapons, located in Europe, which U.S. policymakers maintained were essential to reinforcing the U.S. commitment to NATO. The agreement gave the parties some flexibility to determine their actual weapons mix but included incentives for the Soviets to move from ICBMs to SLBMs. U.S. policymakers hoped that the Soviets would invest in this less vulnerable strategic leg, which would help stabilize the U.S.-Soviet nuclear balance.

The Interim Agreement did not provoke heated or widespread dissent within the U.S. government and policy communities. The Senate registered its support for the agreement with an 88–2 vote on a relevant resolution; Nixon had submitted the Interim Agreement, as an executive agreement (not a formal treaty requiring Senate ratification), to both houses of Congress. The overwhelmingly favorable vote testified to a relatively strong consensus that the agreement was a stride forward in arms control. The agreement engendered fears, however, that the United States had surrendered a significant—perhaps permanent—nuclear advantage to the Soviet Union. Indeed, skeptics gave ground in the debate only with the assurance that the treaty's significant flaws would be rectified in a future treaty. Of less concern at the time was the possibility that the Soviets would cheat on the agreement to build on these (already substantial) advantages.

EVALUATING STRENGTH

The lopsided vote on the Interim Agreement does not communicate the nagging concern, even among those who ultimately supported the agreement, that it had ratified Soviet superiority—that the United States had conceded much under the treaty and received far too little in return. The ensuing debate centered on the significance and the offsetting importance of various asymmetries that were created under the agreement.

For critics, the case against the agreement was straightforward: it gave the Soviet Union a 3–2 advantage in missile launchers and a huge edge in heavy missiles to boot. Even without multiple-warhead missiles, the Soviets maintained a substantial edge in absolute and relative nuclear capability with missiles that could carry three times the nuclear payload of their U.S. counterparts (Newhouse 1973: 263). There was also the danger that the Soviets would build on their lead. Despite the mutual understanding (codified in a statement accompanying the agreement) that the parties could not increase their launcher dimensions by more than 15 percent, the agreement still left unclear exactly which launcher dimensions were involved (Morris 1991: 252), whether increases larger than 15 percent in one dimension were allowed if offset by reductions in others, and whether a 15 percent increase in the length, width, and height of the launcher was still consistent with the agreement. Indeed, the U.S. delegation was compelled to issue a formal statement expressing its "regrets" that the parties could not agree in this regard and announced its own standard for determining whether the Soviets were in compliance with the agreement: a heavy missile was "any ICBM having a volume significantly greater than that of the largest light ICBM now operational on either side."

Critics focused their concerns on the pending Soviet mastery of MIRV technology. Although MIRVs had temporarily given the United States a commanding lead—the United States could deliver over twice as many warheads (and with greater accuracy) against adversary targets than the Soviets could—the prevailing view within the U.S. strategic community was that the U.S. advantage would not hold. Eventually the Soviets would close the gap, with potentially dangerous consequences for the future of the U.S. fixed-site, land-based missile force. Even older Soviet missiles were capable of destroying soft targets, such as radar installations, to improve Soviet first-strike capabilities against U.S. land-based missiles. The accompanying danger (of crisis instability) was that first-strike fears would hasten—perhaps even provoke—the onset of nuclear war: knowing that U.S. ICBMs could not withstand a Soviet first strike and that Soviet missiles were vulnerable on (or in) the ground, U.S. leaders would have no option but to lash out in response to an early warning of a Soviet attack. Still, the most hawkish of critics were less concerned that the United States might act too quickly; they were more concerned that the United States lacked the means to deter a Soviet first strike. They thought that the Nixon administration had settled for sufficiency in the form of a nuclear force that could punish the Soviets—as a final act—for their nuclear transgressions. For these critics, a sufficient force was inherently insufficient. It was neither credible for deterrence nor effective in limiting damage to the United States should nuclear war occur.

In the view of the treaty's supporters, the United States was better off with the Interim Agreement than without it. They highlighted the following deficiencies in the logic of treaty skeptics—but only by creating an illogic of their own.

First, supporters claimed that the agreement was perhaps the best that the United States could achieve under the circumstances. Indeed, for administration officials, it was a better alternative than allowing the Soviet Union to field launchers in sizes and numbers that would soon dwarf the U.S. force. For the Nixon administration, then, the SALT agreement offered the last opportunity for the United States to bargain with the Soviet Union "from a level of equality" (Smith 1981: 30). As Gerard Smith, the chief U.S. SALT I negotiator, subsequently concluded, "The 1972 freeze was an exercise in damage limitation" (U.S. Senate 1979b: 2:3).

Were these supporters correct, though, to worry about the impending imbalance in U.S.-Soviet nuclear forces? True, the Soviet upward-deployment trajectory was unmistakable, had exceeded almost all expectations within the U.S. government, and was undercutting U.S. efforts to bring some semblance of equality to U.S. and Soviet force levels. Yet would the buildup give the Soviets a meaningful strategic advantage? After all, U.S. policymakers had accepted U.S. force ceilings after concluding that more weapons would not significantly augment U.S. destructive capabilities, and they had not unequivocally rejected the logic of Assured Destruction. By this logic, the Soviets were simply wasting resources once they could effectively destroy the United States in a retaliatory strike. So their alleged advantages amounted to "overkill."

Although the Nixon administration had misgivings about AD principles, it had not proposed a clear substitute that could guide U.S. arms control positions. "Sufficiency" was itself indebted to thinking about Assured Destruction, with all of its foibles. Arguably, the administration overcame the implication that "sufficiency" was AD under a new name by pairing the concept with the relativist notion of "essential equivalence," which does not require a force of sufficient capability to deter an adversary. Two parties could achieve essential equivalence with force sizes that do not inflict "unacceptable costs" on each other or that leave the parties vulnerable to a preemptive attack. The administration also distanced sufficiency from AD directly by giving it a relativist flavor—by claiming, in part, that it required "preventing the Soviet Union from being able to inflict considerably more damage on America's population and industry" than U.S. forces could inflict on the Soviet populous and industries in return.[6] Yet the administration's doctrinal revisions were confounded by conceptual and measurement problems that resembled those in prior doctrine: how much relative capability was enough for deterrence was a difficult variant of the question in its absolute form. Now, the answer was sensitive to scenario inasmuch as the attack sequence and sets of targets struck determined the effects of a nuclear exchange. Then, whether the United States could match the damage that the Soviets could impose was a matter of assumption and judgment. What constitutes "considerably more" damage is certainly subjective and is based in any event on squishy estimates of diminishing marginal returns from an attack (due to synergies of society, economy, and governance) and estimates of the cost tolerance of adversary political leaders. Of course, to come up with a reasonable response to the conceptual and operational challenges of damage assessment is to suppose that finely tuned measurement is unnecessary, that the massive scale of destructiveness that U.S. forces can inflict removes any doubt that the United States has met that standard. If true, however, that logic takes us full circle—back to Assured Destruction. Thus, despite the intense debate and the consideration given to doctrinal alternatives, the administration had not surmounted the alleged deficiencies of AD doctrine, let alone crafted a concise replacement.

Second, many supporters viewed the absence of MIRV limitations in the agreement as beneficial because it gave the United States a (temporary) lead in numbers of warheads—on land- and sea-launched missiles—to counterbalance the Soviet numerical edge in ICBMs and antiballistic missiles. Administration officials recognized, in fact, that MIRV limits would fuel significant political opposition. The Joint Chiefs of Staff were loath to accept MIRV limitations, much less in the absence of onsite inspections (to verify compliance with a MIRV ban), a significant reduction in numbers of Soviet land-based missiles, and additional limits on Soviet antiaircraft weapons (Smith 1981: 172). MIRV limits would also have met with intense Soviet resistance. The Soviet Union was unwilling to compensate for limits on (U.S.) MIRVs by reducing Soviet launcher numbers (to equalize the U.S.-Soviet warhead ratio) or to trade away access to MIRV technology when it was still under Soviet development.[7] For these reasons, U.S. leaders never appeared serious about seeking a MIRV limitation (Smith 1981: 157).

Were these supporters correct, though, that U.S. interests were served without MIRV limits? Safeguarding MIRVs promised to weaken the United States by the administration's standard of essential equivalence. The Soviet advantage in land-based missiles—especially heavy ones—would translate into an even larger advantage in ICBM warheads once these missiles were fitted with multiple independently guided reentry vehicles. The Soviet advantage was potentially larger still if the Soviets chose to strike first, to destroy U.S. MIRVed ICBMs in their silos. The danger that U.S. MIRV deployments would feed a Soviet incentive to preempt received scant attention, however, from top U.S. policymakers. They chose to defer the pending warhead problem to future negotiations despite a strong belief within the U.S. arms control community that MIRVs (and ABMs) were primary threats to nuclear stability: the prevailing view in the U.S. Arms Control and Disarmament Agency (ACDA) and the State Department was, in fact, that the United States must push for prohibitions on MIRVs and antiballistic missiles, with or without onsite inspections (Newhouse 1973: 164; Smith 1991: 173), before the parties had invested fully in these technologies, at which point restrictions would be difficult or even impossible to negotiate.

Third, supporters maintained that the agreement would help foster strategic stability. It would do this supposedly by restricting the dimensions of new launchers and the replacement of light with heavy missiles—to prevent the Soviets from increasing their warhead-carrying capacity. It would also promote stability by requiring the retiring of an old missile for each new SLBM deployed and helping, then, to send the Soviet force "out to sea," where the invulnerability of a submarine-based force would ostensibly forestall its precipitous use: freed from a "use-them-or-lose-them" dilemma, the Soviets could afford to wait before striking, with the effect, perhaps, of avoiding a global nuclear catastrophe. In this, U.S. officials assumed that the Soviets had planned to deploy additional submarines, had more aging ICBMs than SLBMs, and had an incentive, then, to reduce their numbers of fixed-site land-based launchers (Newhouse 1973: 247).

Was the administration correct to be concerned, however, about alleged stability problems that stemmed from Soviet dependence on land-based missiles? After all, the United States retained the capability, under all conceivable scenarios, to devastate Soviet cities, industries, and soft military targets in response to a Soviet attack precisely because the pending Soviet missile threat had induced the United States to invest heavily in ballistic-missile submarines and bombers (equipped with cruise missiles to compete with improving Soviet radar and shoot-down capabilities) to retaliate for the "worst-case" Soviet attack. For that matter, the United States should have found little relief in the promise of stability from greater Soviet dependence on submarine-launched ballistic missiles. SLBMs were likely to grow in accuracy, could reduce U.S. warning and response time if launched proximate to U.S. shores,[8] and could thereby target U.S. MIRVed ICBMs, which were inviting targets for attack.[9] More importantly, Soviet fears of the vulnerability of command communications with submarines—or Soviet submarines to U.S. antisubmarine warfare—could prompt Soviet leaders to authorize submarine commanders to launch their SLBMs in the event of a loss in communications or a threat to their submarines or, perhaps, at the onset of a conflict to ensure that the missiles would reach their U.S. targets. U.S. policymakers and analysts worried greatly about the destabilizing threat of high warhead-to-missile ratios; they seemed indifferent, by comparison, to the destabilizing threat from even inaccurate nuclear weapons to adversary command, control, and communication centers—a threat that could push the Soviets to use their SLBMs sooner rather than later (Glasser 1992).

If these stability concerns were in fact warranted, were supporters correct to believe that the agreement gave the Soviets sufficient incentive to move their forces out to sea? The Soviet incentive to sacrifice ICBMs for SLBMs was actually small given the generous allowance for SLBMs in the agreement. Under the terms of the Protocol to the agreement,[10] the United States was restricted to 710 SLBM launch tubes on 44 modern ballistic-missile submarines, and the Soviet Union was restricted to 950 SLBM launch tubes on no more than 62 modern ballistic-missile submarines. Then, the United States was required to engage in one-to-one replacement above a threshold number of 656 (to reach the 710 total), when the Soviets had to engage in such replacement only above a total of 740 SLBM launch tubes. The Soviet incentive to move to SLBMs was further reduced by the overall size and modernity of the Soviet arsenal, the hard-targeting virtues and warhead capacity of Soviet land-based missiles, and the relative benefits to the Soviets of a land- versus a sea-based alternative for addressing the emerging land-based missile vulnerability problem. Given offsetting Soviet assets and the relative vulnerability of Soviet submarines, the Soviets could reasonably choose to address their fixed-site missile vulnerability problem by deploying *mobile* land-based missiles—low-profile and elusive systems that were operationally equivalent to U.S. ballistic-missile submarines. On that score, the Soviets were peculiarly advantaged. Their land mass provided vast space over which missiles could roam; their authoritarian governance limited public disclosure to, and could squelch opposition from, concerned citizens who feared being targeted (due to their proximity to these missiles) in a U.S. attack (Newhouse 1973: 126). From a U.S. standpoint, a large mobile Soviet land-based force was not an appealing (stabilizing) development: albeit lighter and less accurate (given their variable positioning) than fixed-site missiles, they could survive a U.S. attack to target the U.S. fixed-site force (Talbott 1980: 165–166).

Fourth, supporters maintained that the United States had obtained critical exclusions under the agreement. The Soviets had relented (for the time being) to the strongly held U.S. position to omit—from the "strategic" count—British and French weapons and U.S. forward-based systems, including medium-range bombers and weapons on aircraft carriers, that could strike Soviet targets (NAS 1985: 28). The Soviets had dropped their demand for restrictions on forward-based systems as an implicit quid pro quo for the United States dropping its demand that the Soviets reduce their numbers of heavy land-based missiles (NAS 1985: 30). Whereas the Soviet Union had defined "strategic" systems by their potential purposes (targeting the United States or Soviet Union)—which would exclude Soviet intermediate-range weapons that were aimed at Europe—it relented effectively to the U.S. position, then, that the "strategic" character of a system was a function of its range. Supporters correctly viewed this as a significant Soviet concession. After all, (1) a U.S. aircraft traveling from Europe to the Soviet Union could arrive roughly in the same (half-hour) time frame as could a missile fired at Russia from the continental United States; (2) European-based weapons could inflict significant damage on the Soviet Union; and (3) SLBMs—which were counted under the agreement—could be launched from European shores (to reduce travel times, for example) and operate effectively as European-based systems against Soviet targets.[11] The Soviets could rightly ask, then, why the United States should maintain nuclear weapons in Europe when it had fought Soviet efforts to place nuclear-armed missiles in Cuba (Smith 1981: 184). But had the United States achieved a truly meaningful Soviet concession? As we shall see in chapter 4, the contribution to deterrence and war-fighting of forward-based systems was at best murky—and controversial.

Fifth, supporters pointed to U.S. technological advantages that offset U.S. concessions in the agreement. These offsets were apparent in system-to-system comparisons. For instance, the Soviets benefited in numbers of nuclear-armed submarines and SLBMs under the agreement, but Soviet submarines were noisy and easier than U.S. submarines to track, vulnerable as they traversed through choke points, limited in their radius of action by shorter missile ranges, and disadvantaged by the significant U.S. investment in antisubmarine warfare. Unlike U.S. submarines, they also lacked bases for resupply and maintenance that were proximate to deployment zones. Compared to U.S. submarines, Soviet submarines had to travel longer distances to these zones, which limited their missile-carriage capacity; once there, they could not easily sustain a presence, increasing the number of submarines required for rotation (Newhouse 1973: 22–24). Offsets were apparent, as well, in aggregate force levels. U.S. SLBMs, bombers (on alert), and (surviving) ICBMs could retaliate massively for any Soviet attack that capitalized on superior Soviet throw-weight. That you cannot focus on just one component when assessing the U.S.-Soviet nuclear balance—that assessment requires a comprehensive evaluation of forces—was the philosophy behind the U.S. triad, which assumed that U.S. forces could multiply their potency by working in synergy (Smith 1981: 136). It was also behind U.S. AD doctrine, which the Nixon administration had not entirely discredited. Under the doctrine, the specific vehicles and timing for inflicting destruction were irrelevant: what mattered was the "assuredness" and fact of destruction.

Were supporters correct, though, to view these offsets as furthering strategic stability? Despite their attention to equivalencies (via offsets), treaty supporters tended not to consider how U.S. capabilities might look from the Soviet perspective—and, specifically, whether the Soviets might view emerging U.S. counterforce capabilities as a threat to the land-based missiles on which the Soviets relied. Prominent arms control supporters (including McNamara) apparently did not regard MIRVs as a destabilizing technology,[12] and the arms control community appears not, in general, to have been quick to appreciate the counterforce potential of small accurate warheads converging on land-based missiles in numbers (Greenwood 1975: 94, 119, 138).[13] But as long as the Soviets maintained a relatively large number of fixed-site launchers—and the United States possessed MIRVed missiles—the Soviets had reason to fear that the United States might preempt and therefore resist reductions in the Soviet land-based missile force and its potential MIRV capability. After all, MIRVed Soviet missiles helped to ensure the survivability of some requisite number of Soviet warheads in the event of a U.S. attack.[14]

Finally, supporters noted, as always, that the United States retained the right to withdraw from the treaty—here, with six months' notice. Presumably, the United States could exert its right should a more equitable agreement prove elusive in subsequent negotiations. Accordingly, the United States issued a unilateral statement (attached to the agreement) that the United States—and, in its view, the Soviet Union—intended the agreement as a step toward more complete limitations on offensive weapons. But would the United States walk away from the agreement knowing that the Soviet Union, given its capability to produce large numbers of systems, held an advantage in an ensuing arms competition?

TRUST AND VERIFICATION

Because the treaty focused on observable features of a nuclear arsenal, it did not provoke widespread fears of Soviet cheating within the U.S. policy community. Not only could the United States monitor Soviet compliance with national technical means (NTM), the parties had also agreed "not to interfere" with NTM through "deliberate concealment measures which impede verification."[15]

Given the parties' reliance on NTM for compliance monitoring, the agreement did not technically limit numbers of missiles. Instead, it limited numbers of launchers. Fixed, land-based missile launchers had known characteristics that were detectable with satellite reconnaissance, and SLBM launchers were susceptible to tracking indirectly by counting the numbers of Soviet submarines, which contained a known number of launch tubes. Such indirect counting was itself facilitated by impediments to reload capability—that is, the inability to reuse launchers (within relatively short time frames) and their likely destruction, regardless, in a U.S. retaliatory attack. If missiles could have been used and moved quickly to launch facilities for rapid-fire attack, like bullets, the problems of counting systems for arms control would have increased enormously.

This should not be construed to suggest that the negotiating parties strove for total transparency or an ironclad agreement. To the contrary, the agreement was enabled further by the Nixon administration's deemphasis (as within the larger arms control policy community) of the complete verification of compliance with agreements. Nixon had relaxed the parameters for verification in his charge to the SALT I delegation: by his standard, the United States must be capable of identifying "evasion if it occurs on a large enough scale to pose a significant risk" and to do so "in time to mount a sufficient response" (Morris 1991: 258). In principle, the United States need not expend scarce time and resources on fine-tuning the U.S. detection apparatus to pick up small, inconsequential violations. The focus instead was on detecting major violations in time for the United States to compensate.[16] In addition, the agreement was facilitated by a recognition, by both parties, that compliance disputes would inevitably arise and that it was necessary to develop mechanisms for resolving them. For that purpose, the parties drew on the Standing Consultative Commission (SCC) that had been created by the ABM Treaty. Its roles included addressing emerging compliance issues and serving as a forum for exchanging information to build confidence that the parties were complying with the treaty.

Strong treaty supporters were convinced that the United States could detect meaningful Soviet violations. Their optimism was bolstered by the "visibility" of characteristics that required monitoring under the agreement, the commitment to greater transparency under the agreement, longstanding U.S. experience in monitoring Soviet nuclear capabilities, improving U.S. reconnaissance, and the inconsequential edge that the Soviets could obtain from building their arsenal through small, undetectable violations. Their optimism was boosted further by the logic that each Soviet violation increased the probability of detecting widespread or large-scale Soviet violations of the agreement. Their faith drew, here, from simple math: if the probability of detecting any single violation is .05, the probability reaches .50 with around a dozen Soviet violations.

That the agreement appeared to play to U.S. monitoring capabilities did not mollify critics, who were especially troubled by the possible discrepancy between what U.S. intelligence assumed it knew and what it actually did know about Soviet actions and capabilities. Indeed, critics feared that verifying compliance with the agreement—which depended heavily on aerial surveillance—would foster overoptimism and complacency about the U.S. capability to detect Soviet noncompliance. They insisted that the Soviets had acquired a working understanding of U.S. monitoring technology and practices, that is, they knew what the United States had and had not previously detected. Thus, by capitalizing on U.S. intelligence blind spots and monitoring U.S. intelligence-gathering propensities and routines, the Soviets could build up their forces surreptitiously—warehousing missiles, hiding launchers in inconspicuous places (buildings), and creating useful distractions—all the while feeding a false U.S. sense of security. On this score, critics sought implicitly to dispel the reasoning that each Soviet violation increased the likelihood of U.S. detection. In their view, each Soviet violation was not an independent event that combined with other events to increase the overall (cumulative) probability of detection: in actuality, a skilled evader can coordinate its actions to work in effective synergy, that is, to create a pattern that is hard to decipher or detect.

The ABM Treaty

In the late 1960s and early 1970s, the debate over deploying a U.S. antiballistic missile system ended somewhat paradoxically. Defenses that had been promoted with significant domestic controversy to protect against Soviet or Chinese *offen-*

sive nuclear capabilities were curtailed under the ABM Treaty, with relatively light U.S. domestic opposition, in large part because the treaty would restrict Soviet *defensive* deployments. In general, the road to the ABM Treaty was rough and rocky, before it ended in a sharp curve.

The U.S. missile defense debate occurred, however, against a backdrop of concerns about the Soviet "defensive threat." In the 1960s, the capabilities attributed to developing Soviet antiballistic missile defenses varied dramatically throughout the U.S. government. For some, including the Strategic Air Command and the Defense Intelligence Agency, Soviet upgrading of the Tallinn system—initially developed as an air defense system—was a critical nuclear threat. To them, it was inconceivable (despite a sanguine CIA assessment) that the Soviets would invest heavily in air defenses when U.S. nuclear-armed missiles threatened Soviet survival and when their existing (air) defenses offered a potential foundation on which to construct an effective missile defense (Newhouse 1973: 11–12). To others, including McNamara, an expansion of the Soviet Galosh system—which was, in fact, an antimissile system—appeared the more pressing threat (Newhouse 1973: 64, 74–75). Yet both threats eventually receded: from Tallinn, when its limitations were better appreciated; from Galosh, when it was recognized as little more than a Moscow defense. More generally, the Soviet antiballistic missile "threat" abated once U.S. policymakers came to appreciate the formidable challenges to constructing an effective missile defense.

The Johnson administration pursued its Sentinel antiballistic missile program, having recognized the impediments to defending against an all-out Soviet attack with available technology: the Soviets could easily counter a U.S. defensive system by building more missiles. Thus, the administration announced, in 1967, that its program was intended to offer a "light" defense of U.S. cities from a possible (small-scale) Chinese nuclear attack, sometime in the mid-1970s, or the accidental launch of a small number of Soviet missiles. Inasmuch as program objectives emerged through default, the outcome was controversial: some backers viewed the program wishfully as a down payment on a robust and extensive strategic defense network that would greatly enhance U.S. security; opponents viewed Sentinel as a wasteful investment that could hurt U.S. security. Efforts to win public support for the program were not helped by its call for deploying nuclear-armed interceptor missiles near major U.S. cities. With fourteen ABM sites protecting twenty-five cities, from Seattle to Boston, the plan required an interceptor missile, with a five-megaton warhead, to destroy incoming warheads above the atmosphere and a faster-moving missile, with a lower-yield warhead, to destroy surviving warheads in the atmosphere (Earle 1989: 28–29; Pike et al.

1998: 287).[17] Many in these cities loudly protested the onerous price—nuclear weapons in "their own backyard."

Although Congress funded Sentinel, the reservations about the program were not lost on the Nixon administration. The administration's "Safeguard" system, proposed in 1969, was intended primarily to deflect a Soviet first strike (by SS-9 missiles, in particular) on U.S. retaliatory capabilities: the administration had concluded that the Chinese threat to U.S. cities was less severe, and the Soviet threat to U.S. retaliatory capabilities greater, than had been supposed. Drawing on Sentinel technologies, the program was planned in two stages: the first centered on protecting U.S. ICBMs, and the second offered a defense of U.S. cities against a Chinese attack (Labrie 1979: 6–10)—on the assumption that the United States was currently ill equipped to accomplish more than a point defense of hardened targets against a Soviet ballistic missile attack. In essence, Nixon reversed the Sentinel priorities by seeking a defense initially to augment deterrence as traditionally understood. Yet the plan offered the "worst of both worlds" politically for the administration: the system was insufficiently ambitious to appease strong supporters of a U.S. nuclear defense (who hoped to protect U.S. cities from an attack), and its modest contribution, at best, to a land-based missile defense conveyed the hopelessness and cost-ineffectiveness of ballistic missile defense to program critics (Rovner 2011: 89–112). U.S. Vice President Spiro Agnew cast the tie-breaking vote in the Senate to keep the first phase of the Safeguard program alive (Pike et al. 1998: 287).

Still, the issue of defense subsided quickly (albeit temporarily) when the United States and the Soviet Union signed the 1972 Antiballistic Missile Treaty (with the Interim Agreement), which severely constrained the development of missile systems that could shoot down adversary missiles. The rapid diplomatic movement owed in large part to Nixon's decision to use U.S. ABMs as a bargaining chip, to be traded away for limits on Soviet systems. Whereas Kissinger tried to tie U.S. concessions on missile defense to Soviet reductions in offensive capability—indeed, U.S. plans for a missile defense appear to have pushed the Soviets to the negotiating table—he had limited success (at best) in acquiring these concessions given Soviet strategic priorities and views of the strategic balance. Kissinger's bargaining ruse—an opening offer to limit defenses bilaterally to national capitals ("National Command Authorities")—left the United States without leverage when the Soviets, having concluded that an ABM system would not work effectively, unexpectedly accepted the proposal. The U.S.-Soviet offensive agreement was forged, then, after the issue of antiballistic missiles had been settled.[18]

Under the terms of the ABM Treaty (and the accompanying agreed statements), the parties were restricted to two missile-defense sites (with no more than 100 launchers and missiles and six radar complexes per site), a specified deployment radius (of 150 kilometers), and a mandatory separation distance between sites (of no less than 1,300 kilometers, to prevent their complementary performance).[19] Limits on hardware included prohibitions on multiple independently guided warheads, launchers with rapid-reload capabilities, and more than two large phased-array ABM radars (with further limits on radar potential). Other limits were specified to hinder cheating and to aid the monitoring of treaty compliance: radar, launchers, and missiles that were tested in an ABM mode were considered parts of an ABM system, ABM system components were restricted to ABM deployment zones, and so forth. Although the parties were permitted to defend their national capital and one missile site, the United States preferred to deploy a missile defense to protect U.S. missile silos; the Soviet Union sought to retain the antiballistic missile system that had been constructed around Moscow. In a Protocol to the treaty, signed in 1976, the United States and the Soviet Union ratified their preferences by reducing the number of permitted missile-defense sites from two to one.

Although not as contentious as the Interim Agreement, the ABM Treaty touched on sensitive political matters—appropriate U.S. nuclear strategies, the promise of U.S. technology, and Soviet perfidy. The place of antiballistic missiles in the larger debate is appreciated, again, by examining U.S. beliefs about relative advantages from exploiting the terms of the treaty and Soviet cheating.

EVALUATING STRENGTH

Treaty proponents clearly outnumbered treaty opponents. That the United States and the Soviet Union had agreed to constrain missile defenses was largely viewed as a favorable development within the U.S. policy community.[20] Although treaty opponents argued that the United States had conceded much in both the short and the long term under the treaty, treaty supporters won the day by arguing that any U.S. strategic advantage from a missile defense would be costly, short-lived, and counterproductive. Yet the issue of defense, hardly settled, erupted (with a vengeance) in subsequent decades (as discussed more fully in chapters 4 and 5). In the ABM Treaty debate, the basic points of contention were as follows.

First, treaty supporters and critics differed in their net evaluation of the agreement. Critics charged that, under the terms of the treaty, the United States had made major concessions on defense and received little on offense in return: the ABM Treaty constrained U.S. defensive options via a permanent agreement (though with periodic review and a right of withdrawal) when the Interim Agreement institutionalized Soviet offensive advantages that might not diminish through subsequent negotiations. Critics charged that the United States was hurt in the negotiations by the apparent U.S. desire to close a deal, failure to treat a missile defense as a counter to Soviet offensive superiority, and tepid commitment to a defense that gave the Soviets little incentive to negotiate in earnest. In response, supporters maintained that the United States used what negotiating leverage it had to stem a Soviet offensive buildup that had significant momentum: the United States had little to offer to acquire additional Soviet offensive concessions, which already included accepting the U.S. position on forward-based systems. Indeed, if U.S. policymakers eventually concluded that U.S. security was harmed by adhering to the ABM Treaty, then the United States need not be bound by it. The United States attached a (unilateral) statement to the agreement stating its right to withdraw from the treaty if a more complete agreement on offensive arms was not forthcoming within five years.

Second, treaty critics and supporters debated Soviet defensive advantages under the treaty. Critics argued that the treaty ratified the Soviet lead on defense. Whereas the Soviets were using their permissible defense to protect Moscow, the so-called National Command Authority, from a U.S. attack and had constructed a dense nationwide defense against bombers, the United States planned to defend a small fraction of U.S. retaliatory capability (that is, land-based missiles) and lacked an antiaircraft missile network to counter Soviet bombers. But supporters were more impressed by the limits than by the strengths of Soviet defenses. They argued in particular that fears of the Soviet Galosh defense of Moscow overstated Soviet optimism about the likely performance of the system, understated Soviet concerns about a Chinese attack on the Soviet leadership, and ignored the negative domestic effects of dismantling a system that offered some protection to Russians who knew well the pain of war.

Third, treaty critics and supporters debated the value of a U.S. defense, unrestricted by a U.S.-Soviet agreement. Their arguments centered on whether the system could perform as advertised and contribute to U.S. security.

Many critics maintained that missile defense was a realizable goal. As such, it held the potential for shielding U.S. cities from attack and protecting U.S. retaliatory capabilities. Their hope was that a "thin" U.S. defense that was designed to serve relatively modest goals might someday morph into a "thick" defense to protect the United States against a substantial Soviet strike. Indeed, some critics maintained that a robust defense was not elusive, despite claims to the contrary. If anything, the United States was hamstrung by its own lack of vision and fortitude, not by the inherit limits of defensive technology. The Nixon administration had sought to close the distance between plans for hard-target defense and a thin urban defense by committing to technology that was not optimized for either role. A defense that was designed around technologically incommensurate purposes would eventually produce an underperforming system at an exorbitant price. Unlike hard-target defense, urban defense was an extremely demanding task due to the enormous human cost should any Soviet warhead strike near a U.S. city. Such a defense required a heavy investment in ambitious technologies—for tracking, identifying, and destroying warheads under extraordinarily challenging conditions—to obtain a high warhead-kill rate.[21]

Of course, these arguments did not sway strong treaty supporters. They minimized the strategic value of the U.S. defensive concessions that were needed to forge the agreement. In their view, defenses were a wasteful expenditure of resources: the competition between defense and offense will always be won by the offense given the relative ease and cheapness with which the United States or the Soviet Union could build multiple-warhead missiles to thwart defensive gains. On this point, Wolfgang Panofsky, a prominent U.S. scientist whose judgments had weighed heavily in the test ban debate, testified persuasively in 1969 that even if the Safeguard system components "performed as intended, they would only provide protection over a very narrow range of threats over a very limited period of time" (Halsted 1971: 26). Others stressed the ease with which U.S. adversaries could circumvent defenses by employing fairly pedestrian modes of delivery and the disabling vulnerabilities of a missile defense system—especially soft radar installations that could not perform in a nuclear environment.

Separate from whether the system *could* perform in its defensive role was the question of whether it *should* be made to perform that role. Even if the United States were capable of accomplishing the least formidable defensive task—the "point defense" of U.S. land-based missiles in hardened silos—treaty supporters insisted that the United States would not have made a wise investment: U.S. SLBMs and bombers could survive any Soviet attack (without a U.S. missile defense) to retaliate with overwhelming force (despite Soviet defenses). For that matter, even the destruction of the U.S. land-based missile force would not significantly degrade U.S. counterforce capabilities given the relatively small size and low accuracy, at the time, of U.S. land-based missile warheads. The cost-effectiveness of investing in defense was impugned further when looking beyond the first-order consequences of a U.S. defense. For the staunchest ABM opponents, the prohibitive costs of a defense included the fueling of a destabilizing arms race between U.S. and Soviet defenses, U.S. defenses and Soviet offenses, and U.S. offenses and Soviet defenses, based on the illusion that defenses will work.[22] Even a thin defense against China might provoke offsetting Soviet responses.

TRUST AND VERIFICATION

As always, treaty proponents and critics debated the potential Soviet advantages from cheating on the treaty. The arguments would survive largely unchanged into the next decade, though the level of acrimony would intensify significantly.

Many skeptics were convinced that the treaty created abundant Soviet opportunities to cheat (as the Soviets surely would, given these opportunities). They worried in particular that the Soviets would capitalize on their existing defensive infrastructure to break out effectively from the treaty. By doing so, the Soviets could allegedly seize the initiative, catch the United States off-guard (since the United States would—of course—adhere to the letter of the treaty), and build on the offensive advantages that the United States had conceded under the Interim Agreement.

In response, proponents emphasized the formidable challenges to constructing a missile defense quickly or effectively that were hardly reduced through cheating. In their view, the U.S. capability to monitor Soviet treaty compliance would prevent a successful Soviet breakout from the treaty: a nationwide defense system required too many high-profile, interdependent parts—which would have to be subject to visible testing—to permit the Soviets to accomplish their goals in secret. A more limited defense—say, of Moscow—was just that: it could not even shield the Soviet capital from destruction.

SALT II

The SALT II negotiations commenced in November 1972, around half a year after the signing of the Interim Agreement and just weeks after its approval by the Senate. Seven years passed, however, before the SALT II Treaty emerged from the negotiations. As signed by President Leonid Brezhnev and President Jimmy Carter in 1979, the treaty was long and complex by prior standards. At 78 pages, the "treaty" was actually a collection of documents: it was composed of a Treaty that would remain in effect until the end of 1985; a Protocol (consisting of 4 articles) that would remain in effect until the end of 1981; 98 Agreed Statements and Common Understandings that applied to the Treaty and the Protocol; a Joint Statement of Principles and Basic Guidelines for the next round of negotiations (SALT III); a Memorandum of Understanding on an agreed database for various types of offensive strategic arms; and statements by Brezhnev and Carter related to the Soviet Backfire bomber (U.S. Senate 1979c: 3). Rather than allay concerns, the substance and intricacy of the documents provided ammunition for the ensuing policy debate.

The main negotiating issues were resolved in principle in November 1974, when President Ford and President Brezhnev accepted a framework for SALT II at Vladivostok. The fundamentals involved a ceiling for each side of 2,400 ICBM launchers, SLBM launchers, and heavy bombers, including mobile ICBMs and air-launched cruise missiles; a limit per party of 1,320 MIRVed systems; and a ban on new launchers (which would prevent the deployment of new heavy missiles). The Soviets also agreed to omit U.S. nuclear weapons that were based in Europe from the negotiations in exchange for a U.S. concession that the Soviets alone could possess heavy missiles (Talbott 1980: 279–280). Unresolved was how to count cruise missiles or whether to restrict the Soviet Backfire bomber, which the Soviets insisted was not meant for strategic missions.[23] Thus, the Carter administration was left to bring the negotiations to an acceptable conclusion. It plotted a new course with that intent: after considerable internal debate, the administration offered the Vladivostok terms to the Soviets, with a deferral on cruise missiles (apart from a proposed 2,500-kilometer range limitation) and the Backfire bomber to the SALT III round of negotiations. It also offered the Soviets a comprehensive alternative. That proposal would reduce U.S. and Soviet force levels to well below the Vladivostok numbers (to between 1,800 and 2,000 allowable strategic nuclear delivery systems), impose a sub-limit of 550 MIRVed ICBMs and 150 heavy Soviet missiles (cutting that force by half), and ban new land-based missiles, mobile or otherwise (Talbott 1980: 60). Although the Soviet rejected the proposals—they preferred to adhere to the Vladivostok parameters—subsequent negotiations led to the SALT II Treaty.

Under the SALT II Treaty, the parties accepted various limitations that would remain in force until 1985, constraints on problem weapons (cruise missiles and mobile ICBMs) that would remain in force through 1981, and ground rules for the next negotiating round. In numerical terms, the parties accepted a ceiling of 2,400 deployed delivery systems but only through 1981, at which point the ceiling would drop to 2,250. Beyond that, it created a set of ceilings within ceilings: these included a 1,320 limit on MIRVed missile launchers and heavy bombers with cruise missiles;[24] a 1,200 ceiling on MIRVed ballistic missile launchers; and a limit of 820 on MIRVed ICBM launchers. Thus, the treaty was meant to control the size of U.S.-Soviet strategic nuclear arsenals and to reduce the threat of a first strike both by limiting the number of MIRVed ICBMs (apparent "first-strike" weapons) and first-strike targets (warheads in allegedly vulnerable, fixed-site locations). The stabilizing effects of the treaty were ostensibly enhanced by the ceilings on the numbers of permissible ballistic-missile warheads, which favored submarine-launched systems,[25] and the numbers of air-launched cruise missiles on heavy bombers, which favored them over ballistic missiles (because bombers were viewed as second-strike weapons due to their relative slowness and vulnerability). The treaty also included a ban on other weapons (including heavy SLBMs, heavy mobile missiles, and surface-ship-borne ballistic missiles), tests of air-launched cruise missiles (of a given range) on aircraft other than heavy bombers, and (via the Protocol) the deployment of longer-range sea- and ground-launched cruise missiles and testing and deployment of mobile ICBM launchers and air-to-surface ballistic missiles (through 1981). To allay U.S. concerns, the treaty was accompanied by a statement from Brezhnev that the Soviet Union would limit Backfire production to a maximum of 30 bombers a year and a statement from Carter that the United States would essentially hold the Soviets to that commitment.

Despite the Soviet concessions, the SALT II Treaty triggered a maelstrom of criticism within the United States. A main point of contention was the principle of equality that the Senate had written, years before, into its conditional acceptance of the Interim Agreement. Whereas "equality" was seen by SALT II critics as a desirable basis of agreement, the standard left much to subjective evaluation and assumption and required that negotiators reconcile profound asymmetries in U.S.-Soviet force structures, weapon technologies, strategic cultures, and perceived interests. The treaty's proponents and opponents disagreed vehemently, then, over whether that standard should be met and whether the terms of the treaty would prevent Soviet cheating. Of course, the debate was fueled in no small part by deteriorating U.S.-Soviet relations and concerns about the eroding U.S. global position. The spirit of détente—expressed in the summit diplomacy and high-profile U.S.-Soviet agreements of the Nixon administration[26]—had given way to suspicions that the Soviets viewed their "political equality" with the United States as a basis for U.S.-Soviet competition. Soviet behavior before and during the 1973 Middle East war (in which they failed to notify the United States of the impending conflict and militarily resupplied local allies), evidence of alleged Soviet misbehavior elsewhere in the developing world (including the "discovery" in August 1979 that thousands of Soviet troops were stationed in Cuba),[27] and even events that were not linked directly to Soviet transgressions (including the takeover, in November 1979, of the U.S. embassy in Tehran, which sparked a prolonged hostage crisis) stoked fears that the Soviets would employ their newfound strength to capitalize globally on U.S. vulnerabilities.

Against this backdrop, the Senate ratification debate dragged on for over half a year, yielding many thousands of pages of testimony before multiple Senate committees. The traditionally more hawkish Senate Armed Services Committee—its chair was persuaded by Senator Henry Jackson of Washington to hold hearings—issued a report denouncing the treaty as contrary to U.S. national interests (Caldwell 1991: 315, 318). Even the Senate Foreign Relations Committee split (by a vote of 9 to 6) on the issue of recommending ratification. Although it voted to support ratification—and warned that, given Soviet reticence to concede ground on key points, renegotiating the treaty would cause it to unravel (U.S. Senate 1979c: 81)—it also attached thirty-six conditions to its positive recommendation and sought assurance from the administration that it would abide by the Senate's treaty interpretation.[28] For two of these conditions, the committee required explicit Soviet approval. Thus, the committee supported an agreement that it backhandedly conceded was flawed on key points. Its mixed support could only fuel the debate over whether the United States had surrendered critical advantages to the Soviet Union in the negotiations.

The debate came to a dramatic end, however, when in December 1979 the Soviets invaded Afghanistan. Seeing the writing on the wall and bowing to widespread sentiment that the United States should not appear to reward the Soviet Union for its increasingly aggressive behavior, Carter asked the Senate in January 1980 to defer its consideration of the treaty. In consequence, the treaty languished in legal purgatory.

The lukewarm to hostile Senate reception to the treaty owed to the perception that it gave the Soviets an unequal advantage, endangered strategic stability, and created substantial loopholes and deceptive opportunities that the Soviets could (and would) exploit. Thus, the debate over the treaty centered once again on its favorableness of terms and openings for cheating.

Evaluating Strength

For supporters, the benefits of the treaty outweighed its costs; for critics, the treaty extended and exacerbated problems found in the Interim Agreement. The contours and logical failings of the contending positions come into focus when assessing their implications for essential equivalence, strategic stability, and the administration's countervailing strategy.

ESSENTIAL EQUIVALENCE

Supporters argued that the treaty produced essential equivalence between U.S. and Soviet forces because unfavorable asymmetries on some dimensions were offset by favorable asymmetries on others. In their view, such equivalence did not require that the United States and the Soviet Union achieve equality on any nuclear capability measure (such as throw-weight) or in the numbers and types of nuclear weapons. Thus, the United States could design its forces efficiently around U.S. comparative advantages: rather than answering Soviet missiles with U.S. missiles, U.S. bombers equipped with air-launched cruise missiles could destroy Soviet ICBMs in their silos, and mobile basing of U.S. ICBMs could foil attacks by Soviet missiles (Secretary of Defense Brown in U.S. Senate 1979a: 1:19). Indeed, the SALT II Treaty allowed the United States to substitute quality (the alleged U.S. advantage) for quantity and to retain theater-nuclear capabilities without restraint.[29] In all, supporters were loath to concede that a U.S.-Soviet imbalance was created or reinforced by the SALT II Treaty. Instead, they viewed U.S.-Soviet force asymmetries as the intended byproduct of U.S. plans to diversify and modernize U.S. forces for enhanced performance and survivability.

Their arguments are fairly unproblematic when tied to AD doctrine: its advocates had always insisted that the United States required only a survivable retaliatory force of a given destructiveness and need not match Soviet acquisitions. The arguments are problematic, however, when tied by high-profile treaty supporters to relativist thinking about a "psychological balance"—in Defense Secretary Brown's words, the "reality that nuclear forces have a political impact influenced by static measures" such as warhead numbers and throw-weight (U.S. Senate 1979c: 137). The logical issue is not *whether* the psychological should count in assessments but *how* it counts.

By Brown's accounting, the United States had to maintain both a military and a psychological balance to safeguard deterrence. On this score, Brown (U.S. Senate 1979a: 1:63) argued, for instance, that equivalence requires a U.S. lead on some criteria to counter specific Soviet advantages but "goes beyond the purely military balance to the question of perceptions of United States and Soviet strategic strength." Likewise, Brown deferred to the psychological when he identified key "conditions" for equivalence (U.S. Senate 1979a: 1:12). By this standard, equivalence meant that the Soviets could not employ their nuclear capabilities for "coercive" or military advantage, that Soviet force advantages are offset by identifiable U.S. advantages, and that the U.S. position "is not *seen* as inferior in performance" to Soviet nuclear forces (U.S. Senate 1979a: 1:12, emphasis added).[30] Still, the psychological was entirely missing from other assessments of the nuclear balance. Its absence was felt when Brown suggested that denying the Soviets their gains militarily is sufficient to achieve essential equivalence, that is, the countervailing strategy is "one way of assuring essential equivalence." In his words, "If you can deny [the Soviets] the ability to gain their strategic goals, then you have got essential equivalence" (U.S. Senate 1979a: 1:64–65). The psychological was downplayed further, for instance, when Chief of Naval Operations Thomas B. Hayward (U.S. Senate 1979a: 1:177) predicted that "the Soviets will attain a first-strike capability in the next few years" and concluded that "if that is not a loss of essential equivalence, I don't know what is." Efforts to reconcile the psychological and the military components were hardly a friend of clarity. The confusion only mounted when Brown argued that "essential equivalence does have to consider the perceptions problem" and that essential equivalence "perhaps takes care of the perceptions problem" while the countervailing strategy "takes care of the military problem" (U.S. Senate 1979a: 1:64). By giving essential equivalence a substantial basis in perception, Brown appeared to support at least three conclusions that would not sit well with many treaty supporters. These include (1) that U.S. nuclear weapons are instruments of deterrence, not war-fighting; (2) that U.S. nuclear deployments should mimic Soviet deployments; and (3) that nuclear deterrence is actually quite fragile insofar as having the capability to destroy or defeat an opponent is insufficient to deter it. Many treaty supporters would likely take exception to one or more of these implications; prominent administration officials—including Brown—would likely have rejected all of them.

The intellectual challenge for the administration was greater, here, than determining the role of perceptions. Even without a psychological component, essential equivalency remained an amorphous concept, for it lacked clear reference points. Having shifted the focus from the weapon-to-weapon or aggregate matchups of "equality," U.S. policymakers were left to perform assessments in a vacuum. They were struggling to compare U.S. and Soviet assets without asking the all-important question: equivalence for what purpose?

Their reluctance to pose that question is understandable. A useful response required a complex analysis of the various factors—including Soviet goals and wartime strategies—that would determine the effectiveness of U.S. offsets. For that matter, it required that U.S. policymakers actually commit to a nuclear strategy, which they appeared unable to do. Brown testified, for instance, that "a credible deterrent is achieved when our enemies believe that if they start a course of actions that could lead to war, they will either pay an unacceptable price *or* be frustrated in their attempt to achieve their objective" (U.S. Senate 1979c: 137, emphasis added). Likewise, PD-59 stated that, should deterrence fail, the United States "must be capable of fighting successfully so that the adversary would not achieve his war aims and would suffer costs that are unacceptable" (NSA 2012). Even had officials fully embraced a denial over an AD strategy, questions would remain: Why should the United States settle for "equivalence"? After all, in fighting, is not the goal to "win"? Shouldn't the United States seek land-based missiles in numbers to absorb and survive the Soviet onslaught and deliver a knock-out blow in return? Conversely, the United States might achieve security with a nuclear force that fell short of Soviet capabilities. On this point, dovish critics could reasonably ask, What good is equivalence if hard-target capable, U.S. land-based forces are decimated in a Soviet first strike or if the Soviet attack has left few remaining hardened, counterforce targets for surviving U.S. ICBMs to hit? In other words, What has the United States achieved, then, of "equivalence" to warrant the prior pursuit of offsetting U.S. capabilities?

For the administration, then, equivalence offered only vague and contradictory guidelines for configuring and sizing the U.S. nuclear arsenal and assessing U.S. benefits and costs under a treaty. But their critics were no less hobbled by their own logic.

Critics set their sights on the treaty's unequal treatment of U.S. and Soviet nuclear forces. Paul Nitze (U.S. Senate 1979a: 3:878)—the Defense Department's former SALT representative—surmised that, by the treaty's expiration (in 1985), the Soviets would have "twice the area destructive capability, five times the ICBM plus SLBM hard target kill capability, three times the megatonnage, and twice our throwweight." In consequence, the Soviets could well destroy 90 percent of the U.S. land-based missile force (with a 2–1 Soviet warhead-to-U.S. launcher allocation); the U.S. could destroy perhaps only half of the Soviet force using all Minuteman III warheads (U.S. Senate 1979a: 3:881). In essence, Nitze and other critics concluded that the treaty constrained only the United States—that Soviet Union could proceed with its planned force buildup (Rowny in U.S. Senate 1979a: 2:670). To quote Nitze again, "What we have gained from these concessions has been a series of relatively unimportant adjustments in what otherwise would have been the Soviet program for deployments over the next six years, more than offset by limitations on our programs for future deployments. In essence, most of the negotiating process has been one of trading marginal adjustments to their large strategic program versus more significant adjustments to our much smaller one" (U.S. Senate 1979a: 3:881).

To make their case, critics advertised the treaty's bias, which gave the Soviets "unilateral rights"—exemptions that applied only to the Soviet Union. The egregious bias allowed the Soviets alone to possess heavy missiles—in particular, the SS-18, the multiple-warhead successor to the SS-9 (Rowny in U.S. Senate 1979a: 2:671). U.S. ICBMs were dwarfed in comparisons of U.S. and Soviet missiles under the treaty: the SS-18 was apparently six times more powerful than the U.S. Minuteman and had three times the payload capacity of the MX missile, which was yet to be deployed. The Soviet SS-18 force reputedly exceeded the destructive power of the total U.S. ICBM and SLBM force.[31] Critics also read bias into the Backfire's omission from the Soviet strategic count even though the bomber could deliver a significant payload against U.S. targets, when U.S. aircraft (armed with cruise missiles) were counted against the U.S. MIRV ceiling of 1,320 (Rowny in U.S. Senate 1979a: 2:675). This Soviet exemption was allegedly made more one-sided still, because of the relative U.S. reliance on bombers (indeed, only the United States required cruise missiles) and because superior Soviet air defenses would take a toll on U.S. aircraft before they could strike their targets (Rowny in U.S. Senate 1979a: 2:678). Likewise, critics assailed the treaty's range limit of 600 kilometers on sea- and ground-launched cruise missiles, which made them theater weapons, and the absence of a range limit for Soviet SS-20s, theater-based ballistic missiles with a range exceeding 3,000 kilometers (Alexander Haig in U.S. Senate 1979a: 1:361). Indeed, given unfavorable geography, the treaty would still place much of the U.S. population and military capability within Soviet sea-launched cruise-missile range while keeping much of the Soviet infrastructure at a safe distance from similar U.S. systems.[32] For critics, the U.S. disadvantage only grew when considering attack timing and targeting, "including the fact that the initiative is apt to be theirs; that their command, control, and wartime intelligence facilities are substantially harder and more diverse; that they have more and harder hard targets; that their active defenses and their civil defense preparations are substantially greater than ours" (Nitze in U.S. Senate 1979a: 3:878–879). All of this did not bode well for U.S. force survivability. U.S. aircraft would be slow to arrive on their targets, if they arrived at all; U.S. submarines in port would have been destroyed, and those out to sea would lack "secure and redundant" communications and effective firepower.[33]

The critics had a point: the United States and the Soviet Union were not treated "equally" under the treaty. But critics had not made their case that the Soviet Union would achieve meaningful superiority: they too conducted their comparative assessments in a strategic void. Rather than performing net assessments of wartime payoffs to the parties, based on their respective goals, they relied on unfavorable scenarios and assumptions (for instance, that the Soviets had destroyed the U.S. land-based force, U.S. submarines in port, and B-52 bombers on the ground) and then focused narrowly on the unfavorable aggregate balances (for instance, in megatonnage and hard-target capability) that would exist after an exchange. In this, they failed to ask, what precisely had the Soviets gained from the exchange? Critics had yet to establish that the resulting "imbalance" brought the Soviets closer to achieving their goals. A telling consequence was that critics disagreed over whether the Soviets had "enough" capability. Some critics thought not. Edward Rowny, the former JCS SALT representative, asserted that the Soviets could produce Backfire bombers in quantities that would "add another one-third of the total destructive potential that the Soviets could inflict upon the United States"—what he described as "not an insignificant threat" (U.S. Senate 1979a: 3:1194). Still other critics maintained that the Soviets had gotten everything they wanted from the treaty and had no need to pad their lead. In Senate testimony, Nitze asked rhetorically, "Why should they want more of it? They would just waste resources?" Echoing that remark, Senator Henry Jackson observed that the United States might actually be "better off if the Soviets squandered their resources on ICBM's beyond the treaty limits" (U.S. Senate 1979a: 3:947).

Without a standard for capability assessment, critics had to depend on the Soviets themselves to establish, by their behavior, that they had achieved a "meaningful" edge. The Soviets were expected to signal their advantage by becoming bellicose, combative, and war-prone—perhaps even by launching a "disarming" nuclear attack on the United States—when, in the early 1980s, a "window of vulnerability" opened because Soviet MIRVed ICBMs threatened the survival of the U.S. land-based missile force. Yet, even on this point, critics were vague. They did not insist that the Soviets would attack. For that matter, they did not necessarily claim that the Soviets would try to retain their advantage if the United States pushed back. As one hard-line critic maintained, "A primary lesson from SALT should be that the real threat is what the Soviets are allowed to do by the agreements, not what they might hypothetically do in the absence of the agreement" (William Van Cleave in U.S. Senate 1979a: 3:1181). Despite the overriding importance to the Soviets of obtaining superiority and the costs (with such superiority) that the Soviets would supposedly incur in war, the Soviets would dutifully stick to their plans (as codified in the treaty) and oddly allow the United States to close the gap.

STRATEGIC STABILITY

The SALT II Treaty reassured treaty supporters who relied on the AD threat to safeguard deterrence. Under its terms, these supporters maintained that the U.S.-Soviet nuclear balance was stable: the Soviets would not tempt fate, knowing that in the worst-case scenario, the United States retained thousands of SLBM warheads and cruise missiles (on B-52 bombers) that could devastate Soviet industries and society. Yes, U.S. policymakers had moved away from AD principles in search of wartime options, but Soviet leaders could not assume that the United States would hesitate to use overwhelming and indiscriminate nuclear force, when responding to an unprovoked Soviet nuclear attack, given the costs to the Soviets of underestimating U.S. resolve.[34] For these supporters, the U.S. "window of vulnerability" was an illusion. To quote Paul Warnke, the U.S. ACDA director and chief SALT II negotiator, the window was but a "theoretical vulnerability" based on an unrealistic scenario—one that "staggers the imagination" (U.S. Senate 1979b: 2:71–72). But for many officials in the Carter administration—and its hawkish critics—strategic stability was a real and ongoing concern. This is apparent from their focus on nuclear trends and Soviet first-strike incentives.

For administration officials, the SALT II Treaty promised to strengthen U.S.-Soviet deterrence by capping destabilizing nuclear systems. Whereas hard-target kill capability was far more sensitive to improving accuracies and numbers of warheads than to their yield, the treaty's per-missile warhead and land-based missile ceilings would ultimately reduce the Soviet missile threat to the U.S. land-based force.[35] Thus, supporters argued that the United States was better off with the treaty than without it. As Brown (U.S. Senate 1979a: 1:18) concluded, "I do not see how the magnitude of the Soviet threat would be diminished, or how our ability to respond would be improved, by rejecting SALT II; no solution to our problems would be any easier to fashion in the absence of an agreement." By his estimates, absent a treaty, the Soviets would likely possess a force one-third larger (with a third more MIRVed missiles) by 1985 than they could have under the treaty (U.S. Senate 1979a: 1:14). Soviet missile throw-weight guaranteed that the force growth would disproportionately benefit Soviet hard-target capabilities inasmuch as the SS-18 missile alone could potentially carry as many as thirty warheads (U.S. Senate 1979a: 1:15). Moreover, by their accounting, the United States had not paid a stiff price for the Soviet concessions. For example, the Protocol banned mobile ballistic missiles through 1981, when the United States had not planned to flight test the MX until 1983. Then the treaty allowed the United States eventually to close the alleged window of vulnerability after it opened in the early 1980s. In subsequent years, the United States would increase its hard-target capabilities courtesy of the MX missile (to offset the Soviet SS-18), improved Minuteman III warhead guidance, and enhanced missile survivability through a new basing scheme (Brown in U.S. Senate 1979a: 1:19, 1:21).

But why was it necessary, then, for the United States to close the window? After all, administration officials had minimized the dangers to the United States that were present in the interim. If the United States could deter the Soviets in the period of maximum vulnerability, was this not strong evidence that deterrence was robust and did not require fine-tuning or enhancing? Indeed, if the United States was dangerously vulnerable in that period, should it try to close the window? Faced with a fading opportunity, the Soviet Union might do the unthinkable and attack the United States while it was still susceptible to a disarming strike. True, for some who focused on U.S. vulnerabilities, the Soviet threat was more coercive than existential. Henry Kissinger, a net treaty supporter, argued that "a continuation of these dangerous trends will leave us helpless in future crises and unable to shape events" (U.S. Senate 1979a: 2:829). In his view, the correctives centered on improving U.S. strategic and theater nuclear forces and insisting on equality in future SALT negotiations (U.S. Senate 1979a: 2:830). A skeptic could ask whether the Soviets, if perceived to be unwilling to use nuclear weapons, could actually obtain coercive benefits and, if they could, whether the United States was then positioned to demand anything, much less equality as a future basis of agreement.

Administration officials did have some reasons to assume that the Soviets would not press their advantage: the United States could still launch its land-based missiles against Soviet targets upon warning of a Soviet attack—accordingly, PD-59 contained a "launch-on-warning" (LOW) option (NSA 2012). Although they preferred not to place U.S. weapons on hair-trigger alert—tying the fate of the United States to a potentially faulty detection system—such a posture supposedly reinforced deterrence by feeding uncertainty about the likely U.S. response to a Soviet attack (Brown in U.S. Senate 1979a: 1:26). This uncertainty, combined with the catastrophic damage to the Soviet Union that the United States could inflict, presumably gave Soviet leaders abundant incentive to forgo attacking the United States. But did a LOW posture really serve U.S. security? A U.S. decision, instead, to "launch-under-attack"—when the fact of a Soviet attack was no longer at issue—would not jeopardize U.S. capabilities to destroy softer targets including much of the Soviet military and civilian infrastructure (and the Soviet launcher-reload capability) and would obviously be no less effective than a LOW posture against Soviet missiles that had already been launched. Even with LOW, the effectiveness of U.S. missiles in destroying the reserve Soviet ICBM force would depend on its size and the U.S. capability to discriminate between spent and empty silos. With increases in the size of the Soviet reserve force or uncertainty about missile locations, a LOW posture would require a huge U.S. investment in prompt counterforce capability—indeed, a U.S. ICBM force that could plausibly threaten the Soviet ICBM force in a first strike. Thus, despite U.S. efforts to stabilize the U.S.-Soviet nuclear balance, the strategy could undermine deterrence. It could provoke the Soviets to strike first (given war-fighting arguments) to counter the U.S. advantage if they believed that the United States might hold its fire (not launch missiles on warning of a Soviet attack), a realistic possibility given official misgivings about the policy (see Nolan 1999: 48).

Of course, treaty critics avoided these contradictions by eschewing the "quick fix" of the LOW option. According to critics, the United States confronted a profound asymmetry: the Soviets would have many warheads aimed at a considerably smaller number of hardened U.S. targets; the United States would have relatively few warheads aimed at a large number of Soviet hard targets—missile silos, command and control bunkers, nuclear storage sites, and so on (that were hardened well beyond the levels of comparable facilities within the United States).[36] Thus, improvements in Soviet capabilities and the sluggish pace of U.S. modernization programs created a very real opening that the Soviets might exploit. But were critics on solid logical ground when they insisted that the United States should therefore reject the SALT II Treaty and push the Soviets in subsequent negotiations? If their dire assessment was accurate, what could the United States gain from renouncing the treaty, let alone from pressing the Soviets to make concessions? If the Soviets were willing to accept the potential costs for the unclear gains from an unprovoked counterforce attack on the United States, what reason would they have to negotiate with the United States? For that matter, if the dire assessment was valid—and a window of vulnerability would soon open—did the United States have any recourse but to accept its fate? After all, critics did not claim that the United States could reverse the negative trends in time to prevent the window from opening.

THE COUNTERVAILING STRATEGY

Under the countervailing strategy, administration officials sought the capabilities to "fight" a protracted nuclear war with the Soviet Union. From their perspective, the strategy was aided by the SALT II Treaty's allowance for U.S. force modernization and restrictions on Soviet launchers. Hawkish critics insisted, however, that the administration's negotiating concessions had placed the United States at a counterforce disadvantage that left the United States critically vulnerable if the Soviets struck first. Both positions in this debate were on shaky logical ground.

Throughout the 1970s, U.S. officials voiced support for war-fighting principles, based on a military or political logic or some unwieldy composite of the two. The military logic assumed that the United States could boost deterrence and improve U.S. war outcomes by acquiring the means to deny the Soviets gains from a nuclear attack. It therefore had the United States employing its nuclear weapons to weaken the Soviet Union, perhaps forcing its capitulation. It thus pressed for a relativist approach to weapons deployment for the purpose of countering (or exceeding) Soviet acquisitions. In turn, the political logic assumed that the United States could boost deterrence and improve U.S. war outcomes by acquiring the capability to inflict punishment of growing severity on the Soviets to demonstrate to them the perils of continuing to fight. The political logic had the United States employing nuclear weapons to establish U.S. resolve (and restraint) in the hope of deescalating a conflict, so it pressed primarily for an absolutist approach to weapons deployment. Drawing from AD precepts, it assumed that accumulating nuclear weapons beyond some point served no useful purpose. If anything, U.S. counterforce weapons were meant to buy time, through force-on-force exchanges, to reinforce the reality of *mutual* assured destruction.[37]

The problem, however, was that U.S. officials shifted between the opposing logics without recognizing their incompatibility. These tendencies were apparent under the Schlesinger Doctrine, which favored limited nuclear options (LNOs), ostensibly to support the political logic. Although U.S. officials spoke of the accompanying need to use nuclear weapons to terminate conflict "at the lowest possible level of violence," they sometimes heralded nuclear attacks for their strictly military effects. As a result, LNOs were pursued for a political purpose—to compel the Soviets to deescalate—but the strong emphasis on military strikes blurred the line between strategy and tactics (see Davis 1975; U.S. Department of Defense 1975). The question remained: was the military effort designed to influence the decisional calculations of the Soviet leadership or to disarm it physically? The tendencies surfaced again when Carter administration officials articulated the countervailing strategy. Although Brown denied that nuclear weapons were ultimately of military use and that victory in nuclear war was possible, he insisted that the United States must maintain a relative balance with Soviet nuclear forces and counterforce capabilities to deny the Soviets a postwar military advantage (Brown 1983: 51; Department of Defense 1982). His reliance, then, on competing political and military logics raised fundamental questions. If U.S. strategy was meant to convince the Soviets of U.S. resolve, why would the United States engage in "measured retaliation" (U.S. Senate 1979c: 137) with selective military strikes? After all, engaging in military attacks arguably communicated that U.S. policymakers recognized that hitting civilian targets was a suicidal proposition. Conversely, if U.S. policymakers were serious about fighting a "war," why not pursue it as such, without trepidation? Engaging in limited attacks surrendered the initiative and exposed the United States to a disarming Soviet attack.

Most definitely, the administration relied on the political logic when enforcing a distinction in U.S. war plans between military and civilian-industrial targets.

But that distinction defied practical realities that undermined the political targeting strategy by making it hard for the Soviets to show "restraint." These complicating factors were as follows.

First, damage in a nuclear strike was simply hard to contain. In part this was because targeting distinctions blurred in practice. Thus, targeting Soviet economic recovery in the Nixon administration led to wholesale target proliferation with (1) uncertainty about which targets, when destroyed, might produce the greatest effect; and (2) the high proportion of target destruction that was assumed necessary to thwart recovery. As an example of these problems, fertilizer plants were considered prime targets (Sagan 1989: 46). Whereas strategists distinguished military from civilian targets in the abstract with ease, then, many of the same targets qualified as both, as was apparent in the targeting of war-supporting industries: petroleum refineries, railway yards, and other "dual-use" facilities were included in the mix (Ball and Toth 1990: 70–71). Containing the ravages of a nuclear strike was complicated further by the geographical overlap of targets. Because national economies are constructed for efficiency and thus the virtues of proximity, centralization, and economies of scale, the destruction of a military target would take a huge toll on civilians and industries. Ironically, the Soviet Union—which renounced the principle of limits in a nuclear war—was advantaged over the United States if observing limits was the goal: whereas the United States banished its ICBMs to sparsely populated areas, many Soviet ICBM fields were located in the most heavily populated parts of the Soviet Union, west of the Urals. Adding to the U.S. challenge, the Soviets were comparatively less equipped technologically to assess the scope and severity of an enemy attack—and thus to recognize any U.S. "limits" that were observed (Ball 1982/83: 40).

Second, military targets had "value" to the Soviet leadership. Inasmuch as military instruments allowed Soviet leaders to maintain and extend their territorial control and to stay in power, they would actually incur high "costs" with the destruction of these targets. If so, the United States—by targeting the Soviet military infrastructure—was effectively engaging in the countervalue strikes that U.S. policymakers had explicitly rejected. At some level, administration officials understood this. Brown argued that by attacking Soviet nuclear and conventional forces, war-supporting industries, and military and political control targets, the United States would destroy what Soviet leaders "prized most." Indeed, he testified that survival of their power structure meant more to Soviet leaders than their own lives or the lives of as many as 50 million Soviet citizens (Glaser 1989: 130–131). But such an acknowledgment still challenged the logical foundation of a U.S. (countervailing) strategy that was predicated on observing limitations in nuclear war. After all, "the more valuable the Soviet targets destroyed, the smaller the remaining Soviet incentives for restraint" (Glaser 1989: 130).

Third, hitting nuclear targets per se could still facilitate an unlimited response. Although U.S. policymakers sought to enhance "crisis stability" through arms control—that is, structuring arsenals for reduced vulnerability to lessen incentives to launch weapons precipitously—they were insensitive to the Soviet incentive to launch weapons in actual combat, when U.S. military intentions were no longer in doubt and the launch window had closed significantly. Indeed, a U.S. assault on Soviet military targets could directly trigger a war without limits. U.S. policymakers failed to appreciate that precise and limited counterforce strikes—when directed at military-control targets—could create a Soviet "use-them-or-lose-them" predicament that produced an unrestrained Soviet response or could deprive Soviet nuclear forces of centralized command and thus the capability to exercise restraint (Glaser 1989: 138). If so, the United States quest for limits could actually produce the spasmodic and unrelenting Soviet nuclear response that U.S. policymakers had, in moving away from AD doctrine, sought to avoid.

Fourth, nuclear weapons were no more fine-tuned to send messages than were command, communication, and intelligence networks equipped to receive, process, and transmit messages accurately in a "noisy," that is nuclear-charged, environment—indeed, when these networks were themselves under attack and thus disintegrating and fragmenting (see Brown in U.S. Senate 1979c: 143). Any message that the United States sought to send through astute target selection could be contravened by the weapons that struck those targets (Brown in U.S. Senate 1979c: 143). Most of the U.S. nuclear force (more than half of U.S. warheads) was located on submarines that were not well suited to implement the countervailing strategy. These submarines lacked prompt communication and retargeting capabilities, and their missiles lacked the precision to destroy Soviet hard targets such as silos, launch-control centers, and leadership bunkers. Indeed, these submarines were unlikely to stagger their fire to assist a counterforce or bargaining strategy; any limited SLBM launch could risk the weapons held in reserve by exposing a submarine's position (Ball 1982/83: 47–49). Even if SLBMs were used selectively for political effect, the Soviets had good reason not to read messages into their targeting or rates of fire: U.S. officials had consistently tried to sell the Soviets on the stabilizing effects of submarines by emphasizing what they could not do. For instance, Henry Kissinger remarked to President Brezhnev in a private session that "to coordinate an attack from submarines dispersed all over the ocean—to coordinate a plausible attack—is so difficult as to be virtually impossible" (U.S. Department of State 2012: 224). Under the circumstances, the

Soviets had good reason, then, to see any and all U.S. submarine-borne "signals" as sending but one clear message: the time for messaging had passed and the end was at hand.

Fifth, the Soviet Union was inclined to resist U.S. entreaties. After all, it presumably had initiated the nuclear conflict (or the train of events that led to conflict) by attacking the United States or invading Europe (perhaps with the knowledge that the war would go nuclear). If so, the United States would now have to compel the Soviets to back down. Social scientists have long assumed that inducing a party to renounce gains is more difficult than convincing it to forgo gains: people are more inclined to value what they have than what they do not yet possess, are disinclined to accept the costs of a public retreat, and are unable to grasp easily the exact set of actions that will satisfy a compelling party.

Sixth, Soviet leaders would likely suffer decisional maladies that afflict individuals under stress (Jervis 1982/83; Jervis et al. 1985). Experts on human decision-making tell us that leaders (that is, people) tend to exaggerate the latitude that opponents have for choice and to attribute their hostility to malevolent intent. In consequence, leaders tend to ignore the domestic and international political pressures that prevent adversaries from backing down. Once they commit to a strategy, they tend not to look back or to perform tradeoff assessments that could highlight the downside of preferred options. Given these decisional biases, Soviet leaders would likely conclude that the United States is determined to fight and will not reciprocate Soviet concessions. The risk for Soviet leaders of cooperating, then, is appearing weak or creating openings—for instance, through a cease-fire—that the United States could exploit militarily.

Seventh, Soviet leaders might simply do what they said they would do. Champions of the political war-fighting logic assumed that the Soviets would observe limitations in a nuclear exchange—PD-59 presumed, in fact, that the Soviet Union had limited nuclear options (NSA 2012)—despite a Soviet military doctrine that stressed the importance of seizing the initiative and going on the offensive.[38] Even were the Soviets inclined to play by U.S. doctrinal rules, they would be hard pressed to understand them. The U.S. preference for keeping options open—not committing fully to a political or military targeting strategy in advance—could only provoke the Soviets to fight on their own terms.

Finally, the United States itself would be challenged when trying to show the restraint that the political strategy required. Brown acknowledged that a Soviet counterforce attack might kill 10 million Americans and that a "US response that does not in that circumstance contemplate some retaliation for the 10 million Americans killed is not an acceptable response" (U.S. Senate 1979a: 1:30).[39]

By his calculations, U.S. options in nuclear war involved "degrees of catastrophe" (U.S. Senate 1979c: 137).

Champions of the military (or damage-limitation) logic believed that "limits" in war ensued from incapacitating the enemy and deflecting its blows, not from signaling, avoiding casualties, or fighting wars expressly within defined limits. Their logic was also problematic in multiple respects.[40]

First, the logic suffered because a nuclear war was not "winnable" in a traditional sense. A counterforce exchange would still leave the parties—the alleged "victor" and "loser" of a counterforce exchange—each capable of destroying the other. Thus, the victor in that exchange would be left with no option but to try and break the will of the loser by threatening or attacking its cities—as long as the loser could retaliate in kind. At this point, the parties were effectively on an equal footing: in a countervalue competition of pain infliction, inaccurate or slow-moving weapons—launched from submarines or aircraft—are a match for land-based missiles. The upshot, then, is that the initial counterforce exchange would not free the parties from the mutual-hostage relationship that was envisioned under AD doctrine. At best, it would postpone it.

Second, the logic rested on the untenable assumption that the Soviets were motivated purely by gains or were sensitive only to those costs that would compromise these gains. But proponents of a damage-limitation strategy undercut that argument when they fell back on the threat to punish Soviet leaders directly because they valued their own lives or hold on power (Glaser 1989: 130). They could not consistently argue both that the Soviets were indifferent to costs and that the United States had to fine-tune its methods of punishment in order to inflict the "right type" of cost by targeting the Soviet leadership. Indeed, when arguing along those lines, they had to accept strategic consequences that would only undercut their arguments. The accompanying dangers of shifting the focus back to punishment was that the war-fighting strategy now (1) no less than AD doctrine, would lack credibility, for targeted Soviet leaders, with nothing left to lose, might retaliate against U.S. cities; or (2) would have credibility and would lead Soviet leaders to plan for the worst—by preparing, as they apparently did, to unleash Armageddon in the event of a U.S. attack (see chapter 4).

Third, the logic drew from the heroic proposition that the Soviets were unrelentingly aggressive—even out for world domination—and would pay a huge price (including enormous numbers of civilian casualties) to achieve their goals (see Gray 1979; Gray and Payne 1980; Pipes 1977). The logical problem here was that the costs that the Soviets were supposedly willing to incur had to compromise Soviet gains. As Charles Glaser asked, "What possible use could military forces and political control have if one's country were destroyed?" (1989: 132). Whereas these war-fighters insisted that Soviet leaders would reap no reward from a war that left the Soviet Union without a "head," they failed to ask whether the same was true if Soviet leaders were left without a body—an economy, society, and population, a "Soviet Union" in any true sense of the term. At the very least, U.S. targeting of the Soviet civilian and military infrastructure risked the destruction of Soviet conventional forces, which Soviet leaders would require to collect their prizes of war.

Finally, the logic placed its adherents in the untenable position of avoiding solutions that followed from diagnostics. They argued that, to achieve its goals, the Soviet Union would commit monstrous acts, accept unfathomable costs, and capitalize on a post-exchange nuclear force balance that would swing in favor of the side that struck first. If they were correct, the only question is, why were these war-fighters not advocating an all-out, preventative U.S. attack on the Soviet nuclear infrastructure? Their hesitancy—though understandable—was telling.

Trust and Verification

Fears that the SALT II Treaty gave the Soviets a substantial advantage were reinforced by concerns that the treaty would allow the Soviets to cheat. Although treaty supporters were fairly confident that the United States could monitor Soviet compliance and detect significant Soviet violations, critics were not. Their points of disagreement were as follows.

First, proponents and critics argued over the treaty's fundamental premise that compliance with the treaty could be monitored using national technical means. As supporters would note, restrictions were imposed on things that could be counted or measured with reasonable certainty, and conservative numerical rules were employed to compensate when counting or measurement was proscribed. For instance, the treaty did not limit numbers of missiles; instead it limited visible launchers: these were present in fixed sites, with known physical properties, or on submarines, with known numbers of launch tubes. Similarly, the treaty did not require a visual warhead count; instead, it limited telemetry encryption in missile tests—the electronic signals on missile performance that were relayed to earth—so that the monitoring party could determine the number of warheads that had been released from the warhead bus of a given type of missile. Then, all missiles of a type were presumed to be equipped with the maximum number of warheads that had been tested on that missile type. For supporters, the task of treaty monitoring was eased, as well, by requiring "functionally related observable differences" (for example, between the frames of heavy bombers and other aircraft) to help the monitoring party discriminate between systems that were restricted versus unrestricted by the treaty and by banning weapons that did not allow for such observable differences. Even if the Soviets tried to cheat, they could not succeed given various "observation points" for the United States in a sequence of evasion.[41] The monitoring of Soviet compliance with the SS-16 missile ban demonstrates the point. The Soviet Union was prohibited from producing, testing, or deploying the SS-16 (or producing its third stage) because the SS-16 was effectively a SS-20 missile—an unrestricted theater-based system—with a third stage added for intercontinental range. Although critics feared that the Soviets would cannibalize their SS-16 stocks (which the Soviets could retain) to give the SS-20 intercontinental range in advance of an attack, treaty supporters argued that the Soviets had never deployed a system without first testing it. That would immediately raise the profile of the Soviet ruse.

But critics assailed each and every one of these assumptions. They denied that the United States had effectively surmounted Soviet resistance to onsite inspections by engineering a treaty around U.S. national monitoring capabilities. In their view, the Soviets had various options to hide illicit actions under the treaty. Most importantly, they could use permissible activities to cover illicit ones. For example, the Soviets could launch air-launched cruise missiles from the ground or from ships to circumscribe range restrictions on land- and sea-launched cruise missiles (Nitze in U.S. Senate 1979a: 3:886); they could test ICBMs that were restricted under the treaty in the guise of testing SLBMs (permitted under the treaty); they could employ the "intermediate-range" SS-20 (with roughly the same throw-weight as the U.S. Minuteman missile) with a single warhead (rather than three warheads) to enhance its range (making it technically an ICBM);[42] and so on and so forth. They could also engage in restricted activities and cheat effectively by avoiding illicit activities where the "light is brightest"—that is, where U.S. monitoring capabilities are strongest—and capitalizing, instead, on opportunities to prepare in the "dark." For instance, the Soviets could augment the SS-20 for intercontinental range—without testing—because working with the SS-16 gave the Soviets the operational experience to judge the reliability and performance of the SS-20 in its extended role; they could modify Soviet aircraft surreptitiously to accommodate large numbers of cruise missiles that were maintained in storage; and so forth.

Second, treaty supporters and critics argued over whether the Soviets were positioned to win any game of "hide-and-seek" with U.S. intelligence. Supporters insisted that U.S. intelligence capabilities matched up well against Soviet subterfuge given the challenges of disguising a nuclear buildup. They maintained, for instance, that all of the Soviet Union's ballistic missile submarines were manufactured in a single shipyard—in the open, over a period of many months; that submarines are observable in port and out at sea; that heavy bombers are built at a small number of plants and deployed at a small number of bases; and that a significant number of new ICBM launchers would be difficult to hide even if the Soviets changed their deployment practices to avoid telltale indicators (Brown in U.S. Senate 1979c: 207–208). Where U.S. intelligence was challenged—for instance, in determining whether Soviet ICBM dimensions had exceeded the treaty allowance—the United States could rely on surrogate measures to assess Soviet compliance. Brown noted, for example, that despite possible increases in Soviet missile throw-weight, the United States could still monitor numbers of warheads as well as their weight in order to ensure that the Soviets were not designing extra warhead capacity into missiles (U.S. Senate 1979c: 210). Although supporters conceded that the United States could not detect each and every Soviet violation, they did insist that the United States could detect major treaty violations, given their palpable signatures, scale, scope, and necessary recurrence. Echoing a refrain from the Limited Test Ban treaty debate, Brown described the "double bind" in which the Soviets were placed: "To go undetected, any Soviet cheating would have to be on so small a scale that it would not be militarily significant. Cheating on such a level would hardly be worth the political risks involved. On the other hand, any cheating serious enough to affect the military balance would be detectable in sufficient time to take whatever action the situation required." (U.S. Senate 1979c: 221).

Then, in the view of supporters, the United States had a nonzero probability of detecting even small Soviet violations, which could deter them. This probability stemmed from a variety of factors including sheer happenstance, limited Soviet knowledge of U.S. monitoring capabilities, and redundancies within the U.S. monitoring system. The latter allowed the United States to track various data streams (drawn from human and technical sources), cross-check them for inconsistencies, and seek out additional information when anomalies are detected. As Brown observed, "What we learn from one source—photography, for example—can often be checked against information from other sources such as radar or telemetry monitoring. The use of multiple sources complicates any effort to disguise or conceal a violation" (U.S. Senate 1979a: 1:16). Even Soviet uncooperativeness with U.S. monitoring efforts contains clues about Soviet veracity or evasiveness—the tone and nature of responses in the SCC to U.S. concerns, denials of access to information that was previously available, and so forth.[43]

Overall, supporters shifted the focus of debate to U.S. strengths in monitoring Soviet behavior and away from the weaknesses of U.S. intelligence. When conceding that Soviet cheating could occur, they argued that Soviet secrecy came with a price: mission performance would suffer if the Soviets chose not to test their systems, to deploy systems without support equipment and personnel to avert suspicion, to avoid training personnel with prohibited weapons to keep them under wraps, and so forth.

In contrast, critics were struck more by the unknowns and the limits of U.S. intelligence capabilities. Accordingly, they alluded to the numerous instances in which the U.S. intelligence community was caught by surprise: it failed to predict the fall of the Shah of Iran in 1979, it repeatedly failed to predict the pace and scale of the Soviet nuclear buildup, and so on. For critics, the story was consistently about what lay beneath the surface, not what was protruding through the cracks. Therefore, critics were greatly troubled by the Soviet breakout threat. They argued that the Soviets could prepare for a major, far-reaching breach of the treaty by engaging in low-profile (seemingly "excusable") activities before shifting into high gear—through massive deployment—leaving the United States with no time to counter effectively. Such fears were hardly reduced by claims that U.S. intelligence agencies had successfully monitored Soviet deployments. An apparent track record of success only increased the risk that these agencies would overrely on mechanisms and practices that had "worked" in the past. It also bred hubris that could blind analysts to a Soviet strategy of deception—meant by the Soviets to disguise their activities—and instill false confidence within the U.S. intelligence community.

For critics, the intelligence problem was fundamental: the U.S. intelligence community had no way of knowing independently how good it was at tracking Soviet behavior. It might point to its successes—however numerous they might be—but it could never know its overall rate of success. That requires knowing the full extent of U.S. intelligence failures, which cannot be known with certainty. Indeed, alleged successes might be failures in disguise. Implicitly, critics asked, "Do we know it because they want us to know it?" Or else, "Now that they know we know it, what will they do instead?"

Third, supporters and critics battled over the reputed benefits of transparency that were created under the agreement. For supporters, the treaty would give the United States access to information by requiring the sharing of information and by limiting the Soviet ability to impede detection.[44] Whether or not U.S. policymakers accepted the veracity of Soviet-supplied data, the inflow of information allowed the United States to calibrate and validate its own methods, employ a baseline against which future or newly detected Soviet activities could be assessed, and determine areas of the treaty that required further clarification to strengthen the treaty.[45]

But critics treated alleged Soviet transparency under the treaty as illusionary at best and deceptive at worst. The United States lacked critical Soviet data on missile dimensions to establish a baseline against which modifications could be compared (Nitze in U.S. Senate 1979a: 3:921). A case in point was the Soviet refusal to release information on essential weapon characteristics, such as missile throw-weight (Rowny in U.S. Senate 1979a: 3:987). Regardless, the "release" of data by the Soviet government was a poor gauge of its transparency. Despite Soviet "cooperation" in generating an agreed database on the numbers of Soviet systems, the Soviet-supplied figures could not be accepted on their face. Any data that the Soviets disclosed were likely incomplete and always suspect, and they could not compensate for a fundamental "asymmetry" between the open U.S. and closed Soviet societies. The U.S. democratic system guaranteed that critical information about U.S. nuclear war planning would flow freely into the public domain. The United States had no such assurance about Soviet war planning: U.S. policymakers could only know what Soviet policymakers were willing to reveal. As former JCS chairman Admiral Thomas Moorer noted, the United States must invest hundreds of millions of dollars in intelligence to procure the kinds of information about the Soviet Union that the Soviets could acquire about the United States by reading an issue of *Aviation Week* (U.S. Senate 1979a: 2:580).

Fourth, supporters and critics argued over the threshold at which Soviet violations threatened U.S. security. Supporters maintained that the treaty required only "adequate" verification, that is, sufficient to detect "strategically significant" treaty violations. They presumed, accordingly, that the United States did not require the capability to detect each and every Soviet violation—that it required only the capability to detect violations that would give the Soviet Union a meaningful nuclear advantage. Critics responded that this "standard" amounted to forgoing all standards. The standard risked allowing little violations (1) to add up to big violations (which would indeed hurt the United States militarily); and (2) to undermine U.S. credibility to challenge any and all Soviet misconduct. Indeed, the danger was that no Soviet violation—regardless of its severity—would meet the standard that was set. This was because supporters appeared to evaluate violations in light of U.S. AD doctrine, which meant that the Soviets could flagrantly violate the treaty as long as the United States retained the capability to impose prohibitive retaliatory costs upon the Soviet Union. In Nitze's words, "If one assumes that no capabilities beyond those required for a city damaging role are significant, then none of the SALT II limitations are 'strategically significant':

they may assure the Soviet Union of strategic nuclear superiority without denying us a city damaging capability" (U.S. Senate 1979a: 3:885).

Fifth, supporters and critics sparred over the costs to the Soviet Union of cheating. Supporters argued that the consequences to the Soviets of being caught in deception were sufficient to deter Soviet misconduct even if the United States could not monitor Soviet compliance with all treaty provisions with confidence. In other words, the heavy costs of disclosure could compensate for even a small probability that the United States will detect a Soviet violation. Although the SALT II Treaty stipulates, for example, that a 5-percent change in the critical characteristics of an ICBM make it effectively the "new" missile that each party is allowed under the treaty—though the United States is better equipped to detect 15-percent changes with certainty—the United States would benefit whether the Soviets stuck to the letter of the agreement or tried simply to keep improvements below 15 percent to escape detection. As Brown put it, "I think it is in our advantage to have those limits as narrow as we can make them, even if we cannot monitor precisely to that level of accuracy" (U.S. Senate 1979c: 211). Of course, critics did not buy that logic: they were generally unimpressed by the overall U.S. capability to detect Soviet treaty violations. In their view, the current monitoring task was far more difficult than simply determining the number of stages or type of propellant that a missile employed; it involved challengingly precise judgments about small degrees of change in various quantitative dimensions—missile length, largest diameter, throw-weight, or launch-weight. Critics argued that the limited U.S. capability to verify Soviet compliance with prohibitions on such small changes meant that the Soviets could freely introduce entirely new designs for all of their missiles, though the treaty permitted the parties to acquire only one new type of missile (Nitze in U.S. Senate 1979a: 3:877, 3:884).

Should the United States catch the Soviets in a violation, critics were unconvinced that the United States would lower the boom: the U.S. track record in enforcing the SALT I accords was hardly persuasive on that count. Over U.S. objections, the Soviets had interpreted restrictions on changes in launcher dimensions to permit changes of the allowable magnitude in each of a full set of dimensions. This allowed them to pass off the SS-19 missile as a lightweight system when its resulting volume made it, in the U.S. view, a heavy missile (Nitze in U.S. Senate 1979a: 3:951).[46] That the SS-19 was a prohibited missile—with many times the throw-weight of the U.S. Minuteman (Rowny in U.S. Senate 1979a: 3:1205)—was Exhibit A when critics charged that U.S. policymakers would not do the "right thing" in the face of Soviet transgressions. Critics doubted, then, that U.S. officials would take strong and decisive action to hold the Soviets accountable for even willful treaty violations. U.S. officials could too easily excuse Soviet violations by claiming that they were an "anomaly," "technical" in nature, or the result of a legitimate difference in the interpretation of a treaty provision.[47] In the judgment of these critics, the treaty would effectively bind only the United States.

Sixth, supporters and critics diverged when assessing the value of terminological definitions in the treaty. For supporters, conceptual definitions of ICBM launchers, SLBM launchers, heavy bombers, air-launched cruise missiles, and so forth ensured that the parties would not talk past each other in the negotiations or act on different interpretations when implementing the treaty. The common reference points would prevent the Soviets from hiding their noncompliance in claims that the United States had misunderstood or distorted the rules. Even then, supporters argued that treaty ambiguities do not necessarily harm U.S. interests. They maintained that ambiguities allowed the parties to overcome their differences to secure a useful agreement (and, perhaps, to later resolve their differences in the SCC). One such difference involved the encryption of telemetry (Duffy 1988: 273, 279–280; Talbott 1980: 237). The SALT II Treaty "prohibits either party from *impeding* the ability of the other to verify compliance with treaty provisions by using deliberate concealment measures, including the encoding of ballistic missile flight telemetry" (emphasis added). Although the language permitted some ambiguous level of encryption, it preserved U.S. options to encrypt some telemetry for reasons of national security and still required access to Soviet telemetry data when necessary to verify Soviet treaty compliance (as discussed in chapter 4).[48] Indeed, supporters recognized that tight restrictions could undercut U.S. interests and were sometimes avoided by U.S. negotiators for that reason (Morris 1991: 258). For example, U.S. officials accepted a short-term restriction on the deployment of mobile land-based missiles (in the treaty's protocol) to keep U.S. deployment options open. They also accepted imprecision in the definition of a missile "launcher" in part to allow the United States to shuttle the MX missile among multiple protective shelters (Talbott 1980: 166, 175).

Such disputes were cause for treaty supporters to acknowledge that ambiguities are inevitably present in negotiated text. In the absence of absolute prohibitions, the distinction between permissible and impermissible conduct is often subject to competing interpretations.[49] The SCC was constructed, in fact, with that in mind. Put simply, all possible interpretations of a clause cannot be anticipated when it is negotiated. For that matter, exceedingly precise language and terms—meant to avoid disputes—would ultimately only create them: "Too precise a definition would leave insufficient flexibility to deal with problems brought about by evolving technology [and changing conditions] and might create a loophole that would pose a large security risk with no legal recourse" (Morris 1991: 258–259). A precise listing of impermissible behaviors can legitimize functionally similar behaviors that are omitted from the list, just as a general proscription might leave violators some wiggle room for disputing the application of the rule. A parent can warn a child not to run with scissors—or, instead, with sharp objects—in hand. Which offers the better prohibition? The first—a specific restriction—which might allow the child to run with a knife, a stick, or a pen? Or, the second—a general one—which might lead the child to dispute that an object is "sharp"? Inevitably, drafters of legal text encounter tradeoffs in balancing overspecificity and underspecificity, leaving terms open to different or rival interpretations.

For critics, though, the reality was quite simple: the Soviets had a strong incentive to cheat when ambiguity—intentional or not—provided a cloak for deception. A grievous example of an exploitable loophole involved the treaty's limitation on impeding access to telemetry: critics feared that the Soviets would deny the U.S. access to necessary telemetry by claiming that the United States already had sufficient information to verify Soviet treaty compliance (Rowny in U.S. Senate 1979a: 3:1208). An additional alleged loophole involved the explicit labeling of particular aircraft as "heavy bombers," which allowed the Soviets to exempt the Backfire and comparable aircraft from the treaty despite the technology, dimensions, and performance of the aircraft (Rowny in U.S. Senate 1979a: 2:686, 2:726–727). Still another irksome loophole involved the definition of a missile launcher. Because the Soviets housed their modern missiles in canisters for "cold launch," some critics feared that the Soviets would build an unlimited number of missile silos, claiming that the canisters were effectively the "launchers" (Nitze in U.S. Senate 1979a: 3:884). In sum, critics were loath to describe such disputes as "differences in opinion." Doing so would only legitimize Soviet duplicity: according to Rowny, the Soviets "went to great pains to avoid precise definitions and concrete terms" (U.S. Senate 1979a: 3:1200).

Seventh, supporters and critics battled over whether the treaty had actually limited Soviet cheating on consequential military dimensions. Treaty supporters emphasized that the United States could effectively monitor Soviet compliance with the treaty terms that mattered most. Thus, Brown argued that, because hard-targeting capability was most sensitive to improved warhead accuracy, the Soviets would not benefit inordinately from increasing missile sizes to accommodate greater warhead yields (U.S. Senate 1979b: 2:254). If the Soviets tried, the United States would know: even an absence of data on Soviet missile dimensions was not a major cause for concern because the United States could make relative judgments based on its prior assessments of missile characteristics. This would allow the United States to monitor the terms of the treaty and play to its technological strengths: "we can detect a change of 5 percent with greater confidence than we can measure an absolute value within 5 percent" (Jones in U.S. Senate 1979a: 4:1560).[50] Conversely, critics emphasized the military significance to the Soviets of various treaty exclusions—command and control capabilities, accuracy improvements, and missile stockpiles for reloading Soviet launchers.[51] These exclusions also included key weapon parameters. Critics claimed, for instance, that five parameters that were not covered in the treaty were more important to determining whether a missile was entirely new than was the treaty's 5-percent change allowance in the accepted parameters (Rowny in U.S. Senate 1979a: 3:1212). In their view, the Soviets had intentionally rejected restrictions on vital missile parameters in order to permit the building of new Soviet missiles in the guise of old ones (Rowny in U.S. Senate 1979a: 3:1206). From their perspective, the SALT II Treaty was a monument to tunnel vision. Yes, bombers that carried cruise missiles externally were "distinguishable" from aircraft that did not, but what about bombers that carried these missiles internally? How could they be distinguished from bombers that did not? Yes, Backfire bomber production was limited by the treaty, but what about other Soviet bombers that could arguably serve in a "heavy bomber role" (Rowny in U.S. Senate 1979a: 3:1203)? Yes, the treaty limited the number of hard-target capable warheads that the Soviets could place on their heavy missiles, but what if the Soviets chose to break out from the treaty? The Soviets could then quickly place as many as thirty warheads on their SS-18 missiles and effectively triple their capability—assuming, of course, that they had previously complied with the ten-warhead treaty limit (U.S. Senate 1979a: 1:198). Under these conditions, the warhead limit was an imaginary constraint.

In this context, the Backfire loomed large, with treaty supporters and critics debating the consequences of the treaty's prohibition on increasing the bomber's "radius of action." Whereas the Soviets focused on the inherent technological deficiencies of the bomber (for instance, its lack of a unrefueled round-trip capability) that made it unsuitable for a strategic mission (as opposed to theater or naval-strike missions), administration officials focused on the operational inhibitions (for instance, on aerial refueling and geographical areas of deployment) that would prevent the bomber from performing in a strategic role. They argued that these factors would prevent the bomber from being used strategically: the

Soviets had a critical deficiency in the numbers of refueling aircraft, operational units had not conducted necessary refueling exercises, ancillary aircraft were employed in other roles, and so forth. They argued, as well, that a strategic use for the bomber would come with clear warning signs such as the redeployment of maritime aircraft to support the longer-range bomber force. Yet critics challenged each and every one of these "limitations." They insisted that the Backfire was no different from the U.S. B-52 bomber, which actually was part of the strategic count in the treaty: no U.S. bomber could deliver nuclear weapons, without refueling, in a round-trip, intercontinental attack. They argued further that understandings concerning the bomber were insignificant or revokable: the Backfire bomber could easily be redeployed to Soviet bases nearer to the United States; flying longer distances and refueling were fungible pilot skills that could be acquired from other Soviet aircraft; and the Soviets could work around existing restrictions. For example, the Soviets could station the Backfire in the central Soviet Union "and still refuel, or even pick up their nuclear weapons, at bases closer to their opponent" (Rowny in U.S. Senate 1979a: 2:672, 2:727).

Finally, supporters and critics battled over whether the United States had rendered itself vulnerable overall to Soviet cheating under the agreement. As always, supporters argued that the United States is not bound by the agreement if it ultimately believes that it endangers U.S. security. Critics responded that U.S. policymakers were too wedded to arms control and too naive about Soviet intentions to withdraw from the treaty. If anything, the Soviets would leave first, when they were ready to act, or would simply allow the treaty to expire (with its MIRV limits), whereupon "it is difficult to imagine what leverage the United States will possess" (Rowny in U.S. Senate 1979a: 2:670).

In the end, issues of treaty compliance featured heavily in the SALT II Treaty debate. But these issues were largely a sideshow to the grand treaty debate, regardless of how they were perceived by the participants at the time. Judgments about U.S. costs and benefits under the treaty were far more sensitive to assumptions about the nature and stability of the U.S.-Soviet nuclear balance than to assumptions about Soviet cheating. Indeed, the critics themselves suggested that the Soviets would gain little of value from cheating when they argued that the Soviets would soon achieve a first-strike capability against the U.S. land-based missile force under the terms of the SALT II Treaty; that the Soviets had received everything they wanted from the SALT negotiations (without compromising); or that the Soviets were simply wasting their resources by adding nuclear capabilities that were permitted under the treaty.

The Power of Belief in U.S.-Soviet Arms Control in the SALT Period

The SALT I and II debates had a familiar ring: they drew substance and sustenance from decades-old assumptions about Soviet aspirations and interests. The impact of these assumptions is apparent when examining the competing perspectives on Soviet goals, the changing political prominence of these perspectives, and the arguments about U.S. relative capabilities that treaty proponents and opponents made to bolster their claims.

Soviet Intent

As in years past, treaty critics focused their concerns on the likelihood that the Soviets would capitalize on favorable treaty terms or openings to cheat; treaty proponents based their support on the presumably shared U.S.-Soviet aversion to nuclear war and interest in stabilizing the nuclear balance. In the SALT debate, though, even administration officials voiced some pessimism about Soviet motives.

For critics, the SALT I agreement enshrined the various Soviet advantages that emerged from the relentless Soviet nuclear buildup of the prior decade: that was the Soviet intent. The Soviets would not relax their hardware preferences, which placed the United States at a numerical disadvantage, nor were they willing to make long-term concessions to forge the agreement. In a unilateral statement in the agreement, the Soviet Union indicated that it had not relented on the issue of whether to count the nuclear-armed submarines of U.S. NATO allies against the allowable total; it pronounced a right to match any increases in that overall number during the lifetime of the agreement; and it claimed that future negotiations should address an unfair U.S. advantage in submarine bases in third countries. Critics feared, then, that the Soviet Union would only pad its lead in future negotiations. They could not help but view the negative outcome of the negotiations in light of gratuitous Soviet demands and behavior; a long Soviet track record of deceit, perfidy, and hostility toward the West and its interests; and the plausible military advantages that the Soviets would obtain from the treaty. Indeed, critics claimed that the Soviets had established, through their behavior, that they believed that nuclear advantages were within reach. If nuclear "superiority" was not meaningful, as treaty supporters claimed, why were the Soviets so keen on acquiring and safeguarding it? After all, the Soviets could have stopped procuring weapons once they caught up to the United States and could later have conceded their advantage knowing that the treaty would freeze U.S. forces in place.

The SALT II Treaty only increased the critics' concerns. Skeptics argued that the treaty did little, if anything, to slow the momentum of the Soviet nuclear buildup—that the Soviets had made at most small sacrifices in the negotiations to realize larger strategic gains. From their perspective, the evidence was overwhelming, again, that the Soviets were using arms control to obtain unilateral advantages: the Soviets could continue to modernize their forces, deploy additional warheads, and improve their accuracy under the terms of the treaty; the Soviets had rejected symmetry as a basis of agreement despite U.S. efforts to achieve more equitable terms; and the Soviets had continued to arm despite constraints (delays and freezes) on U.S. procurement. This could only mean that the Soviets had embraced the war-fighting assumption that more capability was better than less capability: for critics, it was telling that U.S. policymakers were now discounting the value of nuclear superiority, which U.S. policymakers had once sought ardently to retain (for more on this, see Katz 1979: 16–18). Whatever U.S. policymakers might believe, critics insisted that Soviet beliefs are what counted—that the Soviets *think* that superiority matters means that it *does*. The most hawkish of these critics feared that the Soviets aspired, through superiority, to neutralize the U.S. capability to inflict damage on the Soviet Union in the event of a nuclear war—that the Soviets might initiate to realize their global ambitions. In their view, the Soviet leadership, while not suicidal, would accept grave risks—accepting some chance that the United States would retaliate by destroying the Soviet Union—to accomplish its goals. Even critics who doubted that the Soviets could achieve a military victory in nuclear war still voiced concerns that the Soviets might seek a "coercive advantage" (before or after a nuclear exchange) from a Soviet force that appeared to be superior to U.S. forces in head-to-head comparisons. With such a force, the Soviets would presumably try to bargain with the United States from a position of strength, employ their conventional forces abroad without fear of U.S. intervention, and gain the acquiescence of U.S. allies, who would now discount the worth of U.S. promises of support and military commitments.

Critics insisted once again that the quantitative and qualitative Soviet nuclear threat was exacerbated by the nature of Soviet deployments, which clearly signaled malevolent Soviet intent. They maintained that there was simply no other explanation for the Soviet refusal to relinquish an overwhelming nuclear advantage in (especially heavy) land-based missiles. That the Soviets invested heavily in silo-killing weapons that were highly vulnerable to a U.S. first strike indicated that the Soviets planned to strike first. Such concerns about Soviet motivation obtained urgency from the anticipated opening of the so-called window of vulnerability in the early 1980s, when Soviet land-based missiles would be equipped with multiple independently targetable warheads in numbers that could overwhelm the U.S. land-based missile force. These concerns—on offense—were worsened by U.S.-Soviet asymmetries in missile defense. That the Soviets had chosen to construct a missile defense of Moscow and had invested considerable resources in civil defense and protecting the Soviet leadership indicated further that the Soviets were guarding against the U.S. retaliatory strike that U.S. AD doctrine had promised to deliver against urban industrial targets. For critics, that spelled trouble for the United States in two respects: it suggested that (1) the Soviets had good reason to fear such a strike (because they were planning to attack the United States); and (2) the Soviets did not buy the U.S. argument (implicit in AD doctrine) that there would be no winners, only losers, in a U.S.-Soviet nuclear war.

Suspicions about Soviet goals were raised further by apparent Soviet violations of prior arms control agreements and supposed "loopholes," ambiguities, and openings for cheating in various treaties that the Soviets could exploit—indeed, supposedly designed into the treaty for that purpose. For critics, the implications of Soviet deception, noncompliance, and refusal to accept intrusive verification measures went well beyond the immediate military significance of the Soviet violations: they indicated a serious lack of Soviet commitment to arms control. Indeed, critics concluded that Soviet behaviors across the full range of global issues were inseparably driven by an overarching Soviet strategy. Thus, the unapologetic Soviet assisting and bankrolling of Cuban forces operating in Africa, obstructionism in the Middle East, and support for Marxist elements in Central America spoke to the Soviet willingness to accept meaningful bilateral limitations on nuclear arms. As Senator Strom Thurmond asked in Senate hearings, "Is it wise at this time to enter into an agreement with a nation that is spreading its aggression throughout the world?" (U.S. Senate 1979a: 1:33). Capitulating to Soviet arms control terms—as by ratifying the SALT II Treaty—would only reward and encourage Soviet malfeasance. In the words of Senator John Tower, "The simple ratification of a treaty which confirms Soviet nuclear superiority would provide an expression of encouragement and approval of Soviet behavior and destroy any prospect of restoring the original basis of detente" (U.S. Senate 1979a: 1:8). This was troubling because "history reflects that the Soviet Union seeks to expand its influence by probing for weakness, advancing where it finds it, and stopping only when opposed" (U.S. Senate 1979a: 1:6–9).

In the view of hard-line arms control critics, the Soviet Union had consistently stood unopposed, given the U.S. policy of appeasement through "unilateral arms control." Thus, by its "zeal" to consummate a SALT II treaty, the United States had only encouraged Soviet uncooperativeness. Whereas the United States saw an arms control agreement as "an end in itself," the Soviets viewed SALT II as a "means to an end"—one that these critics charged was incompatible with U.S. interests (Rowny in U.S. Senate 1979a: 3:979). For domestic reasons alone, the United States now had to hold its ground: critics feared that the treaty would breed widespread complacency—that is, a "euphoria," "pacifier," or "tranquilizer" effect that would leave the United States even less capable of recognizing—much less addressing—the Soviet challenge (see Tower in U.S. Senate 1979a: 1:9).

Critics did leave one important question unanswered—in part because they were not of one mind on the issue. Whereas SALT supporters assumed that interests of the United States and the Soviet Union converged (that they were both served by armament constraints), critics were unclear or divided about the implications of a tougher U.S. negotiating stance. High-profile SALT critics—including former arms control negotiators, such as Rowny and Nitze—insisted that, by rejecting the SALT II Treaty, the United States could strengthen its hand in future negotiations and achieve better terms. But if the critics were right and the Soviets valued the treaty only because it boosted their military power and thereby helped them to compete globally with the United States, why would the Soviets compromise? After all, they allegedly had the momentum and, in a nuclear buildup lacking negotiated constraints, could compete at an advantage.

For their part, supporters of the SALT treaties maintained that the United States and the Soviet Union shared an interest in avoiding nuclear instability, which had been reduced under the agreements (see Brown in U.S. Senate 1979a: 1:141). They argued, in fact, that the treaties had fostered the growing convergence in U.S. and Soviet views about the dangers of a U.S.-Soviet nuclear exchange: for example, under the ABM Treaty, the Soviet Union had accepted limits on ABMs and were implicitly buying into the assumptions of deterrence based on AD principles. To quote Gerard Smith, "The best evidence that they are moving in that direction is their acceptance of these very low levels of ABMs, which in effect indicates that they do not calculate that they can make a first strike and then handle a ragged retaliatory strike and keep it at tolerable levels" (Labrie 1979: 133). For him, the change in Soviet beliefs was "one of the most important things" about the ABM Treaty. Even if the Soviets had not come around entirely to the U.S. view, some treaty supporters could understand Soviet trepidations about accepting the U.S. perspective: that protecting missiles was stabilizing and that protecting people was destabilizing were hardly intuitive or obvious conclusions for the Soviets given their bureaucratic culture and painful experience in war. Supporters maintained that the Soviets would eventually warm to the U.S. perspective; indeed, by ratifying the treaty, the United States would aid the Soviet learning process. Rather than embolden Soviet leaders who would take U.S. concessions for weakness, observable benefits from U.S.-Soviet cooperation would strengthen the hand of moderate Soviet leaders who sought to shift budgetary priorities away from the military and to adopt economic reforms (W. Averell Harriman in U.S. Senate 1979b: 2:311).

Countering the prominent argument that the United States should not appear to reward Soviet interventionism through arms control agreements, supporters insisted that arms control—and the SALT II Treaty in particular—was important enough in its own right to preclude linkage with other U.S.-Soviet issues (Brown in U.S. Senate 1979a: 4:1491). If anything, arms control was a necessary first step in a continuing U.S.-Soviet conflict-reduction process. Through arms control, the parties could gradually allay their concerns about each other's intentions and actions and come to recognize the limited advantages, and major disadvantages, of nuclear arms competition. Accordingly, the United States and the Soviet Union could eventually obtain a stable military equilibrium and realize benefits from an improved global political climate. Thus, the Soviets had everything to gain by upholding the SALT II Treaty. Indeed, it had shown—from its record of treaty observance—that it took treaty obligations seriously and would not risk undermining the SALT II Treaty (given U.S. monitoring capabilities) by seeking illicit benefits. Supporters noted, for example, that the Soviets had stayed within the SALT I Treaty's limits by dismantling submarine-based launchers that were newer than those deployed on U.S. submarines.[52]

To be sure, treaty supporters were not entirely consistent in their logic. Carter administration officials were on soft intellectual ground when balancing optimism and pessimism about Soviet behavior. They had devised a nuclear doctrine that assumed that the Soviets might do the "unthinkable"—that is, launch a first strike against U.S. counterforce capabilities to obtain a nuclear advantage—even as they hoped to stabilize the nuclear balance and realize shared U.S.-Soviet interests through arms control. What was required, then, was a thorough examination of Soviet goals—why and when the Soviets might employ nuclear weapons or change their behavior over the course of a nuclear war. These treaty supporters should have asked, for example, whether the Soviets—if they did go nuclear—would be acting in response to NATO's first use of nuclear weapons (to beat back a Soviet conventional attack). In shirking the relevant questions, supporters assumed—by default—that the Soviets would engage in high-risk conduct.

In consequence, these supporters could as easily have opposed as supported the SALT II Treaty.

The Politics of Arms Control

The Nixon and Carter administrations offer a study in contrasts in arms control. The two administrations differed markedly in their negotiating and selling of the SALT treaties, and each labored within a different domestic arms control environment.

THE NIXON AND CARTER ADMINISTRATIONS

Decision-making in the Richard M. Nixon administration was highly centralized. Nixon's National Security Advisor, Henry Kissinger, controlled the interagency process that produced U.S. negotiating positions; guided the U.S. team through the negotiations; outflanked these U.S. negotiators by setting the negotiating parameters and bridging impasses through "back-channel" discussions with Soviet leaders; and tightly held and selectively distributed information about the negotiations to avoid domestic political (including intragovernmental) interference. For example, in the period between the U.S. announcement of the ABM "breakthrough" in May 1970 and the signing of the ABM Treaty in Moscow a year later, "would-be critics—inside and outside the government—were limited in what they could do or say by their lack of detailed information and access to closely guarded policy developments" (Platt 1991: 246). Kissinger even circumvented the high-level Verification Panel, an interagency group that was ostensibly created to coordinate the U.S. negotiating stance, when he used it only to announce or to ratify his own decisions (Smith 1981: 109–111). He was no more forthcoming with Congress. Although he actively participated in the post-negotiation selling of the Interim Agreement to the legislature, Kissinger had previously attempted to keep key members of the Senate in the dark, away from the proceedings and relevant data (Platt 1991: 235–239). To be sure, Kissinger was constrained by military opinion: he could not deal away the U.S. advantage in MIRVs, forward-based systems, strategic bombers, and next-generation SLBMs without generating opposition from this critical constituency. Indeed, he sought limits on Soviet systems in response to military concerns.[53] But Kissinger retained considerable leeway in the negotiations, which helps explain his success in forging the SALT I Treaty.

The administration sought to sell the agreements by appealing to all sides in the debate. It varied its public appeals to resonate with different ideological groups (Platt 1991: 251) as it promoted arms control as an intermediate path—between an arms race of unlimited proportions and unilateral U.S. disarmament—that promised bilateral cuts and reduced global conflict if the United States retained its military bargaining chips. In consequence, hawks were presented with a persuasive package—an Interim Agreement that came with an increased funding request for the host of "bargaining chips"—the B-1 bomber, the Trident submarine, and cruise missiles—that were permitted under the treaty (Platt 1991: 254). The administration argued that these systems were a must to preserve the integrity of the SALT agreement (Smith 1981: 30).

Hawkish critics vented their concerns about the negotiating process and the resulting treaties. They maintained that the administration had presented them with a fait accompli, in the form of finalized agreements that did nothing to reverse the unrelenting Soviet nuclear buildup. But Senate hawks were willing to hold their fire in exchange for a promise that the treaty would be "fixed" through future negotiations. Hawks made their concession in no small part after reading the political writing on the wall: opposing the treaty would undermine a Republican president who would not welcome a political defeat in advance of the election and had been under pressure to reach an agreement (Rice 2012: 4). The public was split deeply by the Vietnam War, and the administration's dovish opponents thought the treaty did not go far enough—that it failed to cut offensive systems and ban destabilizing weapons such as MIRVs and antiballistic missiles (Platt 1991: 269, 246). Officials within the U.S. Arms Control and Disarmament Agency and Congress had argued for banning both (Platt 1991: 246). For hawks, the Interim Agreement and the accompanying ABM Treaty provided a basis at least for pursuing controversial weapon systems, maintaining healthy defense-procurement budgets, and keeping defense liberals at bay. As the chief U.S. negotiator at SALT, Gerard Smith, described their predicament: "Nothing concentrated the minds of American leaders on the advantages of SALT as much as the clear and present danger of one-sided arms control in the form of congressional cuts in U.S. defense budgets" (1981: 29). Indeed, hawks would score a political victory of sorts when the administration silenced its dovish voices after the 1972 election by purging ACDA, reducing its staff, and curtailing its role in negotiations (Platt 1991: 259–260).

Given the politics and expectations of the SALT I hearings, the Carter administration had an uphill battle acquiring support from a Democrat-controlled Senate for the SALT II Treaty. The battle lines were drawn early: the relatively close Senate vote on Paul Warnke's appointment as chief U.S. SALT negotiator—by less than the two-thirds vote required for treaty ratification—warned of the tough treaty ratification battle to come (Talbott 1980: 56).[54] Headcounts indicated that the administration had to win at least two-thirds of the roughly forty undecided Senate votes to achieve ratification (Sartori 1985/86: 148). The administration had only made its job harder by appearing weak and indecisive on defense when it canceled the B-1 bomber program and neutron-bomb deployment in Europe (Talbott 1980: 160). It was hurt further by its own internal disharmony and lack of political adroitness. Secretary of State Cyrus Vance battled consistently and contentiously with National Security Advisor Zbigniew Brzezinski over first principles: whereas Vance viewed arms control as a preeminent U.S.-Soviet issue—worthy of attention in its own right—Brzezinski was more inclined to link arms control to other superpower disputes (Daalder and Destler 2009: 107). The multitude of voices, clumsiness, slow political response, and openness of the administration left it unable to control the message or the flow of information to the Senate. But the administration was challenged as well by external events that were beyond its control. The Senate debate over the merits of the SALT II Treaty was shaped by revelations of the presence of a Soviet combat brigade in Cuba, Soviet actions in the Third World, and the takeover by an Iranian mob of the U.S. Embassy in Tehran (and the drawn-out hostage crisis to follow)—before the Soviet invasion of Afghanistan proved fatal to the treaty.

To its credit, the administration actively promoted the treaty and reached out to skeptics. It sought to placate hard-liners—for instance, by keeping Henry Jackson and his staff in the policy loop, engaging in outreach to Paul Nitze, and allowing Edward Rowny to serve as the JCS representative on the U.S. SALT delegation (Caldwell 1991: 291–294). It also adopted the time-honored strategy of committing to a major defense program to build political support for an arms control treaty. Carter announced that the United States would eventually deploy two hundred MX missiles, for shuttling among thousands of hardened shelters, after concluding that the SALT II Treaty would not be ratified without such support (Caldwell 1991: 307). Still, the administration's efforts were hampered significantly from without. Nitze and Rowny became powerful and articulate treaty ratification opponents. Rowny's service on the U.S. negotiating team and Nitze's negotiating experience, reputation, knowledge, and ties to Democratic administrations gave credibility to the dissent.[55] Their testimony proved an effective counter to testimony from the administration's star witness, Secretary of Defense Brown. Within the Senate, the SALT II Treaty opposition had a formidable champion in Senator Henry Jackson (and his committed staff, which included Richard Perle) and was galvanized nationally by a network of public interest groups such as the Committee on the Present Danger. The opposition capitalized successfully on growing public suspicion of the Soviet Union and backing for stronger U.S. defenses in the aftermath of the Vietnam War.

Given the determined opposition, the SALT II Treaty was conceivably doomed from the start. Although it is impossible to know with certainty whether the task of selling the treaty was too big or the administration's effort was too small, it does seem likely that a treaty that could have won support from the U.S. Senate would not have been acceptable to the Soviet Union. Indeed, for many hawks, the ideal arms control treaty was based on terms that the Soviets were bound to reject as a matter of definition: if they did not, either the United States had conceded its interests or had failed to recognize the "catch."

THE CHANGING INSTITUTIONAL CONTEXT: THREAT ASSESSMENT

The Nixon and Carter administrations each devised their policies within a different intragovernmental context. Whereas the Nixon administration proactively restructured the formal apparatus for assessing the Soviet threat, the Carter administration was on the defensive. It inherited the changes that were institutionalized under Nixon and suffered under widespread criticism—from outside the executive branch—that these reforms were insufficient. In consequence, the Carter administration had to cope with an inflated Soviet "threat" that the administration was accused of underestimating. These challenges only increased the administration's difficulty winning support for the SALT II Treaty.

Kissinger shared President Nixon's wariness of the CIA (and its ostensible links to the liberal establishment) and expressed disdain for what he viewed as the unprovocative, unsubstantiated, and overly consensual inferences of the National Intelligence Estimates, which relied heavily on CIA inputs (Cahn 1998: 75, 88). Indeed, despite improving intelligence collection, U.S. analysts, throughout much of the Johnson administration, had grossly underestimated the pace of Soviet deployments[56] and had denied explicitly—despite the growing Soviet arsenal—that the Soviets were seeking superiority (DCI 1968: 5–6).[57] Consequently, the early 1970s brought a decline in CIA influence and bureaucratic standing; the demise of the Office of National Estimates (ONE), which was charged with overseeing the initial crafting of these intelligence documents; and the restructuring of the NIE drafting process (Freedman 1977: 52–56). Through the power of appointment at all bureaucratic levels and the redesigning of the bureaucracy for drafting NIEs (allowing for greater input of alternative viewpoints), the NIEs recorded the preferences of the new administration (Cahn 1998: 102–107). Even these changes could not placate hawkish critics. Their indictment of past estimates led the director of central intelligence to appoint groups of outside conservative experts (U.S. Team "B" 1976) to reassess prior intelligence estimates and scrutinize the drafting of the 1976 NIE (see U.S. Congress 1978). Admittedly, there is little evidence that the Team B report, which broadly criticized NIE assumptions about Soviet objectives (Betts 2003: 68; Prados 1993: 28–29), swayed high level officials or affected more than the "tone" of NIEs to follow (Cahn 1998: 159–162, 173). Still, the view that the Soviets were seeking a nuclear war-fighting and -winning capability and subordinating deterrence to this effort became NIE mainstays until the Cold War's end.

The 1970s and 1980s saw a return to the pattern of the 1950s and early 1960s: overstatements of expected growth in the Soviet nuclear arsenal. In 1973 and 1974, the NIEs offered "high" predictions of double the actual number of reentry vehicles that the Soviets deployed (roughly) over the next decade, and from 1978 to 1985, the "low" predictions for the numbers of reentry vehicles were still higher than those achieved by the Soviets in later years (U.S. DI 1989: 7–9). Even predictive "successes" point to an exaggerated Soviet deployment threat. The NIEs of the 1975–77 period offered high and low figures that framed and closely approximated the number of reentry vehicles that the Soviets actually deployed, yet the high estimates of ICBM reentry vehicles, which most concerned U.S. policymakers, exceeded the actual number by a couple of thousand.[58] In the 1970s and 1980s, much of the estimating error resulted from inflated projections about when new systems would replace older systems. The Soviet Union did not field new systems at the time and pace that the U.S. predicted (if it introduced them at all) and unexpectedly retained older land-based and submarine-launched missiles despite the availability of newer models. For that matter, analysts continued to forecast relatively rapid modernization rates despite mounting evidence of predictive error. The 1985 NIE echoed predictions in the 1975 NIE of a nearly complete turnover in the Soviet ICBM force within a decade even though prior Soviet modernization rates did not support that inference (U.S. DI 1989: 14).[59] The estimates also tended to discount the lasting impact of U.S.-Soviet arms control agreements. With the signing of the SALT I and II agreements, NIEs typically contained sets of predictions based on competing assumptions about whether the Soviets would continue to observe the negotiated force ceilings. (Predictions of the early 1980s mostly reflected assumptions about exactly when the Soviets would exceed these limits.)

The overestimating pattern was arguably attributable to the increasing difficulty of the predictive task, that is, judging Soviet modernization and warhead deployment rates (rather than the Soviet missile buildup). But that explanation cannot account for the changing tone of the estimates. By the late 1970s, the main NIE text expressed a far more pessimistic view of Soviet intentions.[60] Despite considerable disagreement, especially between U.S. civilian and military analysts, the consensus textual judgment was that the Soviets possessed darker motives than had been supposed. The Soviets, it was said, grudgingly accepted parity as a reality, not a policy objective (DCI 1977: 2) and did not view deterrence as a mutually beneficial arrangement. From the Soviet perspective, "powerful strategic capabilities offer foreign policy advantages, and superior capabilities to fight and survive a nuclear war constitute the best deterrent as well as the best preparation for the contingency of nuclear war should it occur" (DCI 1978: 24). The Soviet Union would preempt only if believing that a "U.S. strike was both imminent and unavoidable," but at least some Soviet leaders believe that "victory in general war is possible" (DCI 1980: B-3, B-4).[61] Soviet goals seemed ominous, here, in light of alleged Soviet global ambitions and aggressiveness that could spark a nuclear confrontation.

The evidence is, then, that assessments were drafted within the intelligence community to reflect the ascendance of a particular strategic view that was only tenuously related to the facts. Once ascendant, the prevailing view was insulated from change, leaving dissenters to shoulder a substantial burden of proof.

Assessing, Safeguarding, and Improving U.S. Relative Capabilities

The Johnson administration had to confront the grim reality that the age of U.S. nuclear superiority had passed. But McNamara fought the implication that the United States was without nuclear options short of triggering a nuclear holocaust. Like his successors, he planned for nuclear war with some hope that its destructiveness could be limited by selectively targeting the Soviet nuclear infrastructure. U.S. policymakers did not simply resign themselves to the "assured destruction" of the United States in the event of nuclear war: they refused to be placed in the position of having to "press the button," to alter the trajectory of life in the United States (indeed, the planet), and worried that their nuclear trepidations would hurt the credibility of a U.S. policy that was based on the suicidal pledge. The practical effect was to muddle the logic of U.S. nuclear doctrine and thinking about Soviet goals and to divorce both from the U.S.-Soviet nuclear balance assessments that informed U.S. arms control positions.

Without question, predilections toward SALT-era treaties were driven by assumptions about Soviet goals. Yet these goals were poorly linked to actual U.S. policies on nuclear acquisition, deployment, and arms control. These policies were based on assessments of various balances and "imbalances" that only begged the questions of whether, when, and how a nuclear war would be fought—and, then, to a U.S. advantage. The Nixon administration tied U.S. nuclear arms policies to new standards—sufficiency and essential equivalence—and moved to give the United States additional flexibility, through limited nuclear options, in the event of a nuclear war. At the same time, these standards were defined, and the options were devised, without much effort to determine the specific Soviet (wartime or peacetime) objectives that necessitated the shift in standards and strategy. Thus, fundamental questions remained. For instance, why did the United States have to field a nuclear force that was the aggregate equivalent of the Soviet force—in appearance—when the effectiveness of these forces was determined either by the available target set and the exchange sequence (in one view) or some fixed amount of survivable retaliatory capability (in another)? The tensions in U.S. policy only increased as U.S. nuclear capabilities appeared to improve. Accordingly, the Carter administration embraced the SALT II Treaty, which froze in a Soviet advantage in prompt counterforce capability, despite (1) arguing that the Nixon administration was overly deferent to AD principles; and (2) embracing a countervailing doctrine that centered on preparing to fight a nuclear war. One consequence was that U.S. officials focused on military and political advantages of the treaty without appreciating the disadvantages in light of this doctrine.

Many SALT II Treaty supporters—including key members of the Carter administration—placed themselves in an impossible logical position. They insisted that the United States had much to gain from preparing to engage in a hard-targeting competition with the Soviet Union despite its edge in counterforce capabilities; they saw advantages in a treaty that was ostensibly based on U.S.-Soviet "equivalence" when presumably the purpose of the "countervailing strategy" was to improve the U.S. position in war; they scaled and configured U.S. forces without attending fully to the likely pace and consequences of a counterforce exchange; and they failed to appreciate physical and conceptual entanglements that muddied the distinction between military and civilian targets (or force and value targets), which had the effect of raising the price of conflating the two. Rather than address these issues, Carter administration officials fell back on ("discredited") AD doctrinal assumptions. They were certainly correct that the United States had more than enough capability to eviscerate the Soviet population and industrial base in response to a Soviet attack: even under unfavorable retaliatory conditions, the United States retained a sufficient number of warheads in the surviving U.S. land-based missile force alone to destroy two hundred of the Soviet Union's largest cities, with thousands of U.S. SLBM warheads held in reserve.[62] But they did not appreciate that by resorting to such arguments, they were impugning the premises of war-fighting doctrine.

In adhering more strictly to counterforce principles, war-fighting critics of the SALT II Treaty exhibited logical deficiencies of their own. They failed to demonstrate that rejecting the treaty would improve the U.S. war-fighting position when, absent a treaty, Soviet nuclear capabilities could continue to grow. But their logical deficiencies stemmed, in the main, from their adherence to war-fighting principles and their accompanying reliance on an unrealistic war scenario. In this stylized nuclear encounter, the parties considered only potential *gains* from attacking adversary military targets, not the costs that the adversary could inflict in retaliation. Wantonly missing from the nuclear scenario was an appreciation that the United States would impose catastrophic human costs upon the Soviet Union (by virtue of the dual nature of targets, their co-location, the spread of nuclear fallout, and so forth), whether measured in casualties, social disorder, economic recovery capability, or a loss of military manpower and weapons for promoting and protecting Soviet national security interests. Thus, whatever war-fighters might think (and hope), the inflicting of costs was an unavoidable feature of war and should loom large in thinking about war outcomes. Even if surgical counterforce exchanges reduced the ravages of war, the combatants would inevitably confront the costs of continuing the conflict: with counterforce targets destroyed on one side or the other, the parties would eventually encounter the AD ("kill-*and*-be-killed") scenario that U.S. policymakers had sought to escape.

Treaty critics only exacerbated the logical problems when they worried about Soviet treaty violations. Although critics detected a wide variety of ways that the Soviets could acquire illicit advantages, they failed to establish that the illicit gains were worth the price to the Soviets—that is, the unraveling of these treaties—should the cheating be discovered. After all, the Soviets had not brazenly sought to undercut the treaty's limits on launchers, missiles, and warheads, which suggested, at the very least, that the risk of discovery limited the scope and severity of Soviet cheating. Even critics suggested that the Soviets had everything to lose from undermining these treaties insofar as they were written to Soviet advantage. The former chief U.S. negotiator in the SALT I talks, Gerard Smith, was correct to ask, then, "why those who are most concerned about possible Soviet evasions usually also hold that the proposed theory strongly favors the U.S.S.R. . . . Were this true, why would the U.S.S.R. violate it?" (U.S. Senate 1979b: 2:4). Certainly, critics could not be faulted for wanting to impose tough verification standards and for worrying about surreptitious Soviet cheating: after all, realists assume that parties will engage in cheating when profitable, based on calculations of benefit, cost, and probability of discovery. Thus, treaty compliance is impossible without accountability. But critics must concede that verification measures are also subject to cost-benefit analysis. They must ask, then, whether a tough verification standard is actually essential for U.S. security and whether all prior Soviet cheating counts equally when the United States must decide whether to accept or continue to abide by a treaty. Put simply, they must ask whether the United States is better off, overall, with some imperfect treaty than without it. In this case, it appears so. To quote Smith again, "I do not understand the thesis that the United States cannot rely on its intelligence systems for accurate information about what the other side is doing under agreed limitations which include restraints on counterintelligence measures, but could rely upon the same intelligence systems" when the opposite conditions held (U.S. Senate 1979a: 2:4). In the absence of a SALT II treaty, for example, the Soviets could encrypt all telemetry and impede U.S. monitoring of Soviet behavior through national technical means; make ICBMs and other strategic nuclear weapons indistinguishable from other weapons to confound U.S. military planning; modify weapon platforms (including transport aircraft) to carry cruise missiles; deploy large numbers of mobile missiles that would be more difficult for the United States to track; and so forth (U.S. Senate 1979c: 204–205). Then, the United States would have no recourse: the United States would lack the legal standing to protest Soviet actions or to press the Soviets to explain their actions, let alone possess the institutional mechanisms (through the SCC) to seek redress. Of course, the United States had one major avenue of recourse: it could arm in response to the perceived Soviet threat. But the United States always retained that option (once formally withdrawing from the treaty). For that purpose, the United States was actually better off with a treaty that facilitated the flow of information about Soviet actions and provided a means to gauge Soviet objectives, through the absence or detection of Soviet treaty violations.

It is clear from the evidence, then, that U.S. policymakers divided primarily on the issue of Soviet goals. Hawkish skeptics argued that the Soviets had committed to nuclear superiority, not deterrence per se, and sought legally and illegally to further their advantage. These skeptics assumed that the SALT treaties would—at best—buy the United States a small respite that carried the danger of lulling U.S. policymakers and the Western public into complacency. Administration officials countered based on an opposing reading of Soviet goals. They argued consistently that the Soviets—by accepting procurement restraints under these treaties—had implicitly accepted the principle that there were no winners, only losers, in a nuclear exchange. They argued further that the Soviets had a strong interest in adhering to the terms of the treaty and would not risk it, then, for the limited gains that were possible through cheating. Based on their reading, U.S. officials expressed optimism that the Soviets would abide by the terms of the various SALT-era treaties. Indeed, had these officials been pessimistic about Soviet intentions, they could easily have found common ground with treaty critics.

In the end, the U.S. story of the SALT negotiations is not one that realists could easily tell: it is not a story of U.S. policymakers resolving uncertainty about Soviet capabilities or coming to understand how the changing nuclear balance would affect war outcomes. It is a story, instead, of policymakers differing in their assessments of relative U.S. strength under the treaties and, specifically, in the extent to which the United States was disadvantaged by the size and heaviness of the Soviet land-based missile force. Hawks feared that in a worst-case scenario, the United States could marshal only thousands of nuclear warheads—many times the yield of the weapons that flattened Hiroshima and Nagasaki—to retaliate against Soviet targets. More significantly, however, it is a story of U.S. policymakers differing in their willingness to trust the Soviets to adhere to the terms of the agreement. In consequence, the main storyline of the SALT period involves (1) U.S. government officials shedding their war-fighting impulses to accept agreements—based on terms that the Soviets would accept—because they believed that the Soviets preferred nuclear stability to the unbridled quest for nuclear superiority; and (2) their domestic critics successfully dashing hopes for a ratified agreement by arguing that the Soviets will continue to press for advantage, with or without a treaty.

But this is not to say that arms control policies and advocacy were coherently tied to beliefs about Soviet goals. Assumptions about Soviet goals informed the U.S. policy debate but did not discipline its logic. When successive administrations struggled with standards of sufficiency and essential equivalence and doctrines of varying military emphasis, they did not ground their arguments and assumptions in an understanding of the precise goals for which a nuclear war would be fought. Thus, neither administration officials nor their hawkish critics made a compelling logical case that the pursuit of war-fighting doctrines would permit the United States to escape the dilemmas of Assured Destruction. At best, they established that the revised plans for nuclear war would prolong the nightmarish consequences of nuclear war in a sequence of nuclear exchanges that amounted to Assured Destruction either (1) in "slow motion," as the parties battered each other in a battle of wills; or (2) with a "prelude," as the parties exhausted their counterforce capabilities before facing the choice (embodied in

AD doctrine) of whether to die first or second. In other words, the U.S. flexibility to act—sought ardently under the countervailing doctrine—served no real purpose. Indeed, "flexibility," itself, was the focus "because it is very hard to construct a convincing case for any of the proposed options" (Jervis 1984: 79).

Nuclear Arms Reductions in the Final Cold War Decade

The Reagan Years

The controversy over the terms of the SALT II Treaty spilled inevitably into the 1980 presidential election and, of course, the positions and policies of the Reagan administration to follow. On the campaign trail, Reagan claimed that the Soviet Union was aggressive and unrelenting and a serious security threat to the United States due to its own prior mistakes. In office, Reagan did not let up. He staffed his administration with key personnel who were deeply suspicious of Soviet intentions and overtly hostile to prior U.S. arms control concessions, which had allegedly placed the United States at a severe disadvantage. Unsurprisingly, then, the early 1980s were a nadir for U.S.-Soviet relations and for arms control.

In Reagan's first term, the administration pushed the Soviet Union strongly—and unsuccessfully—to accept a dramatic restructuring of its forces. It maintained that the United States had to hang tough in negotiations and to improve its military strength if it was to secure a better treaty. Administration officials insisted that their predecessors had been too anxious to get a deal: treaties were virtual ends in themselves—written around what the Soviets would accept, not U.S. interests (Talbott 1985: 8). They argued that the United States would have been better off walking away from the negotiating table than accepting the deeply flawed agreements that resulted. They insisted, for that matter, that the United States would have benefited from holding the Soviets to their commitments and standing up to willful and systematic Soviet violations. In their view, no violation could be dismissed: small violations could add up to big Soviet advantages and impugned the general Soviet commitment to arms control and international legal obligations. Thus, administration officials seriously questioned whether U.S. security interests were best served by working outside the framework of formal arms control treaties or by interpreting treaties to permit the deployment of new U.S. weapon systems. Indeed, the Reagan administration announced formally that it would not seek ratification of the SALT II Treaty and put forth an interpretation of the ABM Treaty that permitted the United States to pursue defensive technological options, short of deployment.

The Reagan administration was willing, however, to accept the constraints of "unpalatable" treaties—the very limits that administration officials had claimed were precisely the problem for having locked the United States into an inferior position. The administration maintained that it "would not undercut existing agreements" (a thinly veiled reference to the SALT II Treaty) as long as the Soviets did the same and that the United States had no immediate plans (or need) to withdraw from the ABM Treaty (Sartori 1985/86: 149). The administration deferred implicitly to the SALT II Treaty, even when exceeding its ceilings. In May 1986, the Reagan administration announced that the United States would scale its strategic forces to address the Soviet strategic threat rather than stay within SALT-imposed limits (given the deficient Soviet commitment to SALT and arms control) and, by the end of the year, broke through the SALT limits by deploying an additional heavy bomber that was equipped with cruise missiles. Yet the administration continued to stay generally within the SALT II ceilings and announced that it had no plans to increase U.S. force levels appreciably except to match Soviet quantitative improvements (U.S. Senate 1988a: 1:45).

The fact is that the Reagan administration was sufficiently committed to arms control with the Soviet Union to win significant concessions from it. With the Soviet Union under the new leadership of President Mikhael Gorbachev, the Reagan administration is credited with helping forge a revolutionary treaty: the 1987 Intermediate-Range Nuclear Forces (INF) Treaty banned an entire class of nuclear weapons and established rules for intrusive onsite inspections that would become staples of future agreements. By that year, in fact, the United States and the Soviet Union had agreed to the basic outlines of a Strategic Arms Reduction Treaty (START) that drew heavily on INF principles.

The Changing Strategic Nuclear Threat

In the 1970s, the arms control debate centered on the anticipated size and capabilities of the Soviet nuclear force and specifically on the "window of vulnerability" that would supposedly open in the 1980s, with the full deployment of Soviet MIRVed missiles (the fearsome SS-18s and SS-19s). The hundreds of SS-18 missiles in the Soviet arsenal alone were presumed to be sufficient—with two warheads aimed at each U.S. silo (to ensure a kill) to destroy most of the U.S. land-based missile force and leave the Soviets with a healthy SS-18 reserve.

In critical respects, the U.S. nuclear force of the 1980s was a product of design. Although the U.S. strategic arsenal was a shadow of its former self, in sheer megatons—down considerably from its peak yields of the early 1960s—the U.S. military (with civilian support) opted consistently for quality over quantity—pursuing platform mobility and weapon accuracy over explosive punch.[1] The B-52—the workhorse of the U.S. strategic bomber force—had acquired new avionics, short-range capabilities, and stand-off attack capabilities (with cruise missiles); the three-warhead Minuteman III missile was deployed with an upgraded guidance system for targeting Soviet missiles in their silos; and Poseidon submarines were back-fitted with the Trident I (C-4) missile for improved accuracy and range. To support them, newer systems were under development. The MX missile—roughly the equivalent of the Soviet SS-19 in size and the Soviet SS-18 in warhead capacity (as limited to ten warheads under the SALT II Treaty)—was planned for deployment in the mid-1980s.[2] It would soon be joined by the Trident ballistic-missile submarine, which could launch the accurate (silo-busting) Trident II (D-5) missile and an intercontinental-range stealth bomber (the B-2). The question remained, however, whether the United States had conceded a knockout advantage to the Soviet Union.

The administration faced a quandary. In 1980, Reagan had campaigned in part on his opposition to the multiple-shelter, horizontal-basing plan for the MX missile. Carter had announced that plan in 1979, within months of his decision to proceed with full-scale MX development. The plan amounted to a shell game: as designed, a single missile was to move along tracks among multiple shelters. The underlying principle was simple: if the United States would not compete with the Soviets in numbers of missiles, it could compete in target proliferation by creating decoy silos to absorb Soviet missiles. The Soviets would have to target each shelter (empty or not) more than once to destroy the MX force with confidence. The Carter administration had not come to its decision quickly or lightly: the solution emerged from many dozens of alternatives, each of which suffered from one disadvantage or another—some combination of expense, poor reaction time, and potential vulnerabilities (which included a weakening of the U.S. triad, as would occur, for example, if the United States opted for an aerial-basing mode). By rejecting the Carter alternative, the Reagan administration had painted itself into a corner. It wanted to move rapidly to address the perceived Soviet threat; at the same time, it could not reverse itself easily after having unequivocally staked its position—in part, to placate Republican constituents who, by merit of their proximity to the MX bases, would absorb a Soviet attack and suffer the social and economic disruptions that base construction would bring.

The "fix" came early. In 1981, Reagan announced plans to place the MX in existing Minuteman silos after they had been superhardened; then, in 1982, the administration announced its desire to proceed with a "dense pack" (or "closely based spacing") scheme.[3] The proposal was disadvantaged, however, by widespread skepticism over its basic premise. The dense pack scheme challenged the conventional wisdom that launchers should be spaced adequately to prevent multiple launcher kills from a single strike; it assumed, instead, that bunching silos together would allow the United States to capitalize on the fratricidal effect of one Soviet warhead upon another to impair a Soviet attack and permit the United States to launch its missiles. Whether or not the scheme was based on sound science, it was certainly premised on an untested principle and an exceedingly poor sense of what Congress would tolerate. The proposal became an object of derision for its seemingly "magical" solution to the basing problem. Its case was certainly not helped in Congress by strong resistance to the MX from a substantial minority, intolerance for "hypothetical solutions" to a "hypothetical problem," and a desire by many members to retaliate against the administration for its "political" manipulation of the Soviet threat. In consequence, the Congress refused to buy into the scheme or to release MX funding until the administration had deliberatively studied various basing alternatives. With the advice of a presidentially supported commission headed by Brent Scowcroft, the administration decided to deploy the MX in existing missile silos (which the commission claimed were less problematic than had been supposed given the diversity of the U.S. retaliatory force) and to proceed with the development of a smaller, mobile missile (the Midgetman).

Although MX production began in 1984, the first fifty missiles were not deployed in Minuteman III silos until 1988—at which point the scheduled deployment of another fifty missiles was blocked by Congress, again out of concern for the vulnerability of the U.S. force. In response, the administration prepared to base the remaining missiles in railroad garrisons for dispersal on the U.S. railway system (two missiles per car) in times of national emergency. The secretary of defense gave the go-ahead, in the final months of the administration, for full-scale development of the system.[4]

Despite intense and lasting concern about the U.S. window of vulnerability, the Reagan administration was unable (and perhaps unwilling), then, to move with urgency to address the problem. Consequently, hawks within and outside the U.S. government continued to trumpet the threat that the Soviets posed to the U.S. strategic force. By one Air Force analysis, the "window of vulnerability" had actually widened during Reagan's presidency: the Soviets could employ their SS-18 missiles, with more warheads than the United States possessed on all its land-based missiles, to wipe out the U.S. force and still retain a significant SS-18 reserve force.[5]

U.S. Strategic Goals: Declaratory Doctrine

In some respects, the Reagan administration departed incrementally from past doctrine. Although Reagan officials argued incessantly that they were seeking to correct the mistakes of the past, they built their nuclear strategy and targeting policies around the practices of prior administrations. Beginning in the Kennedy administration, successive administrations had attempted to increase the president's wartime nuclear options. Their efforts decreased the U.S. reliance on the cataclysmic response—a spasmodic attack on Soviet urban industrial centers—that U.S. declaratory doctrine of the mid-1960s promised that the United States would deliver in retaliation. Accordingly, the Reagan administration paved the path of the Carter administration by casting the rationale for U.S. nuclear weapons decidedly in terms of "denying" the Soviet Union gains through war. The goal was not to deter the Soviets by threatening to impose unacceptable costs (or to achieve Soviet cooperation in war to observe certain limits) but instead to damage the Soviet military so severely that it could not accomplish its wartime goals, whatever they might be. These ideas were articulated in a key Defense Department document (the Defense Guidance) and the President's National Security Decision Directive (NSDD-13), which asserted that the U.S. goal was prevailing in a protracted nuclear war (Talbott 1985: 255). In his 1984 Report to Congress, Defense Secretary Caspar Weinberger stated that a primary principle of U.S. strategy was to end hostilities "at the lowest possible level of damage to the United States and its allies" and to "restore peace on favorable terms" (quoted in Blacker 1987: 141). Despite originating in prior policy, this orientation toward war-fighting brought various significant policy departures.

First, the Reagan administration departed from prior practice by no longer treating Soviet leadership targets as "withholds." Whereas prior administrations had shied from targeting the Soviet leadership immediately—hoping that it would control its forces to limit the effects of war—the Reagan administration treated the Soviet leadership as a critical counterforce target. In its view, attacking the Soviet leadership was an effective means of disrupting command and control of Soviet forces and deterring Soviet aggression. In this, the administration gave voice as well to criticism within the U.S. strategic community of the "mirror imaging" that was implicit within AD doctrine, that is, the assumption that U.S. and Soviet leaders shared a desire to avoid provocations that could bring harm to their own citizenry. The critics assumed that, unlike U.S. leaders, their Soviet counterparts valued only their own lives, prerogatives, and hold on power. Thus, deterring the Soviet Union required placing its leaders directly at risk.

Second, the administration departed strategically from its predecessors by elevating the role of the defense. For the administration, a strong defense was no less essential to the U.S. denial strategy than was a strong offense. This was the message, in 1983, when Reagan announced his "Strategic Defense Initiative" with the hope of avoiding the risks and very high potential costs of a policy based on AD principles. For defense advocates within the administration, a potential aggressor had nothing to gain from attacking an effective defense. At the very least, a strong U.S. defense could tip the balance toward deterrence by limiting potential Soviet gains from an attack and reducing the damage that the United States incurred in war. If deterrence failed, a defense could save U.S. lives directly—or indirectly, by protecting U.S. (offensive) capabilities to respond to a Soviet attack. These were ostensibly worthy goals, for the United States had to assume that the Soviets would under some conditions willingly accept the costs of attacking the United States for the alleged benefits. A prominent hawkish scenario had a collapsing Soviet state launching a nuclear attack as a final act of retribution against the United States. Inasmuch as Soviet leaders presumably had nothing left to lose from attacking, they could at least take the United States down with them.

Third, the Reagan administration placed fresh emphasis on prompt weapons delivery, accuracy, survivability, and command and control. These were critical assets if the United States was to compete with the Soviet Union in the battle for survival—and victory—that a nuclear war was assumed now to have become. To prevail in a nuclear war, the United States would have (1) to locate and destroy Soviet targets, including mobile missiles, before they were launched against U.S. targets; (2) to process vast amounts of information quickly and efficiently to retarget U.S. weapons during the course of the conflict; (3) to protect sensors, communication links, and command and control facilities despite their assorted vulnerabilities; and (4) to observe some limits, perhaps, to avoid a catastrophic Soviet response when U.S. attacks on the Soviet military infrastructure would leave the Soviet industrial base in ruins, kill tens of millions of Soviet citizens, and sorely test the Soviet willingness to exercise restraint. Even attacks on the Soviet leadership per se, if extended to the lower ranks, might have had the United States targeting a hundred thousand people (Ball and Toth 1990: 73).

As Coit Blacker surmised, "The explicit endorsement in U.S. declaratory policy in 1983 of a deterrent posture based on the twin goals of limiting damage and the termination of nuclear hostilities on terms favorable to the United States constituted one of the most significant revisions to American nuclear strategy since McNamara's abandonment of the 'no-cities' doctrine in the early 1960s" and the acceptance of the principles of Assured Destruction, which Weinberger had pointedly rejected (Blacker 1987: 142–143). These shifts only increased the challenges for U.S.-Soviet arms control. The administration's embrace of denial principles hardened the U.S. negotiating terms, while the administration's pursuit of a missile defense only increased the Soviet reluctance to accept those terms.

Arms Control: Backdrop, Negotiations, and Consequences

The Strategic Arms Reduction Treaty (START) talks, which started in June 1982, were initially meant as a SALT follow-on round that would result in nuclear arms reductions. To break with the past, Reagan repackaged the "SALT III" negotiations as the START negotiations with the intent of negotiating dramatic reductions that would equalize U.S. and Soviet forces. Early success was proscribed, however, by the administration's preoccupation with SALT compliance issues, enthusiasm for missile defense, and hard-line negotiating positions.

The SALT Legacy

The START talks were shaped by the SALT legacy. In the aftermath of the SALT ratification debate, treaty critics—many of whom obtained prominent positions in the Reagan administration—challenged the Soviet Union on its wholesale cheating on the ABM, SALT I, and SALT II treaties. Charges of Soviet cheating (and Soviet countercharges) continued throughout much of the Reagan administration. Even on the eve of Reagan's heralded 1987 breakthrough—the Intermediate-Range Nuclear Forces Treaty—top officials in the administration harshly criticized the Soviets for assorted treaty violations.[6]

In their view, the Soviets were duplicitous: they exploited ambiguities in treaties with overly narrow, legalistic, and obviously self-serving interpretations of provisions; they capitalized on loopholes that they had intentionally constructed; and they engaged in what, by any reasonable standard, was flagrant cheating. Its scope, frequency, and variety could only signal that the worst was yet to come, when the Soviets improved their strategic position through repeated treaty violations. Even "militarily insignificant" violations served Soviet grand strategy: to quote Richard Perle, then an assistant secretary of defense, "They would not be making these significant investments . . . if they did not think it made a significant contribution to their military capability" (U.S. Congress 1987: 52).

These skeptics detected frightening consistency in Soviet behavior. They cited the full litany of Soviet violations going back at least to the Limited Test Ban Treaty[7] to argue that the Soviets show no regard for legal obligations: the violations—both big and small—occurred without a hint of Soviet contrition or concern. As Kenneth Adelman, the director of ACDA, remarked, "What has impressed me over the years is how the Soviets lack even the interest, the seriousness in the [SCC] to come up with credible explanations of what they are doing" (U.S. Congress 1987: 25). Instead, the Soviets attributed the resulting controversy to imprecisions in the treaty text. But the truth, according to Richard Perle, was that "the Soviets count on controversy to obscure their violations so that they can be confident of getting away with them" (U.S. Congress 1987: 5). In this, the Soviets could depend on support from overzealous U.S. policymakers (and policy advocates) who embraced the cause of arms control, trusted that the United States and the Soviet Union shared perspectives and interests, resisted military competition when it was required, and could excuse any Soviet treaty violation. Thus, the Soviets were twice blessed: they could count on the United States abiding by stringent interpretations of an agreement while they were effectively unconstrained.[8]

For treaty proponents, the case for Soviet violations—let alone willful ones—was not open and shut. Most of these violations were "technical" in nature and hardly signaled a Soviet push for a nuclear advantage. As one prominent expert concluded, many of these alleged violations stemmed from "ambiguous" behavior or the inherent vagueness of treaty provisions: "It is not possible to negotiate a perfect agreement, the provisions of which will not be subject to differing interpretations by the parties" (U.S. Congress 1987: 65). Parties differ in their understanding of the terms of the agreement, raise issues that were unanticipated when the agreement was negotiated, and push its boundaries—as the Reagan administration did in (re)interpreting the ABM Treaty. For that matter, parties must inevitably revisit issues that negotiators sought to work around to craft a mutually agreeable treaty: "Several of the compliance disputes in the first half of the 1980s concerned provisions of agreements that were an imperfect compromise at the time they were negotiated. . . . Nearly all the charges of noncompliance were either patently invalid or somewhat questionable" (Duffy 1988: 272–273). Soviet "violations" were sometimes based on U.S. treaty interpretations that the Soviets had rejected (or not explicitly accepted) during the treaty negotiations.

One longstanding subject of disagreement involved the Soviet deployment of the SS-19 missile despite the understanding on the U.S. side, under the SALT I agreement, that the Soviets would not deploy a new heavy missile—which the

United States had defined as a missile with a volume substantially larger than the Soviet SS-11, the heaviest of the Soviet light missiles (NAS 1985: 53). Drawing from that experience, Reagan administration officials charged repeatedly that, despite the SALT II prohibition on deploying more than one new missile, the Soviets were acquiring new missiles in the guise of modernizing their older designs. The issue came to a head when the Soviets deployed the mobile SS-25 missile, which the Soviets claimed was a modernized version of the SS-13 missile. The Reagan administration insisted that the SS-25 exceeded the 5-percent throw-weight allowance under the treaty, which effectively made the SS-25 a new missile. As elsewhere, U.S. experts disagreed over whether the Soviets had actually violated the treaty and then over the severity of the offense. Administration critics noted, for example, that the United States and the Soviet Union employed different baselines (what to include and exclude and which past test to use as a reference) when determining missile throw-weight, that U.S. estimates for past tests contained large margins of uncertainty, and that the missile's throw-weight was in any case insufficient to accommodate another warhead for a planned Soviet breakout from the SALT II Treaty (Sartori 1985/86: 159–160; U.S. Congress 1987: 98).

Another dispute followed from the Soviet encryption of missile telemetry, arguably hindering the U.S. verification of Soviet compliance with treaty restrictions on new missile deployment and numbers of warheads. Although the United States could obtain relevant data from unencrypted channels, hawks charged that the Soviets might supply false information on those channels and accurate information on encrypted ones. As long as the Soviets continued to encrypt information, Soviet behavior was incriminating as a matter of definition. In response, administration critics contended that the SALT II Treaty was not meant to "prevent" encryption—even the U.S. Air Force had opposed the idea of giving the Soviets unrestricted access to U.S. telemetry—but to restrict actions that would "impede" the verification of compliance with treaty provisions (Schear 1985: 163). Indeed, if "impede" was taken to mean doing anything that would make verification more difficult, then all encryption was banned (Sartori 1985/86: 161)—which the qualified text and negotiating record establish were not the prohibition's intent. By this reading, the Soviets could legally encrypt all of their telemetry, if the United States could judge Soviet treaty compliance through other means (U.S. Congress 1987: 98). Not only was Soviet encryption allowable, it was even reasonable, given the amount of information on Soviet systems that the United States had on hand: after all, U.S. officials had described Soviet violations in very specific (numerical) terms when charging, for instance, that SS-25 throw-weight exceeded SALT II allowances. Administration critics were probably correct, therefore, to conclude that the encryption dispute was driven in no small part by military intelligence gathering: the United States wanted as much information as it could acquire; the Soviet Union wanted to supply as little as it could and to learn as much as was possible about U.S. monitoring capabilities. Thus, the Soviets responded to U.S. criticism essentially by saying, "Tell us what channels you need," and the United States basically declined to do so.

Some of the more contentious compliance disputes pertained to Soviet adherence to the ABM Treaty. Hawks maintained that Soviet treaty violations established, individually and collectively, that the Soviets were engineering a nationwide missile defense. The alleged violations included employing antiaircraft radar concurrent with tests of (ABM) interceptors contravening the treaty's prohibition on testing radar "in an ABM mode" (meant to prevent a party from integrating radar quickly into a national defense system). The Soviets claimed that their actions were permitted under the treaty, which allowed radar for range safety and instrumentation to keep aircraft from straying into test areas and to check the performance of missile navigation systems. A more bothersome challenge was the Soviet deployment of a large phased array radar (LPAR) at Krasnoyarsk that was not, as the treaty required, located on the Soviet "periphery" and "oriented outward"—for the permissible activities of early attack warning or monitoring U.S. compliance through national technical means. The U.S. fear was that the Soviets would network the radar with battle radar and antiballistic missiles to track, target, and intercept U.S. warheads as part of a missile-defense system.[9] Although U.S. experts tended to agree that the Krasnoyarsk radar was a "clear" treaty violation, opinion divided over its military significance. Administration officials argued that LPAR permitted the Soviets to lay down the expensive, long lead-time portion of a missile-defense system in advance of a treaty breakout. Others viewed the radar more benignly given its vulnerability to attack; its inability to operate at required frequencies in a nuclear-charged environment; its distance from other portions of the Soviet missile-defense system; its anomalous location relative to Soviet missile fields; and its solitary existence apart from a network of other such radar to create a nationwide defense. The expert verdict was that the radar was intended for early warning—perhaps plugging a detection hole for U.S. submarine-launched ballistic missiles (see Schear 1985: 157–158). In other words, they concluded that the radar was illegal—as the Soviets would later concede—but its apparent function was not. Indeed, some experts argued that the U.S. legal position was compromised by the modernization of U.S. early-warning radar at Thule, Greenland, and Flyingdales Moor, England, which were obviously not on the "U.S. periphery." U.S. officials claimed that these radar were "grandfathered" in; the Soviets claimed that the United States had installed new radar there in violation of the treaty.

So administration critics viewed the U.S. "response" to the alleged violations as disproportionate to the severity of the Soviet offenses and their strategic significance (Duffy 1988: 281–282). The Soviet violations occurred at the edges of agreement, could not change the strategic balance, and would only raise U.S. suspicions and provoke U.S. responses that would make it even harder for the Soviets to profit from cheating. An actual Soviet breakout from the treaty would send unmistakable signals that would leave no doubt about Soviet intent and would give the United States sufficient lead time to respond effectively. That the United States had detected lesser violations should boost confidence that the Soviets could not get away with major violations.[10] For that matter, the evidence was that the Soviets were not trying to "get away" with anything. To the contrary, the Soviets modified their behavior in light of U.S. criticism and concerns: "When the U.S. asked for clarification of ambiguities, the Soviets explained the purpose of their activity, providing information to buttress their position—sometimes in great detail . . . on other occasions, they adjusted their actions . . . to meet a specific U.S. complaint" (Schear 1985: 152). For example, the Soviets did curtail their use of air-defense radar when conducting ABM tests.[11] Thus, coming into compliance—along with an overwhelming record of compliance by both parties—had to be considered in any net assessment of treaty conformity (see Gloria C. Duffy in U.S. Congress 1987: 64).[12] Under the SALT treaties, the Soviets dismantled over a thousand of their ICBMs and SLBMs missiles to stay within the required limits (Philip J. Farley in U.S. Congress 1987: 117). As Schear surmised at the time, the quality of compliance matched the impressive quantitative record: "The array of SALT limitations that both sides have observed since 1980—including the aggregate limits on strategic launchers, the limits on the numbers of missile-carrying submarines, and the warhead ceilings for land-based ballistic missiles—are strategically far more important than the treaty provisions presently in dispute" (Schear 1985: 173).

At some level, the administration also recognized the limits of the Soviet violations: they focused more on U.S. disadvantages under SALT than the extent and severity of Soviet cheating. Charging the Soviets with violations gave officials a pretext for disavowing treaties that reputedly froze in U.S. inferiority and foreclosed U.S. options. Thus, charges that the Soviets had violated the SALT II agreement by deploying the mobile SS-25 missile should be seen in light of administration plans to develop the so-called Midgetman missile, which was not permitted under the SALT II Treaty;[13] charges that the Soviets had violated the ABM Treaty should be seen in light of the administration's dissatisfaction with the treaty's restrictions on defensive technology. As one prominent arms control expert concluded, "The U.S. and Soviets currently interpret the ABM Treaty loosely with respect to some of their programs, but restrictively with respect to the programs of others" (John Rhinelander in U.S. Senate 1985: 266).

Strategic Defense

For supporters of missile defense, the ABM Treaty did not seal the primacy of the offense over the defense. In their view, the United States had to compete on defense to address the Soviet offensive and defensive threat and to realize the growing promise of defensive technology—scientific and technological advances in information processing, radar, lasers, and so on. The alternative was to concede a substantial Soviet defensive advantage. The Soviets, already offensively superior, were actively pursuing defensive technologies (legally and illegally) and investing heavily in passive nuclear defense. Indeed, the United States required a robust defensive R&D program if only to appreciate the potential of defensive technology and thus the full dimensions of the Soviet threat.

With Reagan's public announcement of the Strategic Defense Initiative—or "Star Wars" proposal, as it was (often derisively) known—the administration offered the hope that defensive technology would make nuclear weapons "impotent and obsolete."[14] Toward that end, it sought to explore a wide range of exotic technologies for a hard-point defense of U.S. land-based missile sites or—more ambitiously—an extensive nationwide defense to protect U.S. population centers. Critics assailed these plans on legal and strategic grounds.

LEGAL ISSUES

The Reagan administration sought to determine "what science had to offer" while keeping the ABM Treaty in force (in part to placate domestic critics). Consequently, the administration walked a fine line—crossed it, critics insisted—when it defined permissible and impermissible action under the treaty. In the ensuing controversy, the meaning of Article V of the ABM Treaty was front and center. Under Article V(1), the United States and the Soviet Union had committed "not to develop, test, or deploy ABM systems or components which are sea-based, air-based, space-based, or mobile land-based."[15]

For administration critics—that is, those who subscribed to the "traditional" or "restrictive" view—the text of Article V was clear, inclusive, and prohibitive. Simply put, the pursuit of exotic defenses was not allowed under the treaty. Other parts of the treaty supported and elaborated these restrictions, most importantly (1) Article II(1), which defines an ABM system as "currently consisting of" interceptor missiles, launchers, and radars; (2) Article III, which limits the ABM deployment area of the parties to two confined areas (later reduced to one); and (3) Agreed Statement 1, D, which states that to "insure" the fulfillment of the obligation under Article III, the parties agree "that in the event ABM systems based on other physical principles and including components capable of substituting for ABM interceptor missiles, ABM launchers, or ABM radars are created in the future, specific limitations on such systems and their components would be subject to discussion in accordance with Article XIII [which involved discussion in the SCC] and agreement in accordance with Article XIV [which involved amendment] of the Treaty." The traditional view was that Article II recognized that ABM systems were possible that were based on exotic technologies (hence, "*currently* consisting of") and thus that the restrictions in Article V applied to ABM systems of all types, whether employing new or old technology. In turn, Agreed Statement D (that is, 1, D) was clearly meant to apply to new land-based technologies, such as lasers, that might confound the application of Article III; it was not meant to open the door to discussion of all potential technologies, regardless of their basing. Otherwise, claimed critics, there would be no logical reason for having prefaced the statement by referring to Article III.

The administration, however, offered its own "broad" interpretation of the treaty. In its view, the treaty was not meant to restrict the development and testing of exotic technologies, only to subject their actual deployment to discussion and negotiation (under Article XIII and Article XIV), which could lead to the treaty's amendment. To make their case, administration officials argued that Article II of the treaty associated ABM systems and their components with the technology that was currently available and therefore that Article V merely limited that technology to the sites that were specified under Article III. They noted further that Agreed Statement D was thus written as the sole reference to exotic technologies and was intended to leave their disposition open to discussion and negotiation.[16]

The debate centered, then, on fine points. Was the comma before "currently consisting of" in Article II meant to be read as an "and," as administration officials maintained, or as a "comma," as their critics argued? Does mention of current technologies in the document, in reference to ABM systems, imply that ABM systems are those that employ current technology? Still, the debate went beyond the parsing of words and grammar; indeed, the administration's critics argued that a textual focus played to the administration's strategy. Whereas the administration made its case by reinterpreting text, trumpeting logical inconsistencies, and revealing "clues" to textual interpretation in the "secret" record of negotiations, Senate testimony, and official statements, critics argued that the administration's interpretation of the ABM Treaty contravened the prevailing understanding—held by Soviet officials and key U.S. policymakers, including Secretary of Defense Caspar Weinberger and the chief arms control negotiator, Gerard Smith—when the treaty was negotiated and ratified. That the treaty was not more explicitly restrictive, then, was easily explained: the prohibitions on exotic technologies were so clearly understood at the time that they required no elaboration. Accordingly, critics argued that senators across the political spectrum (including prominent hawks such as Henry Jackson) had subscribed to the restrictive understanding of the agreement during the 1972 ratification hearings and that one of the lone Senate ratification opponents of the treaty, Senator James Buckley of New York, had predicated his negative vote on his belief that the treaty restricted new technologies. That the Reagan administration had developed its opinion without consulting (inside or outside) experts—let alone Soviet officials—only belied the administration claims to understand the text.

Notably, the administration argued that the developing and testing—not the deploying—of exotic technologies was permitted under the ABM Treaty. Indeed, it argued that deployment was prohibited unless expressly allowed by subsequent treaty amendment, when it could have insisted that Agreed Statement D required only the discussion and proposal of amendments before a party could proceed with deployment. In other words, it could have insisted that the treaty gave the United States the right to develop, test, and deploy exotic technologies.[17] Presumably, the administration thought it wise not to press the case for deployment before knowing more about U.S. technological options and advantages vis-à-vis the Soviet Union. Maybe both sides in the debate appreciated, then, that the stakes were higher than the future of the ABM Treaty. Whereas administration critics voiced concern that the new interpretation would bring all treaties into question and complicate the negotiation of new ones, the administration recognized implicitly that the ABM Treaty served U.S. interests by constraining Soviet action.[18]

THE POLICY DEBATE

Administration officials maintained that their policies on missile defense served U.S. security: the potential gains were high relative to the costs. Their critics charged that these policies endangered U.S. security by threatening U.S.-Soviet arms control. The competing sides argued as follows.

First, administration supporters and their critics voiced opposing views of the promise of defensive technology. Supporters maintained that a functioning missile defense system was in reach. To make their case, they highlighted U.S. ingenuity, resources, technological prowess, and problem-solving capabilities; the nonlinear performance gains that new technologies deliver over time; and the full range of potential options—of varying cost, promise, and ambitiousness—that increased the prospects of producing a viable U.S. defense. Critics responded that defending hardened U.S. missile silos—let alone U.S. cities—against a Soviet attack required an extremely high rate of effectiveness in an unforgiving and uncharted nuclear-conflict environment. Here, the defense was competing, not just against nature, but against an adaptive opponent that would adjust its (offensive) tactics to compensate for defensive improvements. To thwart a defensive system, the Soviets could launch warheads in numbers that could overwhelm a defense; it could saturate the defense and open attack corridors at defensive points of weakness; it could defeat defensive measures by changing missile trajectories or adopting inexpensive counters at each phase of a missile's flight trajectory;[19] or it could dispense with missiles altogether in favor of other means of delivery. In sum, the challenge for the defense was overwhelming: the defense had to cover the entire range of offensive options while the offense could play to its own strengths and exploit defensive weaknesses.

Second, administration supporters and their critics disagreed over the advantages of a partial defense. Supporters asserted that any defense of U.S. missiles or citizens was an improvement over no defense: even the limited defense of the United States could help save American lives or stabilize the U.S.-Soviet nuclear balance. Supporters claimed that a defense that offered some protection of U.S. land-based missiles—that is, U.S. second-strike, counterforce capabilities—could dissuade the Soviets from launching an attack and might decrease Soviet reliance on land-based missiles given their vulnerability, now, to a U.S. counterattack. In response, critics stressed the impediments to potential defensive improvements. They argued that a perfect defense was unachievable and that even a defense that approached 90–95 percent effectiveness (a standard thought reasonable by defense enthusiasts) would not prevent the Soviets from inflicting catastrophic damage on the United States: the 5 to 10 percent of surviving Soviet warheads—out of a force of ten thousand—could destroy much of the U.S. urban-industrial base. Then, the Soviets could undercut any U.S. defense easily and cost-effectively by building more missiles.

Third, supporters and their critics argued over whether a defense could destabilize the nuclear balance by provoking Soviet offensive and defensive improvements. For supporters, the dangers were minimal. The United States could draw on its superior economic and technological base to construct a defense that would thwart Soviet offensive countermeasures. They insisted, regardless, that the Soviets marched to their own drummer and did not respond to U.S. behavior, positive or negative, on offense or defense. Indeed, that was the problem. Thus, in 1985, Secretary of State George Shultz described the Soviet defensive threat in bleak terms:

> In the past 20 years, the Soviets have spent about as much on strategic defense—missile defense, civil defense, and air defense—as they have spent on strategic offense. They deploy the world's only operational ABM system, and are continuing to modernize it. Their propaganda about the so-called "militarization of space" rings rather hollow when one considers that they have the world's most active military space program; last year they conducted about 100 space launches and nearly 80 per cent of them were military in nature, while the United States had only about 20 total space launches. The Soviets also have the world's only extensively tested and fully operational anti-satellite system. And their own research efforts into SDI technologies—high-energy lasers, particle-beam weapons, radio-frequency weapons, and kinetic-energy weapons—long antedate our own.[20]

Seen from this perspective, it was forgoing defenses that posed the greatest danger to the United States because Soviet offensive and defensive improvements combined to give the Soviets an incentive to attack the United States. Indeed, pursuing a defense was a no-loss proposition. If defensive technology failed to live up to its promise, the United States would be no worse off for its efforts.

Critics insisted, however, that U.S. missile defenses could stoke a dangerous arms race: potential instability existed in a defensive-defensive and offensive-defensive arms competition that could conceivably give one side an edge; it existed in the possible closing of a U.S. window of opportunity, when the Soviets might strike the United States while they still could; and it existed in the illusory belief that the defense could dominate the offense, which could fuel U.S.-Soviet tension and encourage high-risk behavior (including the renouncing of arms control agreements).[21] That U.S. officials publicly and consistently repudiated AD principles—by suggesting that missile defenses could shield populations from nuclear attack—had to reinforce Soviet misgivings about surrendering an offensive advantage in heavy, MIRVed, land-based missiles (for penetrating the defense). If anything, it could prompt a buildup in Soviet offensive forces. The United States could not expect the Soviet Union to adhere to offensive limits when the United States, by pursuing a defense, was increasing the challenges for the offense. Ironically, given the cost-effectiveness of Soviet offenses over U.S. defenses, the Soviets might emerge offensively in a stronger relative position through the competition.

Fourth, supporters and their dovish critics argued over the necessity of moving beyond the "mutual hostage" relationship that was embodied in AD principles. Supporters maintained that the Soviets might just do the "unthinkable" and attack the United States—perhaps in response to a U.S. first strike to thwart a conventional Soviet push into Europe. Critics answered by insisting that the nuclear balance was stable—that the Soviets had not jumped through the "window of vulnerability," when it allegedly opened, demonstrated that deterrence was robust. Parties would not dare strike one another in a world in which nuclear offenses trumped defenses. Thus, investing in missile defense would waste scarce resources that could serve other useful purposes.

Certainly, administration critics were not consistent in their logic when claiming, at once, that defenses (1) are destabilizing and will fuel an arms race; and (2) cannot supplant the offense and will not work. Still, they were correct if they assumed that a mistaken belief that defenses work could destabilize U.S.-Soviet relations beyond repair. Administration supporters could not as easily excuse their insensitivity to the liabilities of a defense—its economic costs, illusory gains, and potentially dangerous strategic consequences—nor their own logical inconsistencies. Indeed, by seeking to free the (hostage) U.S. population from the threat of nuclear incineration, Reagan officials suggested that the Soviets would inflict unacceptable costs on the United States in the event of nuclear war, implicitly accepting an (AD) assumption that the administration had explicitly rejected.

The START I Proposal

The administration viewed the START talks as an opportunity to reverse a U.S. disadvantage that was created (or reinforced) by prior arms control negotiations. It focused its concern on the overwhelming Soviet edge in throw-weight and land-based missiles—especially the "heavies"—that threatened the U.S. land-based missile force. Its early efforts were unsuccessful, however, if the goal was to produce a treaty.

The administration proposed, initially, that the United States and the Soviet Union cut their forces by over a third, to 5,000 warheads per side—with a limit of 850 deployed ballistic missiles, restricted further to no more than 110 heavy missiles and 210 medium and heavy missiles—to be followed eventually by the imposition of an equal ceiling on throw-weight. Conspicuously, the administration left U.S. cruise-missile-equipped bombers, restricted under SALT II, out of the U.S. proposal. The U.S. proposal challenged prior practice, both in the size of the required cuts and their relative distribution, for it was written to secure restrictions on missile launchers and throw-weight, in which the Soviets had an overwhelming edge. Indeed, the proposal was written to reflect current U.S. deployment plans while imposing severe cuts in the size of the Soviet missile arsenal. Under the proposal, the United States could increase the number of warheads on its land-based missiles (and add up to 210 new MX missiles) and continue to modernize all three legs of the triad.[22] Needless to say, the Soviets, seeing no merit in the U.S. proposal, summarily rejected it. They favored modest reductions that were based on the ceilings and sub-ceilings of the SALT regime (NAS 1985: 59–60, 74–75).

With public and congressional pressure building for a relaxation of the U.S. negotiating stance, the administration in 1983 modified its proposal to include arms reduction incentives to stabilize the nuclear balance. With these incentives, the parties would presumably want to send their forces out to the sea and deploy single-warhead ICBMs rather than acquire multiple-warhead, land-based missiles (NAS 1985: 64). Structured around the dismantling of existing weapons for new warheads that were introduced, the proposal served (1) the growing sentiment within Congress and the arms control community to "build down" U.S. and Soviet force levels; and (2) U.S. plans to develop a single-warhead missile (the Midgetman)—for deployment, perhaps, on mobile launchers—to reduce the destructiveness of a Soviet first-strike attack on U.S. land-based missiles. Yet the proposal was again one-sided: it was structured to permit the United States to capitalize on its qualitative advantages and existing force configuration, especially the U.S. reliance on SLBMs. Indeed, under the proposal the United States could retain its planned bomber force, with its sophisticated avionics, short-range missiles, and cruise missiles (NAS 1985: 75). Conversely, given the numerical ceilings and throw-weight restrictions, the Soviets were required to jettison most of their ICBM warheads, the mainstays of the Soviet strategic nuclear arsenal. As before, the Soviets dismissed the U.S. proposal as a thinly veiled effort to profit at their expense. They sought to capitalize on global antinuclear sentiment, in turn, by advocating a "freeze" on procurement, which Reagan officials argued would lock in the Soviet nuclear edge.

Ironically, had the Soviets accepted the U.S. proposal, the resulting configuration of forces would apparently not have improved the U.S. capability to prevail in a nuclear war (which would have the United States absorbing the effects of a Soviet nuclear strike, attacking the Soviet leadership, and targeting and retargeting Soviet military capabilities). Moreover, the administration's revised START proposal permitted the Soviets to maintain a land-based force that could still threaten U.S. ICBMs: the permissible number of Soviet ICBM warheads would still greatly exceed the number of U.S. ICBM launchers. The administration's plans to target the Soviet leadership alone were enough to bring the premises of Reagan's arms control policies into question. Could a headless Soviet military control its actions, or would it release its nuclear might in a massive spasmodic wave? Would a targeted Soviet leadership—which was now paying the ultimate price—have any incentive to limit its retaliation? Indeed, the doomsday script had already been written and might well have confounded all administration efforts to limit the damage that the Soviets would inflict upon the United States in war. Unbeknownst to U.S. policymakers at the time, Soviet leaders had devised their own system to address the leadership decapitation threat. Life imitated art in 1984, when they effectively built the "doomsday" device of *Dr. Strangelove* fame. When activated by Soviet leaders, the "Dead Hand" (or Perimeter) system would pass the critical decision to launch Soviet missiles—in a final spasm against U.S. targets—to a few junior officers who were buried in a hardened bunker within a granite mountain. With a cutoff of command links and positive sensory indications that the Soviet Union was under nuclear attack, they would "decide" whether to comply with instructions to launch an ICBM containing a signaling device that would trigger the launch of remaining Soviet missiles (Hoffman 2009: 143–154).[23]

Despite its weak doctrinal foundations and inauspicious beginnings, the fortunes of arms control improved greatly in Reagan's second term in office. The late 1980s brought a profound turnabout in U.S.-Soviet arms control negotiations—in no small part due to a change in Soviet leadership under Gorbachev. Although a START treaty did not take final form for another five years, Reagan and Gorbachev agreed on the treaty's essentials at Reykjavik in 1986 and follow-up negotiations through 1987. The breakthrough resulted from Soviet concessions in the INF Treaty that opened the door to a new era of intrusive onsite inspections.

The Intermediate-Range Nuclear Forces (INF) Treaty

In Reagan's first year in office, the United States and the Soviet Union began to negotiate limits on intermediate-range nuclear forces capable of striking targets within ranges of a few hundred to a few thousand miles. These forces were a growing concern for NATO countries with an unfavorable shift in the European balance. The withdrawal of U.S. missiles (including the Jupiter missiles from Turkey after the Cuban Missile Crisis) left a range "gap" in European-based U.S. weapon systems: they tended thereafter to divide between the tactical and the strategic (U.S. Senate 1988b: 11). In 1977, the balance shifted—dramatically, from NATO's perspective—when the Soviets introduced mobile SS-20 missiles, with their three independently-targetable warheads, as a replacement in theater for aging (single-warhead) SS-4 and SS-5 missiles. NATO leaders on both sides of the Atlantic were greatly distressed that the Soviets had achieved a regional monopoly on an entire class of weaponry. In 1979, NATO responded by adopting a two-track approach: the United States would press the Soviets diplomatically to reduce their intermediate-range missiles to the lowest possible levels and commence the deployment in Europe of 464 ground-launched cruise missiles (GLCMs) and 108 single-warhead, Pershing II ground-launched ballistic missiles (GLBMs) to reverse the NATO disadvantage. Presumably, the parallel military effort would give the United States negotiating leverage and improve the U.S. position, in theater, should the negotiations fail.

Late in 1983, the United States made its "zero-zero" offer to cancel the deployment of GLCMs and GLBMs in Europe if the Soviets would dismantle their SS-20s, SS-4s, and SS-5s. But the United States was willing to accept a "non-zero" compromise, with numbers as close to zero as possible, as long as it met certain conditions—exclusivity (of third-country systems), universality, symmetry, and verifiability (Secretary of State George Shultz in U.S. Senate 1988a: 1:19). In consequence, the talks brought into focus various issues that had proven intractable in the prior SALT negotiations, when the Soviets were unwilling to accept U.S. conditions. The main disagreements were as follows.

First, the United States and the Soviet Union disagreed over whether any settlement should include third-country forces. As in the SALT negotiations, the Soviets consistently voiced their view that European systems count against the allowable U.S. totals. From their perspective, it made no sense to exclude nuclear systems held and operated by countries that were allied with the United States, when those forces would most likely be used in coordination with U.S. forces in time of war. The Soviets argued, in fact, that the U.S. position was logically contradictory: the United States insisted that the U.S. deployment of intermediate-range missiles in Europe was a decision by NATO—of which the United States was the critical member—yet ruled out the consideration of non-U.S. forces in the negotiating formula (NAS 1985: 132). The United States was determined, though, not to bring other parties (or their holdings) into the negotiations. As the United States saw it, these forces were rightly excepted from a U.S.-Soviet treaty: they were under the control of sovereign states with their own decisional processes, considerations, and sensitivities.

Second, the United States and the Soviet Union disagreed over whether a treaty had to apply universally (globally), that is, whether it required the demobilization and dismantlement of intermediate-range missiles that were based outside of Europe. The United States and the Soviet Union clashed repeatedly over various Soviet proposals that would allow the Soviets to maintain SS-20 missiles in the Far East. In the Soviet view, SS-20 missiles that were located in Asia were intended to address threats on that front, including U.S. air and naval forces in the Pacific (U.S. Senate 1988a: 1:113); in the U.S. view, the SS-20s had the mobility and range to target Europe (NAS 1985: 128–129).

Third, and most significantly, the United States and the Soviet Union disagreed over whether the United States and the Soviet Union should be held to equal ceilings. The difference in view stemmed from diverging U.S. and Soviet assessments of the theater-force balance. The Reagan administration insisted that the Soviet SS-20s were a substantial threat to NATO military facilities—air bases, ports, conventional and nuclear forces, and so on—for which the United States did not currently have an answer;[24] the Soviets maintained that the United States had fixated on the numerical imbalance in intermediate-range missiles. In the Soviet view, the United States did not account for other U.S. theater-based systems that could deliver nuclear weapons against Soviet targets, nor did the United States consider a qualitative U.S. advantage: the United States could hit the Soviet Union from Europe when Soviet intermediate-range systems lacked the capability to hit the United States in turn. To the Soviets, then, the U.S. deployment of Pershing II and cruise missiles in theater was nothing less than a U.S. effort to circumvent SALT limitations by adding hundreds of warheads to the U.S. strategic force. The Soviets would have no recourse if it stayed within those limits.

Finally, the United States and the Soviet Union disagreed over whether a treaty required intrusive verification measures. Whereas the Soviet Union viewed verification as a less important issue, the United States maintained that a treaty had to permit measures for ascertaining compliance with the agreement (although an outright ban would be easier to police).

With U.S. deployment to commence in late 1983, the Soviets held their ground: they insisted that NATO could not deploy any intermediate-range missiles, that a treaty must incorporate aircraft and third-country weapons, and that limits should not apply globally, that is, to Asia (Shultz in U.S. Senate 1988a:

1:20).[25] Although both sides gave some ground—for instance, the United States indicated its willingness to include aircraft in a settlement—a breakthrough did not occur until late 1986, when President Reagan and President Gorbachev reached a tentative agreement on the basic treaty parameters in Reykjavik. These were U.S.-Soviet equality,[26] exclusion of third-country systems, no reduction in NATO's conventional capabilities, global limits on relevant missiles, and provisions for verification (Shultz in U.S. Senate 1988a: 1:22). By the following year, the Soviets had accepted the double-zero approach, favored by the United States, which would include shorter-range missiles that could still hit NATO targets (U.S. Senate 1988a: 1:115–116). After agreeing that the eventual treaty would prohibit all ground-launched missiles with ranges between 500 and 5,500 kilometers, the parties moved rapidly toward developing the treaty's stringent verification procedures.[27]

The Treaty, consisting of text (a Preamble and 17 Articles), a Memorandum of Understanding (pertaining to the establishment of a database), and Protocols on the procedures for eliminating missiles and the conduct of inspections, was signed by Reagan and Gorbachev in December 1987 and was submitted to the Senate for its "advice and consent" in January of the following year. The finalized treaty—of unlimited duration[28]—broke entirely new ground. It (1) banned the possession, manufacture, and flight-testing of all ground-launched missiles in the 500–5,500 kilometer range; (2) required the elimination (in phases) of missiles, launchers, and support structures within three years of the treaty's entry into force; (3) prohibited the parties from engaging in any concealment, whether deliberate or not, that would impede verification of compliance using national technical means; (4) detailed the schedules for missile dismantling and the procedures for missile destruction and warhead removal (in order to create transparency without compromising security); (5) required that the parties exchange missile data in detail; (6) mandated for the first time that the United States and the Soviet Union submit to onsite inspections of military bases and facilities so as to validate initial data, establish that proscribed support activities have ceased and missiles have been eliminated, and verify compliance with the treaty (through short-notice inspections); (7) set the rules for the continuous monitoring of portals and perimeters at a U.S. missile-production plant and a Soviet (SS-25) missile final-assembly plant; and (8) created a Special Verification Commission to address problems in treaty implementation. In sum, the treaty prohibited a whole class of weapons and established an inspection regime so that the United States and the Soviet Union could count each other's missiles, monitor their destruction, determine whether the other was abiding by the agreement, and resolve issues of treaty implementation. By the treaty's disarmament deadline in 1991, the parties had destroyed all of their missiles.

So the United States and the Soviet Union overcame their considerable differences to reach a lasting agreement. Its acceptance was due to the Reagan administration's growing receptivity toward arms control and, more significantly, a profound change in Soviet leadership.[29] The Gorbachev era would bring a dramatic restructuring of Soviet domestic policies and external relations and, in Gorbachev's last year in office (1991), the demise of the Soviet Union itself. For that matter, U.S. arms control proponents and critics overcame their differences to provide widespread support for the INF Treaty. In May 1988, the Senate gave its consent to the treaty with an overwhelmingly favorable vote (93–5), which followed strong support in the Senate Arms Services Committee and Foreign Relations Committee.

Still, the agreement gave critics of U.S.-Soviet détente an opportunity to express their fears and vent dissatisfaction with the Reagan administration's turn toward accommodation (Nolan 1991: 358). Indeed, even some treaty supporters voiced concerns about Soviet relative advantages and benefits from cheating under the terms of the treaty.

Evaluating Strength

Oddly, the zero formulation was embraced by U.S. doves (and the European left) and by hawkish officials within the Reagan administration—albeit for different reasons. Neither held, however, to entirely coherent positions.

Doves valued the treaty for its important precedent in arms control: for the first time, the United States and the Soviet Union had agreed to meaningful cuts in nuclear arms by banning a whole category of weaponry. For doves, the double-zero solution represented a critical and necessary step toward disarmament: if anything, they were concerned that the treaty would fail to deliver on its longer-term promise of spurring strategic arms reductions.

Unsurprisingly, doves had for various reasons doubted the need for deploying U.S. missiles in Europe in the first place. First, doves expressed concerns about the U.S. reliance on nuclear weapons to compensate for NATO conventional deficiencies. They were suspicious of "bean counts" that pointed to enormous Soviet numerical advantages over NATO in troops and hardware and expressed some faith that NATO could defend Europe without relying on nuclear weapons. They argued that superior Western technology, substantial NATO aerial capabilities, abundant reserve assets, and the burdens of (Soviet) offensive operations might allow NATO to overcome its quantitative disadvantages. When acknowledging

NATO's limitations, they looked first to conventional solutions: even the limited application of nuclear force, they argued, could spark a global conflagration. Second, doves maintained that missile-deployment advocates had exaggerated the Soviet military and political threat. In their view, the Soviets would cautiously avoid military confrontations: the United States and the Soviet Union were well aware that conflict could escalate or spread, that they could lose control in the "fog of war." Tinkering with this reality with some deployment gimmick was counterproductive: placing U.S. intermediate-range missiles in Europe could fuel the arms race, exacerbate U.S.-Soviet tension, and promote a false and dangerous belief that nuclear war can be limited. Third, doves assumed that the United States already possessed a robust nuclear deterrent—a strong, invulnerable U.S. strategic force that obviated the need to match Soviet weapons in quantity, kind, or location. For doves, the alleged imbalance in theater nuclear weapons could not override the reality that the United States and the Soviet Union had at their disposal tens of thousands of strategic nuclear warheads that could hit the very same targets that intermediate-range missiles would strike and still destroy other essential targets (Talbott 1985: 43). The U.S. deployment of hundreds of single-warhead missiles in Europe thus promised only illusory gains.

But many doves conceded that U.S. strategic and theater-based nuclear weapons served the U.S. defense commitment to Europe—that the Soviets would act reservedly in Europe (and elsewhere), fearing that a military confrontation will become an all-out nuclear war. When the Kennedy administration offered its "flexible response" posture as an alternative to U.S. reliance upon tactical nuclear weapons, it did not reject the nuclear option, nor did it back a conventional-force buildup to support the doctrine (Gavin 2012: 30–56). In principle, the administration remained dependent on nuclear weapons. Although it proposed that NATO conventional defenses could raise the nuclear threshold, it argued nonetheless that the United States would ascend the escalation ladder—for example, by using nuclear weapons against concentrated Warsaw Pact armored divisions—if necessary to thwart an enemy advance. In consequence, the nuclear and the conventional did not converge seamlessly in administration thought, nor in the thinking of dovish policy proponents who embraced the administration's arguments in the years to follow. Doves argued that any use of nuclear weapons might spark an all-out nuclear exchange even as they relied on a flexible-response policy that gave the United States a nuclear first-strike option; they argued that the specter of nuclear incineration might permit a purely conventional U.S.-Soviet war even as they insisted that the potential for unbridled escalation helped to deter a U.S.-Soviet war at any level. It is no wonder, then, that doves focused their attention on the deterrence benefits of nuclear weaponry, not the consequences should deterrence fail.

By comparison, hawks were more conflicted in their assessment of the INF Treaty's merits. This was certainly true in the negotiating period. Whereas some Reagan officials maintained that a zero-based solution would ameliorate the threat from the roughly one thousand Soviet warheads on intermediate-range missiles that could hit a smaller number of lucrative NATO targets, they received somewhat disingenuous support from officials who viewed the "zero proposal" as a no-cost concession that the Soviets would surely reject. In the latter's view, the proposal allowed the United States to seize the moral high ground (to appease antiwar sentiment domestically and abroad) while avoiding a compromise that would prevent the United States from procuring and retaining intermediate-range nuclear weapons. Still other officials (centered in the State Department) worried about the inflexibility of the U.S. (zero) approach and sought an agreement that would permit the United States and the Soviet Union to deploy some equitable number of intermediate-range missiles.

Notwithstanding these differences, hawks tended to support the zero-zero formula—many enthusiastically—with the finalization of the treaty. Their support owed primarily to another precedent that the treaty set: for the first time, the Soviets had relinquished their overwhelming lead to accept a position of U.S.-Soviet equality. In a word, the Soviets had finally accepted "asymmetric" Soviet reductions as the basis of agreement. This Soviet concession was insufficient, nevertheless, to allay the concerns of some hawks about the treaty. They feared that the treaty would deliver on its promise—that it would create momentum for additional cuts and undermine the U.S. strategic position. The traditional warnings about a false "euphoria" featured again in the Senate ratification debate. The fear was compounded by concerns about the reaction in Europe—whether the improved political climate might fuel demands for reduced military spending and troop levels and undermine NATO defenses (U.S. Senate 1988b: 21). But hawkish concerns about U.S. disadvantages under the treaty centered mainly on its specifics—whether the zero-zero outcome would leave gaps in NATO defenses and weaken deterrence.

These concerns dovetailed, to some extent, with those expressed by various European leaders who were "always uneasy about the zero option" but "could not afford politically to be in favor of less arms control than President Reagan" (Davis 1988: 726). In point of fact, the prevailing sentiment within NATO at the time of its 1979 deployment decision was that the United States would have to boost its nuclear deployments in Western Europe to counter the threat that existed by merit of Soviet proximity to Western Europe—however those deployments were sold to a wary European public (Talbott 1985: 39; Davis 1988: 726). These concerns derived from the challenges of "extended deterrence" that so bothered U.S. and European policymakers of the period. They wondered whether the Soviets really believed that the United States would do whatever it would take—accepting its own nuclear incineration—to defend Europe. The issue surfaced repeatedly over the decades. In the early 1960s, it led U.S. policymakers to question the political wisdom of withdrawing outdated (liquid fuel) U.S. Thor and Jupiter missiles from Europe and of placing a Multilateral Force (MLF) with nuclear-armed submarines and warships under NATO command (Bertram 1981/82). The issue provoked the United States, later, to dedicate five Polaris submarines to Europe and then to allocate SLBM warheads for targeting to the NATO command (Maloney 2007: 326; U.S. Senate 1988b: 13). In the late 1970s, the same issue led NATO to conclude that the United States must boost its direct nuclear support for the alliance.

How these front-line weapons might boost deterrence was another matter; indeed, arguments for deployment derived from competing logics.[30] Advocates agreed that the nuclear deployment in Europe had military value but disagreed over whether it exceeded the deployment's political value. The diverging opinion had important implications for arms control. The political argument gave the United States some flexibility to negotiate a permissible (nonzero) number of intermediate-range weapons but strong reasons for the United States to resist the zero-zero formula. In turn, the military argument (associated with a hard-line war-fighting or "damage-limitation" view) gave the United States reasons to support the zero-zero formulation but also reasons to reject it.

Those who embraced the political argument insisted that the U.S. missiles tied (or "coupled") the United States to the defense of Europe. For them, a pure military/deployment justification rang hollow: after all, U.S. and Soviet strategic systems—which were unconstrained by a (ratified) strategic arms control treaty—could be developed or retargeted to cover the aim points of intermediate-range missiles. Indeed, "most actors in Washington regarded the INF negotiations as a question of 'alliance management,' and discounted the military importance of both the SS-20 and the Western Pershing II and cruise missiles" (Risse-Kappen 1991: 177). From their perspective, the Soviet threat was profoundly political: the Soviets had placed SS-20s in Europe to drive a wedge in the Western alliance. The presumed Soviet goal was to exacerbate age-old fears that the United States would not "trade U.S. cities for European ones" when launching U.S. strategic weapons against Soviet targets was the only available means to thwart a Soviet offensive. Intermediate-range missiles served, then, as a reassuring symbol of the U.S. commitment to Europe, in large part because they signaled that Soviet aggression in Europe would invite an all-out, U.S. nuclear response. A leading-edge presence of these missiles would trigger a first use of nuclear weapons, which would lead inevitably to an all-out nuclear war. With the U.S. finger now tight on the nuclear trigger, the Soviets were presumably unlikely to attack Europe.

By this logic, a political threat required a politically constructed response. A relatively small number of missiles—based on the European continent in exposed positions—would present the United States with a "use-them-or-lose-them" dilemma and signal to allies and adversaries that the United States would invoke its nuclear capabilities in defense of Europe. Consequently, the best nuclear trigger for coupling was a relatively weak, vulnerable U.S. nuclear force on the front lines of the conflict. Once a nuclear war had started, the United States would presumably be forced to "go all in," that is, to use its strategic nuclear assets against Soviet strategic targets, perhaps to spark an all-out nuclear conflagration.

But this argument did not satisfy those hawks who viewed nuclear weapons first and foremost as instruments of war. War-fighters relied on U.S. theater-based weapons, as an option of first recourse, to counter a Soviet conventional attack and, more generally, sought nuclear deployments to establish U.S. "escalation dominance." By this, they meant that, in a nuclear war, the United States had to "prevail" over the Soviet Union at the higher level of engagement. U.S. efforts to win in Europe—at the conventional or nuclear level—would otherwise be thwarted if the Soviets could "win" a war at the "intermediate-level," which would have left the United States without escalation options short of a suicidal strategic nuclear exchange. In a word, these hawks were looking for militarily effective options that would "decouple" U.S. strategic forces from Europe.

Political concerns apparently drove the Carter administration to deploy the missiles in Europe. Militarily, the U.S. position in Europe had improved. In the years prior to the NATO decision, the United States dramatically increased the number of warheads on SLBMs, from 80 to 400, that were available to the NATO Supreme Allied Commander Europe, and Secretary of State Cyrus Vance testified before Congress that the United States did not require additional sea- and land-based systems in the European theater given the target coverage that was then available from U.S. SLBMs and forward-based aircraft (Garthoff 1983: 198–199). This suggests that linkage concerns were behind the U.S. push to deploy these missiles. Indeed, the Carter administration apparently took the lead in forging the NATO consensus due to President Carter's prior mishandling of the neutron-bomb deployment decision: Carter decided against deploying the bomb after it had been supported, at U.S. urging, by European leaders. The intermediate-range missile deployments gave the administration a chance to prove its mettle domestically on a matter of national security and to address concerns abroad about a weak U.S. commitment to Europe (Garthoff 1983: 203–204). The U.S. hope, it seems, was to tighten the "coupling" of the United States to Europe—or, at least, Europe to the United States.

But the NATO deployment defied a single logic. For political reasons, Germany insisted that it alone would not harbor the U.S. intermediate force, and mobile, low-profile cruise missiles were dispersed to a few countries in Europe—160 in the United Kingdom, 112 in Italy, 96 in Germany, 48 in Belgium, and 48 in the Netherlands—where they were arguably less exposed to disarming Soviet attacks (assuming they were dispersed from their bases in a crisis). Although NATO had carefully calibrated the deployment numbers—not too big or too small—to be true to the coupling logic, it was less committed to that logic, then, in selecting the manner and location of the bulk of the intermediate force. Thus, the U.S. deployment decision—as a compromise between the political logic of coupling and the military logic of decoupling—arguably offered the worst of both worlds. The U.S. missile force in Europe was too undersized, range-impaired, and slow-moving to prevent the Soviets from striking NATO military targets, yet it was still present in numbers and (dispersed) locations—with backup from U.S. nuclear-capable tactical aircraft—to create the appearance that the United States sought to confine a nuclear war to Europe.[31] Even had the United States restricted its deployment to front-line Pershing II missiles in Germany, it might well have undermined coupling as a deterrence strategy. The United States had simply replaced its Pershing I missiles at U.S. bases in West Germany with the same number of Pershing II missiles (Garthoff 1983: 204–205). These vulnerable missiles, aimed at Soviet military targets, could have induced "crisis instability," if the arguments that had long informed U.S. nuclear strategy and arms control held true. Their short flight time, range, and accuracy had to stoke fears within the Soviet Union that the United States might strike first in a conflict, which could lead the Soviets to preempt.[32]

In the end, hawks of all stripes placed far too much emphasis on the peculiar performance (virtues) of intermediate-range missiles—the "gap" that they fill—and too little emphasis on the political or military logic that tied the deployment, retention, or dismantlement of these weapons to U.S. security (U.S. Senate 1988b: 26). The result in the 1970s was to bias conclusions toward the deployment of U.S. intermediate-range missiles. James Schlesinger dubbed this intellectual failing the "illusion of concreteness" when he challenged the excessive "weight" that U.S. deployment advocates had placed on intermediate-range missiles despite the peace that had prevailed for decades in Europe in the absence of these missiles (U.S. Senate 1988a: 1:27). A feature of such weapon-centered thinking is that U.S. weapons—once deployed—appeared irreplaceable to some policy advocates: to quote Schlesinger, "they take on presumed virtues and an apparent indispensability that did not exist prior to such deployment" (U.S. Senate 1988b: 27).[33] For other advocates, affected differently by such narrow thinking, the weight had been lifted once the Soviets agreed to get rid of their own missiles.

A consequence of weapons-centered thinking was that policy advocates were not entirely consistent in their logic. Individually, they did not hold various weapon programs to the same standard. For example, U.S. policymakers ignored the decoupling potential of a U.S. missile defense system—that it might signal that the United States sought, above all else, to limit damage to U.S. territory and therefore that the Soviets could attack Europe with impunity.[34] They also ignored the complicating presence of a huge assortment of other U.S. nuclear weapons in Europe. Even at zero-zero, the United States retained a formidable nuclear-strike force of four thousand theater-based nuclear weapons carried by aircraft, artillery, and short-range missiles.[35] Collectively, they reached opposing conclusions from the same premises. This came through in the INF Treaty debate when advocates assessed the strategic nuclear implications of an outright missile ban. Richard Burt, a former high-ranking arms control official in the Reagan State Department, maintained that the Soviets would not make up for the loss of SS-20s in Europe by retargeting their intercontinental-range missiles because that would weaken the Soviet capability to target the United States (U.S. Senate 1988a: 2:180). Similarly, Paul Nitze, an arms control advisor to the administration, suggested that the Soviets were unlikely to employ intercontinental-range systems to cover SS-20 targets, once the INF Treaty was in effect, because "one loses something here," "it is not an intelligent thing to do," and "that is not the way one would do it" (U.S. Senate 1988a: 1:300). Given alleged Soviet strategic force advantages and the paltry size of the Soviet intermediate-range force that had nonetheless concerned U.S. policymakers, the retargeting (or enlarging) of Soviet strategic forces to compensate would seem a useful political investment. Indeed, former secretary of defense Harold Brown doubted that the Soviets would build SS-20 missiles, in violation of the treaty, because "the Soviets can build as many SS-25s as they wish to carry out the role of the dismantled SS-20s" (U.S. Senate 1988a: 2:112).

Another result of weapon-centered thinking was that policy advocates insufficiently developed their logic. In consequence, the logic provided an inadequate basis for concluding that the presence or the absence of U.S. missiles would couple *or* decouple the United States to Europe.[36] True, champions of the political logic argued, in the main, that the removal of Soviet SS-20 missiles vitiated a major Soviet threat that could drive a wedge in the NATO alliance. On this score, Ambassador Maynard Glitman, the U.S. negotiator on Intermediate Range Nuclear Arms, observed that the United States profited overall from ridding the world of the SS-20s and their unique decoupling capabilities: the SS-20s were dedicated to attacks on the Soviet periphery, whereas the mobile SS-25s—which the Soviets might employ in their place—could target either the United States or Europe (U.S. Senate 1988b: 38). Thus, reversing the U.S. missile deployment in Europe was a fair price to pay for the dismantling of the Soviet SS-20s. Yet such narrow analysis could also support the opposite conclusion. Eugene Rostow argued for reducing the numbers of U.S. and Soviet intermediate-range missiles to some equal nonzero number so that U.S. intermediate-range missiles would continue to couple the United States to Europe (U.S. Senate 1988a: 3:376).[37]

Drawing from the political logic, neither set of advocates argued convincingly that the Soviet SS-20s uniquely threatened U.S. interests in Europe, let alone that the SS-20 threat had required the "offsetting" deployment of U.S. missiles. For various reasons, they could well have come to opposite conclusions about the U.S. deployment and thus its implications for arms control.

First, given Soviet proximity to Europe, the U.S. weapons were—at best—a partial solution to the extended-deterrence problem. Henry Kissinger suggested as much when he argued that the withdrawal of U.S. missiles from Europe would create a critical imbalance: the Soviet Union can threaten Germany with nuclear weapons on Soviet territory, but NATO cannot threaten the Soviet Union with nuclear weapons on German territory in return. Thus, removing Pershing I and II missiles from Germany would further decouple the country from NATO (and NATO more completely from the United States).[38]

Second, the U.S. missiles were arguably irrelevant to Soviet strategic calculations because, with or without these weapons, the United States could credibly commit to defend Europe at all costs. U.S. missile deployments added little to the U.S. credibility equation because (1) the United States maintained substantial U.S. political and economic ties to Europe; (2) the U.S. policy community held strongly to the belief that U.S. interests were intrinsically tied to an independent Europe; and (3) a "trigger" for U.S. nuclear retaliation within Europe resided in the large presence there of U.S. troops, which served as a virtual hostage population.[39] Even if deployment advocates were correct that the Soviets would be tempted by the perhaps small probability that U.S. strategic weapons would actually be used in Europe's defense, the phenomenal cost to the Soviets, if they were, had to chill risk-conscious Soviet officials and war planners.

Third, the U.S. missile deployment could well have been counterproductive. These missiles could signal to the Soviets that NATO was incapable of defending Europe with conventional force or that the United States sought to stay clear of the fighting by bolstering NATO's nuclear capabilities. If the latter, a more convincing coupling signal was weakening, not strengthening, the U.S. nuclear and conventional position within Europe. A reduction in conventional capability would increase U.S. reliance on U.S. theater-based nuclear forces and a reduction in those forces would increase U.S. reliance on strategic nuclear forces, with the net effect of placing Europe clearly under the protection of the U.S. strategic nuclear umbrella. But even this strategy is flawed if the United States is actually reticent to accept the costs of a nuclear exchange with the Soviet Union. Then, the coupling of European defense to the U.S. strategic nuclear arsenal might undermine the overall credibility of the U.S. commitment to defend Europe: "If American leaders thought a war in Europe would lead to world war, they would feel enormous pressure to find a peaceful solution in a crisis, even if doing so meant sacrificing other values" (Jervis 1984: 93).

Finally, these missiles were arguably an ineffective signaling device. Although Kissinger, among others, believed that the triggering potential of the missiles would deter Soviet aggression—that the United States would "use" these missiles early so as not to "lose" them to attacking Soviet forces—his argument rests on dubious logic (U.S. Senate 1988a: 4:180). It assumes that the United States would foreclose all of its options—and put its reservations about using nuclear weapons aside—so as not to miss an opportunity to use weapons that were not militarily essential in the first place. Why should the Soviets buy that logic, and why should the United States be bound to it? After all, U.S. policymakers did not plan to retaliate automatically with nuclear force for conventional Soviet attacks on airfields where nuclear-capable U.S. aircraft were based.[40]

For champions of the military logic, the unanswered question was whether the United States should rely more on its strategic or, instead, on its theater nuclear weapons to keep the peace (or win a war) in Europe. The logic could actually support conclusions that some or all war-fighters would reject.

First, war-fighters could argue that theater nuclear weapons were largely irrelevant to the U.S.-Soviet nuclear balance and the extension of deterrence. Indeed, some war-fighters saw the intermediate-force controversy as a sideshow that distracted from the "real problem"—U.S. strategic nuclear vulnerability. In their view, the Soviets could simply respond to the equalization of theater nuclear forces by taking the confrontation to the "next level," precipitating a strategic nuclear exchange, in order to capitalize upon their strategic "dominance."

Second, war-fighters could argue (even if they rarely did) that U.S. missile deployments would have little effect on the nuclear balance in Europe. Although these missiles arguably complicated Soviet war planning, permitted the United States to redirect its strategic assets and dual-use theater-based aircraft to other targets, and provided NATO significant in-theater nuclear capability for blunting a Soviet attack (U.S. Senate 1988c: 21), they might not have countered the fundamental threat that Soviet intermediate-range missiles posed to NATO bases, ports, and other facilities that were essential for resupplying NATO forces.[41]

Third, war-fighters could argue (even if they typically did not) that theater nuclear weapons compromised U.S. interests by increasing the probability of an all-out U.S.-Soviet nuclear war. Relevant here is that the Soviets feared that U.S. intermediate-range missiles in Europe were first-strike weapons: they could arrive at their targets quickly to target Soviet aircraft on the ground, missiles in their launchers, or the Soviet leadership in or outside its shelters. The Soviets had reason to suppose, then, that the United States would employ these missiles in tandem with their strategic nuclear counterparts. Soviet fears in this regard were nurtured and validated by the Reagan administration's emphasis on military and leadership targeting and reinforced by their own predilections toward overwhelming force: the Soviets had consistently claimed, as a matter of doctrine, that a nuclear war would know no limits. After all, a nuclear war fought in Europe was a total war for the Soviet Union, by merit of geographical proximity.[42]

Finally, war-fighters could argue (even if they never did) that the U.S. missile deployments were an insufficient response because the United States should boost its nuclear forces in theater at the expense of U.S. strategic forces. If the Soviet priority was conquest of Europe—implied by U.S. concerns about "extending deterrence"—the Soviets would presumably not welcome the enormous costs of attacking the United States, a secondary target. By redirecting its capability to Europe, in consequence, the United States would strengthen its overall global position: the U.S. bombers, air-launched cruise missiles, and SLBMs—which war-fighters depreciated in strategic assessments—would constitute a formidable force for confronting Soviet aggression on the front lines of the conflict.

Trust and Verification

The INF Treaty's revolutionary inspection regime failed to allay concerns, in some quarters, about potential Soviet cheating on the agreement. Hard-line treaty opponents, like Senator Jesse Helms of the Committee on Foreign Relations, argued that under the terms of the treaty, the Soviets had abundant motive and opportunity to cheat—and *would* cheat, to significant advantage. Even some treaty supporters conceded that the Soviets could cheat on the treaty or contravene its spirit. The ensuing controversy centered on several key points.

First, treaty critics and supporters debated whether the United States could determine existing Soviet missile holdings to know whether the Soviets had actually dismantled all of their banned missiles. The disagreement reflected very different assessments of the constraints on U.S. intelligence.

Critics doubted that the United States had adequate knowledge of Soviet missile stocks. To make their case, they pointed to the highest of the outlying U.S. intelligence estimates of Soviet missile totals; they highlighted the discrepancy between the reload capability of Soviet SS-20 missiles and the small number of surplus missiles with which the Soviets were credited in U.S. tallies;[43] they warned of the deficiencies of baseline figures that were derived from inspections of known Soviet facilities; and they challenged the utility of validating data through concurrence between the U.S. and Soviet figures when the two sets of figures were not truly independent of each other. They gave particular attention to the restrictions on permissible U.S. inspections, for instance, that the United States could not conduct inspections "anytime/anywhere" and was limited to a small number of short-notice inspections at specified facilities. Thus, in their view, U.S. intelligence was privy only to what the Soviets wanted the United States to know and was disadvantaged further because the Soviets knew—from available U.S. sources—what the United States "knew" about Soviet capabilities and could play to existing U.S. perceptions. So the new monitoring system under the INF Treaty was rigged: it would allow the Soviets to destroy their "known" missiles and hide the rest. Worse still, the United States had so little knowledge of the quantities and qualities of Soviet SS-20 holdings that the Soviets could substitute functioning missiles with dummy or defective ones and destroy only the latter. The Soviets could therefore retain much of their intermediate-range force after the United States had destroyed its missiles.

Treaty supporters responded that critics greatly overstated the limits of U.S. knowledge of Soviet activities. They supported their assertions by pointing to the general consensus within the U.S. intelligence community on numbers of Soviet intermediate-range nuclear missiles; the useful opportunities that inspections permitted for validating U.S. data and establishing baselines against which to assess Soviet holdings; and the convergence between Soviet-supplied figures and U.S. estimates that were drawn from various sources, including national technical means. They assumed, then, that the United States could count on a large number of independent and overlapping checks to ensure that the Soviets were complying with the treaty. In Nitze's words, the treaty worked "by creating a network of interrelated constraints and measures that allow careful monitoring and reinforce one another in such a fashion as to raise the cost and difficulty of cheating and the risk of getting caught" (U.S. Senate 1988a: 1:290). They developed this argument by echoing a familiar refrain: the greater the scale of the violations, the greater the chances of exposure. Each illicit Soviet missile multiplied the chances of discovery; and the disclosure of a single missile would implicate the Soviets in deception.

Second, treaty critics and supporters disagreed over how easily the Soviets could override the prohibitions on producing new intermediate-range missiles. Critics asserted that the treaty's safeguards were much less rigorous than they appeared; treaty supporters conceded that the safeguards were imperfect but downplayed the negative consequences.

Critics argued that the United States did not know whether the Soviets maintained secret production and storage facilities in some parts of the vast, uninspected portion of the Soviet land mass. Even James Schlesinger, a treaty proponent, conceded that the Soviets could produce banned missiles under the treaty: the United States was restricted to onsite monitoring of the exterior of a single missile assembly plant, allowing the Soviets to assemble their missiles illicitly in uninspected facilities. Some critics saw additional opportunities for Soviet subterfuge in the resemblance and interchangeability between the stages of the Soviet SS-20 and other Soviet missiles: of particular concern was that the Soviets would pass a new SS-20 off as a two-stage SS-25 missile—currently a three-stage weapon (perhaps armed with SS-20 warheads that had been retained legally, under the treaty). Inasmuch as the Soviets had considerable experience in the production, testing, and deployment of SS-20 missiles, they could lie low—with their secret stocks—until the time was right to challenge U.S. interests. For that matter, the Soviets could legally obtain intermediate-range missiles by staying within the terms of the treaty: they could test missiles at longer ranges—to qualify them (legally) as strategic systems—and modify them subsequently for intermediate-range performance. Thus, some critics surmised that the United States should not ratify an intermediate-range forces treaty without a satisfactory strategic nuclear arms reduction treaty in place to prevent the Soviets from getting around restrictions on (the production, testing, and deploying of) intermediate-range missiles by claiming that they are "strategic" weapons.

Although treaty supporters were willing to concede some of these points, they were not swayed by the overall logic. They stressed that the Soviets would have to overcome substantial treaty hurdles to produce missiles illicitly: the treaty gave the United States the right to weigh, measure, and image containers exiting an SS-25 assembly facility and randomly select a small number to be opened; it required the opening of SS-25 shelters, for designated intervals, to permit their inspection through U.S. national technical means; it restricted the similarities between missiles—permitted and banned under the treaty—to a single missile stage (and, then, required that they exhibit observable differences and be non-interchangeable); and it precluded the deployment of the Soviet SS-16 missile, which, minus its third stage for intercontinental range, was essentially the SS-20 missile.[44] Supporters argued that even a secret missile arsenal would do the Soviets little good: missiles were effectively unusable if not tested and integrated into ongoing Soviet military training and exercises and would eventually fall into disrepair. They conceded that the Soviets could circumvent the rules by testing missiles at longer ranges and deploying them to perform at intermediate distances. But, in their view, the cure for the Soviets was worse than the disease: it was expensive, had significant opportunity costs (in lost strategic capability), and would yield weapons that were not clearly threatening to Europe as was required if the Soviets were to obtain the necessary political leverage.

Third, treaty critics and supporters debated whether the United States had conceded too much to secure a verifiable treaty. One dispute centered on the U.S. concession of "anytime/anywhere" inspections. Where critics saw Soviet opportunities to cheat in any and all limits to the U.S. right of inspection, supporters emphasized that the United States would lose much, when the Soviets were obtaining reciprocal rights with more robust inspection provisions: ceaseless requests for inspections could trigger interminable disputes, and the Soviets could engage in military and industrial espionage in the guise of verifying compliance with the treaty. In point of fact, it was the U.S. defense establishment that voiced opposition to unrestricted inspections once they threatened to become a reality (Nolan 1991: 370–371). Another dispute centered on the treaty's ban on the production, testing, and deployment of all GLCMs because their conventional and nuclear variants were indistinguishable. Whereas some skeptics insisted that the United States had thereby sacrificed a significant conventional-force multiplier that could assist the United States in far-flung military operations, treaty supporters argued that forgoing conventionally armed GLCMs was a small U.S. concession: the United States could still draw on cruise missiles, launched from other platforms, and substitutes for cruise missiles in the robust U.S. conventional arsenal. Still another dispute centered on the fact that the parties could retain the warheads of dismantled missiles under the treaty. Critics stressed that this gave the Soviets an additional relative advantage, of 4 to 1 in warheads and 12 to 1 in fissile materials (due to the high yields of the Soviet weapons). Some critics argued, in fact, that the Soviets could rapidly modernize their strategic arsenal by reusing these warheads given the modular construction of Soviet weapon systems. In response, treaty supporters claimed that warhead retention was a blessing in disguise for the United States, as the United States had the greater need for reusing the nuclear materials (given abundant Soviet production capabilities and stocks) and would incur great expense and challenges in disposing of them safely. Indeed, in their view, the transparent destruction of these materials would threaten U.S. security: warhead technologies would surely be exposed—and compromised—in order to allay Soviet concerns that the United States was complying with the treaty (U.S. Senate 1988c: 24, 66). Supporters claimed, in fact, that critics exaggerated the ease with which the Soviets could reuse warheads, which were actually customized for the SS-20 missiles that were now destined for the scrap heap. Regardless, they argued, the United States was hardly disadvantaged by a treaty that took large numbers of Soviet warheads out of the active inventory. Were this only a temporary treaty benefit—and the Soviets were to seek "strategic" replacements for the lost missiles—the Soviets could not do so without incurring substantial economic costs (which would only increase if the Soviets tried to reuse SS-20 warheads and guidance systems).

Fourth, treaty critics and supporters debated the net strategic value to the Soviets from cheating. For critics, treaty loopholes and allowances created abundant opportunities for the Soviets to increase—quite dramatically—the numbers of Soviet nuclear missiles while the United States was disarming to comply with the treaty. In response, treaty supporters claimed that critics put far too much emphasis on what the Soviets *could* do and too little emphasis on the ultimate effect. In their view, the real issue was not whether the Soviets maintained a secret missile stock but whether it would yield an effective Soviet advantage. Supporters argued that a host of factors—the presence of U.S. tactical nuclear systems in Europe, the backup support from the British and French nuclear arsenals, the lower risk to the Soviets of pursuing longer-range missiles in place of intermediate-range ones, the sheer size of U.S. and Soviet strategic arsenals—made it quite unlikely that the Soviets would strive, again, for advantage in intermediate-range missiles (Schlesinger in U.S. Senate 1988c: 158). A force of many dozens of illegal triple-warhead, SS-20 missiles would still constitute a small fraction of the warheads and bombs that were available to the United States. As Schlesinger concluded, "If the Soviet Union is not deterred by the 12,000 warheads in America's strategic forces that can reach Soviet soil, then the Soviet Union will not be deterred by the 12,400 warheads that could reach Soviet soil when we throw in that handful of weapons presently based in Europe that will be withdrawn under this treaty" (Schlesinger in U.S. Senate 1988c: 142).

Finally, treaty supporters and critics debated the overall value of the treaty-based inspection regime. Critics focused on potential Soviet gains from cheating, convinced that the Soviets would cheat. After all, that was the Soviet pattern: once again, critics recited the litany of Soviet treaty violations, with great emphasis on the SALT legacy, to argue that the Soviets had constructed loopholes and openings—now, in the INF Treaty—with which to cheat. They assumed that, with sizable opportunities for illicit gains, the Soviets would stick to their pattern. In response, proponents argued that weak protections against cheating had to be assessed against gains for the United States under the terms of the treaty and the risks to the Soviets from cheating. Schlesinger had a point, then, when he testified that the INF verification regime was actually "quite weak" but was "satisfactory," nonetheless, "given the outcome of the treaty" (U.S. Senate, 1988a: 2:140–141). So did the State Department when it argued that verification requirements could actually be loosened in light of reduced Soviet incentives to cheat (Nolan 1991: 371). Supporters stressed, as well, that the United States had much to gain from the long-term cooperative benefits that the inspections promised, which extended well beyond the dismantlement of intermediate-range forces. In their view, the treaty set the useful precedent of robust inspections for future agreements (most immediately, the START treaty), could offer lessons and skills through implementation that could further U.S.-Soviet cooperation, and helped the parties to build trust through consistent and active compliance (see Nitze in U.S. Senate 1988a: 1:295–296).

The problem, however, was that positions on cheating did not necessarily mesh with the arguments that were used previously to support the U.S. missile deployment in Europe. That the Soviets could cheat on the treaty should have been a primary concern given the political argument that Soviet intermediate-range missiles would fuel the decoupling of Europe from the United States. At some point, the Soviets could disclose their heretofore hidden capability—once the United States had destroyed its intermediate-range missiles and support infrastructure and dismantled its related production capabilities—to acquire a monopoly in intermediate-range missiles. Although such perfidy, so clearly demonstrated, might drive Europe closer to the United States, that was not the likely result if political (linkage) arguments held true: the unrelenting Soviet buildup, in the face of an accommodative U.S. response, was the kind of signal that political war-fighters believed would fray the lines that bound the United States to

Europe. Military war-fighters should have been no less concerned about Soviet duplicity. If war-fighting arguments were valid, the Soviets had a strong incentive to cheat and to exploit illicit gains for military advantage. After all, by their reasoning, the United States, having destroyed its own stockpile and unable to threaten credibly to escalate attacks to the strategic level, would have no answer to these Soviet missiles.

The Power of Belief in U.S.-Soviet Arms Control in the Reagan Administration

U.S.-Soviet strategic relations soured significantly in Reagan's first term, only to produce dramatic breakthroughs in Reagan's second term in office. The source and impact of these changes are appreciated when examining (1) prevailing U.S. beliefs about Soviet goals; (2) the U.S. intragovernmental politics that gave some of these beliefs prominence over others; and (3) overall U.S. assessments of relative nuclear capabilities.

Soviet Intent

In the Reagan years, arms control skeptics and proponents voiced now familiar arguments about Soviet intent. Through the end of the Cold War, the positions of many of these advocates remained remarkably unchanged by the forces that eventually brought down the Soviet Union.

In the early 1980s, hawks voiced a decidedly negative view of the Soviet Union. Its obstreperousness confirmed their suspicions that the Soviets were not serious about negotiating meaningful arms control or holding to their existing agreements. Kenneth Adelman, as ACDA director, spoke for many when he observed that Soviet treaty violations amounted to nothing less than a "brazen Soviet disregard for arms control commitments" (1984: 245). In this view, Soviet violations were especially worrisome because they were so flagrant: the Soviets had planned their violations in the period of "detente," "knew" that the United States would detect them, and obviously could care less. The violations were more worrisome still because the Soviets were pushing the envelope, seizing opportunities that were allowed by treaties, while the United States stood still. As Adelman surmised, "Since the strategic arms talks began in 1969, the Soviets have introduced four new classes of land-based missiles, upgraded them seven times, and launched at least five new or improved classes of ballistic missile submarines." The pace was actually quickening: "Since the first strategic arms accord was signed, the Soviets have added more than 6,000 nuclear warheads, just from the time of the second was signed (1979), they have added 3,850" (1984: 247).

Doves challenged these dire conclusions. They had strong misgivings about current U.S. policies that rested on overly pessimistic assumptions about Soviet intent. They acknowledged Soviet obstinance but were inclined to read Soviet actions as responses to harsh administration policies or reflections of a (perhaps slow) learning process that, despite potential setbacks, would eventually yield greater U.S.-Soviet trust. In their view, claims of Soviet perfidy had to be examined in light of the robust and ongoing U.S. nuclear-force improvements that had made U.S. forces more survivable, mobile, capable, and numerous.

Whereas dovish arms control proponents saw the INF Treaty as another opportunity for the United States and the Soviet Union to realize their common interests, most hawks provided a qualified endorsement of that view. They saw the INF Treaty as proof that U.S. determination and pressure could force the Soviets to the bargaining table and then to negotiate seriously. As Senator Alan J. Dixon of the Senate Armed Services Committee put it, "I believe many will agree that the Soviet Union began serious negotiation of an INF Treaty because they clearly realized their vulnerability to nuclear attack, with marginal warning time, from intermediate nuclear missiles based in Europe" (U.S. Senate 1988c: 21). Secretary of Defense Frank Carlucci—in observing that the "Soviet Union respects strength and scorns and exploits weakness"—echoed these conclusions: "Had INF opponents succeeded in blocking our deployments, we would be faced with a Soviet monopoly in INF missiles, rather than have before us a treaty eliminating them on both sides" (U.S. Senate 1988a: 2:6–7).

Many hawks were convinced, however, that the INF Treaty was a charade: in their view, Soviet concessions were never what they seemed and in practice would disappear. The Soviets, as always feigning compromise to lull the West into complacency, would soon press and extend their advantage to capitalize on U.S. vulnerabilities under the agreement. After all, in the view of most hawkish critics, the Soviets had pursued a massive unprovoked nuclear buildup in Europe and then sought to maintain a sizable advantage in nuclear delivery systems.[45] Eugene Rostow warned, then, that the INF Treaty might well amount to a Soviet Trojan horse, and Henry Kissinger cautioned that no Soviet leader was positioned to reverse longstanding Russian policies or to establish full control of the Soviet government. Indeed, Gorbachev would not have risen to prominence from within the Soviet bureaucracy if he had been inclined to challenge its views and interests (U.S. Senate 1988a: 3:385, 4:185). The danger of being played by the Soviet leadership was that the United States would confront the Soviet Union from a much weaker position once antinuclear sentiment took hold in the West and NATO had disarmed. Even leading administration officials warned against optimism in the post–INF Treaty environment. Carlucci cautioned that the Soviets might use the treaty "to convince Western European nations to distance themselves from the United States and to neglect their military preparations" (U.S. Senate 1988a: 2:6).

Yet the administration that had once championed such hawkish rhetoric did change its tune, decidedly and unmistakably. With the INF Treaty, administration officials implied that, given converging U.S. and Soviet interests, the Soviets would likely abide by the terms of an agreement. Chairman of the Joint Chiefs of Staff Admiral William J. Crowe argued, for example, that Soviet cheating on the INF Treaty was extremely risky for the Soviet Union because "our discovery of cheating would run counter to everything General Secretary Gorbachev is trying to do in his public diplomacy, e.g., improve the Soviet image; revitalize the Soviet economy in cooperation with the West; and achieve more openness and candor in Soviet society" (U.S. Senate 1988b: 43). A chorus of such pronouncements—that the Soviets would have little to gain and everything to lose from violating the INF Treaty—spoke volumes to a fundamental shift in assumptions. In consequence, Reagan officials downplayed Soviet behavior that was previously heralded as signaling malign Soviet intent.[46] For Secretary of State George Shultz, the "pattern of Soviet behavior is not one of wholesale violation of arms control treaties" but rather one of "selective and specific" violations that necessitate a like U.S. response (U.S. Senate 1988a: 1:27). Accordingly, the administration relaxed its standard for judging the significance of Soviet treaty violations: it fell back on "effective" treaty verification despite insisting previously that an identical standard ("adequate" verification) let the Soviets off the hook.[47]

Significantly, officials expressed these beliefs despite the relative ease with which the Soviets could cheat on the treaty or work around its prohibitions. That the Soviets had relaxed their previously intractable positions on asymmetric force reductions and onsite inspections appears to have signaled to a broad U.S. audience that the Soviet Union was changing and that the United States could—at some level—trust it to comply with a negotiated treaty.

The Politics of Arms Control

The Reagan administration was hardly of one mind on arms control.[48] It recruited heavily from both the ranks of arms control critics and establishment figures, including former officials of administrations that these same critics had once assailed for being soft on the Soviets. Thus, its early forays into arms control were impaired by maneuvering, infighting, and backroom dealing. Internal agreements were typically fragile and short-lived: advocates shifted positions often to deflect new internal initiatives, revised Soviet stances, or pronouncements by the president or members of his inner advisory circle (Talbott 1985). Still, the administration broke from the Carter administration by adhering to a hard-line stance.

In the early 1980s, the sluggish pace of U.S.-Soviet negotiations and the Reagan administration's dismissive attitude toward arms control fueled vocal opposition. The administration was cognizant of rising public sentiment for a (bilateral) freeze—which had become a local, state, and national electoral issue—and feared losing the public relations battle to liberal arms control proponents. It was well aware that the lack of progress on arms control with the Soviet Union had given liberal congressional critics the ammunition to challenge the administration's stances and potentially deny research and development funding for the MX missile program. The consequences, within the Congress, of the rising tide of dissent included a push for the mobile, single-warhead Midgetman missile as an alternative to destabilizing multiple-warhead missiles like the MX; a "nuclear freeze," which involved legislation to curtail funding for the testing, production, or deployment of new nuclear weapons; and a "build-down" formula in arms control to induce a shift from destabilizing to stabilizing nuclear weapons. The proposed measures threatened to constrain the positions and prerogatives of an administration that was wedded to the MX missile, opposed to a freeze that would lock in U.S. inferiority, and suspicious of proposals that would allow the Soviets to retain their throw-weight advantage.

The pressure on the administration receded, in part, through its own political maneuvers. It embraced a build-down in principle (in mid-1983, the president pledged to structure it into a U.S. START proposal; see NAS 1985: 58); it advertised the "deep cuts" in force levels that were required under U.S. proposals; and it sought to frame force increases as potential reductions by suggesting that key U.S. weapon systems, like the MX, were bargaining chips for getting the Soviets to respond seriously to U.S. arms control proposals. In the end, the most stringent freeze proposals could not garner the necessary congressional support: even legislators who voted in favor of (watered-down) freeze resolutions voted to support the MX missile. After narrowly beating back a nonbinding resolution in the House that called for a comprehensive freeze, the administration pushed successfully for an alternative resolution calling for a freeze only after the United States and the Soviet Union had reduced their forces to equal levels. Months later, the House passed a freeze resolution that was severely weakened by amendments (NAS 1985: 84–85). To deflect disarmament pressures, the administration could count on backing from the military, which sought to preserve and improve the U.S. military position. For instance, the Joint Chiefs of Staff favored limiting launchers to enable the United States to cover targets with available multiple-warhead missiles, and the military expressed reservations about INF negotiating concessions that would sacrifice valued U.S. conventional weapons, including cruise missiles (Talbott 1985: 253–262, 66, 242).

The administration had to contend, again, with legislative pressure and resistance. In 1987, the Democrats retook control of the Senate, and Sam Nunn, the powerful leader of the Senate Armed Services Committee, challenged the administration's position on the ABM Treaty. As a supporter of strategic defense and of a cautious approach to arms control, Nunn's protests carried substantial weight. He felt strongly that the administration undercut the Senate's constitutional authority by rejecting the Senate's understanding of the treaty as the basis for assessing its meaning. Nunn warned Reagan pointedly that continuing to hold to a broad interpretation of the treaty would provoke "a constitutional crisis of profound dimensions."[49] Under Nunn's Committee leadership, the Senate demanded (and obtained) the treaty negotiating record that Reagan officials claimed supported their own judgments, prepared a legal analysis that challenged the administration's treaty interpretation, funded strategic defense at levels well below the administration's requests, and prohibited the administration (in fiscal year 1988) from conducting tests that breached the narrow interpretation of the treaty.[50] Eventually, the administration—facing dissent from within (foremost, from Secretary of State Shultz) and seeking to maintain program funding—backed off from its demands that Congress accept the administration's perspective on the treaty.[51]

The Reagan administration's positions were bolstered nevertheless by indirect support from the intelligence community, which retained suspicions about Soviet motives, strategies, and plans. This was clear from its inflated estimates of Soviet strategic deployments. For instance, the 1983 National Intelligence Estimate predicted that the Soviets would deploy 120 SS-24 ICBMs in silos by 1988 and a rail-mobile version by 1989, whereas the Soviets had deployed none of these missiles in silos and nine on trains by 1988. In the interim, adjustments to these estimates were incremental (U.S. DI 1989: 29). By the 1980s, the prevailing view in the NIEs remained that the Soviets were striving for "global political and military domination" and perceived the United States "as the principal strategic threat, the greatest obstacle to their political-military activities and the achievement of their goals" (DCI 1981: 1). Given this consensus judgment, the only question was, did the Soviets believe that dominance was obtainable in the foreseeable future?

General assumptions of this sort were protected from scrutiny by supportive beliefs that were not held to an evidentiary standard. Beliefs related to Soviet tradeoff decisions enjoyed this "privileged" status. NIEs asserted that, in these decisions, security considerations trumped civilian concerns and Soviet strategic forces trumped all else, reflecting the centrality of these forces to Soviet global military and political strategy, their relatively small claim on Soviet resources, and their dependence on a military infrastructure that had little relevance to the civilian economy. NIEs increasingly recognized the moribund state of the Soviet economy but not its limiting effects on Soviet strategic capability (U.S. DI 1982: 36). Even into the late 1980s, the state of the Soviet economy was recognized as constraining only the most ambitious efforts to expand Soviet strategic forces, as NIEs continued to predict growth and refinement in Soviet nuclear war-fighting capabilities (DCI 1988: 5). Perversely, then, the U.S. intelligence community offered predictions in the 1980s without due regard for great concerns within the Soviet Union about its capabilities and competitiveness and for changes in Soviet thinking: Soviet political and military leaders now discounted the contribution of nuclear weapons to the force balance, accepted deterrence principles, and acknowledged (under Gorbachev) that Soviet military capability contributed to U.S.-Soviet antagonism and drained the Soviet economy (Wohlforth 1993: 229, 239, 253–272). Not until the last gasps of the Cold War did analyses incorporate Soviet economic troubles into force projections in the form of slower modernization rates (U.S. DI 1989: 31). Only then did these analyses acknowledge that Soviet leaders believed that their past military efforts had been costly and ineffective, their goals had been too ambitious, and the Soviet economy could no longer sustain existing force levels (e.g. U.S. DI 1988: vi–viii; DCI 1989).[52]

Still, the Reagan administration managed to move forward on arms control. Although it adhered to controversial positions (most obviously on missile defense) that continued to complicate U.S.-Soviet (and U.S. executive-legislative) relations, it came to embrace more traditional thinking about arms control. For example, it accepted the principle of offsetting asymmetries—that the U.S. edge in bombers and cruise missiles counterbalanced Soviet advantages in land-based missiles (Talbott 1985: 338–339). With changes in the Soviet leadership and a personnel shift on the U.S. side, with visible administration hard-liners, such as Richard Perle, Kenneth Adelman, and Eugene Rostow, no longer in the administration, a reconciliation of U.S. and Soviet views proved possible. Yet the administration's success provokes an interesting question: would the Senate have given its advice and consent to the INF Treaty had it been negotiated under a more liberal-leaning (Democratic) administration? The answer—as always with the counterfactual—is unknowable with certainty. Weighing toward an affirmative response is the dramatic shift in the Soviet negotiating stance and transformation of the Soviet state. These changes provoked a widespread reassessment of Soviet goals within the U.S. policy establishment. Also weighing in that direction is the Democratic takeover of the Senate. The opposition hindered the administration's plans for the MX missile and missile defense and pressured the administration to show flexibility in arms control (Nolan 1991: 368, 376). But weighing toward a negative response is the faith that was required, in accepting the treaty, that the Soviets would actually observe its terms. The question, then, is, Would hawks have believed that Soviet violations were checked by the INF Treaty had it been negotiated by a Democratic administration?

The fact is that critics were hard pressed to challenge a treaty that was negotiated under Reagan given his hawkish credentials and reputation for sticking to his guns. Republican opposition was encumbered further by Reagan's political popularity and staunch backing for the treaty (Nolan 1991: 372). Yet high-profile treaty "supporters" still offered only a qualified endorsement of the treaty. For instance, Perle voiced concern about "specific provisions" that "deserve close consideration, either because they are ambiguous, because they invite differing interpretations, because they create loopholes whose exploitation by the Soviets would alter substantially the military consequences of the treaty, or because they have important implications for future negotiations or the evolution of our military forces" (U.S. Senate 1988a: 3:3–4).[53] Some who had served in the administration came out flatly against the treaty, and high-profile moderates (such as Brent Scowcroft) and almost all of the candidates vying for the 1988 Republican presidential nomination expressed reservations about, or opposition to, the treaty (Nolan 1991: 368–369).[54] Thus, a less stringent agreement or a less credentialed administration might well have faced a more hostile Senate reception.

Assessing, Safeguarding, and Improving U.S. Relative Capabilities

The Reagan administration arrived in office seeking to erase the mistakes of the past. In its view, the U.S. strategic position had seriously eroded through longstanding neglect, misguided priorities, and unreciprocated U.S. concessions. The administration proposed to correct the nuclear imbalance specifically by engaging the Soviets in hard bargaining and scaling and configuring U.S. strategic forces to serve war-fighting principles. It offered an initial START proposal that was a bold departure from the U.S. positions in the SALT II negotiations, and it continued to modernize the nuclear triad by pushing ahead with the

B-2 stealth bomber, multiple-warhead MX missile, single-warhead Midgetman (mobile) missile, and Trident II SLBM programs. But the early administration efforts were ultimately unsuccessful. The bold proposals failed to win Soviet support, and subsequent proposals would arguably have done little, by war-fighting standards, to improve U.S. outcomes in war. Under the proposed terms, the Soviets would retain a large multiple-warhead, land-based missile force that could hypothetically destroy its U.S. counterpart in a first-strike attack. Although the administration improved its absolute counterforce capabilities through ongoing procurement, it did not reduce overall U.S. vulnerability to a Soviet counterforce attack. Indeed, the hard-line policies of the administration could have undercut its counterforce strategy by hurting the prospects for arms control. Given the superior Soviet competitive position, the administration only increased the Soviet incentive to build up Soviet forces, as a counter to potential U.S. force improvements, by accusing the Soviets of multiple treaty violations, circumventing the ABM Treaty by moving forward on a U.S. missile defense, and engaging in hostile rhetoric. (The latter included Reagan's labeling of the Soviet Union as an "evil empire" and holding the Soviet government responsible for the downing by a Soviet military interceptor of a Korean commercial airliner that had strayed accidentally into Soviet territory.)

Of course, the contemporary take on this period is that the renewed U.S.-Soviet competition was a product of design: Reagan's plan was to bankrupt the Soviet Union by engaging it in an arms race that only the United States could win. That Reagan "won" the Cold War soon became a mantra of administration supporters who saw, in the Soviet collapse, redemption for Reagan's tough stances, policies, and actions.[55] The reality is, however, that few analysts foresaw, in the early 1980s, that the Soviet Union would soon implode from its internal tensions or believed that the Soviet political apparatus could provide the leadership that would instigate, oversee, and navigate these cataclysmic changes. Although U.S. officials in the Reagan administration were cognizant of changing Soviet behavior, they did not accept increased Soviet cooperativeness on its face: indeed, Reagan administration officials spoke disparagingly of cooperative Soviet signals as a feint—a thinly veiled Soviet "peace offensive" that was meant to obtain unilateral Western concessions. The fear was that the Soviets would achieve in "kindness" what they could not accomplish with bluster and force. Soviet President Gorbachev was thus viewed with suspicion by U.S. arms control hawks because of his apparent flexibility in dealings with the West. Eugene Rostow, who had left the administration, warned that Gorbachev knew that the

Soviet Union was "now on the verge of achieving overwhelming strength" and "was determined to utilize this military superiority" (Rostow 1987: 26).

To be sure, a reading of administration statements and testimony suggests that U.S. policymakers recognized that the United States was blessed with abundant economic assets and could outspend the Soviet Union. Some U.S. officials even believed that the maldistribution of Soviet resources, as induced by an arms competition, would force the Soviets to change under internal duress. Yet all such readings must take note of the nonspecificity and atypicality of these views: in general, hawks were not predicting the Soviet Union's imminent collapse. To the contrary, administration officials asserted with great frequency that the Soviet military enjoyed first claim on national resources, that this testified to the political strength of the Soviet establishment, and that the threat from the Soviet Union was enhanced, not reduced, by the burden of military spending on the Soviet economy. Indeed, U.S. nuclear procurement plans assumed that the United States had to acquire the capability to engage in a protracted nuclear war to restrain—and perhaps to combat—a Soviet leadership that was wedded to its belligerent strategy and goals and was incapable of meaningful change (Kirkpatrick 1982). When, in the late 1970s, the great bureaucratic battles were fought over the reputed underestimating by the CIA of Soviet military spending, hawks argued that such spending reflected intractable Soviet positions and hostility toward the West: they did not greet such spending joyously in the knowledge that the Soviets were sowing the seeds of their own destruction. Ironically, the doves who argued that high Soviet military spending spoke to Soviet economic inefficiencies—as some did—appeared to appreciate best the fragile underpinnings of the Soviet system.

The fact of the matter is that Reagan's policies were hardly optimized to transform the Soviet Union. If U.S. policymakers had believed that conditions were ripe for the Soviet Union to change, they would have adopted more appropriate policies. The deficiencies of U.S. policy are clear, for example, in the U.S. missile defense plan, which is often viewed as the leading edge of the administration's "spend-them-till-they-drop" strategy because it played to U.S. technological and economic advantages. But the program was not conceived to force the Soviets to increase their defense expenditures: the program was largely confined to research and development, where the budgetary costs for the United States and the Soviet Union were relatively small. Then, the program arguably worked to the U.S. disadvantage should the Soviets counter an expensive U.S. missile-defense system cheaply by building more missiles. Thus, the internal administration debate pitted hard-line advocates like Caspar Weinberger and Richard Perle—who saw Reagan's SDI, apart from its technological promise, as useful for sabotaging U.S.-Soviet arms negotiations—and moderates like Robert McFarlane, the deputy National Security Advisor—who viewed U.S. defenses as a potential bargaining chip for achieving Soviet offensive reductions (Earle 1989: 32). The political "transformers" who viewed a U.S. defense as valuable for pushing the Soviets to their spending limits—they were not represented in the debate. Regardless, if they had been present, they would likely have argued for a different set of policies. Assuming that the Soviet Union was ripe for change, they would have advised the administration to tread softly: hostile U.S. rhetoric and a renewed U.S. military buildup could strengthen the position of Soviet hard-liners, who could point to a U.S. threat to justify staying the course.

This is not to minimize the extent and importance of the shift in the administration's attitude and approach toward the Soviet Union in Reagan's second term, with the signing of the U.S.-Soviet Intermediate-Range Nuclear Forces Treaty and significant progress toward a START treaty. Under new leadership, the Soviet Union accepted (1) asymmetrical reductions (through the zero-zero formula) that would exact more significant cuts in Soviet than U.S. forces; and (2) intrusive inspections on the sovereign territory of the Soviet Union to verify its treaty compliance.[56] These revised Soviet positions swayed the administration by signaling a profound shift in Soviet goals. There is no other plausible explanation for the administration's willingness to accept the resulting treaty.

The threat that war-fighters believed that the Soviets presented to Europe—which had necessitated placing U.S. missiles there—had not abated with the departure of Soviet SS-20 missiles. Indeed, by the political logic of coupling, the INF Treaty weakened the U.S. deterrence position by removing the link between U.S. forces and Europe's defense; by the military logic of war-fighting, the treaty arguably gave the Soviets an incentive to warehouse missiles secretly or to build up Soviet strategic forces to cover European targets and to gain a significant advantage over a U.S. force that was upwardly constrained by U.S. domestic politics. As one analyst observed, "None of the issues that the original dual-track decision in 1979 had set out to solve were in fact resolved, and the role of nuclear weapons in Europe, though now vastly diminished, remained open to controversy" (Nolan 1991: 388). Treaty proponents and critics were correct to point out that the Soviets had abundant avenues to cheat on the agreement or violate its "spirit" by pursuing strategic weapons to fill the gap that was left by the exodus of intermediate-range missiles. Certainly the Soviets could have found a way to "repackage" these strategic missiles so that they would substitute for the SS-20s, in order to send the signals that would supposedly drive a wedge in the NATO alliance. Their qualitative imperfectness for the task could have been overcome easily by producing these weapons in quantity. Overall, the (legal and illegal) opportunities for circumventing the INF Treaty exceeded those under prior agreements and would have sorely tempted the Soviets to cheat if one accepts the logic behind the missile deployments. The Soviets would come into possession of invaluable political weapons, for which the United States had no immediate answer.

That this logic did not sway U.S. officials suggests that they believed that the Soviets intended to abide by the treaty given the formal Soviet acceptance of the terms. Even administration officials, who had set the bar at a level that they believed the Soviets would not cross, had calculated that doing so would require a significant change in Soviet goals. Admittedly, the administration was hemmed in by its own commitment to the zero formula. A belated U.S. rejection of the treaty would not have gone over well with the European public or with a U.S. Congress that doubted the administration's commitment to arms control. But the administration did not sign the INF Treaty reluctantly having made a proposal that it hoped would fail. With its prior hard-line stances, the administration clearly established that it could oppose treaties that it believed hurt U.S. interests.

Still, the administration's successful negotiation of an INF Treaty bears essential similarities with the administration's less successful record in strategic nuclear arms control. In the INF negotiations, administration officials never reconciled numerical proposals with ostensible U.S. policy goals. This would have required, for instance, that they consider the tradeoff between the military and political goals that nuclear weapons supposedly serve. In strategic arms control, the administration placed itself in a similarly untenable position. Although Reagan insisted throughout the 1980 presidential campaign that the SALT II Treaty was "fatally flawed" and his administration later hammered that point home by challenging the Soviet willingness to accept or respect a fair agreement that would reverse a Soviet throw-weight advantage that threatened the U.S. retaliatory force,[57] the administration generally adhered to the terms of the SALT II Treaty and the strategic modernization plans of prior administrations.[58] The administration was no more attentive to these goals when seeking major changes in the Soviet force structure. Ostensibly, correcting various "imbalances" would improve the U.S. counterforce position. Yet the U.S.-proposed terms would not meaningfully reduce the vulnerability of U.S. land-based missiles to a Soviet first-strike attack nor the residual U.S. throw-weight disadvantage after a nuclear exchange. Moreover, the U.S. START proposals would improve U.S. wartime performance only in a stylized conflict in which the participants played by the same rules, stuck to them, and accepted an outcome that, as in a boxing match, was decided on "points." As Reagan officials saw it, the combatants would seek to neutralize each other's land-based missile capabilities; then, when the land-based missiles of one side were exhausted, the parties would calculate residual throw-weight to determine the winner. The "loser"—capable still of destroying the "winner"—would have to accept the outcome "by decision." Was that, however, its only recourse? Following AD logic, could it not threaten, instead, to destroy the "winner"? What options would the latter have to respond, other than either reciprocating the threat or acting upon it and then suffering the consequences?

So what does all of this say about the validity of realist thinking about the security dilemma, as manifest in the propositions "peace through strength" and "trust but verify"? The evidence impugns key realist assumptions.

The administration tended to evaluate U.S. strength by generally ignoring conditions of use. Indifference to these conditions was apparent when the administration (1) promoted arms control positions without dutifully considering their strategic impact or fit with U.S. declaratory nuclear doctrine; and (2) embraced principles of U.S.-Soviet force equality—at "zero-zero," in the case of intermediate-range nuclear forces—with little sense of how correcting an "imbalance" would affect deterrence or change the course of a nuclear conflict. The viability of the administration's arms control positions—both early and late—hinged, as a result, on underdeveloped assumptions about Soviet goals that would determine whether, when, and how nuclear weapons would be used.

By the same token, the administration exhibited growing trust of the Soviet Union. The administration's positions drew initially from decidedly hawkish assumptions about Soviet intent and then, with a profound shift in Soviet INF negotiating terms, from a relaxing of those assumptions. Had the administration not relaxed its view, it might well have worried about (and opposition to the treaty might have galvanized around) the loss of U.S. missiles in the European theater and the openings in the treaty to Soviet cheating. After all, some hawks continued to believe that Soviet proximity to Europe and substantial Soviet conventional and nuclear holdings threatened the U.S. capability to extend deterrence to NATO allies and that the Soviets would yield to temptation and manufacture or store intermediate-range missiles (or retarget strategic missiles) to boost the Soviet military and political position in Europe. Still, the administration does not appear to have considered fundamental tradeoffs between trust and verification by acknowledging that changing Soviet goals had reduced the need to worry about Soviet treaty violations. To the contrary, it adopted intrusive mechanisms to monitor treaty compliance when they were least needed, even as the Soviet willingness to accept these measures rendered them somewhat superfluous.

Nuclear Arms Reductions after the Cold War

The George H. W. Bush through Obama Years

The end of the Cold War was swift and unexpected. When President Gorbachev became general secretary of the Communist Party of the Soviet Union in 1985, no one within the U.S. policy community was predicting the momentous change that was in the offing—that, in the very near future, the Soviet Union would allow the nations of Eastern Europe to plot their own course (into NATO, no less), the Soviet leadership would surrender its power, the Soviet empire would fragment into a myriad of independent republics (all but one denuclearized), or the United States would emerge as the world's sole superpower. U.S. policymakers were understandably slow to respond to events given their uncertain trajectory. Less understandably, the arms control momentum slowed significantly after the initial flurry of cooperative U.S. and Russian military gestures and dramatic measures and cuts that were intended for nuclear stability. Indeed, the nuclear debate of the post–Cold War period was much like its Cold War–era counterparts. The strategic debate pitted those who wanted to avoid arms control concessions against those who believed that the United States would benefit from force reductions. Missing, again, from the policy debate was a clear articulation of how a given number of strategic nuclear weapons might serve, or not serve, U.S. security interests.

The George H. W. Bush Administration

The George H. W. Bush administration is credited with a major arms control achievement in the form of the START I Treaty. The significance and contribution of the treaty are apparent when examining (1) the strategic conditions under which the treaty was negotiated; and (2) the terms of the treaty and the intragovernmental conflict that it engendered.

Backdrop: International Context and U.S. Doctrine

The beginning and end of the Bush administration almost exactly frame the series of momentous events that marked the end of the Cold War. Bush arrived in office in January 1989, the month after the Soviet leadership had abandoned the Brezhnev Doctrine and announced that the countries of Eastern Europe could decide their own course; he left office in January 1993, roughly a year after the collapse of the Soviet Union and its replacement by four separate nuclear-armed republics. The pace of events was fast and furious—almost certainly too fast for U.S. policymakers to absorb the full impact of the change or predict its course. Thus, administration officials were initially reluctant to concede that the Soviets had reevaluated their priorities. Eventually, they did acknowledge a tectonic shift in the U.S. threat environment: the Soviet Union, as the United States had known it, was gone.

The imperative, then, was to keep the reforms going. Administration officials remained concerned about recidivism in Russia, given its economic challenges, authoritarian history, conservative military, and tumult that could abet the rise of forces hostile to U.S. interests. U.S. policymakers hoped, then, to keep Russia on its new course with a series of unilateral gestures. In September 1991, the Bush administration announced, for example, that it would bring home and destroy various battlefield and theater nuclear weapons; remove tactical nuclear weapons from submarines, surface ships, and naval aircraft; take U.S. (B-52) strategic nuclear aircraft off alert;[1] and cancel the Peacekeeper (MX) rail garrison and mobile portion of the Midgetman programs. The following month, President Gorbachev announced similar measures, among them eliminating battlefield nuclear munitions, removing tactical nuclear weapons from submarines and surface ships, de-alerting heavy bombers, and decommissioning three ballistic-missile submarines. The cooperative reciprocation continued after the failed 1991 coup attempt by Russian hard-liners and Boris Yeltsin's subsequent emergence as Russian president. Bush announced the cancellation of the Midgetman program and the capping of U.S. B-2 bomber production (at 20); Yeltsin announced the terminating of bomber and cruise-missile programs. The U.S. unilateral gestures were paired with proposals for far-reaching, negotiated cuts in strategic nuclear weapons (Secretary of Defense Richard Cheney in U.S. Senate 1992b: 100–103) and efforts to reduce the threat from Russia of unauthorized weapons use and proliferation. In 1992, the United States initiated the Cooperative Threat Reduction Program (known commonly as the Nunn-Lugar initiative) to assist the securing and dismantling of the Soviet infrastructure for nuclear, chemical, and biological weapons.[2]

Suddenly, U.S. policymakers had to determine the nuclear requisites of defending the United States with it now lacking peer competitors. As long as the Cold War survived, U.S. policymakers could structure and scale the U.S. arsenal to the presumed demands of the central conflict. But U.S. civilian and military policymakers, to this point, had not asked whether the United States must retain its basic force structure or an essential level of nuclear capability if Russia ever sought to cut its arsenal dramatically. Ironically, the U.S. military now resisted even favorable asymmetric reductions, insisting that it had to retain the capability to perform critical functions even absent a clear threat (that is, it was a "capability-based," not "threat-based" military). In this view, the United States no longer had the "luxury" of addressing a single threat—it had to look in multiple directions and prepare accordingly. Uncertainty about the threat was believed by some to be reason to expect—and prepare—for the worst. To quote JCS Chairman Colin Powell, "We have not called the threat right yet. Nobody told me 2 years ago that you better be ready for war with Iraq. . . . Nobody was able to anticipate what would happen in Korea, during World War II, or lots of other times and places" (U.S. Senate 1992a: 54). The military raised the bar further by arguing that the United States required sufficient capability to forestall the emergence of threats. The classified U.S. Defense Guidance called initially for a "new world order" supported by U.S. capability sufficient to deter "potential competitors from even aspiring to a larger regional or global role."[3] Although the Defense Department removed these controversial statements from the final document, it still called for a robust capability, which, among its functions, could preclude "any hostile power from dominating a region critical to our interests, and also thereby to strengthen the barriers against the reemergence of a global threat to the interests of the U.S. and our allies."[4]

The general threat level was heightened by the danger that was posed by particular countries as expressed in frequent reference to "regional threats." The U.S. military services insisted that regional threats provided strong reasons to preserve Cold War–era budgets and weapon systems—as demonstrated, for instance, by their decisive role in the 1991 Desert Storm operation that pushed Saddam Hussein's forces from Kuwait. The necessity of staying the course—and retaining essential nuclear capabilities—was driven home by revelations of Iraq's prewar progress toward acquiring the bomb and by North Korea's emerging nuclear reprocessing capabilities, which promised a plutonium-based device in the near future. In the last half of the Bush administration, Secretary of

Defense Richard Cheney tasked the military with developing plans for using nuclear weapons against possible proliferators, and U.S. nuclear war plans included options for targeting countries that acquired or might acquire weapons of mass destruction (Kristensen 1997: 23–24; Paul 2009: 85). Perversely, U.S. policy officials, who had once trumpeted the Soviet threat, now spoke wistfully of the Soviet Union as a model competitor that actually played by the rules. They were unwilling to let U.S. security hinge on whether Saddam Hussein—or his kind—would act as responsibly.

With concerns about the growth in the Chinese arsenal and the proliferation of nuclear weapons to new states, the administration went on the offense and on the defense. On defense, the administration saw an eventual need to amend the ABM Treaty to accommodate the pending deployment of the Global Protection Against Limited Strikes (GPALS) system, which had evolved from Reagan's Strategic Defense Initiative. Albeit less ambitious than Reagan's vision, the system was still meant to protect against up to "about 200 reentry vehicles from whatever source" to address the emerging threat of the global proliferation of ballistic missiles (Henry F. Cooper in U.S. Senate 1991a: 9). Specifically, it was intended to integrate tactical, theater, and strategic missile defenses for complete and continuous protection of U.S. allies and forces overseas and the United States from "accidental, unauthorized, and limited ballistic missile strikes" (U.S. Senate 1991a: 5). As conceived, it required, in clear violation of the ABM Treaty, the deployment of multiple ground-based sites and space-based sensors and interceptors. As it was, the United States continued to offer creative interpretations to keep the United States ostensibly in compliance with the treaty.[5] On offense, the administration sought to reorient U.S. strategic nuclear forces to confront emerging threats. Whereas U.S. officials in the Carter administration had once tried to build support for the Nuclear Nonproliferation Treaty (NPT) by pledging that the United States would not use nuclear weapons against a non-nuclear state (that was acting independently of a nuclear power), Bush administration officials were not about to renounce U.S. options. In their view, the United States lacked equivalent means to respond should U.S. adversaries employ biological or chemical weapons on civilian populations or U.S. conventional forces. Much was made, in fact, of the reputed effectiveness of a thinly veiled threat to Saddam Hussein before Desert Storm that the United States would employ nuclear weapons in response to Iraq's use of chemical weapons.

Early in the George H. W. Bush presidency, Secretary of Defense Cheney initiated a review of U.S. targeting, which, in turn, generated a study and briefings that apparently "appalled" Cheney and Powell. They were purportedly struck by the inefficiencies, excesses, and incongruities that were built into the plans, for instance that "nearly forty weapons were designated just to hit Kiev" (Nolan 1999: 29–30). The Cheney initiative would eventually result in the dropping from the SIOP of thousands of targets, located largely in (non-Russian) former Soviet republics (Nolan 1999: 31). But the military took these levels—still driven by the Russian threat—as approximating the floor coverage that was necessary to ensure U.S. security. The U.S. military continued to plan its nuclear offensive against Russia based on the matching of weapons against the same basic target set. Indeed, it would support the START I Treaty not because the Russian political transition had reduced the demands on U.S. forces and the risks of disarmament but because the treaty and the shrinking adversary land mass had reduced the number of nuclear targets. Military planners had concluded, then, that they could cover the military target set now with a smaller number of weapons. To quote JCS Chairman Colin Powell,

> When we compared the level of damage against the smaller target base that results from the START reductions, we determined that our modern, more capable weapons systems will allow us to maintain approximately the same levels of damage and target coverage that we can achieve today. When we examined the mix of weapons in the case when all of our forces are generated to full alert, we determined that even though the aggregate numbers of weapons decline, the percentage of survivable warheads increases because of the higher ratio of submarine and aircraft warheads compared to ICBM warheads. Of the land-based and sea-based missiles on a day-to-day alert, the percentage of survivable warheads will also increase in the post-START force. . . . Our analyses of the reduced target base, of target coverage, damage expectancy, survivable warheads, reserve weapons, and the status of day-to-day and generated forces, all suggest that our national security is enhanced and deterrence improved as a result of the START treaty. (U.S. Senate 1992b: 2:120–121)

Such analysis would impede future negotiations for arms reductions.

The START I Treaty

The length, facets, detail, and complexity of the START I Treaty—or Treaty Between the United States of America and the Union of Soviet Socialist Republics on the Reduction and Limitation of Strategic Offensive Arms—testify to its long and arduous negotiating history. As signed in July 1991 in Moscow, it includes a text with nineteen Articles, two Annexes, six Protocols, and a Memorandum of Understanding. It would later include the Lisbon Protocol—between the United States and Russia, Ukraine, Kazakhstan, and Belarus (the four nuclear-armed successor states that emerged from the Soviet Union)—and it was offered to the U.S. Senate for its advice and consent with a host of executive agreements, declarations, and statements that were not an "integral part" of the treaty (U.S. Senate 1992c: 3–7). Nine years in the making, the treaty's negotiating process spanned two U.S. presidencies, four Soviet presidencies, and—of course—the transition from the Cold War era to the post–Cold War era.

Signed as the Soviet Union was crumbling, the agreement was actually overtaken by events. With the official demise of the Soviet Union in December 1991 (the month after the treaty was sent to the Senate), Senate consideration had to await the negotiating and signing (in May 1992) of the Lisbon Protocol. With the Protocol, what had been a bilateral treaty effectively became a multilateral treaty, as the new states assumed Soviet obligations under the treaty and agreed to maintain former Soviet nuclear weapons under the "control of a single unified authority," while Ukraine, Kazakhstan, and Belarus pledged, as non-nuclear states, to become parties to the Nuclear Nonproliferation Treaty.[6] (Russia predicated its own ratification of the treaty on its ratification by Ukraine, Kazakhstan, and Belarus.) The result was a delay in U.S. Senate consideration and Russian ratification of the START I Treaty and the submission of the START II Treaty to the U.S. Senate for consideration. The delay in START II ratification was necessary because it required collective adherence to the START I Treaty (to ensure the denuclearization of the three former Soviet republics) and because the treaties were to run concurrently, with the verification provisions passing from START I to START II. The pending START II Treaty—and its promise of deep and meaningful cuts—provided a strong inducement for Senate ratification of the START I Treaty. At the same time, the still-unspecified START II terms provoked some U.S. senators to doubt the wisdom of prior ratification of the START I Treaty.

Certainly, the treaty represented a dramatic break with the past: it imposed extensive and intrusive verification procedures and deep cuts (by roughly two-fifths) in U.S. and Russian forces that reduced the alleged disparities between them. Few doubted that START I was anything less than a remarkable achievement. Even Cold War–era hawks agreed: by their narrative, the treaty was clear evidence that Reagan "got it right." Negotiated largely during his presidency, the treaty was unquestionably a symbolic and practical arms control victory (or "win") for the United States: Reagan had held his ground on key positions and the Soviet Union ultimately relented. The United States had insisted that the Soviets must concede their advantages in MIRVed, land-based missiles—especially in heavy ICBMs—and close various openings for cheating. The Soviets acquiesced to both

U.S. positions and generally compromised far less grudgingly in these negotiations than in the past. The START I Treaty is constructed, then, around the longstanding U.S. desire to reduce first-strike incentives by curtailing dependence on land-based multiple-warhead missiles and to strengthen verification measures to ensure Soviet treaty compliance. Consequently, the treaty imposed a low warhead ceiling on land-based missiles and restrictions on Soviet "heavies," and it devoted many hundreds of pages to elaborating verification procedures, requirements, and obligations.

The essentials of the START I Treaty are detailed in its 19 Articles. Of these, a number are especially noteworthy.[7]

Whereas Article I obligates the parties to adhere to arms limitations and reductions as specified in the treaty, Article II establishes limits (and sub-limits) on delivery vehicles (missiles and bombers) and "attributed" warheads.[8] These limits were to be reached over a seven-year period (with three- and five-year intermediate ceilings). Under the treaty, the parties were restricted to 1,600 deployed delivery vehicles and 6,000 accountable warheads: of the latter, only 4,900 were permitted on ballistic missiles, with a limit of 1,100 on deployed mobile (ballistic) missiles and 1,540 on a maximum of 154 Soviet heavy (SS-18) missiles, a number that would be reached by reducing the SS-18 force at a rate of 22 per year over the seven-year period. Despite Soviet efforts to pinch the United States by constraining SLBM warheads and bombers, the United States successfully shifted the focus of sub-limits to land-based missiles, the heavies in particular, on which the Soviets relied: the treaty does not contain explicit sub-limits on the numbers of bombers (Woolf 1992: 265). Although the treaty does not prevent the development, testing, or deployment of "new types" of missiles, it calls for a throw-weight restriction (at 54 percent of the current aggregate Soviet throw-weight).

Article III articulates the rules for deployed warhead counting. By attributing warheads to a type of launcher, the treaty moved beyond the Cold War–era practice (under SALT II) of simply crediting the number of warheads tested on a type of missile to all missiles of that type. Instead, warhead numbers are set for specific types of existing missiles.[9] As a compromise for new types of missiles, warhead counts are set to the numbers that were flight-tested, if they equal or exceed the number derived through a mathematical formula (based on warhead weight and missile throw-weight).

The treaty allows the parties to reduce their attributed warhead numbers through downloading—decreasing the number of warheads per missile—to a maximum of 1,250 warheads (divided among three types of weapons) so as to increase strategic stability by distributing warheads over a larger number of weapon systems (to decrease their vulnerability to an attack).[10] Ironically, the United States had to deflect a Soviet push for a generous downloading allowance, after the Soviets had initially resisted the idea of downloading altogether. The United States feared that the Soviets would break out from the treaty by storing warheads for later uploading, that is, increasing the number of warheads per missile. To address such fears, the treaty limits the number of warheads that can be downloaded (per the U.S. proposal), although it allows 4 warheads to be downloaded per missile (per the Soviet proposal). To guard further against uploading, it requires the replacement (and elimination) of the old warhead platform (when more than 2 warheads are downloaded from a missile) with a platform designed for the smaller number of warheads.[11]

Bombers, however, receive favorable treatment. The first 150 U.S. heavy bombers are each credited as carrying 10 warheads when carrying a maximum of 20 cruise missiles; the first 180 Soviet heavy bombers are credited as carrying 8 warheads when carrying a maximum of 16 missiles.[12] To penalize bomber deployments beyond these numbers, additional bombers are credited with their actual number of missiles (though bombers, armed solely with short-range weapons, count as having a single warhead).

Articles IV–VII cover various allowances and prohibitions. They include a ceiling of 250 on the numbers of non-deployed mobile missiles (and 110 launchers) to prevent a rapid breakout from the treaty; weapon locating and conversion restrictions; exclusions for training, test, or conventional systems; and an elimination requirement—for mobile-missile launchers, SLBM launchers, heavy bombers, and so forth—to conform to the treaty's numerical limits.

These articles impose additional constraints related to the production, deployment, and testing of new weapon types, the deployment and operation of mobile missiles, and so on. But the primary novelty of the treaty is found in Articles VIII through XII, Article XV, and the various Protocols that focus on verification and compliance. They require nine types of onsite inspections (plus exhibitions), data exchanges among the parties, noninterference with national technical means, assorted cooperative measures, a ban on all encryption of missile telemetry, and the establishment of a Joint Compliance and Inspection Commission to address issues of compliance and treaty implementation. The specifics regarding definitions of terms, procedures for conversion and elimination, onsite inspections, calculation of throw-weight, and so forth are contained in the various additional documents that are integral to the treaty.

The treaty was to remain in force for fifteen years (a period that could be extended by agreement) unless the treaty was superseded by another treaty or a party withdrew from the treaty. That remained an option, providing that a party gave six months' notice that "extraordinary" events "jeopardize" its "supreme interests."

EVALUATING STRENGTH

The START I Treaty was generally greeted with praise and anticipation. Indeed, it received Senate approval, in 1992, with a vote of 93 to 6. The treaty had certainly gone a long way toward deflecting the routine claim that U.S. negotiators had settled for terms that "the Soviets would accept." At the very least, it was viewed as an important "work in progress"—in fact, a necessary down payment to further arms control and safeguard the critical changes in Russia. It did provoke some worries and criticism.

First, some worried about the uncertain course of events. Wary analysts and legislators wondered if U.S. officials had duly considered the pitfalls of dramatically reducing U.S. strategic force levels in a period of instability and uncertainty about the future of Russia and arms control. Events continued to overtake the treaty: its fate within the U.S. Senate was complicated by the ongoing negotiation of the START II Treaty and by the travails of START I ratification in the former Soviet republics. The republics had yet to agree on sharing the costs or the procedures for implementing the treaty. But treaty proponents argued that it was imperative that the treaty move forward sooner rather than later—that the United States could not simply wait for a better (START II) treaty. The START I Treaty was essential for (1) gaining the adherence of Ukraine, Kazakhstan, and Belarus to the Nuclear Nonproliferation Treaty; (2) binding the governments of these republics to a non-nuclear posture and the Russian government to the numerical specifics of the treaty; and (3) implementing the intrusive verification measures detailed in the agreement. The United States had to act before new realities were created, that is, before the new states sought security and benefits from their nuclear arms holdings and before nuclear rivalries and suspicions took hold. That nuclear holdings could increase competition among the republics was a real and potentially serious problem: Ukraine, Kazakhstan, and Belarus had pressed hard for U.S. economic and military assistance, security guarantees, and a resolution that would not convey their subordination to Russia (inasmuch as the START I Treaty allowed Russia alone to keep nuclear arms). In consequence, the United States had to settle for legally binding bilateral letters that, in conjunction with START treaty obligations, committed these republics individually to destroy their nuclear holdings or transfer them to Russia.[13]

Second, concerns were raised about unnecessary constraints that were imposed on the United States by negotiating and implementing formal arms control treaties. Many hawks concluded that the end of the Cold War had freed the United States to act unilaterally to address existing and emerging threats. For example, Richard Perle claimed that the appropriate approach was to take "unilateral actions that we deem necessary and wise, adjusting them if necessary in light of what the other side does" (U.S. Senate 1992b: 1:235). In this, hawks revealed little trepidation that U.S. unilateralism would drive an arms race. By their thinking, the "arms race" was a Cold War myth: the defining armament pattern of the period amounted to massive, unprovoked Soviet force deployments and a U.S. failure to respond to them (see Wohlstetter 1974a, b). Hawks acknowledged that U.S. and Soviet weapons were designed as offsets for adversary acquisitions, that is, MIRVs were intended to counter Soviet antiballistic missiles, missiles were moved out to sea to offset their vulnerability on land, and so forth; they would concede, however, only that Cold War–era arms acquisition was driven by Soviet (ideological) goals. As Perle surmised, "the weapons resulted from the politics," not "the other way around" (U.S. Senate 1992b: 1:243). So regardless of U.S. actions, the adversary threat would now recede: "Not only is it unthinkable that Russia would increase its nuclear ballistic missiles beyond where they are today—if anything the numbers are going to come down radically—but they have no desire to offset ballistic missile defenses if they should be deployed with increasing offensive forces" (U.S. Senate 1992b: 1:236).

Throughout the Cold War, hawks had used Soviet reliance on their land-based forces—and heavy missiles in particular—as a litmus test of Soviet objectives. That the Soviets depended on these ostensibly vulnerable forces—silo-killers, no less—betrayed their willingness to launch a first strike against U.S. nuclear forces. Why else would the Soviets invest in vulnerable forces unless they planned to use them first? But, if the hawks were correct, should not the relatively large Russian land-based force now provoke the same basic concerns about Russian goals? Thus, of primary note is not that hawks had reevaluated the adversary threat with the end of the Cold War; instead, it is that hawks had changed the basic rules for evaluating the threat. Whereas Soviet capabilities and objectives were once viewed as entirely in sync—as reinforcing aspects of the Soviet threat—Russian objectives could now be invoked to overlook Russian capabilities.

A critical implication of the shift in focus to objectives is that hawks implicitly downplayed the effects of weapons technology on nuclear stability. As always, they paid little heed to destabilizing developments that might give the United States a military advantage, including U.S. SLBMs with hard-target capabilities (the Trident II) and the U.S. employment in non-nuclear conflicts of conventionally armed ballistic missiles (which were indistinguishable at launch from nuclear-armed ballistic missiles). Now they ignored the destabilizing potential of Russian force deficiencies, which included deteriorating Russian early-warning and command and control capabilities (from neglect and territorial losses). In 1992, Secretary of State James Baker testified with apparent delight that the "illegal radar" at Krasnoyarsk had been dismantled and that the Russians had asked if they could convert part of the structure into a furniture factory (U.S. Senate 1992b: 2:18–19). Why the deteriorating Soviet early-warning system was viewed as a positive development when the United States had no plans to strike Russia and no one suspected that Russia intended to build a nationwide missile defense system is truly curious. Was U.S. security enhanced if Russia was forced to act *under the suspicion* that it was under attack?[14]

Third, concerns were raised about the adequacy of U.S. strategic forces under the treaty. Some hawkish critics noted that the treaty had not ameliorated the threat from Russian heavy missiles and, more generally, MIRVed land-based missiles. The Russians would retain a substantial land-based missile force despite cuts under the treaty, including the number of SS-18s by half. In point of fact, the ratio of SS-18 warheads to U.S. missile silos declined, under START I, only from 3.1:1 to 2.8:1 (U.S. Senate 1992c: 15).[15] (The 154 SS-18s were each credited with ten warheads to prevent the Russians from quickly boosting their nuclear force through warhead uploading.) START I imposed no limits on (non-mobile) ICBMs or SLBMs, and the parties could store thousands of these missiles for a possible breakout from the treaty. True, these missiles arguably held little value to the Russians compared to stored warheads that could be placed quickly on existing missiles. The treaty restricted the locations at which missiles could be stored, for possible reloading, which would be impeded, in any case, by U.S. counterstrikes.[16] But critics still constructed scenarios in which stored Russian missiles were used in successive waves of attack.

Thus, hawks and doves found some common ground in arguing that the START I Treaty had not broken appropriately with the past. Under the treaty, both the United States and the Soviet Union could retain a robust nuclear arsenal of thousands of strategic warheads, could employ their substantial holdings of tactical nuclear weapons in place of strategic weapons, and could store (non-mobile) missiles, their warheads, or fissile materials for future uses. Doves could reasonably press for substantial reductions—far more constraining than the START I ceilings—in the size of the U.S. force given the lessened (1) demands of deterring the Russians; and (2) stakes over which any U.S.-Russian conflict would be fought. After all, as we shall see, even hawks argued that Soviet goals—not Soviet weapons per se—had previously threatened the United States and its interests, and those goals were now more transparently benign as, for instance, a Russian invasion of Europe was unlikely.

Missing on all sides was a deliberative assessment of U.S. force requirements in light of the doctrinal commitments of the past. Whereas war-fighting principles would bind U.S. force levels to the existing Russian target set composed of nuclear forces and leadership, industrial, and conventional-force targets, assured-destruction principles would tie U.S. force levels to the declining Russian willingness to accept the costs of war. U.S. officials hardly sent clear signals in this regard. They accepted START-imposed warhead levels that were deemed necessary for the United States to cover military targets, yet they implied that U.S. security was ultimately ensured by a U.S. capability to lash out and destroy Russia under all contingencies. Note, for instance, Powell's judgment of the U.S. safeguard against Russian cheating: "Even if they had 20,000 SS-25s, I am not sure what that truly does for them. As long as we have very survivable systems at sea, for example, what would they do with these? What incentive is there for them to move in this direction?" (U.S. Senate 1992b: 2:148). Cheney's response to concerns that the Russians would upload warheads secretly for military advantage was similar:

> It does not make sense in the warfighting sense. Our bombers are off alert. It does not seem logical to me that they would make a major investment to try to catch those bombers by building up.
>
> [Moreover] if you look at the downloading that has been permitted, they could break out from that downloading but it seems unlikely that they would do that because there is really no target to send these uploaded warheads against. (U.S. Senate 1992b: 2:128)

In essence, Cheney (1) argued that Russia had no interest in launching a strike that could annihilate the land and air legs of the U.S. triad; and (2) recognized that, beyond ratios of advantage that were (a bit) lower than those that the Soviets possessed before START, additional counterforce capability did the Russians no good—for they would still have to cope with the immense retaliatory force of the naval leg of the U.S. triad.[17] Whether Cheney recognized it or not, he had come close to embracing the controversial principles of AD doctrine that a long line of U.S. administrations had sought to discredit.

TRUST AND VERIFICATION

The task of verifying compliance with the START I Treaty was vastly more complicated than verifying compliance with the INF Treaty: whereas the INF Treaty banned intermediate-range missiles entirely, the START I Treaty established numerical ceilings for various weapon systems. With a ban, the detection of any proscribed weapon implicates its possessor in a treaty violation. Not so with a ceiling. Detecting a violation requires (1) distinguishing among weapons to avoid double counting; and (2) collective monitoring of weapons to determine whether their numbers exceed the allowance. Verifying compliance with the START I Treaty also required the capability to "peer into" weapons (to ensure that individual missiles did not exceed their allowable warhead numbers) and to discriminate among weapons of the same type (to distinguish nuclear-armed from conventionally armed bombers). The monitoring of compliance with both treaties was confounded, of course, by the potential for hidden production and stockpiles and uncertainty about the fate of weapons that had supposedly been destroyed or converted for conventional use. In various ways, treaty negotiators rose to the challenge.

Verifying compliance with the START I Treaty eased considerably when the Soviets accepted the principle of monitoring the perimeter and exit points (portals) of mobile-missile production factories as part of the INF agreement. The issue in START of which facilities to monitor had taken years to settle given resistance to "anytime, anywhere" inspections, U.S.-Soviet force asymmetries, and differences in missile-assembly procedures. But the parties eventually worked through their differences: for instance, the United States agreed to declare the MX a "mobile" missile so that the Soviets would obtain reciprocal monitoring rights, the Soviets agreed to the (continuous portal and peripheral) monitoring of the missile's first-stage assembly plant in exchange for the U.S. monitoring of Soviet final assembly plants (because the United States assembled the MX in its silo), and so forth. In addition, the parties agreed to full access to missile telemetry, regularized data exchanges, the display of new weapons to reveal their essential characteristics, unique identifiers for each mobile missile, and regular inspections of weapons (at identified sites) to verify their numbers and characteristics. The treaty gave a party the right to request an inspection of undeclared facilities (and the suspect party a right of refusal), and it required that the suspect party follow various procedures to allay the accuser's concerns.

Treaty critics were not convinced, however, that the START I Treaty had sufficiently blocked Russian cheating. They expressed their concerns, as always, by constructing scenarios in which the Russians could effectively cheat—focused primarily on the threat from the production and storage of undeclared Russian mobile missiles, viewed by the U.S. intelligence community as the principal compliance concern (U.S. Senate 1995a: 56). Skeptics noted that U.S. intelligence could not conclusively determine prior Soviet production quantities and thus the potential scale of hidden stockpiles that Russia could use to an ever-increasing advantage, as U.S. warhead numbers declined under the treaty. Skeptics built on these concerns by criticizing various treaty asymmetries that had emerged through compromise: the Russians could monitor the first-stage MX assembly plant, but the United States was not entitled to inspect Russian rocket assembly facilities, which allowed the Russians to stockpile rockets for future assembly. These concerns were magnified by allegations that the Russians could maintain secret manufacturing and storage facilities.

For their part, treaty supporters made their case by advertising the treaty's multiple departures from prior practice. These were as follows. First, the treaty brought transparency in behavior that was previously opaque. Whereas the Soviets had once encrypted telemetry, claiming that the United States already had sufficient information to verify Soviet compliance under SALT, the START I Treaty required unimpeded access to missile telemetry information (through its open broadcasting) and the supplying of data tapes after missile tests to ensure that all relevant information was acquired. Transparency was facilitated, here as elsewhere, by national technical means: the Russians could not risk trying to deceive the United States with false information that the United States, through its own sources, could possibly invalidate. Second, the treaty brought a dramatic increase in intrusive activities and host-government obligations for active monitoring of treaty compliance. Monitoring was permitted outside two missile assembly plants, weapons were subject to identity and capability checks, and parties were notified when mobile missiles were dispersed and they could conduct post-dispersal base inspections of these missiles. These procedures would permit cross-checks and repeated observation to inhibit cheating. Third, the treaty facilitated accuracy in record-keeping for catching discrepancies. Its various reporting requirements allowed the inspecting party to establish baselines for assessing change from preestablished levels and evaluating its own intelligence, detection methods, and calculating methodologies. Fourth, the treaty shifted the burden of proof to the party under inspection. Although a party could refuse to allow the inspection of an undeclared site, a refusal to accede to an inspection request or to allay suspicions of a violation could endanger the treaty and was itself evidence that impugned the veracity and integrity of the suspect party. Finally, the treaty increased the probability of detecting a violation by boosting the numbers and sensitivity of monitoring mechanisms. Each procedure raised the probability of detection, if only by triggering actions (increased surveillance, a focused search for confirmatory evidence, or a challenge to the Russians for an explanation) that would increase the probability of detection. That detection probability increased further should a party attempt to obtain a large (meaningful) advantage through cheating.

Treaty proponents made a strong case that treaty mechanisms would catch all but small or occasional—perhaps unintended or technical—violations. Yet, for verification purposes, proponents and critics made too much of these mechanisms and too little of the political context in which the treaty would be implemented. The relevant question was not how to create absolute transparency—which is impossible—but rather how to design relatively efficient monitoring mechanisms that limit cheating to some acceptable level.[18] After all, U.S. policymakers routinely accepted risks of Russian noncompliance in exchange for relative gains in U.S. military capability.[19] The irony of START verification, then, is that the parties accepted higher costs of verification through more intrusive means when the need for verification was decreasing: the United States relied primarily on national technical means to assess Russian compliance, could still not prevent the Russians from cheating, and had less reason than ever to accept the treaty's verification costs, given the declining risk of cheating.

The risk was decreasing for the United States because cheating would yield the Russians only marginal military benefits. This was true because under the treaty (1) the United States would retain a formidable force of 6,000 nuclear warheads; (2) U.S. force-survival percentages (for a second strike) were increasing while the number of targets that U.S. forces had to cover was decreasing; and (3) the Russians retained the capability—with or without cheating—to inflict devastating destruction on U.S. society or to launch a "disarming" counterforce strike on U.S. land-based missiles. No less importantly, U.S. exposure to cheating had declined because Russia was now less of a security threat: the Russian political system was opening to scrutiny, Russian economic capabilities were declining, and the Russian government had clearly embraced nonmilitary priorities. To quote Sydney Graybeal, "While negotiating these provisions has contributed to greater openness and mutual understanding, I doubt that they would be, or need to be, of the same comprehensiveness and intrusiveness if they were being negotiated in the present post–cold-war environment." Put simply, the Russians had neither the incentive nor resources for significant cheating (U.S. Senate 1992b: 1:152).[20]

The Clinton Administration

With the world in flux, the Clinton administration was pulled in multiple directions. It had to contend with the four nuclear-armed states that had emerged from the former Soviet Union; the possible dissemination of Soviet nuclear weapons, materials, and knowledge to other states; and the potential development of nuclear weapons (or other weapons of mass destruction) by apparently risk-prone states such as Iraq and North Korea. In response, the administration sought to manage the U.S.-Russian relationship while confronting proliferators and building multilateral support for measures that would impede proliferation. It had a mixed record of success: Saddam Hussein did not bow to U.S. (and UN) demands that Iraq open its suspect WMD sites more fully to inspections, the U.S. deal with North Korea (the 1994 Agreed Framework) on its nuclear program remained fragile, the Russians deflected U.S. attempts to renegotiate the ABM Treaty, the U.S. Senate refused to ratify the 1996 Comprehensive Test Ban Treaty, and the United States and Russia failed to formalize the U.S.-Russian strategic arms reductions that Clinton sought in his last years in office. Even the much-anticipated START II Treaty failed to deliver on its promise. The treaty was ratified by the United States in 1996 but fell into oblivion when, in 2000, the Russian Parliament attached conditions to the treaty that the U.S. Senate refused to accept.

Perhaps the administration's travails were forewarned by the context in which the START II Treaty was forged and approved and by the controversies that surrounded the treaty. Yet the environment and reception were seemingly more felicitous for a U.S.-Russian deal than at any point in the nuclear era.

Background: The Changing Threat and U.S. Doctrine

The Clinton administration made nuclear weapons a policy priority though retaining as well as changing past strategies and policies. In seeking a permanent extension of the NPT in 1995, it basically reiterated Carter's pledge in stating that the United States would forgo nuclear attacks on non-nuclear states that adhered to the treaty (Simpson 2012: 63, 67); it supported deep arsenal cuts (as proposed under the START II Treaty) and created space for cuts by modifying the guidance on employing nuclear weapons "to accommodate existing war fighting demands at lower levels" (McKinzie et al. 2001: 8); it extended the scope of the U.S. nuclear targeting of China (Kristensen et al. 2006: 163); it sought to comply with the terms of the ABM Treaty until it could be amended in light of the architecture that the United States had selected to address a defined threat (John D. Holum in U.S. Senate 1997a: 15–18); and it jettisoned the brazen, war-fighting rhetoric and guidelines of the Reagan era. A 1997 Presidential Decision Directive (PDD-60) excised references to "prevailing" in a nuclear war from U.S. doctrine. Nevertheless, the administration resisted some basic changes. It did not alter "the fundamental axioms" of the SIOP and continued to plan options around the requisites of nuclear war-fighting (McKinzie et al. 2001: 7–8). In the tortuous internal government debate that ensued early in the administration, in which everything was initially on the table, the Clinton administration's initiative was most notable for what it did not accomplish. As Janne Nolan put it, Clinton's 1994 Nuclear Posture Review "started out as a very ambitious effort to scrub all of the assumptions of both declaratory and operational doctrine, to examine whether we needed a triad, why we needed to continue to rely on prompt counterforce, and so on. For many reasons, the review ended up as a pallid, little document that was not briefed around for very long and that essentially ratified the status quo" (Nolan quoted in Arms Control Association 2002; see also Nolan 1999: 35–62). The many hundreds of Russian conventional military, leadership, and industrial targets slated for a high level of damage continued to dominate the U.S. target list.[21] For that matter, the administration appeared to counter its apparent policy shifts. PDD-60 weakened the U.S. assurance of U.S. non-use of nuclear weapons against non-nuclear states by preserving the option to use nuclear weapons against an attack that involved chemical or biological weapons (Simpson 2012: 69), and the U.S. military developed war plans and target lists to address a growing threat from the Third World that included biological and chemical weapons (Kristensen 1997; Paul 2009: 86–87).

The administration struggled when explicating the abstract purposes that nuclear weapons served in the post–Cold War era. It acknowledged that the purpose of nuclear weapons was first and foremost to deter nuclear war, with confidence that the United States could dissuade even malevolent, risk-prone foreign leaders from attacking the United States (U.S. Senate 2000: 21). The key, according to JCS Chairman John Shalikashvili in endorsing the START II Treaty, was to maintain an arsenal sufficient "to hold at risk those assets which any foreseeable enemy would most value—the core determinant of effective deterrence."[22] In this, U.S. policymakers only appeared to embrace AD principles. Shalikashvili donned the hat of the war-fighter when he stated approvingly that the U.S. force (under the START II Treaty) was "sufficient to prevent any foreseeable enemy from achieving his war aims against us or our allies" (U.S. Senate 1995a: 81). Official statements consistently begged the question, Did the United States intend to *deny* gains to the adversary or to *punish* it by inflicting pain beyond its threshold of tolerance? The answer was unclear when Undersecretary of Defense Walter Slocombe noted that "United States nuclear forces must be capable of, and be seen to be capable of, holding at risk those critical assets and capabilities that a potential adversary most values." Why distinguish between assets and capabilities? Tellingly, it indicated that he recognized at some level that the two concepts were grounded in distinct logics, with diverging implications: a leader might fight to the end, exhausting its *capabilities;* it might concede defeat, short of exhaustion, to preserve its remaining *assets.*[23] The logical liabilities of conflating strategies had not abated despite the large nuclear advantage that the United States held over potential adversaries. If anything, they had increased because a U.S. denial strategy had to assume that U.S. adversaries—who could not meaningfully reduce U.S. retaliatory capabilities with counterforce strikes—would act irrationally or would strike only to inflict as much damage as possible on the United States and its interests. If that were true, any policy that held assets at risk was wrongheaded: an adversary that will attack to inflict damage for its own sake cannot be deterred—once it can assuredly inflict some sought level of destructiveness. The only reasonable *offensive* strategy for the United States, then, is either preemptive or preventative.

Thus, U.S. policymakers had to address new threats when they had not resolved critical tensions—or forged a consensus—in thinking about the old threat. That was bound to confound the reducing of nuclear force levels through the START negotiating process.

The START II Treaty (Toward START III?)

Just as the task of finalizing and obtaining ratification of the START I Treaty had passed from Reagan to Bush, the responsibility for ratifying the START II Treaty passed, in turn, from Bush to Clinton.[24] Having emerged from a June 1992 joint summit agreement between Presidents Bush and Yeltsin, the treaty was signed just weeks before Bush's term ended and was formally transmitted to the Senate on President Bush's last day (and President Clinton's first day) in office. Senate consideration of the START II Treaty was slowed by the enormous diplomatic challenge of getting the former Soviet republics to ratify the START I Treaty, which did not enter into force until December 1994 with the exchange of ratification instruments (Holum in U.S. Senate 1995a: 23). Under the terms of START I, the parties committed to completing their arms reductions by the end of 2001, that is, seven years from the date that START I went into effect; under START II, they committed to complete the next round of reductions by January 1, 2003, having completed the first phase of START II reductions by the earlier date. The two treaties were to be implemented simultaneously and remain in force over the same duration. (In 1997, the deadline was extended to the end of 2007.)

Although the START II Treaty required that the parties reconfigure and cut their forces from START I levels by half—a reduction of thousands of deployed warheads—the treaty built on the START I Treaty in key respects. The START II Treaty consists of the main text (a Preamble and eight Articles), two Protocols (one on elimination and conversion procedures and the other on exhibitions and inspections), and a Memorandum of Understanding on warhead attribution. Compared to START I, it is a considerably shorter document—around thirty pages in length—in large part because it relies on the definitions and verification procedures in START I. But the treaty broke new ground: it banned Russian heavy missiles (the infamous SS-18 force, halved in START I) and land-based, multiple-warhead missile deployments (hence the treaty's additional verification procedures). By the completion date, each party was to have reached the specified ceiling—a range between 3,000 and 3,500 warheads, with the stipulations that (1) no more than 1,750 of these warheads were to be placed on SLBMs; and (2) the maximum number of weapons with which a particular type of heavy bomber was equipped (not "attributed" numbers) would count toward the overall ceiling. For instance, the B-2 bomber counted as one weapon under START I and sixteen weapons under START II (U.S. Senate 1995a: 32). Still, 150 U.S. bombers that were equipped to carry perhaps twenty air-launched cruise missiles counted as carrying half that amount (U.S. Senate 1995b: 17). (Increasing or decreasing the number of warheads on a bomber type required an exhibition to demonstrate the type's weapons carriage.)

The START II Treaty was enabled by the U.S. concession in June 1992 of deeper cuts in SLBMs in response to Russian objections that the U.S.-proposed terms unfairly penalized Russian dependence on land-based missiles (U.S. Senate 1995b: 10) and two subsequent U.S. concessions (in December 1992). The Russians had sought the latter to relieve the economic hardships that were imposed by the dismantling of the Soviet-era, MIRVed, land-based missile force. These concessions were the relaxing of the downloading limitation to permit Russia to retain 105 (of 170) SS-19s in existing silos as single-warhead missiles and the reuse of 90 (of 154) SS-18 missile silos for single-warhead (SS-25) missiles (U.S. Senate 1995b: 3). More generally, the START II Treaty relaxed START I requirements to permit the parties to download a larger number of warheads from ICBMs and SLBMs without replacing the reentry vehicle platform. As with START I, the treaty eliminated launchers—missile silos, bombers, and submarine launchers (through destruction or conversion)—but not warheads or missiles, the SS-18s being the important exception. The production of multiple-warhead missiles was prohibited, however, after January 1, 2003. For its part, the United States could exempt some of its heavy bombers from the count by reorienting them exclusively to a conventional role or by giving them a distinguishing characteristic (detectable through national technical means) and deploying them away from nuclear weapons storage areas and heavy bombers with nuclear missions. Thus, the treaty allowed the United States to exempt 100 B-1 bombers that had counted against the U.S. START I ceiling.

Despite its appeal, the START II Treaty was ultimately a political casualty of deteriorating U.S.-Russian relations. U.S. ratification was delayed until 1996; the Russian Duma did not ratify the treaty until 2000. Then the Duma conditioned the treaty's entry into force on the U.S. ratification of agreements that were made in 1997 pertaining to issues including missile defense. The treaty lapsed—along with its heralded ban on SS-18s and its de-MIRVing provisions—when the U.S. Senate failed to agree to the Russian conditions. Although Presidents Clinton and Yeltsin agreed in 1997 to a framework for reducing each party's strategic force levels to between 2,000 and 2,500 warheads, formal negotiations were blocked by continuing disagreement between the parties on missile defense (U.S. Senate 2010: 3).

EVALUATING STRENGTH

The United States conceded ground in the START II Treaty negotiations. The treaty limited the United States in its areas of advantage—most decidedly, by holding bombers to their actual cruise missile count and capping numbers of SLBM warheads. But even critics acknowledged that the United States obtained much in return. It secured the de-MIRVing of the Soviet land-based missile force—the heralded threat behind the alleged U.S. "window of vulnerability"—and received a long-sought concession in the Russian agreement to dismantle the SS-18 force. These were no small achievements for most champions of U.S.-Russian arms control. As the director of ACDA, John Holum, commented, "In cutting the SS-18 force to 0, START II completes a 20-year quest by the United States to eliminate the most dangerous and destabilizing aspects of the cold war nuclear rivalry" (U.S. Senate 1995a: 23). Then the United States retained flexibility under the treaty for distributing sea-based warheads, permitting the planned retention of fourteen Trident submarines (U.S. Senate 1995a: 31). For treaty proponents, START II met the standard by which prior treaties had long been assessed (and disparaged), that is, a rough "parity" or "equivalence" between U.S.

and Russian forces and "stability" in depriving each side of a first-strike incentive. The survivability of the U.S. force, enhanced under START I, had increased further under START II (U.S. Senate 1995b: 11–13).

For critics, a central concern was whether the United States remained vulnerable under the treaty. Critics recognized that smaller arsenals could dramatically reduce the numbers of U.S. weapons that could avenge a Russian first strike. Their concerns about declining U.S. numbers built on more general concerns that the United States had not duly sought to preserve U.S. competitiveness and reduce U.S. vulnerabilities under the treaty. In their view, the U.S. position was actually weaker than it appeared because U.S. bombers had been taken off alert; a large fraction of the U.S. submarine force was in port at a given time; and the United States, unlike the Russians, was reliant on aging hardware (U.S. Senate 1995b: 13–17).[25] Although congressional skeptics generally believed that the treaty's pluses outweighed the negatives, they worried about the long-term effects of the treaty. More specifically, they posited that the United States—given its far-ranging interests—would be better off, down the road, forgoing arms control to make unilateral adjustments—upward or downward—in U.S. strategic nuclear holdings. Even legislative supporters of the START II Treaty worried that U.S. concessions under START II would create inexorable momentum toward a future treaty that would unacceptably reduce U.S. force levels and compromise the viability of the U.S. triad (U.S. Senate 1995b: 23). That was the concern when the Clinton administration tentatively agreed in a 1997 summit with Yeltsin to reduce force sizes to 2,000 to 2,500 warheads (cutting forces below START II levels by 30 to 45 percent) and when President Putin pressed repeatedly for even deeper cuts, to a ceiling of 1,500 warheads or lower.[26] The Pentagon argued initially that it could not cover the necessary target set with 2,500 warheads (McKinzie et al. 2001: 8), and hawkish critics worried that the United States would increase its vulnerability to challenges from less capable states as the size of the U.S. arsenal dwindled. Their fear was that the United States was vulnerable, at lower numbers, to a threat from China and fledgling nuclear states like North Korea. But these concerns revealed little consideration of the conditions that would provoke a nuclear conflict—the gains that adversaries would seek, the possible role of U.S. nuclear weapons in denying the adversary its gains, or the threshold at which the United States had sufficient nuclear capability on hand for punishing any or all adversary transgressions.

Dovish START II proponents responded that such concerns were unwarranted. They maintained that the lower U.S. holdings would guarantee reductions in the size of the Russian force, decreasing its destructiveness and increasing strategic stability, and would still leave the United States with robust nuclear capabilities.[27] They noted further that, by Cold War–era standards, the United States was well positioned to respond to all non-Russian nuclear adversaries. Not only would the United States maintain a huge absolute and relative edge over any and all Third World competitors, it could unload its full complement of (first-strike) nuclear weapons on an unfortunate challenger, which would lack the capability to deplete the U.S. arsenal through counterforce strikes. Thus, these doves made a compelling case that the United States had the capability to cope under all contingencies. But that was easier than establishing the threshold at which U.S. capabilities were "excessive."

TRUST AND VERIFICATION

The START II Treaty required additional monitoring to verify compliance with its new disarmament provisions. It included methods for destroying SS-18 missiles (and launch canisters) under U.S. inspection; procedures for ensuring that SS-18 silos were permanently modified (for instance, with concrete) for launching the lighter, single-warhead SS-25; an allowance for repeat inspections to ensure that the silos actually contain single-warhead missiles; exhibition and inspection requirements pertaining to the weapons carriage of heavy bombers; exhibition requirements to establish the observable differences that distinguish heavy bombers employed for conventional rather than nuclear missions; a call for additional data exchanges; and the creation of a Bilateral Implementation Commission to address issues of compliance that might arise (U.S. Senate 1995a: 27–28).

As usual, hawks and doves divided on the issue of compliance verification. Ardent treaty proponents insisted that the United States was positioned to catch Russian cheating and would emerge in the stronger position with disclosures of Russian infidelity. Russia could not achieve meaningful gains by adding warheads to those few Russian land-based missiles that could actually accommodate multiple warheads. For that purpose, it would have to excavate a large number of silos to launch the Russian stock of land-based missiles or to field large numbers of mobile missiles. These were comparatively costly options for the Russians that would almost certainly bring premature disclosure. At that point, the United States could offset Russian force improvements easily by adding MIRVs to the U.S. Trident missile force (under START II, the destruction of warhead-mounting platforms was not required). Still, hawkish critics remained concerned about U.S. vulnerability to Russian deception. They recognized the multitude of ways that the Russians could cheat to add perhaps many hundreds of warheads to their deployed arsenal. Beyond warhead uploading and silo excavation, the Russians could reconvert heavy ICBM silos after the U.S. onsite inspection of the initial conversion, develop a MIRVed SLBM (which was permitted under the treaty) and deploy it in ICBM silos, or deploy bombers with larger numbers of warheads than had been counted under the treaty (on some of these possibilities, see U.S. Senate 1995b: 31–37). Because these avenues would invite U.S. detection and an offsetting U.S. response or produce marginal Russian strategic benefits, critics focused their concerns specifically on the mobile missile threat. U.S. intelligence viewed these missiles as a more promising avenue for a Russian treaty breakout, concerns that were echoed by the U.S. Senate's Select Committee on Intelligence (U.S. Senate 1996: 13).

But was their relative attention to mobile missiles warranted? For at least three reasons, the answer is no. First, mobile missiles arguably posed no more of a threat to the United States than did other strategic nuclear missiles in the Russian arsenal. Although these missiles were mobile and could thereby escape U.S. detection and targeting, Russian mobile missiles per se presented a greater U.S. military problem in the unlikely scenario in which the United States struck *first*. A mobile missile was no more a threat to the United States than a fixed-site missile once launched against the U.S. target set. Second, the Russian deployment of mobile missiles was arguably a stabilizing development. It indicated that the Russians valued deterrence and were seeking a force, then, that could survive a U.S. first strike. Like submarines, mobile, land-based missiles are reputedly stabilizing systems: they need not be launched quickly in a crisis (out of fear of otherwise "losing them"). Although the United States sought repeatedly to ban these weapons, Russia has rightly perceived them as an effective counterpart to SLBMs, given the Russian absence of easy port access but an abundance of territory over which these missiles can roam and hide.[28] Third, the United States possessed some capability to monitor these missiles through national technical means and the inspections that were permitted under the treaty. That capability had only grown as Russia, moving toward a more open society, had lifted restrictions on access and movement. Finally, even large quantities of illicit mobile missiles would not destabilize the U.S.-Russian nuclear balance assuming the Russians were sensitive to the human costs of a nuclear exchange. If anything, the Russian leadership had grown more appreciative of these costs with the demise of the Soviet political system.

In the final analysis, the thinking behind verifying compliance with the START II Treaty rested on somewhat contradictory foundations. First, U.S. officials coveted an intrusive verification regime yet chose to limit its purview rather than expose U.S. industrial and military facilities to reciprocal inspections. Thus, the United States accepted some risk that the Russians would violate the treaty even as the United States struggled to negotiate the closing of apparent loopholes and openings to Russian cheating. Second, U.S. officials pushed for more intrusive verification measures as the Russian threat was diminishing: the Russian economy was deteriorating and the Russian military was losing control over national resources. The question, then, was whether the risk of Russian cheating warranted the expense of intrusive compliance monitoring. Third, U.S. officials pushed for a rigid verification regime that would still not reduce Russian payoffs from cheating. Simply put, if Russia had the desire and means to warehouse illicit missiles, it could do so.

Thus, a basic question remained: was the verification regime appropriate given the actual risk of Russian cheating? U.S. officials answered affirmatively without fully considering the relevant tradeoffs.

The George W. Bush Administration: Reassessing Arms Control

Whether or not the Cold War's end had actually produced global unipolarity, the George W. Bush administration was unquestionably responsible for the pronounced post–Cold War shift toward U.S. unilateralism. Although accusations of U.S. unilateralism predated the administration (Huntington 1999), Bush officials unabashedly embraced a "go-it-alone" strategy by shunning arms control treaties and negotiations even before its leap into Iraq in 2003 without UN Security Council support. The administration would not concede its prerogatives by locking the United States into treaties—arms control or otherwise—supposedly with good reason. The tragic terror attacks of September 11, 2001, established beyond a doubt that the United States faced a new enemy that would go anywhere and do anything to hurt the United States.

In this threat environment, the lines blurred between the al-Qaeda terrorists who attacked the World Trade Center in New York and the Pentagon outside Washington, D.C., and so-called rogue states—Iraq, Iran, and North Korea—that had vociferously challenged U.S. interests and had the will and capability to develop weapons of mass destruction. Not surprisingly, the Bush administration's 2002 *Nuclear Posture Review* (*NPR*)—the official statement of the role that is expected of nuclear weapons in U.S. security—had U.S. nuclear weapons serving in various capacities—including destroying North Korean WMD and countering a North Korean conventional offensive. The *NPR* called, in fact, for the development of low-yield, bunker-buster bombs to destroy deeply buried underground WMD storage sites. In the same year, high-profile U.S. policy documents—including the president's State of the Union address and the *National Security Strategy of the United States*—reiterated the principle of "preemption" (more correctly, prevention) by which the United States could respond to emerging threats by taking the offensive. The implication was that the United States might use nuclear weapons first in order to destroy chemical and biological weapons stocks (Simpson 2012: 71). In 2005, the JCS, in a draft document, gave U.S. military commanders the option of requesting presidential approval to use nuclear weapons to respond to a WMD attack (Lebovic 2007: 44). For administration officials, the challenge was rewriting the rules—overcoming the reservations of those who were still "living in the past"—to keep pace with the global transformation.

Whereas prior administrations had chastised the Soviets for ignoring agreements in pursuit of superiority, the Bush administration appeared intent on doing both. Its accompanying attitude toward arms control with Russia is expressed in two major arms control initiatives. The first of these was the U.S. withdrawal from the ABM Treaty; the second was the negotiating of the Strategic Offensive Reductions Treaty (SORT).

ABM Treaty Withdrawal

Missile defense was a contentious issue throughout much of the Cold War and post–Cold War periods. The Clinton administration, which had hoped to amend the ABM Treaty to permit deployment, was criticized nonetheless for its allegedly tepid commitment to missile defense.[29] With concerns about a growing missile threat in Clinton's second term—galvanized by the warnings in 1998 of a pending ballistic missile threat in the report from the Commission to Assess the Ballistic Missile Threat to the United States—the Bush administration was determined to act.[30] For Bush officials, the treaty was an unnecessary constraint: it stood in the way of the missile defense that Bush had promised in his presidential campaign to guard against emerging threats. In December 2001, it announced that in six months, the United States would withdraw from the Antiballistic Missile Treaty.

The United States was certainly acting within its rights: the treaty recognized that a party could withdraw from the treaty with six months' notice if "extraordinary events" threatened its "supreme interests." As Bush put it, "The ABM Treaty hinders our government's ability to develop ways to protect our people from future terrorist or rogue-state missile attacks . . . the events of September the 11th made all too clear, the greatest threats to [the United States and Russia] come not from each other, or other big powers in the world, but from terrorists who strike without warning, or rogue states who seek weapons of mass destruction." But were U.S. interests served by withdrawing from the treaty?

U.S. fears of rogue states were reminiscent of fears, in the 1950s, that Russia—and, in the 1960s, that China—might attack the United States when it could. Although these particular concerns abated with time, hopes that a defense could protect the United States from attack grew, again, as the focus in the post–Cold War period turned to a new set of "bad characters." Indeed, a defense now looked even more promising given the small number of warheads that a rogue state could launch against U.S. targets. Defense advocates insisted that a missile defense positioned the United States, specifically, to (1) capitalize on its enormous economic and technological capacities; (2) sustain its high-technology infrastructure through advanced research and development; (3) disclose the hidden potentials of technology for an improved understanding of the threat environment; (4) upgrade its defensive capabilities as the requisite technology became available; (5) extend deterrence to allies without having to cope with the "trading-New York-for-Paris" dilemma; (6) win allies by offering to place them under the U.S. protective umbrella; and (7) overthrow hostile regimes that were armed with nuclear weapons without fear of nuclear retaliation against the U.S. homeland. Perhaps, most importantly, with an effective missile defense, the United States could shed its dependence on the good will, rationality, and cost-aversion of adversary leaders—or their fragile control over nuclear weapons and materials—to protect the United States and its allies against catastrophe. In the view of the Bush administration and its supporters, the United States could ill afford to forgo the defensive option: the threat to the United States was too great and potential benefits of a defense were unlimited.

In response, missile-defense critics questioned the merits of a wholesale abandonment of the ABM Treaty. They asked whether the alleged security gains from withdrawing from the ABM Treaty were worth compromising U.S.-Russian relations; establishing a dangerous legal precedent; giving the United States a (bad) reputation for not standing by agreements; and provoking third countries, such as China, to build their arsenals to overcome a potential U.S. defense. Some critics maintained, regardless, that a defense was unnecessary because deterrence was robust: Iranian and North Korean leaders were not oblivious to cost, that is, the phenomenal retaliatory destruction that the United States could impose on an offender under any and all contingencies. They also emphasized the enormous challenges that the United States would encounter in devising a successful defensive system. In their view, a missile defense would be (1) ineffective because a high warhead attrition rate would still incur an unacceptably high probability that adversary warheads would survive to devastate one or more U.S. cities; (2) offset—even dangerous—if provoking the adversary to build more missiles to overwhelm the defense; and (3) circumvented if the adversary redirected its fire to unprotected targets or sought to deliver nuclear weapons against U.S. targets through less exotic means. For instance, a device aboard a ship in port could still devastate the surrounding city.[31]

Of course, the Bush administration triumphed, by fiat, in the domestic dispute. It was positioned constitutionally to withdraw from the treaty, regardless of opposition. Still, it sought to reduce the potential fallout from its action. To boost support retroactively for the decision, administration supporters noted the relatively muted Russian reaction to the U.S. withdrawal announcement. Russia stated that it would not be bound by the START II Treaty, which had never taken effect; it did not renounce the SORT Treaty (signed the month before), which reduced force levels below the START II ceilings.[32] Indeed, President Putin called months later for the quick acceptance of a new arms control regime to replace the ABM Treaty. But the issue of missile defense would remain a source of U.S.-Russian tension once the issue—much like the intermediate-range missiles of the 1970s and 1980s—became ensnared in alliance politics. The Bush administration moved beyond its initial plans to place interceptors in Alaska and California—to defend against potential missile threats from Asia and the Middle East (and, specifically, North Korea and Iran)—to plans to place interceptors in Poland and radar in the Czech Republic for additional defense against an Iranian nuclear attack on Europe. Consequently, extending missile defense became a measure of the U.S. commitment to extending deterrence to former Warsaw Pact states that were threatened by Russia—ironically, in part *because* they were under the U.S. defense umbrella.

The SORT Treaty

In May 2002, President Bush and Russian President Putin signed the Strategic Offensive Reduction Treaty (SORT, or Treaty of Moscow). SORT indirectly formalized the demise of the START II Treaty: it stated that the START Treaty would remain in force and made no reference to its successor.[33] It also signaled the end of arms control negotiations as a lengthy, hard-fought process in which parties sought to configure the force balance to advantage: in essence, SORT bound the parties legally to their unilateral decisions and gave them exceptional freedom to determine their own force mix. In other words, the treaty gave legal cover to the United States to do what it had already planned to do. Indeed, the United States engaged in strategic bargaining with Russia—for the first time with the hope of avoiding the strictures of a formal agreement.

In 2001, the Bush administration announced its plans to reduce deployments to between 1,700 and 2,200 warheads, approximating the levels of the 1997 Clinton-Yelstin agreement (Woolf 2008: 2). In response, the Russians (and the U.S. Senate) indicated their preference for a formal treaty.[34] The Bush administration eventually made its one key concession when it accepted the principle of a legally binding agreement. It was unwilling, however, to allow Russia—in a role reversal—to constrain U.S. prerogatives under a treaty. Russia sought ironclad counting rules (for instance, crediting delivery systems with their warhead-carrying capacity and requiring the destruction of delivery systems before a party was credited with a given warhead reduction); it insisted on accompanying inspection procedures and data exchanges to assist verification rather than relying, for that purpose, on the START I Treaty, which would remain in effect until late 2009 (Woolf 2008: 6–7); and it tried (once again) to include prohibitions on missile defense to ensure the effectiveness of the dwindling Russian offensive arsenal. The resulting treaty was hardly a compromise. In its few paragraphs, it gave the administration latitude to act within a single broad ceiling: "it does not include any of the detailed definitions, counting rules, elimination procedures, or monitoring and verification provisions that have become common in treaties signed since the late 1980s" (Woolf 2008: 1). The basics of the treaty reduce, in fact, to two brief sentences in Article I, which read, "Each Party shall reduce and limit strategic nuclear warheads . . . so that by December 31, 2012 the aggregate number of such warheads does not exceed 1,700–2,200 for each Party. Each Party shall determine for itself the composition and structure of its strategic offensive arms, based on the aggregate limits for the number of such warheads." In consequence, the treaty allowed the United States to determine where to place its warheads and whether and how to dispose of warheads that were not actually deployed. Indeed, the treaty permitted the United States to retain most of the delivery vehicles—air, land, and sea—that were planned under (the 3,500-warhead limit of) the START II Treaty (Woolf 2008: 12). Reflecting the Bush administration's desire for short- and long-term flexibility, the treaty did not count U.S. delivery vehicles in overhaul or under conversion for conventional use against U.S. totals; it did not require the destruction of warheads, which allowed their redeployment should international circumstances change (Woolf 2008: 5);[35] it ran for a limited (ten-year) duration and permitted withdrawal with "three months written notice" without an overriding reason; and it did not impose interim constraints, that is, a timetable for force reductions over the course of the treaty.

Under the circumstances, there was little U.S. intragovernmental debate over the terms of the treaty: hawks felt that the treaty protected U.S. prerogatives, and doves figured that some arms control was better than none given the administration's resistance to arms control in principle. The treaty was ratified by the U.S. Senate without formal opposition: two amendments failed—one related to U.S. reporting on Russian compliance and the other to presidential consultation (in leaving or extending the treaty). But both sides of the debate voiced concerns about the treaty's generality, fearing that the "devil was in the *lack* of details."

Of course, the treaty did not resolve outstanding issues in U.S.-Russian arms control. In particular, the United States and Russia continued to hold incommensurate views on the challenges that U.S. missile defenses posed to Russian offensive nuclear forces. Nor did it place the United States closer to resolving the issues of whether, how, and when it might employ nuclear weapons, if not against Russian targets. Despite the administration's protests, the Congress blocked funding for an earth-penetrating (bunker-buster) nuclear weapon—for use, in part, against underground WMD facilities—amid claims that the bomb would spur nuclear proliferation, produce enormous collateral damage when employed, and still not destroy (and perhaps even disperse) the targeted materials (Lebovic 2007: 52). Even if the United States sought to employ nuclear threats only to deter unwanted behavior, critics wondered whether U.S. threats were credible. After all, the United States possessed conventional alternatives, and its nuclear options were normatively problematic. The United States might have to respond to a chemical or biological attack when the responsible party is unknown, after the immediate threat to the United States has passed, when the damage from the biological or chemical attack is modest compared to destruction from a (U.S. retaliatory) nuclear explosion, or when the initial attack was triggered by accident or initiated independently by a nonstate entity.[36] For that matter, critics wondered what the United States might do if its threats *were* credible. Would the United States feel compelled to act on its nuclear threats, regardless of the consequences, out of fear of losing credibility at home and abroad?[37] To be sure, a policy of "calculated ambiguity" could give the United States some freedom to maneuver. But it would only postpone the critical choice of whether or not to use nuclear weapons.

In the end, the Bush administration sought to keep its options open by scaling the U.S. arsenal to some "essential" floor level of strategic nuclear capability. But planning for such a capability-based strategic force was a poor substitute for a formal analysis of the threats that would determine when and how nuclear weapons would be used. Consequently, fundamental questions remained unanswered. Under what conditions would the United States launch a limited or an all-out strike against the Russian conventional or nuclear infrastructure? Would the United States have the time or the need to attack any or all targets before the adversary could strike? Should the United States scale its forces in the expectation that U.S. adversaries would act independently or in unison? Would a strategy that was designed to create options for U.S. policymakers ultimately force them to make heat-of-the-battle decisions under high uncertainty and severe pressure to act?

The Obama Administration

The Barack Obama administration hoped to set the troubled U.S.-Russia relationship on a new course. The Bush administration had refused to concede U.S. prerogatives or defer to the sensitivities and concerns of other states, now that the United States was finally free from Cold War competition and was engaged globally in a war on terror and conflict with rogue states. In its view, new rules—and a jettisoning of old rules that governed U.S. arms control with Russia—were required to address the new global threats. But the Obama administration viewed U.S.-Russian relations somewhat differently. It approached arms control with Russia as an essential component of a larger multilateral effort to address the challenges that had confounded the prior administration. In a historic speech in Prague in the spring of 2009, Obama offered a vision of a world without nuclear weapons and outlined an ambitious agenda that would include ending the production of fissile materials for nuclear weapons, U.S. ratification of the Comprehensive Test Ban Treaty, and new arrangements to stem nuclear proliferation. Through strategic arms control, the Obama administration sought to demonstrate that the United States was actually willing to limit its own prerogatives and coordinate U.S. efforts with other states in order to halt the proliferation of nuclear weapons and to solve global security problems. The immediate product of the administration's initial foray into arms control was the New START Treaty.

The Changing Strategic Context

With a flourish, the Obama administration announced its plans to "reset" U.S.-Russian relations. To the administration, the term, which was introduced by Vice President Joseph Biden, suggested appropriately that these relations had deteriorated badly, albeit not irreparably, under the stewardship of the prior administration. The term also provided a good promotional hook in the form of a physical prop—a "reset button" that Secretary of State Hillary Clinton gave to her Russian counterpart—which the two pressed during a photo opportunity.[38] But the changing atmospherics were arguably insufficient to facilitate U.S.-Russian cooperation. The button was itself transformed into a symbol of Russian grievances. The gift had been mislabeled to read "overload"—for many Russians, an appropriate characterization of relentless U.S. affronts that Russia could not tolerate.

Whereas U.S.-Russian relations had their ups and downs in the Cold War period, falling often into prolonged periods of suspicion and hostility, they were at least predicated on the U.S. assumption that the Soviet Union was a driving force in global affairs. The intensifying post–Cold War conflict between the two powers stemmed in no small part, however, from perceptions in Russia that it was being circumvented or ignored. The disturbing implication of U.S. claims that the "world has changed" since the Cold War (and September 11) was that the age of superpower dominion had passed—that Russia was now too weak to compete. The implication had surely inspired President Putin's public admonishment of "those who would like to build a unipolar world, who would themselves like to rule all of humanity."[39] These sentiments were not solely attributable to Russian oversensitivity. The United States indeed had shown little regard for Russian protests over NATO expansion into Eastern Europe, the U.S. pursuit of missile defense and withdrawal from the ABM Treaty, the disregard for the Serbs in the war in Kosovo, Russian stakes in conflicts with former Soviet republics (such as Georgia), and U.S. unilateralism. Adding perceived insult to injury, the United States expected Russia to fall into line behind U.S. policies, for instance, by imposing sanctions on Iran for its nuclear pursuits. That Bush administration officials had dismissed strategic arms control as a Russian ploy to anchor the U.S. military to Russia's fading glory only added to Russia's consternation. Unsurprisingly, then, U.S. relations with Russia were prone to hostile flareups: U.S. plans to place a missile defense system in Eastern Europe provoked Russian President Dmitri Medvedev to threaten to move Russian missiles closer to Poland and Lithuania; an article written by two U.S. scholars claiming that the United States had achieved a first-strike capability against the Russian nuclear force brought an angry Russian response, as if the article had formally pronounced a U.S. policy; and so on and so forth (Lieber and Press 2006; Waller 2009: 105). That the Russian response was exaggerated said much about the U.S.-Russian relationship, even if U.S. policymakers took it as reason to dismiss Russian protests.

The Obama administration was pressed early to make strategic arms control a policy priority. The START Treaty (formerly the START I Treaty), which had been the cornerstone of U.S.-Russian (post–Cold War) strategic arms control, was set to expire on December 5, 2009. The United States and Russia could not settle for the loose guidance of an abbreviated document, modeled after the SORT Treaty, without considerable sacrifice: that approach was made possible by verification measures that remained in effect under the START Treaty. A new strategic arms control agreement was given urgency, as well, by the approach of the 2010 (five-year) NPT Review Conference. The administration was compelled to demonstrate its commitment to disarmament (under Article VI of the NPT) so as to avoid the disastrous outcome of the 2005 Review Conference, where Iran had challenged the U.S. willingness to forgo nuclear threats against non-nuclear states (Simpson 2012: 72). The administration hoped to build multilateral support for the general principle of nuclear nonproliferation and to gain international support to isolate Iran and North Korea for their illicit nuclear programs. Obama administration officials appeared optimistic that the world's non-nuclear majority could be swayed by a broad-based U.S. effort that included a negotiated reduction in the numbers of deployed U.S. and Russian strategic nuclear weapons, a commitment to multilateral arms control—as exhibited, for example, by pushing for Senate approval of the Comprehensive Test Ban Treaty, and stronger U.S. assurances not to employ nuclear weapons against states complying with nuclear nonproliferation agreements (Simpson 2012: 74).

The task of changing global opinion was obviously difficult. Although deployed strategic nuclear warhead totals were now down to a quarter of their pre-START levels, the United States had endured intense criticism from the world's non-nuclear majority. Notwithstanding frequent references to Article VI obligations to help sell various treaties, the U.S. nod toward the NPT had always lacked sincerity: in the U.S. government, moving to "zero" had never been seen as a policy priority, been viewed generally as desirable, or been regarded as a U.S. obligation under the loose wording of the treaty.[40] The U.S. policy focus instead was on establishing the mix of weapons that would "stabilize" the nuclear balance—with the assumption that small nuclear arsenals were inherently destabilizing—and preserving U.S. flexibility by storing nuclear materials for potential reuse. That the non-nuclear powers were unimpressed, in consequence, by the large cuts in the relative and absolute size of the U.S. and Russian deployed arsenals—from their peak Cold War–era levels to the present—promised an unenthusiastic reaction to the far smaller cuts that were now possible in these considerably smaller arsenals.

Major obstacles remained, as well, in strategic arms control. The United States and Russia continued to disagree over whether U.S. missile defenses threatened Russian security, whether nuclear arms control should be allowed to compromise related U.S. conventional capabilities, and whether large-scale reductions in U.S. strategic forces would increase global security. Whereas Secretary of Defense Robert Gates's *Nuclear Posture Review Report* of 2010 broke some new ground—

for example, by opposing the development of new nuclear warheads—it adhered to various positions of the Bush administration. For example, it pushed for a robust missile defense in Europe, implicitly acknowledged the sanctity of the U.S. strategic triad, retained ambiguity about when and how the U.S. would employ tactical nuclear weapons, rejected a policy of no-first-use of nuclear weapons, and conceded that nuclear weapons have purposes other than deterrence (their "fundamental" purpose). Indeed, warhead coverage was driven—as in prior administrations—by a prompt counterforce requirement that would give the United States the capability (in a first-strike attack, perhaps) to limit the damage that an adversary could inflict in return. When departing from its predecessor, the Obama administration still invited foreign skepticism. It stated, for instance, that the United States would not use or threaten to use nuclear weapons against non-nuclear states that were parties to, and were complying with, the NPT, but it left open the possibility that the United States would employ nuclear weapons against those same countries if they developed other nonconventional weapons—it explicitly carved out an exception for biological weapons—or acquired conventional capabilities that required a U.S. nuclear response. Its initiatives also gave Russia reason for concern. Although the administration scuttled preexisting plans for ten long-range interceptors based in Poland and a radar in the Czech Republic in favor of a broad-based, flexible system that was pegged to the growth of the Iranian threat and designed for widespread—including Russian—participation, it still did not allay Russian concerns about U.S. defensive capabilities and intentions (U.S. Senate 2009). Thus, the question was whether the New START agreement represented a new beginning for U.S.-Russian arms control or its culmination.

The New START Treaty

The Obama administration moved quickly to forge an agreement to succeed the START Treaty. In April 2009, the parameters for a treaty were set in a meeting between Presidents Obama and Medvedev in London and then detailed in July 2009 in a more formal Understanding that the parties signed in Moscow. Although a treaty was still incomplete when the START Treaty expired, the negotiating progress was swift by historical standards: in April 2010, the parties signed the New START Treaty. Its intent was to cut strategic forces to levels below those established by the Moscow Treaty (SORT) and to simplify verification procedures by the standard of START; it would not affect nonstrategic nuclear weapons, nondeployed weapons, or missile defenses. Yet the relatively rapid pace of the negotiations belied the unanticipated Russian objections to portions of the

START Treaty's verification regime—U.S. telemetry monitoring, the U.S. presence at the Votkinsk missile assembly plant, and so forth—and frustrating setbacks from age-old issues—such as missile defense—that impeded the finalization of a treaty.[41] The pace also belied the contentious Senate ratification debate to come. The administration had to answer pointed questions about alleged U.S. giveaways under the treaty and the supposed Russian record of treaty noncompliance. Thus, the relatively compressed (eight-month) time frame (compared to the START hearings) for Senate deliberation—and the alleged pro-treaty cast of witnesses—proved a matter of contention. Critics claimed that the treaty had been virtually railroaded through the Senate without necessary data and support documentation, preventing the legislature from duly performing its constitutional duties (U.S. Senate 2010: 119–120). The treaty received the "advice and consent" of the Senate—barely exceeding the two-thirds standard—with a 71–26 vote in December 2010 (following a 14–4 vote by the Senate Foreign Relations Committee), before it was ratified the following month by the Russian Duma.

Simple by comparison to its SALT- and START-era predecessors, the New START Treaty borrowed from prior treaties and practices. The finalized treaty—17 pages in length, with a 165-page Protocol (containing definitions, specifics on verification, and so on, as well as the Agreed Statements)—drew heavily from the verification procedures found in the START Treaty. (By way of contrast, the briefer SORT Treaty lacked definitions and counting rules, allowing each party to determine the warhead holdings to report.)[42] New START also built on the philosophy of the prior (Bush) administration that the nonadversarial U.S.-Russian relationship—and its inherent stability—gave the parties freedom to mix, that is, to diversify their forces for efficiency and performance. The New START Treaty set a limit of 800 deployed and nondeployed ICBM and SLBM *launchers* and heavy bombers, 700 deployed strategic land-based and submarine-launched *missiles* (ICBMs and SLBMs) and heavy bombers (equipped with nuclear weapons), and 1,550 deployed warheads. (The START Treaty made no numerical distinction between missiles and launchers.) In a dramatic departure from START, New START counted warheads on individual missiles rather than attributing some maximum number of warheads to missiles of a type. The treaty set no limit on numbers of nondeployed missiles or warheads, nor was it structured to provide incentives—hallmarks of prior treaties—to push the parties toward stabilizing systems. Although the treaty did count heavy bombers as carrying a single warhead (regardless of their cruise-missile load)—and thus favored a slower moving, arguably less vulnerable weapon platform—it did so partly as a practical matter insofar as bombers were not typically deployed with their nuclear payload, which made them hard to count (Woolf 2011: 6). To facilitate the verification of compliance, the treaty drew on a set of streamlined procedures and practices: these included fewer but more far-reaching inspections, extensive data sharing, unique identifiers for all missiles and launchers, and onsite inspections that would include the external inspection of all missiles at a given site, checks of their unique identification codes, the determination that nondeployed or non-nuclear systems were based apart from deployed or nuclear systems, and counts of the actual warheads on selected missiles. The treaty, which was to supersede the SORT Treaty, was to run for ten years, with a right of withdrawal under the standard conditions.

In key respects, however, the ratification debate over the New START Treaty was a departure from the past: the assumptions of hawkish critics were newly inconsistent and clashed with hawkish criticisms of the past. The dueling arguments of proponents and opponents concerning the treaty's relative benefits and openings to cheating are as follows.[43]

EVALUATING STRENGTH

The debate between treaty supporters and critics centered overwhelmingly on lost U.S. prerogatives under the treaty. Whereas supporters emphasized that the United States was free to pursue its key military options, critics stressed that the United States had made critical and unnecessary concessions under the treaty, inasmuch as a Russia in decline was in no position to bargain. The debate centered on various points.

First, supporters and critics argued over whether the treaty restricted the U.S. pursuit of a missile defense. The key text in this regard is found among a list of principles in the treaty's preamble: "Recognizing the existence of the interrelationship between strategic offensive arms and strategic defensive arms, that this interrelationship will become more important as strategic nuclear arms are reduced, and that current strategic defensive arms do not undermine the viability and effectiveness of the strategic offensive arms of the Parties." For critics, the statement appeared in the treaty for some reason. Indeed, the Russians had stated (unilaterally) when signing the treaty that the threat to Russia from a U.S. missile defense could provoke Russia's treaty withdrawal (Woolf 2011: 16). Not only had Russia insisted on the language—as a compromise, when the United States refused to accept explicit restrictions—but it had stated its view that the relevant portions of the treaty were "binding" on the parties.[44] At the very least, by acknowledging that nuclear defenses impinge on offenses, the United States implicitly legitimized Russian claims that U.S. missile defense plans must defer to Russia's offensive concerns. Put more strongly, it "handed the Russian government the political tool they have sought for so long to bind our future decisions and actions."[45] Accountability to Russia could prevent these defenses from realizing their potential, to protect the United States even from a small-scale ballistic missile attack, and could leave the United States hopelessly dependent on discredited, outmoded AD principles. Treaty supporters disagreed. In their view, the text simply stated the obvious. It articulated the inherently uncontroversial assumption—long behind the U.S. approach to nuclear arms control, deterrence, and preparedness—that a country's defense helps the country's offense by impairing the adversary's offense. If this was not true, why would the United States want to build a missile defense? In the words of Secretary of State Clinton, the preamble text was not a "constraint" on the United States; it was "simply a statement of fact." Its innocuousness was surely indicated by the absence of articles in the treaty expressly limiting a U.S. missile defense (except for a restriction on placing missile interceptors in existing land-based missile silos) and past Russian deference to U.S. missile-defense plans, as indicated by Russia's continued adherence to the START Treaty after the United States had withdrawn from the ABM Treaty (U.S. Senate 2010: 49). For that matter, treaty supporters could have argued that hawks had shifted the terms of debate by insisting, now, that *the United States* was bound by implicit constraints within the treaty. In the Cold War era, hawks had sought to write binding language into treaties and to strengthen the status of statements attached to them fearing that only ironclad language would legally constrain the *Soviet Union*.[46]

Second, treaty supporters and critics disagreed over the costs to U.S. security, under the treaty, of counting conventionally armed ICBMs and SLBMs against a party's allowable strategic total. For critics, the United States had once again surrendered its critical prerogatives—here, in conventional prompt global strike systems. They maintained that these systems could greatly contribute to U.S. security inasmuch as speed of delivery—to capitalize on available intelligence information—was essential to defeat elusive terrorist groups and mercurial rogue-state opponents. Indeed, given the relatively small size of rogue-state arsenals, a conventionally armed ballistic missile might give the United States the capability to preempt or prevent a rogue-state nuclear strike without resort to nuclear force. But treaty supporters were generally unconvinced that the United States had conceded a critical option under the treaty. They noted that the United States retained the right to deploy these systems—administration officials had successfully fought an outright ban on conventionally armed ballistic missiles (Woolf 2011: 18)—and would do so, regardless, only in small numbers: these weapons would be "so expensive as to warrant use only against the highest priority time-sensitive targets" (U.S. Senate 2010: 53). Indeed, some supporters viewed restrictions on these missiles as quite appropriate: the advantages of these weapons—a hypothetical capability to hit high-valued targets anywhere in the world within an hour—were small given their liabilities. These included the danger that Russia (or another nuclear power) could mistake a U.S. conventional ICBM strike on a third party for a nuclear strike on Russia and the challenges of distinguishing conventional and nuclear versions of the systems in treaty compliance verification (U.S. Senate 2010: 52–53).

Third, treaty supporters and critics disagreed over the relative value, under the treaty, of focusing exclusively on strategic nuclear weapons. Critics asserted that the treaty did not account for the very real threat that Russian tactical nuclear weapons—numbering in the many thousands and positioned proximate to their "strategic" targets—posed to U.S. interests. In their view, the threat from tactical nuclear weapons had only increased with reductions in the size of the U.S. strategic nuclear arsenal, growing Russian dependence on these (comparatively inexpensive) weapons as conventional-force substitutes (U.S. Senate 2010: 58), and breakdowns in Russian security that could provoke their unauthorized or accidental use or spread to third parties. Treaty supporters focused, in turn, on the merits of limiting strategic nuclear weapons, not the disadvantages of focusing singularly on strategic nuclear weapons. Thus, they maintained that some controls over nuclear arms are better than none, that controlling tactical nuclear weapons is a formidable issue given their small size and mobility and value to the United States (for supporting its NATO commitment), that strategic nuclear agreements could further the case and boost momentum for other agreements that might limit tactical weapons, and therefore that the worth of agreements is measured, as well, by their favorable impact on the political environment. To quote Senator John Kerry, "During the worst years of confrontation, we still built up a series of treaties and arms agreements and various other agreements to try to tamp down the potential for hostility."[47] Supporters argued further that the control of *strategic* nuclear arms was essential given their potency (that is, speed of delivery and awesome destructiveness) when compared to many (Russian) tactical nuclear weapons—mines, artillery shells, and so on—that were range-impaired or intended for defense and did not directly threaten Europe (Woolf 2011: 30). Treaty supporters had reason, in fact, to argue that hawkish critics had once again changed the principles of discourse by challenging a war-fighting orthodoxy. These critics had always maintained that the Soviet Union, with its superior strategic counterforce capability, could coerce concessions or secure wartime gains from the United States and therefore that strategic nuclear weapons trumped all others. With the downsized Russian force and the smaller Russian urban-industrial target set, the United States was now arguably in a stronger strategic position relative to Russia than the Soviets had been relative to the United States in the "window-of-vulnerability" period. Why, then, had tactical weapons suddenly achieved primacy in critical analyses?

Fourth, supporters and critics disagreed over whether the treaty constrained the United States in unobvious ways. Indeed, the dispute had critics revisiting the "great debate" over the Reagan administration's "broad interpretation" of the ABM Treaty by doubting the overall value of executive branch interpretations of treaty text. The Reagan administration had partly grounded its interpretation in its own view of the negotiating record: from its perspective, the "actual" meaning of the text—as the administration divined it—trumped executive branch interpretations and Senate understandings of the text at the time the treaty was ratified. For critics, then, the "meaning" of treaty provisions—belatedly revealed—could impose nefarious constraints on the United States. That the administration refused to release the unabridged negotiating record only fueled suspicions that the treaty text had hidden meanings and that the administration was being deliberately deceptive. For treaty supporters, however, the negotiating "record" was a misnomer. What critics took for a record was a compilation of ambiguous and incomplete documents, was based on statements and communications that were made for various political purposes, was not a binding product of U.S.-Russian agreement, and was *always* subject to interpretation. Rather than settle debate, the record would thus provoke endless debate and counterproductive efforts to renegotiate the treaty. Supporters argued, in consequence, that the "shared understanding" between the executive branch and the Senate during ratification is the only interpretation that is relevant for congressional deliberations. Should that interpretation raise Russian objections, the appropriate recourse was resolution through amendment, discussion in the treaty's consultative body, and—in the worst case—a U.S. treaty withdrawal.[48]

Finally, supporters and critics disagreed over the wisdom of reducing arms when nuclear arsenals—outside of Russia—continued to grow. For many critics, the poor state of the Russian economy *was* the basis of arms control, as it was optimally practiced: the Russian military was collapsing under its own weight, and the United States could now scale and configure its military to address emerging threats and prepare for unforseen challenges. Their fear was that U.S.-Russian arms control would (now or eventually) deprive the United States of vital tools that serve U.S. national security interests. But for proponents the issue was simpler: was supporting *this* treaty in the U.S. interest? For them, the answer was obviously yes. Indeed, many supporters hoped that U.S.-Russian cooperation on arms control would lead other countries to reduce their arsenals. That could inspire further U.S. and Russian reductions and increase U.S.-Russian cooperation to address shared security concerns (U.S. Senate 2010: 8).

In sum, advocates on both sides of the debate revealed their differing preoccupations. Doves focused on force reductions; hawks focused on the allegedly disturbing number and severity of U.S. concessions (affecting U.S. conventional options, missile defense, adversary target coverage, and the like)—indeed, that the United States had made any concessions at all. Missing from the debate was a clear sense of the requisites of U.S. security and the circumstances under which more or less nuclear capability was warranted.

TRUST AND VERIFICATION

The New START Treaty's verification provisions deviated from prior practice in various respects. First, New START required that the parties cooperate more actively to establish that they are complying with the treaty. In consequence, the parties need not monitor telemetry to determine the number of warheads that were released in space from a missile's warhead bus, count all missiles of a type as carrying the maximum number of warheads for which a missile of that type had been tested, and so forth. Instead, the parties could count actual warheads on specific weapons, selected with sampling techniques that were meant to increase accountability. Under the treaty, the inspected party would declare the actual numbers of warheads on each missile at an inspected site; the inspecting party would then choose a missile randomly to inspect its warheads or three heavy bombers to inspect their actual numbers of weapons.[49] Presumably, the inspected country had an incentive to declare accurate numbers so as to avoid being caught cheating. Second, by reason of efficiency, the New START Treaty loosened the compliance requirements for eliminating strategic nuclear systems or converting them to non-nuclear uses. New START permitted the parties to eliminate launchers and bombers using less destructive means and to eliminate and convert weapon systems employing new methods after demonstrating them to the other party (Woolf 2011: 7–9). Third, the treaty required the compilation of a comprehensive database containing information about the characteristics, numbers, and locations of weapons. The data were to be supplemented through regular updates and notifications when changes occurred (for instance, when weapons were moved) and were subject to validation through direct inspection at designated sites (deployment bases, maintenance facilities, and so forth).

Not surprisingly, the change in practices provoked debate. Where treaty supporters saw advantages in efficiency and limited redundancy in moving away from the START procedures, treaty critics saw openings under New START that would allow—indeed, tempt—the Russians to cheat.

Critics claimed that the Russians had repeatedly engaged in practices that violated the letter of the START Treaty—encrypting telemetry, impeding onsite U.S. inspections—and had not proven any more trustworthy than their Soviet-era counterparts were. In the minority view of the Senate Foreign Relations Committee, "Russia repeatedly violated START I all the way to its expiration in December 2009" (U.S. Senate 2010: 116). Further laxity in verification procedures, then, would only encourage Russian perfidy. So critics challenged the new verification procedures. They argued that the administration was wrong to suggest that the new measures were effectively comparable to those under START, when openings had now been created for the Russians to cheat. Critics insisted that direct inspections under New START were a poor substitute for preexisting practice and, in particular, that maintaining the prohibitions on telemetry encryption was vital for ensuring that the Russians would not test new systems—with greater warhead capacities—nor equip their systems with undeclared warheads. Although the treaty allowed for eighteen direct inspections a year among given sites, critics maintained that the inspection procedures were far too susceptible to Russian mischief. Only ten inspections a year would be conducted at missile sites (or bomber bases), and then only one missile could be selected by the United States for inspection per site—to check figures that the Russians had provided for a site *after* learning that it was to be inspected. The fear then was that the Russians could falsify figures for uninspected sites (eased by reduced limits on mobile-missile basing) and play the (presumably favorable) odds of being caught in a lie when only a single missile was to be inspected.[50] For critics, the facts of the matter were straightforward: any restraint that the Russians had shown in the past was attributable to sound verification practices that deterred Russian violations. To abandon redundant checks and common verification practices (for instance, in eliminating weapon systems) was now asking for trouble. Diehard critics even questioned whether the United States had abandoned verification altogether under the treaty. Paula DeSutter, the assistant secretary of state for verification, compliance, and implementation for most of the George W. Bush administration, insisted that the inspection regime under New START was sufficiently lax that the United States would find it difficult—maybe impossible—to argue that the Russians *had* violated the treaty. In her words, "There will be very few violations because we have made it virtually impossible for the United States to collect the type of information and weigh it against a solid treaty with solid language that would permit us to say they are cheating" (DeSutter 2010).

In response, supporters claimed that critics had overstated the severity of alleged Russian violations of the START Treaty: Russian noncompliance issues focused exclusively on matters of weapon conversion and elimination, not on illicit Russian weapons in storage or production (U.S. Senate 2010: 30). These issues arose in large part because of the complexity and cost of the procedures required by the START Treaty and could be attributed, then, to confusion and disagreement over the rules and Russian efforts to cut corners for economic reasons. Not only did these violations not betray systematic Russian deceit for strategic gain, they were even likely to decline under New START.

In part, this was because for the Russians, honesty was the best policy. This was true because (1) the costs to the Russians of being caught in a lie, undermining a treaty that critics themselves claimed advantaged the Russians, were prohibitive; and (2) illicit gains would be militarily significant only with widespread cheating, which was hard to hide. Indeed, supporters argued that Russia was an unlikely candidate for cheating if the arguments of critics held true. Claims that Russia was trying to bind the United States through agreement because Russia could not afford to compete (U.S. Senate 2010: 23) and that the Russian threat could now be sidestepped to focus on other, graver threats implicitly conceded that stringent monitoring was no longer required to ensure Russian treaty adherence.

Supporters argued, further, that the United States was advantaged by new material realities: the Russian capability to cheat had actually diminished over the years, while the U.S. capability to catch cheating had increased. Whereas the Russian capability to produce missiles, submarines, and bombers had been severely hurt by the deteriorating Russian economy and redirection of resources away from the Russian military, the U.S. capability to monitor Russian military activity had improved. The improvement resulted from the considerable experience and knowledge that were acquired by the United States from monitoring Russian production, procedures, and START compliance (U.S. Senate 2010: 6) and the growing transparency of the Russian political system. The combination of declining Russian military potential and increasing U.S. detection capabilities meant that the probability of a Russian treaty violation escaping detection was considerably smaller now than in the past.

Supporters bolstered their case by arguing that New START verification procedures were up to their task—that the changes in verification procedures under

New START, for various reasons, amounted to a streamlining of inefficient and counterproductive START practices.[51] First, the prior practices were unnecessarily redundant: the parties did not need to monitor telemetry when they could actually count the number of warheads on a missile. Second, they were unjustifiably cumbersome and expensive: for instance, portal and perimeter monitoring of Russian missile assembly plants, under the START Treaty, involved a large investment of time, resources, and labor when considering the sluggish pace at which Russian missiles were actually produced and assembled. High costs and burdensome procedures were especially problematic in weapons elimination and conversion. In the view of U.S. treaty negotiators, the parties could devise simpler and less costly methods for eliminating and converting weapons when left to their own devices. Third, the practices were simply outmoded inasmuch as U.S. knowledge of Russian weapons had improved, weapons were uniquely identified, Russian inspection sites had declined in number, and verification requirements were lower under New START than under prior treaties. Whereas telemetry monitoring was necessary, for example, to verify Russian compliance on missile dimensions, the lack of restrictions on new types of missiles under New START had relieved the parties of that monitoring burden. Fourth, the preexisting procedures actually exacerbated the military threat to the United States. Supporters noted that the ostensible "gold standard"—telemetry monitoring—of compliance verification had a very significant downside. It fed the warhead inflation (and thus the instability threat) that treaty critics claimed to fear. It did so, essentially, by creating a self-fulfilling prophecy: the Russians were compelled to arm missiles to their hypothetical warhead capacity to realize the full "benefits" under the treaty on the assumption that the United States would do the same.

Whether or not New START represented a step backward in verification, supporters challenged the critics' standard of comparison. Inasmuch as the START procedures were off the table, supporters maintained that the verification measures in New START should not be compared to START measures but instead should be evaluated in light of the absence of *any* such measures that the failure to ratify New START Treaty would bring. Supporters noted further that the United States retained recourse outside the parameters of the treaty and was well positioned to respond to Russian behavior in kind. Whereas critics argued that warhead downloading had created an especially big challenge for verifying treaty compliance because the Russians could "easily" upload warheads to those same missiles, supporters maintained that the treaty stood up well against the Reagan-era standard of "effective verification," given the high probability of U.S. detection and the U.S. relative capability to upload warheads (on land and at sea) to outpace the illegal Russian activity (U.S. Senate 2010: 24). Other potential cheating scenarios suffered similarly under scrutiny. Whereas critics argued that the Russians could gather their nondeployed missiles to reload mobile missile launchers in a nuclear conflict, proponents noted that a significant Russian reload capability was implausible given the barriers to Russian missile production (U.S. Senate 2010: 29), the absence of necessary training and exercises for that contingency, and the challenges of reloading launchers in a nuclear conflict. For the Russians, then, the only viable means to compete with the United States (surreptitiously or otherwise) was through a highly visible and resource-intensive—and, therefore, highly unlikely—effort to build additional missiles and launchers.

Certainly, treaty critics offered some support for their essential argument, summarized in the minority view of the Senate Foreign Relations Committee: "The treaty effectively requires unilateral U.S. reductions and its limitations are so porous and permissive that it does not place effective ceilings on the slowly emerging comprehensive Russian strategic modernization program" (U.S. Senate 2010: 120). But treaty critics were ultimately hobbled by their inconsistent and deficient logic. This was apparent when critics argued (1) that the Russians needed the treaty more than the United States did but supposed that the Russians would endanger the treaty by seeking illicit gains; (2) that the United States had negotiated away critical options to the Russians, though they were no longer a threat, yet protested that the United States had left itself dangerously vulnerable to potential Russian cheating; (3) that the Russians were advantaged if cheating at the margins of the treaty when the United States was actually well prepared to respond; and (4) that the treaty's verification provisions were lax in comparison to procedures under START, when the alternative to New START was not a return to START but no cooperative verification measures at all. The most generous interpretation for these logical failings is that skeptics had thrown up a barrage of criticism in the hopes that some portion of it might stick.

The Power of Belief in U.S.-Russian Arms Control of the Post–Cold War Period

The Cold War came unexpectedly to an end, but the new era also brought its share of somewhat surprising developments in the halting and diverging course of arms control. Appreciating these post–Cold War developments requires an acknowledgment of (1) prevailing U.S. beliefs about Russian goals; (2) the intragovernmental politics that gave prominence to some beliefs over others; and (3) assumptions about U.S. relative nuclear capabilities.

Russian Intent

The U.S. Defense Department was still trumpeting likely improvements in Soviet military capabilities in the 1989 issue of *Soviet Military Power,* an official publication on the subject. In it, Secretary of Defense Richard Cheney wrote of the "extraordinary momentum" of Soviet strategic force modernization and conceded only that the Soviets had changed "strategy and tactics for achieving its national goals." He argued that despite the Soviet "declaration of benign intentions toward the Western democracies, Soviet military capabilities continued to constitute a major threat to our society." But the remarkable turnabout in long-held Soviet positions under President Gorbachev eventually grabbed the attention of even U.S. hard-liners. Cheney himself came to acknowledge momentous changes that were hard to reconcile with a U.S. Cold War–era perspective. By 1991, the Cheney-led Defense Department had replaced *Soviet Military Power* with *Military Forces in Transition* amid doubts that future issues were forthcoming. By 1992, when selling the START I Treaty to the U.S. Congress, Cheney heralded the seismic shifts in U.S.-Russian relations, first under Gorbachev and then under Yeltsin. The changing sentiments were expressed throughout the U.S. government. U.S. intelligence agencies downplayed the threat from the former Soviet republics, noting severe cutbacks in their military spending for research and procurement. The director of the Defense Intelligence Agency—renowned for its deeply pessimistic view of Soviet intentions and capabilities—testified that the military capabilities of Russia and other former Soviet republics were "in profound decline" and that there was "virtually no likelihood" that they would attack the United States or its allies.[52] The tone of official assessments changed accordingly. Whereas "Red Russia" was consistently the subject of questions and testimony in Senate hearings on the Limited Test Ban Treaty, "Democratic Russia" emerged as the (presumably more trustworthy) U.S. negotiating partner in Secretary of State James Baker's START I testimony.

U.S. officials appreciated the significance of Russia's START I Treaty concessions, especially on intrusive verification. In the language of international politics theory, the Russians had sent a "costly signal" that they would not cheat. They did this by agreeing to mechanisms that arguably made cheating cost-prohibitive given the subterfuge that was required to realize even small gains in nuclear capability without incurring any real strategic benefits. For that matter, U.S. policymakers believed that START I offered insurance against Russian recidivism by creating binding legal commitments that would constrain successor governments, regardless of their intentions. Still, U.S. policymakers were far more optimistic about Russian intentions than was warranted, based arguably on a sober (realist) analysis of Russian capabilities. U.S. retaliatory capabilities aside, Russia maintained a formidable nuclear force that could destroy much of the U.S. civilian and military infrastructure, including the U.S. land-based missile force in a first strike. Even the deep cuts that were required under the START II Treaty would have left the Russians—over the next decade—with a large interim force that included MIRVed missiles. Casting aside their Cold War focus on threatening Soviet hardware, hawks became increasingly uninterested in Russian disarmament—and the de-MIRVing of Russian land-based missiles—once Soviet leadership had ended. The bigger fear for hawks was that bilateral arms control would restrict U.S. unilateral options.

This is not to say that U.S. policymakers sought to understand how U.S. policies might affect Russian objectives. True, hawks and doves contested the irreconcilability of U.S.-Russian policy preferences. Whereas hawks sometimes argued that Cold War rules still applied—that Russia sought a relative nuclear advantage over the United States (in part by tying U.S. hands through agreements)—doves typically argued that a sympathetic U.S. response to Russian concerns could promote U.S.-Russian cooperation. But once the Soviet Union faded from view, U.S. policymakers turned their attention to other priorities. They put little emphasis, in consequence, on how U.S. national security policies might create conflicts with democratic Russia and complicate the forging and ratification of arms control treaties. Although U.S. policymakers feared, for example, that regressive forces would seize power in Russia and derail reforms, they showed little concern for the potentially corrosive effects of U.S.-Russian clashes on various issues—or U.S. indifference to Russia, once it was no longer deemed a threat. Thus, over strong Russian objections, the Clinton administration pursued NATO expansion into Eastern Europe (see Goldgeier 1999), and the Bush and Obama administrations sought to incorporate those same countries into U.S. missile defense schemes.

Hawks refocused on Russian intent as the Obama administration sought to mend the deteriorating U.S.-Russian relationship. But hawks often relied on two conflicting assumptions when thinking about Russian goals. First, hawks assumed that these goals were fairly benign because they stemmed from Russia's fundamental weakness. In other words, they assumed that Russian obstinance and resistance stemmed from Russia's lost stature and inability to influence U.S. policies (as on missile defense), not dissatisfaction with the actual substance of that policy or the specifics that Russian leaders cited to make their case. In this view, the Russians were simply trying to drag the U.S. military into the hole that Russia had dug with its inefficient, unresponsive, and outmoded economy. Second, hawks assumed that the Russians were pushing, by all available means, to recover their past glory. Accordingly, hawkish critics assailed the New START Treaty for its openings to Russian cheating. As expressed in the minority report of the Senate Committee on Foreign Relations, "Assuming Russian treaty compliance violates the historical record, and it ignores the very real evidence of renewed Russian nuclear threats to U.S. allies and friends" (U.S. Senate 2010: 111). From this perspective, Russia was little more than the Soviet Union with a friendly face. Indeed, the new Russia was not obviously weaker than its Soviet incarnation: hawkish dissenters made much of Russian tactical nuclear superiority, military modernization efforts, and opportunities to secure military advantages by cheating on the treaty.

Treaty supporters were also hurt by contradictory logic. Although they generally voiced the fairly charitable view that the United States and Russia had common interests, they sometimes attributed Russian cooperativeness to Russian weakness. It is one thing to argue that the Russians will not cheat because they value cooperation; it is quite another to say that the Russians will not cheat because they cannot do so advantageously and are afraid of getting caught.

The Politics of Arms Control

The end of the Cold War did not bridge the divide between arms control hawks and doves: the ratification debate over successive arms control treaties occurred largely along party lines. But the disagreements lacked the sharp edges of the Cold War–era debates, suggesting perhaps that the participants were *trying* to find fault with the treaties. For Democrats, a concern was that Republican-negotiated treaties did not go far enough in their cuts, assurances, and restrictions; for Republicans, a concern was that Democrat-negotiated treaties were a slippery slope of implicit political commitments. These would create political momentum that would cause the United States to give away more than it should.

Erstwhile foes came together to support the START treaties, given hawkish concerns that the arms control process would cease before it produced far-reaching reductions and changes in Russia's force structure. In the end, these fears were realized. As the ratification of the START II Treaty was delayed (to obtain adherence from former Soviet republics), the Republicans gained control of the U.S. Senate. A conservative Republican, Jesse Helms, became chairman of the Senate Foreign Relations Committee with the power to delay or quash treaty ratification. He employed that power, in committee, to bottle up the START II

Treaty (and the Chemical Weapons Treaty) to leverage a reorganization of the State Department.[53] The Clinton administration did record a final victory of sorts. The START II Treaty was approved by committee in December 1995, whereupon it was endorsed by the U.S. Senate in January of the following year. But it was presented in 1995 for ratification to a (now more conservative) Russian Parliament. Its hard-line members maintained that Russia had conceded too much under prior treaties—that Russia had negotiated from weakness and received too little in return from the United States in arms control and other security matters.[54] The Russian legislature did not approve the treaty until 2000, whereupon it conditioned its ratification on the U.S. ratification of various agreements that had been negotiated with the Clinton administration, including modifications and clarifications of the ABM Treaty (Woolf 2001: 2). The Clinton administration had pressed the Russians to renegotiate that treaty to permit a U.S. missile defense (by the middle of the following decade) with the capability to deflect a (relatively small) North Korean or Iranian ballistic missile attack on all fifty states.[55] The Russians had been loath, however, to weaken the treaty, fearing that the initial U.S. investment was a down payment on a system that could eventually neutralize the Russian offensive nuclear force. Although Russia's President Yeltsin surprisingly relented to the U.S. deployment of six interceptor systems as "theater" missile defenses (the basis of the 1997 agreements), the U.S. Senate was unwilling, in turn, to accept conditions that would affect U.S. missile defense plans or capabilities.[56] Indeed, Senate Republican leaders had voiced their concern that Clinton was too anxious to make a strategic arms deal and would compromise missile defense by working within negotiated parameters.[57] Their relations with Clinton were polarized further by the resounding Senate rejection of the Comprehensive Test Ban Treaty (signed by Clinton in 1996 and sent to the Senate in September 1997) and, of course, by Clinton's Senate impeachment trial (in early 1999).[58] The resulting standoff helped doom the U.S. ratification of the START II Treaty and squeezed an administration that found itself battling resistance from within as well. Although the Pentagon believed that it could still accomplish its nuclear targeting goals under the START II ceilings, it feared that negotiating additional offensive arms cuts, as the administration proposed (possibly in a package that included ABM Treaty amendments), would dangerously deplete U.S. nuclear target coverage capabilities. The Pentagon could live comfortably with the three-thousand-plus warheads that were permitted under START II; it doubted seriously that it could do its job with two thousand warheads. It worried, too, that acquiescing to further reductions would lead to ever more onerous cuts.[59]

The earlier demise of the START II Treaty did not hurt the case for ratification of the Moscow Treaty in the George W. Bush administration. In pushing its treaty, the administration enjoyed strong Republican support for having stepped away from the ABM Treaty and for having tied U.S. force levels to U.S. security needs; it built on that support by assuaging Democratic concerns about the administration's lack of commitment to arms control by signing a treaty that formally reduced U.S. and Russian nuclear deployments. Consequently, the SORT Treaty eventually received a strong endorsement, in the form of a unanimous vote, from the U.S. Senate. The treaty did not squelch debate, as Democrats harped on the deficiencies of the treaty. The Democrats held the treaty from a Senate vote, then, out of concern for its lax verification provisions, lack of specificity on the timing of reductions, and limited scope (for instance, it failed to address issues of nuclear safety and proliferation). Senate approval was aided, in consequence, by the accompanying passage of various nonbinding declarations.[60]

The Obama administration engaged in vigorous internal debate over how much the United States should defer to the policies of the past. Ultimately, it departed incrementally from the Bush administration's positions on critical issues such as U.S. missile defense and reliance on nuclear weapons.[61] Yet the administration faced an uphill Senate battle over the New START Treaty. Republicans sought to postpone a vote until after the new Senate, with its extra Republican votes, took office in January 2011; to derail the treaty with amendments (including one rejecting the preamble's link between offenses and defenses); and to tie treaty votes to unrelated bills.[62] In the politicized atmosphere, two Republicans who had supported the treaty in committee voted against sending the treaty to a floor vote.[63] In the end, the fate of the treaty apparently hinged on Obama's concession to kick in tens of billions of dollars (over ten years) to modernize and sustain the U.S. nuclear infrastructure (national weapons laboratories and the like). That still did not allay concerns that the administration was insufficiently committed to a robust U.S. nuclear force posture.[64] Indeed, the treaty was opposed by various Republican presidential contenders and the two top Senate Republicans, though it was endorsed by high-profile moderate Republicans including President George H. W. Bush, Henry Kissinger, James Baker, George Shultz, Colin Powell, and Condoleezza Rice.[65]

Assessing, Safeguarding, and Improving U.S. Relative Capabilities

Ironically, the vastly improved post–Cold War atmosphere for U.S.-Russian arms control that facilitated the forging of treaties impugned their necessity and wisdom. Hawks refused to concede, through negotiations, the preponderance that the United States had "won" through competition. In their view, the United States—in confronting new global threats—would only weaken itself through compromise. Even Russia's continued possession of MIRVed, land-based missiles was acceptable now, if the United States could, in turn, retain its nuclear weapons and freedom of action. Accordingly, a hallmark of Bush administration arms control efforts was the renunciation of prior treaties (the ABM Treaty), the negotiation of less stringent ones (SORT), the reduced thresholds for treaty withdrawal, and the exclusion of U.S. weapon levels from the give-and-take of negotiations. The 2002 Moscow Agreement essentially ratified the deployment decisions that U.S. policymakers had made unilaterally. Indeed, many U.S. policymakers would challenge the Obama administration for having conceded so much to get a deal.

The post–Cold War nuclear debate clearly turned on assumptions about Russian goals. There is no other credible explanation for why doves and hawks alike looked to a world of "lesser" rogue-state nuclear threats rather than negotiate an agreement, first and foremost, that would ameliorate the Russian nuclear threat. How else to explain that the U.S. arms control debate centered less on whether the U.S. nuclear force was appropriately scaled and configured to withstand a Russian assault and more on whether U.S. force modernization was sufficiently funded and U.S. options and technologies (conventionally armed ballistic missiles, missile defenses, and so forth) were excessively constrained through agreement? Indeed, under Obama, two foreign policy officials in the prior administration went on record supporting a U.S. withdrawal from the INF Treaty out of concern that it undercut the U.S. capability to respond to a ground-launched intermediate-range nuclear threat, in kind, from the likes of North Korea and Iran.[66] The Russian threat abated not because Russia surrendered MIRVed, land-based missiles but because the Soviet Union ceased to exist, and those same nuclear weapons were now under the control of Russian leaders who presumably possessed benign objectives.

Still, hawkish doubts about Russia's transformation lingered. In consequence, many hawks continued to warn of Russia's nuclear ambitions. Yet neither U.S. policymakers nor their critics devoted the necessary time and effort to translate those goals into U.S. capability requirements. U.S. policymakers through the Clinton administration continued to hold U.S.-Russian arms control agreements to some unwieldy combination of (Cold War–era) Assured Destruction and war-fighting principles. By the George W. Bush administration, they had dispensed almost entirely with doctrinal justifications. By then, U.S. policymakers simply scaled U.S. forces to cover a global range of targets to create U.S. nuclear options for various contingencies. U.S. force requirements bent to considerations of target coverage and attack timing more than to changing Russian deployment levels or specific assumptions about how or why a strike against U.S. interests would occur. Hawkish critics fared no better in establishing U.S. strategic nuclear requirements. Their position amounted essentially to opposition to change.

So, what does this say, again, about the realist security dilemma? More specifically, what can be said now of the validity of the propositions on strength and verification that stem from that dilemma?

Without question, U.S. policymakers sought—unilaterally—to maintain U.S. strength relative to Russia as its economic hardships and political changes forced a change in budgetary priorities. They scaled U.S. forces for efficiency and target coverage and opposed far-reaching cuts that would weaken the U.S. relative nuclear position. But looks are deceptive. From a realist perspective, it is problematic that U.S. policymakers failed to respond predictably to changing Russian relative (or absolute) capabilities. Alterations in the U.S.-Russian nuclear balance cannot account for the following facts: (1) a major arms control treaty (START I)—heralded as necessary for the passage of a much-awaited, far-reaching treaty (START II) on de-MIRVing—remained the centerpiece of arms control in the years to follow; (2) a hawkish U.S. administration (under George W. Bush) rejected the constraints of arms control and thereby accepted a robust Russian strategic force that included MIRVed Soviet heavy missiles (the much-heralded scourge of the Cold War period); and (3) the U.S. nuclear arsenal appeared impervious to reductions beyond an established floor level of capability. Explaining these developments requires insights into prevailing U.S. thinking—its substance and logical deficiencies—about Russian intentions, the primacy of the Russian security threat, and the adequacy of U.S. capabilities against this and other threats.

Indeed, these same policymakers increasingly depended on trust when evaluating Russian compliance with the terms of arms control treaties. The importance of trust was belied, of course, by the intrusive measures for verification that the parties came to accept (and that treaty critics came to expect) in the START treaties, the increased transparency of the Russian political system that would help the United States detect shifts in Russian nuclear policies, and the arguably limited advantage that the Russians, with their downsized force, could obtain through cheating. Still, the Russians could have cheated—for instance, by manufacturing and storing mobile missiles—to obtain an illicit nuclear advantage. These illicit benefits might well have derailed ratification efforts in earlier decades.

In the final analysis, the nuclear debate of the post–Cold War period was much like its Cold War–era counterpart. Doves made a case for modest strategic force reductions, while hawks focused narrowly on what the United States was conceding and what the Russians were retaining, under the treaty. True, the now-smaller U.S. arsenal—and the potential emergence of new nuclear competitors—had reduced the "slack" in U.S. strategic nuclear forces for covering the full range of potential nonconventional threats. So U.S. policymakers had reason to worry that the United States might lose its margin of advantage over potential competitors. But U.S. policymakers had not established that U.S. force levels had reached the point at which further reductions would endanger U.S. security. After all, the United States maintained an advantage over new post–Cold War competitors that dwarfed any advantage that the United States or the Soviet Union held over the other in the Cold War period. Indeed, the United States could unleash the full wrath of the U.S. force, if necessary, on a challenger that lacked a first-strike capability and would retain the capability to build up the force, by redeploying weapons, if global circumstances were someday to change.

CHAPTER SIX

The United States and Strategic Nuclear Arms Control

Assessing Intentions, Constraining Capabilities

Arms control hawks and doves battled across a central policy fault line. The stakes could not appear higher given the subjects of dispute: the wisdom and likely outcome of negotiating with Russia and the catalysts, probability, and consequences of a U.S.-Russian nuclear exchange. But hawks and doves had more in common than they thought. Across the ideological spectrum, advocates placed far too much emphasis on balances, gaps, asymmetries, openings, windows, and standards of destruction that had no meaning apart from Russian goals. In turn, they put far too little effort into assessing those goals and their various policy implications.

Hawks versus Doves: The Battle over Russian Intentions

The nuclear strategies that informed U.S. arms control positions in the Cold War period drew fundamentally from hawkish or dovish assumptions or some composite of the two. Hawks who tended toward a hard war-fighting posture shared a belief that the Soviets would pursue their interests, at the expense of the United States, despite the great risks and costs; doves who embraced AD doctrine maintained that the United States and the Soviet Union shared an aversion to nuclear war and would avoid a conflict that could spiral out of control. Positioned somewhere in the middle were those who looked for options between surrender and the suicidal consequences of an all-out nuclear war. They expected nuclear deterrence to hold but wanted breathing space, if they were wrong, in the hope that the Soviets might reconsider their course. In their war-fighting scenarios, U.S. leaders would act uncompromisingly in defense of U.S. interests and Soviet leaders would have to concede ground: confronted with strong U.S. resolve—a U.S. willingness to pay the supreme price in a nuclear conflict—the Soviets would presumably seek a way out.

To a man, U.S. presidents of the Cold War period exhibited some mix of hawkish and dovish impulses. Truman and Eisenhower—at the height of Cold War tension—were no exception. They insisted that the Soviet Union would seek gains at U.S. expense and that arms control treaties had to be designed carefully, then, to safeguard U.S. interests. Truman—under his proposal for international control of atomic energy—would have relaxed the U.S. hold on nuclear weapons and technology only with confidence that other states could not seize on U.S. de-nuclearization to obtain a nuclear advantage. In turn, Eisenhower appeared unconvinced, initially, that meaningful arms control with the Soviet Union was possible and feigned interest in negotiations to win over global opinion. He consistently proposed terms that assumed the worst Soviet motives and favored the United States at Soviet expense. Consequently, the proposals required exceptional measures to ensure Soviet treaty compliance (the test ban proposals), could leave the United States in a preponderant position if accepted by the Soviet Union (Atoms for Peace), or would push the Soviet Union's political transformation to obtain greater openness and transparency (Open Skies). Yet both administrations showed some optimism about Soviet intent: at times they took the arms control negotiations quite seriously, believed that their proposals served both U.S. and Soviet interests, and stuck with the negotiations despite stalemate and recurring setbacks.

The Kennedy administration tilted a bit more toward the dovish position, over hawkish resistance. Hawks in Congress remained deeply skeptical of Soviet reasons for signing the Limited Test Ban Treaty. They argued that the Soviets, as always, would cheat and then warned of the U.S. vulnerability to treaty loopholes and openings that the Soviets had designed into the treaty. They insisted more generally that any and all Soviet actions stemmed from a master plan to gain global advantage and refused to assess Soviet behavior in light of similar—even provocative—U.S. actions. Although the Kennedy administration harbored some distrust for the Soviet Union and rejected the Soviet terms for a comprehensive test ban agreement for that reason, it depicted Soviet motives generously when supporting the test ban treaty. In its stated view, the Soviets had an interest in preventing environmental contamination, controlling the spread of nuclear weapons, and impeding a profligate arms race that could lead to war.

The debate between hawks and doves survived the 1960s. Indeed, it increased in intensity, with concerns that the United States had surrendered too much to the Soviets in the SALT negotiations of the early 1970s, and later erupted with a vengeance in the SALT II Treaty ratification debate of the late 1970s. For hawks, the SALT II Treaty—negotiated despite the U.S. Senate's insistence on "equality" as the basis of agreement—was a monument to Soviet malevolence, truculence, and perfidy, not to mention U.S. timidity. In their view, the treaty proved beyond a doubt that the Soviets sought nuclear superiority, planned to acquire it in all ways possible to use for military and political advantage, and now recognized that the United States would not stand in their way. To strengthen their case, hawks recited the litany of ways that the Soviets could—and most certainly would—violate the treaty and pointed to nefarious Soviet activities in the developing world that proved that the Soviets were a threat. These arguments were given urgency by hawkish warnings of dire consequences once the so-called window of vulnerability opened in the early 1980s. Of course, doves rendered a very different verdict. In their view, the SALT treaties were a first step toward reversing the arms race, stabilizing the U.S.-Soviet nuclear relationship, and building trust between the two parties. By their account, both the United States and the Soviet Union had conceded some prerogatives under the treaties to realize the greater benefits of cooperation. But the dovish viewpoint received only a lukewarm endorsement from Carter administration officials when they tried to sell the SALT II Treaty. While denying that the Soviets had obtained nuclear superiority under the treaty, they embraced the central war-fighting precepts that the Soviets would accept great risks and costs to profit at the U.S. expense.

The polarization of viewpoints intensified into the 1980s. Prominent members of the Reagan administration voiced deep distress over Soviet goals. To bolster their argument, they read Soviet treachery and deceit into the Soviet violation of treaties, unwillingness to own up to past misconduct, refusal to accept asymmetrical strategic force reductions to equalize the force balance, and resistance to reasonable measures for verifying treaty compliance. The administration's positions and policies provoked considerable opposition from dovish policy advocates, members of Congress, and public interest groups. They maintained that U.S. intransigence—and the accompanying U.S. arms buildup—had closed the door to fruitful arms reduction negotiations and confirmed Soviet suspicions that the United States was not serious about a deal. The acrimony subsided in Reagan's second term with the negotiating of the INF Treaty. To be sure, some hawks dismissed the treaty as a ruse that would give the Soviets a military and political edge in Europe; other hawks heralded the treaty as proof that the United States would prevail if it stuck to its guns (on the matters of asymmetric Soviet reductions and intrusive onsite inspections). But the treaty led many hawks to temper their assessment of Soviet motives. They were impressed that the Soviet Union—under new leadership—had changed its tune and conceded to U.S. demands (under the "zero-zero" formula). Thereafter, administration officials downgraded the severity and importance of Soviet treaty violations and highlighted the Soviet stake in remaining treaty-observant.

Albeit haltingly at first, the dramatic turnaround in the Soviet negotiating position eventually convinced even hardened U.S. observers that the Soviet Union, as the United States had known it, was gone. U.S. policymakers now looked to the START I Treaty as a means to lock in the pronounced changes in their negotiating partner's outlook, hoping that arms reductions would progress under their own momentum and prove difficult to reverse. Importantly, the dramatic reassessment of adversary goals occurred despite the limitations of the START I Treaty, which would still leave Russia with heavy ICBMs and a hypothetical capability to disarm the U.S. land-based force in a first strike. Even the START II Treaty would have left the Russians with a formidable MIRVed land-based missile force over the following decade. For many Cold War–era hawks, these weapons were not—indeed, by their (post-hoc) claims, were never—the issue: the nuclear threat basically ended, then, with the demise of the Soviet regime. Accordingly, some U.S. policymakers who had voiced fairly hawkish views in the Cold War years argued for U.S. multilateralism and cooperative engagement with Russia and China when both emerged as U.S. post–Cold War competitors (see, for instance, Brzezinski 2012). Yet hawks generally remained of two minds about whether Russia remained a primary U.S. threat, given its political transformations and economic weaknesses. The attitudinal conflict was apparent, for instance, in the debates over ABM Treaty withdrawal in the Bush administration and the New START Treaty in the Obama administration.

In all, positions on arms control in the U.S. policy community divided primarily on the basis of adherence to a relatively simple set of assumptions about Russian goals. These assumptions defied an evidentiary standard, remained largely immune from scrutiny, and therefore varied largely in prominence, not in content, into the post–Cold War transition. Of course, the collapse of the Soviet system suggests that dovish arguments were better grounded in the evidence: hawks consistently assumed a level of Soviet malevolence and aggressiveness that was hard to reconcile with the costs and risks that the Soviet leadership appeared willing to incur. Indeed, dovish arguments have been bolstered, in hindsight, by the opening of Soviet archives and testimony from principal participants in Soviet military decision-making. The emerging evidence indicates that the Soviets built up their forces in the 1960s in order to achieve parity with U.S. forces, viewed nuclear superiority on some metrics as a means to reinforce deterrence, read the vulnerability of the U.S. land-based missile force as an indication that the United States was preparing to strike first (and thus cared little about the risk of exposure), resisted preemption as a means for gaining advantage over the United States in a nuclear engagement, relied on vulnerable land-based missiles as a cost-effective means for enlarging the Soviet nuclear force, and produced a large nuclear force more in response to pressure from the Soviet defense-industrial complex than a strategic imperative (on this, see Burr and Savranskaya 2009). In short, the evidence indicates that the Soviets were on the defensive, not the offensive. Thus, the Soviet leadership's public statements—embracing nuclear parity, not superiority, as a force objective and depreciating the value of capability improvements beyond that level—provided an accurate sense of Soviet intentions. As William Wohlforth concluded, "Once the Soviet Union achieved parity and was recognized to have done so by the West, Soviet leaders and political spokesmen began to evaluate the strategic equilibrium positively, and disclaimed any effort to shift it in their favor" (1993: 190). The new thinking in Soviet policy was, in fact, "not only to *minimize* the allocation of resources" for defense but "to move beyond deterrence and defense to a system of world security built on a much broader basis" (Garthoff 1990: 3, emphasis added).

Although Cold War–era hawks lionized Ronald Reagan for having won the Cold War, their post-hoc celebration of the rightness of his policies cannot obscure their faulty premises. Hawks issued dire warnings about the intractability of Soviet expansionist objectives when the views of the Soviet leadership had dramatically and irretrievably changed—in response to a long-term cumulation of effects: "After decades of rivalry, the new elites conceded to themselves that the U.S.S.R. had lost the political and economic competition with the United States and could not continue unreformed under the burden of its own inner contradictions" (Zubok and Pleshakov 1996: 275).

Assessing, Safeguarding, and Improving U.S. Relative Capabilities

Despite their general consistency, these assumptions about Russian goals provided a deficient guide to policy. Beliefs about U.S. relative capabilities, under given treaty terms, suffered the consequences.

The logical problems were palpable from the beginning. Although the Truman administration's proposal for international control of atomic energy drew implicitly from thinking about a security dilemma, it paid too little attention to the mechanisms through which such control would presumably serve U.S. national security. The proposal provided no real basis for U.S. hopes that, under international controls, the security fears of states would subside, that the defense would be advantaged, that an international inspection agency could compete successfully with state subterfuge, or that states would rally to oppose an aggressor. Moreover, the proposal showed little indication that U.S. policymakers had thought carefully, in particular, about Soviet fears and temptations in light of opportunities for cheating, the possible actions of other states, and the overall risks and costs of treaty noncompliance. Indeed, Truman's belief, that the Soviets would accept terms that effectively froze in the U.S. advantage and left the Soviets at the mercy of an international organization that the United States could control, itself conveyed a lack of due deliberation over Soviet goals.

Similar failings were apparent in Eisenhower-era initiatives. The Atoms for Peace proposal promised to deliver international control of fissile materials, through their gradual relinquishment to an international agency, but nonetheless failed to address important implementation challenges. These included the absence of transparency over the size of initial stockpiles (for establishing whether the parties were donating their fair share); the Soviet unwillingness to participate if the United States would retain a sizable residual stockpile; and the growing U.S. and Soviet incentive to withhold fissionable material, as stockpiles declined, to obtain a relative advantage. The Open Skies proposal promised to reduce U.S.-Soviet tension through overflight provisions and information sharing, but it could have had the opposite effect. Whereas the increased transparency of military facilities might allay concerns about adversary military preparedness, it might actually have increased U.S.-Soviet tension by feeding suspicions and fueling politically inspired accusations. The administration's comprehensive nuclear test ban proposals—which required onsite verification—were arguably necessitated by potential Soviet cheating. But they revealed limited recognition that, by accepting the Soviet negotiating terms, the United States might actually realize sizable benefits through a treaty that would severely restrict (if not foreclose) Soviet testing in three environments and confine Soviet illicit underground tests to the low-yield explosions that could evade detection. The administration's record reveals an inadequate appreciation of the potential (positive and negative) effects of U.S. arms control proposals.

The Kennedy administration embraced a set of assumptions that failed to gain currency in the Eisenhower administration. Kennedy officials concluded that a primary U.S. advantage was in delivery capability, not nuclear weapons technology per se; that major breakthroughs in nuclear science were unlikely to occur through testing; that, in atmospheric testing, the costs (in environmental degradation) outweighed the potential U.S. security benefits (including obtaining useful data for hardening systems against nuclear effects and developing a functioning antiballistic missile system); that the Soviets could not gain overwhelmingly by preparing a breakout from an atmospheric test ban; that cheating on a limited (three-environment) test ban was prohibitively costly and risky; and that, through ongoing tests, the Russians would ultimately close the testing gap with the United States. So the administration concluded that material realities shielded the United States from the untoward consequences of a (three-environment) test ban and could not protect the U.S. lead, treaty or no treaty. The administration was unwilling, however, to accept an implication of these arguments that the United States should embrace the unmonitored ban on all nuclear tests that the Eisenhower administration had rejected. Accordingly, proponents accepted a three-environment test ban without territorial monitoring, while (1) demanding a policed ban on underground tests that would still allow the Soviets to cheat; and (2) rejecting an unmonitored ban on these tests that might have greatly reduced the overall rate of Soviet nuclear progress. The administration's logic was suspect, as well, as it pertained to the political origins and implications of the treaty. Administration officials denied that trust underrode the treaty yet argued that shared U.S.-Soviet interests would induce Soviet compliance, and they claimed that the treaty would help to preserve U.S. nuclear superiority over the immediate term yet insisted that it would lessen U.S.-Soviet competition and tension. Consistency suffered, however, on all sides of the debate. Skeptics claimed that the Soviets sought the treaty to freeze in U.S. inferiority and reverse U.S. advantages in underground testing yet argued that the Soviets would risk these benefits by surreptitiously testing, testing that could provoke the U.S. renunciation of the treaty.

Illogic shaped the debates over offensive-force ceilings under the SALT treaties. The terms of the Interim Agreement ostensibly allowed the United States to meet the Nixon administration's standards of "essential equivalence" and "sufficiency," but the ambiguities and inconsistencies of these standards made them poor guides for scaling or configuring U.S. strategic nuclear forces. Whereas the administration paired its support for the agreement with a push to modernize U.S. strategic forces and the acceptance of "equality" as the basis for future negotiations, the administration could have taken these two standards to support "superiority" or "inferiority," given their amorphous underpinnings.

The deficiencies in strategic logic outlived the Nixon administration—if anything, they grew in severity. This was apparent when the Carter administration (1) sought the requisites (under the countervailing doctrine) to fight a protracted nuclear war with the Soviet Union and embraced the SALT II Treaty even though it would give the Soviets a first-strike, counterforce advantage; and (2) viewed the SALT II Treaty favorably even though it failed to enshrine U.S. superiority, as was arguably necessary to serve the countervailing doctrine; (3) distinguished military from civilian targets without considering factors that muddied the designations; (4) failed to address the consequences of conflating some "force" and "value" targets; (5) deferred implicitly to the AD criteria that the administration had explicitly rejected; and (6) planned to fight a protracted nuclear war even though it claimed that no one could win a nuclear exchange.

Hawkish critics were hardly immune to illogic when assailing the SALT II Treaty. They failed to determine whether Soviet benefits from cheating outweighed the Soviet risk from undermining the treaty, whether the United States was best off accepting the treaty to head off a potential Soviet nuclear buildup, and whether the absence of a treaty would leave the United States ill equipped to monitor Soviet nuclear capabilities (through U.S. national technical means). Indeed, hawkish first principles suffered under scrutiny. Although hawks argued that the fact of U.S. nuclear "inferiority" in counterforce capability would embolden the Soviets and possibly tempt them to attack the United States, they failed to determine whether, when, or how alleged U.S. nuclear deficiencies could benefit the Soviets to provoke their aggression. These imbalances were actually significant only if the Soviets believed that they could achieve victory by eviscerating the U.S. land-based force in a surgical strike. But any such victory would only postpone the moment of reckoning at which the United States and the Soviet Union confronted their impending (assured) destruction. In other words, this hypothetical Soviet attack could not change an essential reality: for the Soviets, attacking U.S. value targets would always come with a prohibitive price.

The Reagan administration furthered the logical disconnects and deficiencies in U.S. arms control policy. It made much of the Soviet history of violating treaties, the threat to the U.S. nuclear force from Soviet land-based missiles, and the Russians' "evil" ambitions. But it impugned these various positions by promising to observe the terms of the SALT II Treaty, if the Soviets did the same. The effect was to bind the United States—to some degree—to a treaty that, by the administration's lights, worked to the Soviet advantage. Admittedly, the administration's perspective changed dramatically once Gorbachev accepted the policed ban on intermediate-range nuclear forces that the Soviets had rejected under prior leadership. Still, the administration never reconciled its negotiating terms and stated policy goals. The zero-zero formula embodied in the INF Treaty was not grounded in the logic of coupling (or decoupling) Europe's defense to U.S. strategic forces. Nor would the various strategic force balances that the United States proposed through START have improved the U.S. capability to "prevail" in a nuclear war.

The Cold War's end did not resolve underlying logical tensions. Hawks challenged strategic nuclear reductions that allegedly conceded advantages to Russia (due to its tactical-nuclear weapon holdings and modernized arsenal) and gave it opportunities to cheat, even as they lamented the "anachronistic" U.S. preoccupation with Russian nuclear capabilities that would hurt the U.S. capability to address "new threats." Treaty skeptics were certainly not alone in their illogical tendencies. Proponents trumpeted mutual benefits that the parties would realize from the New START Treaty even as they attributed Russia's cooperativeness to a faltering economy that left Russia unable to compete. Indeed, illogic reached into U.S. post–Cold War nuclear planning. Through the Clinton administration, U.S. officials evaluated U.S.-Russian arms control treaties in light of some unwieldy composite of (Cold War–era) AD and war-fighting principles. Although the George W. Bush administration finally shed doctrinal pretenses, in assessing various nuclear options it appears only to have stopped wrestling with the "big questions." U.S. force requirements were now overwhelmingly sensitive to conventions governing target coverage and attack timing, not to the conditions that would drive potential U.S. adversaries to lash out against the United States or its interests. Neither hawks nor doves put forth an explicit argument of how the United States might gain or lose from further reductions.

In sum, U.S. policy disputes were driven in the Cold War and post–Cold War periods—first and foremost—by assumptions about adversary goals. These goals determined whether Russia would seek or obtain potential benefits in a nuclear war, launch a counterforce strike that left U.S. cities intact, or covet benefits or gain significantly from cheating on treaties. Thus, these goals should have provided direction when U.S. policymakers asked whether the United States had sufficient nuclear capability on hand to deter Russia, should take comfort in the "stability" of the existing nuclear balance, or could limit the costs to the United States should war occur. Yet the specifics of these controversial goals remained strikingly absent from policy debates over appropriate U.S. nuclear strategies and the net benefits of one arms control treaty or another.

Politics as a Complementary or Alternative Explanation?

In the U.S. arms control policy community, the fate and standing of beliefs about Russian goals varied with political-party control of the executive and legislative branches of government and—of course—the political acumen and skills of administration officials and congressional leaders. This was apparent in the Kennedy administration's handling of the Limited Test Ban Treaty. The administration negotiated the treaty with an eye to Senate ratification, sought to present a united political front to Congress and the public, headed off potential military dissent by promising a robust nuclear test program, and orchestrated a broad-based lobbying campaign to promote the treaty. The Nixon administration adopted a different, but no less effective, political approach. Kissinger controlled the U.S. negotiating effort, keeping opponents out of the loop, uninformed, and off-balance. With treaties in hand, the administration then outmaneuvered the opposition: it played to the concerns of arms control critics by supporting equality in a future treaty and the modernization of the U.S. triad; it played to the aspirations of arms control proponents by framing arms ceilings (in the Interim Agreement) as an essential first step toward reductions. Indeed, the administration successfully played the opposing sides against each other. It neutralized dovish efforts to reduce U.S. forces unilaterally by promoting a robust U.S. nuclear force as a bargaining chip for obtaining future Soviet concessions, even as it tempered hawkish criticism by arguing that defeating the SALT I treaties would leave the U.S. military at the mercy of dovish force-cutters (and weaken the president and the Republican Party before the pending election). The Nixon administration stepped adeptly, as well, around the U.S. military's sensitivities by excepting certain systems—MIRVs, forward-based systems, strategic bombers, and next-generation SLBMs—from U.S.-Soviet arms control.

The Carter administration struggled to obtain Senate support for the SALT II Treaty. Its problems stemmed partly from its alleged ineffectualness, having canceled the B-1 bomber program and neutron bomb deployment in Europe, responded tepidly to Soviet adventurism in the Third World and the U.S. global-political decline (as exhibited by the Iranian challenge), and ignored the negotiating standards for the "next treaty" that the Senate had imposed for supporting the SALT I agreement. The administration also suffered from problems that were clearly of its own making: its promotional efforts were undone by the administration's internal disharmony and inability to anticipate or react effectively to criticism. But the administration might well have overcome these obstacles were it not for a critical domestic political development—the rise of a well-organized hawkish opposition that capitalized effectively on growing concerns about Soviet motives and declining U.S. military preparedness.

Although the Reagan administration included, in its ranks, both arms control critics and establishment figures—and its arms control proposals were not entirely true, then, to any one constituency—it managed to adhere initially to a hard-line negotiating stance. It softened its positions marginally, however, with the rise of the nuclear freeze movement, growing interest in a "build-down" of U.S. and Soviet forces, and widespread distaste for the administration's unyielding stance in arms control negotiations. But its insistence on strong verification measures and asymmetric Soviet cuts provided the administration with considerable domestic political latitude when, in Reagan's second term, the Soviets acquiesced to the U.S. positions. Hawkish criticism of the administration's standout accomplishment—the INF Treaty—was muted by Reagan's hard-line, Republican, and conservative credentials (and, of course, his personal appeal).

The ratification debates of the post–Cold War period lacked the sharp edges of prior controversies, although disputes flourished, largely along party lines. Doves (primarily Democrats) sought to keep the negotiation process going with the hope of further reductions; hawks (principally Republicans) sought to dampen hopes and expectations of deepening U.S. strategic force cuts out of fear that the United States would concede more than it should. For that matter, hawks saw no reason for the United States to concede anything: the United States required a full set of capabilities to combat new and emerging threats, and a failing Russian economy would force Russia to reduce its arms, regardless of what the United States did or did not do. By Clinton's second term, opposition had galvanized to downsizing the U.S. strategic arsenal beyond the levels of the START II Treaty due, in part, to suspicions that the administration would curtail U.S. missile defenses to gain Russian support for offensive-force reductions. These sentiments resounded unequivocally when the U.S. Senate later rejected the agreements on which the Russian Parliament had conditioned its ratification of the START II Treaty. True, the George W. Bush administration achieved what its predecessor could not—a treaty ratified by the United States and Russia that would bring strategic nuclear force sizes down below the START I (indeed, START II) numbers. But it did so with an impermanent treaty that set ceilings at levels that the United States had unilaterally determined served U.S. interests and gave the United States and Russia maximum freedom to determine their own weapons' mix. Republicans endorsed the treaty because it had been negotiated by a Republican administration that had convincingly established that it would put U.S. "interests" first (by withdrawing from the ABM Treaty and tying U.S. force levels to U.S. security needs). Democrats endorsed the treaty because it promised to deepen U.S.-Russian cooperation and permitted at least some strategic arms cuts.

Despite its small absolute effect on U.S. strategic force levels, the Obama administration's New START Treaty invited controversy. Critics feared that the leaner U.S. arsenal guaranteed that smaller absolute cuts would now produce large relative declines in the size of the U.S. force, with the effect that new states could challenge the United States in a nuclear arms competition. But the numerical realities of the dwindling U.S. arsenal cannot account for the domestic treaty opposition. Senate Republicans voiced concerns about the treaty's impact on U.S. missile defense and conventional-weapons programs and the overall U.S.-Russian nuclear-force balance. Despite the treaty's endorsement by high-profile Republican moderates, the administration had to resort to a time-honored strategy to obtain Senate backing: it sweetened the pot by committing to modernize the U.S. nuclear infrastructure.

Taken together, the evidence is significant that U.S. domestic politics explains the hawkishness or dovishness of the U.S. approach to arms control. The United States signed and ratified a limited test ban treaty in the Kennedy administration that might well have been blocked had it not gone all-out to promote the treaty; the Nixon administration received Senate approval of a SALT I Treaty that codified asymmetries that proved fatal to the ratification of the SALT II Treaty in a Democratic administration; the Reagan administration, despite its formidable hawkish credentials, encountered considerable resistance to the INF Treaty, which might have doomed ratification in a more dovish administration; the Bush administration jettisoned the ABM Treaty that the Clinton administration had accepted as a key element of the U.S.-Russian arms control regime; and the Obama administration fought an uphill battle to acquire support for a New START Treaty that departed only incrementally from prior agreements and allowed the United States to continue its onsite monitoring of the Russian nuclear arsenal. Indeed, domestic politics also constrained the hawkish agenda. The (Republican) Eisenhower, Nixon, Reagan, and George W. Bush administrations had to control their impulses and get serious about arms control under legislative (and, sometimes, public) pressure.

That said, the evidence is also strong that domestic politics affected U.S. policies mainly on the margin. Neither the Eisenhower nor the Kennedy administration were willing to accept an unverifiable ban on underground testing; the Reagan administration effectively relented to the terms of the SALT II Treaty; the Clinton administration, like the George H. W. Bush administration, planned for a missile defense system that would violate the ABM Treaty (if not amended); and the Obama administration adhered largely to precedent and ultimately received Senate support for the New START Treaty.

These conflicting verdicts are both based, however, on limited perspectives. They assume that domestic politics did or did not matter because hawks and doves competed to pull policy in one direction or another. Thus, neither reflects an evaluation of the actual impact of a political "win" or "loss" on overall U.S. nuclear capability. In point of fact, the key to the growth and resilience of U.S. nuclear forces was not what was contested politically but what was accepted by all sides in the debate—the essential belief that U.S. security was enhanced by a large and diverse nuclear arsenal. Hawkish policymakers sought security in additional qualities and quantities of U.S. delivery capability that would not sizably change the relative capability of the U.S. strategic nuclear force; dovish policymakers were uncomfortable with negotiating outcomes that would give the Russians an overall advantage in delivery vehicles before or after a nuclear exchange. In the end, partisan views converged around the central principles that arms control should (1) proceed in small steps; (2) permit diversity in U.S. strategic delivery capability as a hedge against risk; and (3) strive for "adequate" measures to ensure Russian treaty compliance.

In their "perfect worlds," hawks might have funded an all-out arms competition with the Soviet Union, and doves might have defunded U.S. nuclear modernization programs and made substantial unilateral U.S. force reductions. That U.S. policymakers ultimately conceded to political reality—and adjusted their policy goals to accommodate a determined opposition—is a major part of the *political* story. That they could accommodate the opposition, despite their harsh rhetoric and rigid thinking, is of course a major part of the *ideational* story. Some policymakers saw grave implications in small shortfalls in U.S. nuclear capability; others took solace in small U.S. nuclear advantages. These dueling advocates failed to grasp that, despite the divisions, they shared similar premises and prognoses. Ultimately, even hawks could live (albeit uncomfortably) within the constraints that were imposed by the public and the legislature.

The U.S. nuclear force emerged and survived through a profound consensus, not the loud domestic politics of division or even the quieter politics of compromise. This consensus rested, in no small part, in the illogic of arms control. It fed an intellectual flexibility that generated broad support for a robust U.S. nuclear arsenal and an intellectual inflexibility that safeguarded the U.S. arsenal against dramatic cuts or developments that could threaten the existing arms "balance."

So, Where Does This Leave the Security Dilemma?

In strategic nuclear arms control, signs abound that the United States was trapped in a security dilemma. Throughout the Cold War and post–Cold War periods, successive U.S. administrations sought an arms "balance" with Russia, avoided taking large risks, opposed treaty terms that would permit significant Russian cheating before the United States could effectively respond, crafted policies to meet a largely invariant standard, renounced agreements when they supposedly came to threaten U.S. prerogatives or interests, and overcame political resistance at home to obtain support for negotiated treaties. U.S. security concerns and considerations registered, then, in the negotiating and managing of various treaties. The Limited Test Ban Treaty permitted a robust U.S. underground test program; the SALT I Treaty imposed ceilings that allowed the United States to cover its designated targets and to modernize the strategic nuclear triad; the SALT II Treaty received support (through adherence) from the Reagan administration despite its strongly expressed reservations; the START I and II treaties reduced force levels dramatically and still left the United States capable of hitting a global set of targets; and the New START Treaty received the "advice and consent" of the U.S. Senate over determined opposition. The handling of the ABM Treaty alone offers convincing support for the realist thesis: the United States (and the Soviet Union) accepted the treaty's severe limits on missile defenses only after recognizing the permeability of a military defense, and it walked away from the treaty three decades later, when the Russian threat "receded" and missile defenses promised effectiveness against lesser adversaries. But the realist argument suffers from two major deficiencies.

First, when adopting a strict (offensive-realist) interpretation of the security dilemma, realists fail to account—across time and space—for the selective U.S. response to foreign capabilities. Although U.S. policymakers believed that U.S. strength was the key to global peace and security, they still chose where and when offsetting U.S. strength was required. U.S. policymakers viewed Russia as a grave threat in the early postwar period, when it possessed but a fraction of then-current U.S., or now-current Russian, nuclear capabilities; they downgraded the threat significantly in the late Cold War years when the leadership of Russia—not its capabilities—substantially changed. Indeed, U.S. policymakers redirected their concern in the post–Cold War period to states, with small or fledgling nuclear arsenals, that could not hope to match the size and robustness of the Russian force. Thus, contrary to the strict realist reading, the evidence is compelling that "threats" are predicated on a perception of malevolent intent.

Even then, the Russian "threat" rose and receded with the standard that was used to evaluate U.S. strength. Consequently, early postwar evidence that the United States sought to safeguard its relative capabilities could support the opposite conclusion. Eisenhower rejected an unmonitored, comprehensive ban on nuclear testing that might have benefited the United States by restricting Soviet cheating to the (low) levels that could evade detection in underground tests; conversely, U.S. policymakers proposed terms—under the Baruch plan, Atoms for Peace, and Open Skies—that might ultimately have worked to the U.S. disadvantage. True, evidence that U.S. officials deferred to prior negotiating practices and treaties suggests that they employed a consistent standard, which might reflect the constraining influence of material realities. But administrations differed in their adherence to the status quo: for example, the George W. Bush administration withdrew from the ABM Treaty that the Clinton administration sought to preserve (through amendment). Regardless, why should we assume that, by adhering to a consistent standard, U.S. leaders safeguarded or improved U.S. capabilities? They could well have been wrong to rely on precedent or to refuse to stray from existing practice.

Realist assumptions notwithstanding, the analytical focus on physical capabilities and accompanying balances and imbalances reflects a widespread tendency to defer to the seemingly intrinsic properties of strategic nuclear arsenals. In reality, it reflects the view that these balances reduce to various ad hoc standards. Assured Destruction criteria demonstrate the fragile underpinnings of this practice. The standard emerged mainly from U.S. considerations of cost-effectiveness, not from a studied sense of the costs that Soviet leaders would tolerate. Indeed, by AD criteria, the United States would have effectively destroyed the Soviet Union in a retaliatory attack that spared two-thirds to three-quarters of the Soviet population (from immediate death). An implication is that the United States could have "destroyed" the Soviet Union with a (considerably smaller) force that inflicted lower levels of damage, with less assuredness.

In actuality, terms like *Assured Destruction, essential equivalence,* and *sufficiency* are based on assumptions. These pertain to when, how, and why nuclear weapons will be used, the likely effects of a nuclear war, and the cost tolerance of national leaders. Thus, the usefulness of these terms depends—for starters—on whether those assumptions are made explicit—by posing and answering basic conceptual and operational questions. In a nuclear conflict, what is the payoff from targeting societal assets versus adversary military capabilities? Over what time frame will such a war unfold? Can a nuclear war be "fought"? Should adversary leaders be attacked as military command or as value targets? Or should they be spared from attacks with the hope of terminating a war short of a catastrophic outcome? In evaluating force capabilities, should nuclear weapons be distinguished by their physical characteristics or by their applications? How much destruction is required of a designated target set, at what level of assurance? Is the diversity of the U.S. retaliatory force (that is, the U.S. triad) more important than its sheer size for assuring U.S. retaliation for an attack? Do the stability costs of a multiple-warhead capability outweigh its benefits in force efficiency? Should given targets be hit promptly or left in reserve for subsequent attacks?

Second, realists fail to recognize the extent to which the arms control positions of U.S. doves and hawks depended on trust in the Russian adversary—a belief that it would not act as it was capable. Arms control negotiations yielded agreements when U.S. policymakers trusted that Russia shared the U.S. interest in an agreement—that it, like the United States, had an aversion to war, a desire to reduce the costs and risks of arms competition, and a preference of limiting the human costs should war occur. In other words, they trusted that, at least in the short term, the Russians valued the benefits under an agreement more than the advantages of working outside the agreement. Thus, U.S. policymakers accepted some non-negligible risk that Russia might defect, either by violating the letter or spirit of the agreement. They assumed—with some probability of error—that Russia would not exploit each and every loophole, abide by its own skewed reading of an agreement, cheat because it could get away with it, or capitalize fully on each and every legal opportunity to obtain an advantage.

Certainly, trust was a troubling concept for arms control hawks—doves, too, for that matter. But it was needlessly bothersome to both. One lesson of U.S.-Soviet arms control is that the parties must trust one another, to some degree, to reap the rewards from a treaty. No set of inspections can provide absolute assurance that another is complying with the terms of a treaty. Even with omnipresent inspectors, a potential cheating problem would remain, for "there is no escape from verification uncertainty" (Dunn 1990: 175). Moreover, no treaty can be written with knowledge of the dozens of ways that the text can be interpreted or the future circumstances that will confound the treaty's application. For that matter, efforts to make contracts ironclad by addressing each and every contingency risks creating contradictions, implying that practices that are not explicitly proscribed are permitted and enticing parties to adhere to the specific over the general spirit of a treaty. As Chayes and Chayes conclude, "The main obstacle to the solution of the verification problem is the persistence of the belief that compliance issues are necessarily questions of good and evil. They are not. They are an inevitable part of living under an arms control regime" (1990: 164). A second lesson of U.S.-Soviet arms control is that, despite U.S. best efforts, the Soviet Union could always act as it was capable. It could have prepared to break out from various treaties, which would have left the United States at a disadvantage; in fact, it could have attacked the United States with nuclear weapons to realize some hypothetical goal. Just as doves trusted that the Soviets would not capitalize on alleged loopholes in a treaty because the advantages relative to the risks were small, hawks trusted—to some extent—that the Soviets would not act as they were capable, that is, launch an annihilative first strike on the U.S. military or civilian infrastructure once the Soviet nuclear relative advantage had peaked. Although U.S. policymakers sought to maintain the credibility of a U.S. (nuclear) retaliatory threat for purposes of deterrence, they generally acted on a faith—or trust—that the Soviets believed they had everything to lose from a nuclear confrontation, that is, that no one could "win" a nuclear war.

The role of perceptions of capability and trust is often sidestepped, shunted aside, or addressed reflexively (not reflectively) in a realist analysis (defensive as well as offensive) that gives short shrift to the critical beliefs of U.S. policymakers. Bringing these beliefs to the forefront reveals that ideas about relative capabilities—albeit grounded in material capabilities—explain whether, when, and how states choose to arm or disarm. Central to U.S. capability assessments were assumptions about the military effectiveness and stabilizing potential of certain weapons over others, the value of nuclear weapons beyond some floor level of aggregate retaliatory capability, and so forth. Certainly, states can alter physical realities—seize territory, inflict harm to the societies of others, and so on—whether or not the effects are perceived (or anticipated) by policymakers or analysts. But it is up to individuals, given their policy priorities and capabilities at hand, to determine whether these changes constitute a threat; indeed, it is up to individuals to determine whether, when, and how those changes present a threat and thus what kinds and quantities of capability are necessary to offset it. The point is that U.S. policymakers judged that they had achieved "essential equivalence" and that Russia threatened various "balances." The United States had no need—based on any fundamental metric—to match or exceed the Russians in weapon quantities, qualities, or aggregates.

With a misguided focus on the numbers within the U.S. policy community, all-important assumptions about adversary goals remained oddly removed from policy assessments. These goals provoked disputes but seldom informed them. Even when hawks acknowledged at the end of the Cold War—under the force of compelling evidence—that Russian goals had changed, they were not always clear about whether and how they had changed and whether the United States could now turn its attention to other pressing threats. When they eventually considered these new threats, the old tendencies surfaced: U.S. planners continued to rely on convenient metrics and what had "worked" in the past. For their part, U.S. civilian leaders sought to retain significant margins of "nuclear advantage," to the point that the Russians could realistically fear that the United States was seeking a nuclear first-strike capability against all potential threats.

Absent a focus on when, how, or why an adversary's weapons might be used and whether the United States should employ its weapons to punish transgressions or deny military gains, new questions arose that challenged the consistency and coherence of U.S. policy. Could U.S. efforts to retain a large and robust nuclear force push adversary leaders to relax their control over nuclear weapons—by pre-delegating launch authority to military commanders, shifting to hair-trigger alert status, moving toward preemptive-attack or launch-on-warning modes, or even placing nuclear devices surreptitiously on U.S. territory—to ensure that these weapons survive a U.S. first strike? Might the U.S. desire to retain the option of deploying conventional and nuclear variants of the same delivery systems ultimately confound adversary attack-warning systems and lead to inadvertent nuclear conflicts? Could U.S. attempts to capitalize on U.S. nuclear superiority to deter the use of chemical or biological weapons ultimately place the United States in the position of using nuclear weapons largely to preserve U.S. credibility? Might the U.S. pursuit of nuclear offenses and defenses provoke adversaries to increase their warhead numbers, with deleterious consequences, to ensure that some requisite number hit their targets? Could the potency of the U.S. nuclear force foster a dangerous illusion that the United States could shield itself or its allies from nuclear devastation through a preemptive strike on the adversary's military-industrial infrastructure? Indeed, would U.S. preparations for such a strike—real or imagined—feed the momentum toward war and make such a strike more likely, and also less effective? If the answer to any of these questions is yes, a large and robust U.S. force could well make the United States less—not more—secure.

Introduction

1. Throughout this book, I use the term *Russia*, by way of shorthand, to refer to the contemporary state and to the Soviet Union of the Cold War era.

2. For strong introductions to nuclear deterrence principles and debates in the contemporary context, see Freedman (2004) and Morgan (2003).

3. Variation exists among realists in their regard for intentions and beliefs as independent influences on state behavior. Their various writings suggest that a party (1) responds to the "threat" from another's capabilities and aggressive intentions (Walt 1987); (2) crafts its behavior toward another based on its presumed "type" (Schweller 1994); (3) acts on the basis of its own perception and governmental structures (Rose 1998); or (4) considers another's intentions (Glaser 1997, 2010). Although self-identified realists do sometimes concede a substantial role, then, to perception (Jervis 1976, 1978), realists tend to weight signal quality far more heavily than beliefs—and, certainly, more heavily than psychological dynamics—when explaining state behavior. Accordingly, defensive realists imply that signals—when costly—are highly conducive to a single interpretation.

4. In more elaborate terms, trust is a "willingness to place the fate of one's interests under the control of others in a particular context" despite "some uncertainty" about whether the "trustees will protect the interests placed in their control" (Hoffman 2006: 17). Although trust involves "both uncertainty and vulnerability" (Wheeler 2009, 436), it assumes that another party will "want to reciprocate cooperation rather than exploit it" (Kydd 2000: 326).

5. Planning around the worst case was impossible, regardless, given the abundant worst cases around which to plan that include "worse, worst cases" that will *always* leave policymakers without reasonable alternatives (Garthoff 1978: 23).

6. By opting for technology, U.S. policymakers could reveal their indebtedness to a military (strategic) culture—or, more broadly, American (societal) culture—that seeks technological solutions to policy problems and defines problems around available technology. Nevertheless, a cultural explanation cannot explain policy divisions (between hawks and doves), variance in positions across issues, or evolving positions over time.

7. For an accessible discussion, see Nevid (2009: 248–249).

Chapter 1 • Initial U.S. Nuclear Arms Control Initiatives

1. On their arguments and the differences among them, see Sigal (1978: 331–335).

2. Several prominent military and government officials—including Generals George Marshall and Dwight Eisenhower—apparently had misgivings about the precipitous use of the bomb. How strongly these views were held at the time and whether they got through to Truman is another matter of historical dispute. For a skeptical view, see Hixson (2003: 261–267).

3. Memorandum from R. Gordon Arneson, Interim Committee Secretary, to Mr. Harrison, June 6, 1945, Top Secret. From the National Security Archive. Available at www.gwu.edu/~nsarchiv/NSAEBB/NSAEBB162/14.pdf, accessed February 9, 2013.

4. Notes of the Interim Committee Meeting Thursday, 31 May 1945, 10:00 A.M. to 1:15 P.M.—2:15 P.M. to 4:15 P.M. n.d., Top Secret. From the National Security Archive. Available at www.gwu.edu/~nsarchiv/NSAEBB/NSAEBB162/12.pdf, accessed February 9, 2013.

5. On preventative versus preemptive attacks, see Trachtenberg (2007).

6. The strongest and best-known statement of this historical argument is found in Alperovitz (1965).

7. Almost a quarter of those surveyed in one poll felt that the United States should have dropped many more atomic bombs on Japan before it surrendered (Tannenwald 2007: 89).

8. Truman apparently concluded that it was best to tell the Soviet Union, just not to tell them too much (Broscious 1999: 24).

9. Social scientists argue that, compared to deterrence, compellence is more difficult to achieve, for a variety of reasons. These include the challenges of getting someone to relinquish what they already possess, clearly communicating a compellence demand (as compared to a deterrence demand, which is implicit, for instance, in how a state deploys its forces), and so forth.

10. This conclusion was possible from a selective reading of the Interim Committee's recommendation.

11. The plan was named for Dean Acheson—undersecretary of state at the time—and David Lilienthal, the former head of the Tennessee Valley Authority who would soon become the first head of the U.S. Atomic Energy Commission.

12. The report was meant to guide the negotiations, though Baruch was given the discretion to craft the means for implementing the report's objectives.

13. Evidence to this effect lies in the internal debates over such control within the U.S. government, the exuberance that leading U.S. officials (including the president) showed for the principles of the plan, the apparent evolution of U.S. thinking and policy on the subject, and the extent to which the United States responded to Soviet assertions and offers on the issue.

14. In essence, the United States encountered the "Prisoner's Dilemma" problem in game theory—the basis of the security dilemma.

15. True, the Soviets did not dismiss inspections in their entirety. They proposed the inspection of production and mining facilities—where the United States held the advantage—but excepted research facilities, where the Soviet nuclear program was gestating at the time (Holloway 1994: 165).

16. U.S. policymakers found little in outward Soviet indicators to suggest that these

weapons gave the United States political or military advantages. Stalin did not believe, in fact, that nuclear weapons would be decisive in a war with the United States; to the contrary, he believed that Soviet natural assets would offset the (relatively small) U.S. nuclear stockpile, ostensibly the primary U.S. asset against the Soviet Union (Holloway 1994: 240, 250, 261). For him, a Soviet bomb was necessary to bolster the longer-term Soviet military position vis-à-vis the United States and deter war (Craig and Radchenko 2008: 109–110; Zubok 1999: 53, 60). He had no doubt, however, that these weapons had coercive value in the immediate term. Yet that too was hard to know from Soviet behavior. The Soviet leadership compensated for its initial nuclear inferiority with truculence and then exaggerated its own nuclear capability after the Soviet atomic bomb test (Holloway 1994: 169, 267–269).

17. U.S. policymakers assumed that the Soviet Union would not concede its thermonuclear prerogatives unless the United States was bargaining from strength (Bernstein 1989: 149).

18. See Milestones: 1945–1952. Office of the Historian, U.S. Department of State. Available at http://history.state.gov/milestones/1945-1952/Atomic, accessed February 4, 2013.

19. Memorandum for the Files of Lewis L. Strauss, 20 August 1958. From the National Security Archive. Available at www.gwu.edu/~nsarchiv/NSAEBB/NSAEBB94/tb06.pdf, accessed February 9, 2013.

20. The changes in 1957 included creating and staffing the position of special assistant for science and technology and establishing the President's Science Advisory Committee (Greene 2007: 6).

21. On the "losing battle" in the Eisenhower administration to "conventionalize" nuclear weapons, see Tannenwald (2007: 155–189). Eisenhower's thinking appears to have been influenced heavily by the shift to thermonuclear weapons (Greene 2007: 21). A similar dynamic appears to have taken place on the Soviet side. Soviet "military doctrine pointed to the need to prepare to fight and win a nuclear war, but by the end of 1955 Soviet leaders understood that a Soviet-American nuclear war was, at some fundamental level, unacceptable, and realized that Western leaders understood this too" (Holloway 1994: 369).

22. Produced routinely (or, by request, on special topics), U.S. National Intelligence Estimates are generally accepted as the authoritative voice of the U.S. intelligence community. The organizational structure for producing them has changed over the years. They are currently created with input from the intelligence community under the direction of the National Intelligence Council, which reports to the director of National Intelligence.

23. In the military's view, the massive numbers of casualties that would result—that is, the collateral damage—amounted to a "bonus" effect that could increase the value of a strike.

24. If the United States struck first—with the full wrath of the U.S. arsenal—the plan intended the delivery of twenty times the (400) megatons that, in a few years, were deemed sufficient to bring the "assured destruction" of the Soviet Union. See Fred Kaplan, No More Nukes, *Time,* October 10, 2010.

25. William Burr, ed., The Creation of the SIOP-62: More Evidence on the Origins of Overkill. From the National Security Archive. Available at www.gwu.edu/~nsarchiv/NSAEBB/NSAEBB130/index.htm, accessed February 4, 2013. The SIOP took effect in April 1961, in the first months of the Kennedy administration.

26. On these debates, see Tannenwald (2007: 115–154). According to Greene (2007: 41–45), the documentary evidence reveals that Eisenhower was a strong advocate for em-

ploying nuclear force in Korea and, if necessary, against China in the Taiwan Strait crisis (1954–55).

27. Dwight D. Eisenhower, Atoms for Peace, International Atomic Energy Agency. Available at www.iaea.org/About/history_speech.html, accessed February 4, 2013.

28. The challenge of setting contribution ratios was acknowledged by Eisenhower's advisors (Hewlett and Holl 1989: 216).

29. Monitoring refers to the detection, identification, and measurement of activities of interest; verification refers to judgments about whether the monitored behaviors are consistent or inconsistent with treaty obligations (Meyer 1984: 112–113).

30. Viewed in more academic terms, Eisenhower sought to overcome the oppressive logic of the security dilemma by adopting an iterative solution: participants would cooperate in each round (forgoing the small, short-term benefits from "cheating" on the agreement) to realize longer-term benefits. In this sense, the proposal stemmed from thinking about benevolent cycles, where cooperation begets cooperation (see Osgood 1962), and the cooperative benefits of repeated play in the Prisoner's Dilemma (Axelrod 1984). Eisenhower appears even to have jettisoned strict realist logic (in favor of liberal-institutionalist logic) by arguing that cooperative benefits could be realized—transparency, coordination of effort, concessions made for reputation benefits, and so on—within the framework of an international institution.

31. This was acknowledged by experts at the time (Sokolski 2001: 31–32).

32. The United States came around to this view: the proliferation threat of civilian nuclear power and the challenges of exercising international control over the atom would become major issues within the Eisenhower administration with the establishment of the IAEA and U.S. bilateral support for the nuclear programs of other states and entities (Hewlett and Holl 1989: 317–325).

33. This problem was recognized by some of Eisenhower's advisors (Sokolski 2001: 28).

34. Administration officials created the exact opposite impression, for example, when they insisted that a state would require a fairly large arsenal to endanger the U.S. military-industrial base and implicitly downplayed the potential vulnerability of U.S. airborne retaliatory capability (Sokolski 2001: 32–33).

35. Indeed, U.S. officials looked at Open Skies as a means for acquiring huge amounts of militarily useful intelligence information (Marquardt 2007: 57).

36. This was the plausible result should parties be unwilling to reveal what they knew out of fear of disclosing what they did not or could not know.

37. John S. D. Eisenhower, Memorandum of Conversation with the President January 12, 1959—9:00AM, 19 January 1959. From the National Security Archive. Available at www.gwu.edu/~nsarchiv/NSAEBB/NSAEBB94/tb11.pdf, accessed February 9, 2013.

38. This is not to say that the public embraced a unilateral ban—public support rose and fell with the state of U.S.-Soviet relations.

39. Still, through much of his presidency, Eisenhower publicly minimized the dangers from nuclear fallout.

40. Throughout his first term, Eisenhower had no test ban advocates in his inner circle—though, by the second half of 1956, his advisors were acknowledging the political importance of at least appearing flexible on the issue (Greene 2003: 171).

41. William Burr, "We Can't Go on the Way We Are": U.S. Proposals for a Fissile Material Production Cutoff and Disarmament Diplomacy during the 1950s and 60s. From the

National Security Archive. Available at www.gwu.edu/~nsarchiv/nukevault/ebb321/index.htm, accessed February 4, 2013.

42. In negotiations, the Soviets had conceded that they would allow some relatively low number of onsite inspections.

43. To make that point during the Kennedy administration, the Soviets used the fact of U.S. announcements of Soviet tests as evidence that the United States *could* identify Soviet tests (Seaborg 1981: 144).

44. See, for instance, the conclusion, in 1958, of the Conference of Experts (Seaborg 1981: 13).

45. That the United States changed its demands pertaining to monitoring, ostensibly to reflect the evolving science on the subject, only fueled outward Soviet disdain for the U.S. negotiating position (Seaborg 1981: 18–19).

46. John S. D. Eisenhower, Memorandum of Conversation with the President January 12, 1959—9:00AM, 19 January 1959. From the National Security Archive. William Burr and Hector L. Montford, eds., The Making of the Limited Test Ban Treaty, 1958–1963, The National Security Archives. Available at www.gwu.edu/~nsarchiv/NSAEBB/NSAEBB94/tb11.pdf, accessed February 9, 2013.

47. This turn of events was ironic given the principles of Eisenhower's earlier Open Skies proposal.

48. These differences also hindered the successful negotiation of various other proposals (specifically, international control of nuclear weapons and a comprehensive test ban) that required the Soviet Union to open its territory to inspection.

49. Whereas the Kennedy administration was also unwilling to accept an unverified ban on underground testing, it tended toward a more sanguine view of the consequences of Soviet cheating on underground tests.

50. These were virtually indistinguishable from military explosions and would conceivably be employed within one of the environments that was closed to nuclear testing under the Limited Test Ban Treaty.

Chapter 2 • Early Success at Arms Control

1. See also William Burr, ed., The Creation of the SIOP-62: More Evidence on the Origins of Overkill. From the National Security Archive. Available at www.gwu.edu/~nsarchiv/NSAEBB/NSAEBB130/index.htm, accessed February 4, 2013.

2. The Claremont Institute. Missilethreat.com. Available at http://missilethreat.com/missiles/r-16-ss-7/, accessed February 13, 2013.

3. Doubling accuracy can offset an eightfold increase in yield (Thee 1988: 12).

4. On this, see also the testimony of Harold Brown, Director of Defense Research and Engineering, in U.S. Senate (1963: 532).

5. These tests, which establish whether and how a technology works, require more planning and time than proof tests, which establish whether and how a developed technology works. Accepting his argument that it might take six months' advance notice for effects tests on nuclear weapons (U.S. Senate 1963: 157), the Soviets would have a one-year jump on the United States should they breach a ban with such development tests.

6. The U.S. government inadvertently offered support to these skeptical arguments by announcing the fact of a Soviet nuclear test, which arguably only added to the asymmetry problem by helping the Soviets to calibrate tests to avoid detection.

7. Skeptics argued, in effect, that only the Soviet Union understood the message of the Prisoner's Dilemma: that it was not in a party's interest to cooperate when the other party always defects.

8. In fact, the United States arguably engaged in coercion when it tied the extension of its test moratorium beyond the end of 1959 to progress at Geneva (Seaborg 1981: 21).

9. He appeared more hopeful that a comprehensive would have this effect than a limited ban would (Seaborg 1981: 227).

10. Atomic Energy Commission Chairman Glenn Seaborg, Journal Entry for 5 September 1961. From the National Security Archive. Available at www.gwu.edu/~nsarchiv/NSAEBB/NSAEBB94/tb32.pdf, accessed February 9, 2013. See also Oliver (1998: 40).

11. Admittedly, the treaty was uncomplicated inasmuch as it imposed an absolute ban on testing in the given environments, lacked inspection provisions, and emerged primarily to satisfy U.S. and Soviet (not multilateral) concerns.

12. For instance, the Soviets tried to tie a test ban to a nonaggression treaty and a ban on the use of nuclear weapons (Firestone 1999: 80, 88).

13. William Burr and Hector L. Montford, eds., The Making of the Limited Test Ban Treaty, 1958–1963. From the National Security Archive. Available at www.gwu.edu/~nsarchiv/NSAEBB/NSAEBB94, accessed February 4, 2013.

14. Unsurprisingly, perhaps, the AEC and the Pentagon were among those conveying the difficulty of maintaining a persistent state of readiness (Oliver 1998: 68; Seaborg 1981: 133).

15. The treaty did little, furthermore, to constrain the emergence of new nuclear powers. Both China and France would eventually engage in atmospheric testing: China conducted 23 atmospheric tests before ending them in 1980; France conducted 50 atmospheric tests through 1974.

16. These basic arguments are found in Kaysen (1999: 112). The data used here come from SIPRI (2007: 555–557).

Chapter 3 • The Era of Bilateral Nuclear Arms Limitations

1. On MIRV development and deployment, see Greenwood (1975).

2. Equivalent megatons is used as a measure because the area of destruction does not increase in linear proportion to yield. Eight bombs of equal yield that combine to produce a one-megaton explosion would destroy twice the area of a one-megaton bomb.

3. McNamara viewed AD as a useful rationale for resisting service pressure for more and better missiles and aircraft.

4. On the organizational failure to address these fire effects, see Eden (2004).

5. On PD-59 and its relationship to past doctrine, see Nolan (1989: 126–139). For an excellent critique of the countervailing strategy, see Jervis (1984).

6. For that matter, given the disadvantages to the United States of striking second, equivalence could lead the United States to seek nuclear superiority. On these standards, see Smith (1981: 24).

7. Harking back to U.S.-Soviet wrangling over the Baruch plan, the Soviets were willing to accept limitations on testing—where the United States was perfecting its technology—but not research and development, where Soviet capability was relegated (Newhouse 1973: 181, 183).

8. Soviet SLBMs could arguably not do both. The launching of Soviet SLBMs before

Soviet ICBMs were launched could create sufficient warning to allow some U.S. land-based missiles to escape before Soviet ICBMs had arrived on target.

9. The United States obtained SLBM hard-target capability, in the 1990s, with the Trident II (D-5) missile (Feiveson and Duffield 1984: 188–190).

10. The Protocol (in its text) was deemed an "integral part of the Interim Agreement."

11. Admittedly, the operations of the aircraft would be impeded by their vulnerable flying speeds and altitudes, anti-aircraft systems, and round-trip range limitations. Indeed, the Soviets would argue accordingly in the SALT II negotiations to keep the Soviet Backfire bomber out of the strategic count.

12. In the 1960s and early 1970s, ACDA expressed its trepidations about MIRV but was largely ignored. Indeed, it appears to have suppressed its concerns, to an extent, out of fear of losing credibility in the push to restrict other weapons, including ABM systems (Greenwood 1975: 119).

13. True, some U.S. nuclear experts recognized MIRV's counterforce capability—with large numbers of accurate weapons that could be launched against hardened targets—but that was not the argument that was used to build broad support for the technology (Greenwood 1975: 54). On the destabilizing effects of MIRV as a counterforce weapon, see Potter (1978).

14. Ironically, MIRV was viewed, in the U.S. policy community, primarily as a solution to the U.S. land-based missile vulnerability problem, inasmuch as a Soviet first strike on U.S. land-based *missiles* might spare large numbers of U.S. *warheads* (Greenwood 1975: 101–102).

15. In the prior decade, NTM came to refer to "unilateral" and "non-intrusive" means for monitoring compliance (Morris 1991: 250); with the Interim Agreement, the term formally entered the U.S.-Soviet arms control lexicon.

16. On the philosophy and instruments of verification, see Pieragostini (1986).

17. The system was designed around two interceptors—a Spartan missile that would launch a multi-megaton warhead to destroy incoming warheads (even with "misses") above the atmosphere and a speedier Sprint missile that would launch multi-kiloton warheads at lower altitudes against surviving warheads that had separated from decoys and chaff (NAS 1985: 141).

18. On the validity of U.S. bargaining assumptions, see Grynaviski (2010: 390–401).

19. Because Soviet ICBMs were located near Moscow, the United States pushed for the mandatory distance out of fear that the Soviets would capitalize on this proximity by constructing a missile-silo defense that overlapped in coverage with the urban-defense system for heightened defensive effect.

20. For that matter, the Soviets had done a complete about-face and seem to have regarded ABM as the only issue that was on the table (Labrie 1979: 11).

21. In contrast, for hard-target defense, warheads could be intercepted with nuclear warheads at close distances from targets without fear of collateral effects or a complete success: a missile defense only had to reduce the *probability* of a silo kill—by deflecting, incapacitating, or destroying incoming warheads—to protect U.S. launchers in the aggregate.

22. Of course, the logical compatibility of the arguments that defenses were destabilizing and would not work could be questioned. Supporters could finesse the issue by arguing that defenses might fuel an arms race with a false promise of effectiveness.

23. The bombers physical characteristics placed it in the "gray area, between medium and heavy" (Talbott 1980: 33).

24. In consequence, missiles were effectively equated with bombers.

25. A limit of fourteen warheads were allowed on SLBMs, ten warheads were allowed on one new type of ICBM, and warheads were limited to existing numbers on current ICBMs.

26. The agreements included the 1972 Basic Principles Agreement and the 1973 Agreement on the Prevention of Nuclear War.

27. The administration determined belatedly that these forces had been in Cuba from the early 1960s (Blacker 1987: 121).

28. Among the reservations attached to its recommendation for ratification, the Foreign Relations Committee insisted that the "Agreed Statements and Common Understandings" be given the "same force and effect as the Treaty and Protocol themselves" such that their violation would constitute a violation of the treaty itself and that an unsigned statement by President Brezhnev that pledged to limit the production of the Soviet Backfire bomber, which was not limited by SALT II, be considered to be legally binding (U.S. Senate 1979c: 64).

29. By Defense Department estimates, the U.S. Air Force possessed a thousand nuclear-capable aircraft not limited by the treaty (U.S. Senate 1979a: 1:96).

30. He was not alone in suggesting that the military and the psychological are equally vital elements of U.S. strategic policy. For example, Army Chief of Staff Edward C. Meyer gave indirect support for this view when he proclaimed that even public discussions of the U.S. missile vulnerability problem could produce the "very damaging" (in his view, erroneous) perception that the United States was incapable of accomplishing its targeting goals (U.S. Senate 1979a: 1:302).

31. Consequently, it could allegedly have destroyed 90 percent of the U.S. ICBM force in a first strike.

32. Rowny observed that U.S. B-52 bases can be hit with Soviet sea-launched cruise missiles with ranges of less than 600 kilometers, but the U.S. cannot hit Backfire bases with these range-limited weapons. Furthermore, by his estimates, 50 to 75 percent of U.S. population and industry is located within range of Soviet sea-launched cruise missiles (U.S. Senate 1979a: 2:672).

33. Because U.S. SLBM warheads had a tenth of the yield of a Soviet ICBM warhead and half their accuracy, they had arguably one-fortieth of their overall effectiveness given its sensitivity to accuracy (Rowny in U.S. Senate 1979a: 2:674).

34. In the Cold War–era literature, this argument was associated with "existential deterrence"—the idea that nuclear weapons can deter because they exist.

35. William J. Perry, undersecretary of defense for research and engineering, in U.S. Senate (1979a: 1:134).

36. Nitze predicted that by the mid-1980s, the Soviets would have twice as many hardened targets (averaging twice the hardness) as the United States would (U.S. Senate 1979a: 3:885).

37. To quote Brown, "Assured destruction is necessary for nuclear deterrence, but it is not, in my judgment, sufficient as a strategic doctrine or as a sole basis for determining the characteristics of our strategic forces" (U.S. Senate 1979c: 137).

38. Whereas hawkish critics accused U.S. policymakers of presuming falsely that U.S. and Soviet leaders held the same values—this was the "mirror-imaging" fallacy—political war-fighting proponents were no less guilty of that failing.

39. These conclusions were subsequently bolstered by evidence that a U.S. strike on Soviet nuclear targets would kill 15 million civilians (Arkin 2000: 72; Levi et al. 1987/88).

40. The term *damage limitation,* in this context, borrows from Glaser (1989); elsewhere, the doctrine is labeled "pure war-fighting" (Lebovic 1990).

41. For instance, Brown discounted the likelihood that the Soviets would secretively deploy mobile missiles by stressing the scope of deception that was required for successful evasion: "Covert deployment of a force on a scale large enough to be militarily significant would be a formidable task, requiring successful concealment of a large number of deployed launchers, and of their production, support, and training exercises as well, and deployment without central support facilities would entail significant operational disadvantages" (U.S. Senate 1979a: 1:131).

42. See Rowny in U.S. Senate (1979a: 3:1234). The treaty defined an ICBM as a ballistic missile with a range greater than 5,500 kilometers.

43. As Undersecretary of Defense Perry put it, "We have been monitoring the telemetry for more than 20 years and we know what data they send and what data we need. Therefore, if those data on some new tests show up missing, it is a fair presumption that they are now being encrypted" (1979a: 1:138).

44. Without the treaty, according to Brown, "the deception, concealment, and countermeasures which the treaty bans would then be permitted" (U.S. Senate 1979a: 1:18).

45. Ralph Earle, chairman of the U.S. SALT Delegation (U.S. Senate 1979a: 2:459). Even if gaps in U.S. knowledge remained, the United States might not want to press the issue given the potential costs in U.S. security: sharing information to compile an agreed database risked compromising U.S. intelligence sources and methods (Jones in U.S. Senate 1979a: 4:1560).

46. Although the United States had declared that the treaty's restriction on significant increases in the present dimensions of land-based ICBM silos proscribed increases greater than 10 to 15 percent, the Soviets had taken the restriction to allow increases of that magnitude in multiple dimensions: such increases in the diameter and depth of an ICBM would increase its volume by 50 percent (Nitze quoted in Labrie 1979: 121).

47. These views were expressed by Amron Katz, an expert on verification who was appointed, in 1973, by Nixon as ACDA assistant director (Katz 1979).

48. Supporters conceded that some ambiguities might be exploited by the Soviets to advantage, but only at a prohibitive cost. For example, even if the Soviets could test a prohibited ICBM in the guise of an SLBM, they would have to make compromises—and accept a suboptimal weapon system—to make it a credible SLBM (Brown in U.S. Senate 1979a: 1:99).

49. As Meyer observes, "All else being equal, in monitoring, detection is almost always easier than measurement, and produces less ambiguous results (i.e., less uncertainty)" (1984: 123).

50. Even then, Jones insisted that the United States knew existing Soviet silo dimensions to the degree necessary to monitor Soviet compliance—which implied that the confidence interval for such absolute judgments was considerably less than that for relative judgments.

51. Inasmuch as the Soviets employed a cold-launch technique—ejecting the missile from the launcher before the missile engines fire—the launcher can remain intact, giving it a hypothetical reload capability. The treaty restricted the distance from launchers that

missiles could be stored, but presumably missiles could be moved surreptitiously or in a crisis.

52. See, for example, George M. Seignious, director of the U.S. Arms Control and Disarmament Agency, in U.S. Senate (1979a: 2:455).

53. Kissinger responded to military concerns about an unbridled Soviet buildup at sea by incorporating limits on SLBMs. On JCS pressure on this issue, see Newhouse (1973: 223).

54. As chief negotiator, Warnke was a lightning rod for treaty critics.

55. Nitze was a "moderate" in the Reagan administration and was among those who argued that the administration should adhere to SALT II limits.

56. Extensive Soviet silo construction and deployments of third-generation missiles into the late 1960s provoked upward revisions in U.S. intelligence projections that still fell below actual Soviet deployment levels. Even upward-adjusted "high" predictions offered in 1966 and 1967 fell below these levels.

57. In the intelligence community's judgment, even evidence suggesting otherwise need not provoke alarm: with uncertainties about future U.S. capabilities, the Soviets "are likely to be cautious—to overestimate rather than underestimate the U.S. threat" (DCI 1970: 7).

58. The impact of these overestimates was softened, however, by the Soviet introduction of MIRVs on submarine-launched ballistic missiles at twice the predicted levels (U.S. DI 1989: 7–10).

59. On the U.S. overstating of Soviet missile accuracies, see Podvig (2008: 122–129).

60. Although the NIEs were now structured to give more prominence to an assortment of views, the "consensus" view expressed in the text became more pessimistic.

61. The NIE acknowledged differences within the intelligence community about what "victory" actually meant to the Soviet leadership.

62. For one scenario, see Nitze in U.S. Senate (1979a: 3:916).

Chapter 4 • Nuclear Arms Reductions in the Final Cold War Decade

1. It made this tradeoff in the strong belief that accuracy could compensate for megatonnage inasmuch as (1) high yields bring weight, which compromises range and mobility; (2) accurate hits reduce yield requirements (insofar as large explosions are meant to close the distance to a target); and (3) high yields produce collateral destruction that will make it harder to convince the Soviets to observe limits in war.

2. The MX (or "missile experimental," dubbed the "Peacekeeper" by Reagan) was the single new missile that the United States was permitted under the SALT II Treaty.

3. On the MX and its basing, see Federation of American Scientists, LGM-118A Peacekeeper. Available at www.fas.org/nuke/guide/usa/icbm/lgm-118.htm, accessed February 4, 2013.

4. See, again, Federation of American Scientists, LGM-118A Peacekeeper. Available at www.fas.org/nuke/guide/usa/icbm/lgm-118.htm, accessed February 4, 2013.

5. Mark S. Spacher, Executive Summary: The Soviet Nuclear Threat. From Global Security.org. Available at www.globalsecurity.org/wmd/library/report/1989/SMS.htm, accessed February 4, 2013.

6. For an analysis of different views of the significance of alleged Soviet treaty violations, see Guertner (1988).

7. They accused the Soviets of repeatedly violating the treaty by allowing radioactive materials to vent from underground tests. See Kenneth Adelman in U.S. Congress (1987: 45).

8. Given the assessment, the Reagan administration chose not to use the SCC to overcome differences in interpreting the SALT II Treaty. Although the SCC addressed concerns about treaty compliance effectively through much of the 1970s—questions were raised and then answered, data were exchanged, and procedures were developed to allay concerns about possible treaty violations—the administration argued that the SCC was no place to resolve disputes that stemmed from a basic Soviet unwillingness to adhere to treaties.

9. Soviet claims that the radar was intended for satellite tracking—a permissible activity—were dismissed by U.S. experts because the radar was ill suited for that purpose.

10. James P. Rubin and Matthew Bunn, Analysis of the President's Report on Soviet Noncompliance with Arms Control Agreements, the Arms Control Association, March 12, 1987, reprinted in U.S. Congress (1987: 212).

11. Also weighing against such suspicions was the imperfect U.S. compliance record. For example, when the Soviets complained in the 1970s that shelters impeded the monitoring of U.S. silos by Soviet satellite in violation of the SALT I Treaty, the United States was slow to respond and then reduced the size of the shelters rather than doing away with them completely. For U.S. policymakers, it seems, (pure) U.S. intentions were key to excusing U.S. violations of the agreement (for instance, if the shelters were designed to protect workers against the elements); (suspicious) Soviet actions were sufficient to impugn Soviet intent ("a violation is a violation").

12. To quote one expert, "The overall pattern on both sides was clearly one of compliance rather than noncompliance" (Duffy 1988: 272–273).

13. Its flight-testing (in violation of the treaty) would not occur until after the SALT II Treaty was set to expire (Sartori 1985/86: 156–157).

14. In that vein, Reagan even offered to share U.S. defensive technology with the Soviet Union though, given the military sensitivity of the technology, that possibility was not a serious subject of debate.

15. For this debate, see the testimony and submissions of Abraham D. Sofaer, legal advisor to the Department of State, in defense of the administration's position and Gerald C. Smith and John B. Rhinelander in opposition to that position in U.S. Senate (1985: 135–270).

16. Accordingly, they noted that D does not specifically reference "land-based" technologies and is unnecessary ("superfluous" and "redundant") if meant to augment Article III, as administration critics claimed: the article limits ABM systems to certain sites and restricts their composition to a list of traditional components—mainly, launchers, missiles, and radar.

17. That position was accepted by some within the Department of Defense (Melvin Laird in U.S. Senate 1985: 235).

18. In moving into testing and deployment, they would have to contend with potential violations of multiple treaties. For instance, orbiting hydrogen bombs in space to power an X-ray laser that could destroy Soviet warheads would violate the Outer Space Treaty, and the testing of any such weapon in space would violate the Limited Test Ban Treaty.

19. These counters included spinning a missile upon launch or coating it with reflective paint to defeat boost-phase destruction by laser, employing decoys and chaff to confuse and overwhelm detection systems in the weightlessness of outer space, destroying vulnerable radar installations, and varying the warhead trajectory upon atmospheric reentry.

20. Remarks and Question and Answer Session before the North Atlantic Assembly, San Francisco, California, October 14, 1985, reprinted in U.S. Senate (1985: 156–157).

21. That U.S. policymakers were preoccupied with Soviet defensive achievements effectively communicated that point.

22. The proposal reflected the administration's sentiment that MX missiles (and other improvement to the triad) were necessary for U.S. national security—a view unchanged by the emerging consensus that the United States needed to acquire a small, mobile single-warhead missile to reduce U.S. exposure to a Soviet first-strike attack (Talbott 1985: 302, 315).

23. Although the system was not fully automated, the training of these officers would presumably predispose them toward a positive launch decision. See also Bruce G. Blair, We Keep Building Nukes for All the Wrong Reasons, *Washington Post*, May 25, 2003, B1.

24. U.S. officials also voiced concern about Soviet heavy aircraft (for instance, the Backfire bomber), which were not counted against totals in prior arms control agreements, and Soviet shorter-range missiles (the SS-12 and SS-22) that could target NATO facilities.

25. With the deployment of the first U.S. missile in December 1983, the Soviets had already deployed hundreds of SS-20s.

26. The compromise involved one hundred Soviet INF warheads in Asia and one hundred U.S. INF warheads deployed within the United States (U.S. Senate 1988b: 20).

27. The inclusion of shorter-range missiles benefited the United States because it did not then have such missiles in Europe. After the INF treaty was negotiated, Germany stated its willingness to dismantle its shorter-range (Pershing IA) missiles, with their U.S.-supplied and -controlled warheads, once the United States and Soviet Union had eliminated their systems.

28. The treaty included a right to withdraw, with six months' notice, under extraordinary circumstances related to the treaty.

29. The Soviet leadership had actually changed three times since the start of the negotiations. The Soviet presidency passed from Leonid Brezhnev to Yuri Andropov to Konstantin Chernenko to Mikhail Gorbachev.

30. The harder and softer views were articulated, most notably, by Richard Perle and Richard Burt, respectively, from their positions in the Departments of Defense and State (Talbott 1985: 209).

31. With the INF Treaty, the United States still retained thousands of nuclear warheads in Europe for use by aircraft, short-range missiles, and artillery.

32. In fact, U.S. employment in the European theater of conventionally armed cruise missiles, which were indistinguishable from nuclear-armed missiles, could well have provoked a Soviet nuclear response.

33. Thus, some linkage advocates voiced concerns that the destruction of U.S. intermediate-range missiles would dissolve an essential tie that bound U.S. strategic forces to Europe's defense. Eugene Rostow, who had served as Reagan's ACDA director, argued that given the unfavorable U.S.-Soviet strategic balance, the United States would be hurt

politically and psychologically by the fact of withdrawing its missiles from Europe (U.S. Senate 1988a: 3:385).

34. War-fighters maintained, instead, that missile defenses would increase the credibility of the U.S. promise to defend Europe by protecting the United States against Soviet retaliation.

35. Indeed, the United States maintained 1,700 nuclear bombs in Europe that could be dropped from aircraft (U.S. Senate 1988b: 27).

36. On this point, Schlesinger confessed that he was perplexed by the "damned if you do and damned if you don't" relationship (my words) between U.S. nuclear weapons deployment in Europe and the coupling and decoupling of U.S. strategic nuclear guarantee to deterrence in the European theater (U.S. Senate 1988c: 142).

37. Adding to the confusion, General Bernard Rogers, who served as Supreme Allied Commander in Europe until 1987, testified against the INF Treaty with claims that the use of intermediate-range missiles, unlike SLBMs, would desirably signal to the Soviets that the United States intended to observe limitations in war (U.S. Senate 1988b: 28).

38. Kissinger noted the substantial flaws of the treaty but supported it, arguing that public pressure (especially in Europe) would force the United States to withdraw the missiles—in the absence of a treaty—resulting in unilateral disarmament (U.S. Senate 1988a: 4:180).

39. On this point, Secretary of Defense Frank Carlucci argued that "the most tangible expression of our military commitment in Europe is not nuclear missiles, but the presence of over 300,000 American troops in Western Europe as a tripwire for American involvement in the face of any Warsaw pact aggression" (U.S. Senate 1988c: 24).

40. Intellectual coherence was not helped when Rostow used the same triggering logic to argue for retaining U.S. missiles in Europe when he believed that U.S. strategic nuclear forces were significantly inferior to their Soviet counterparts (U.S. Senate 1988a: 3:376).

41. This assumption led the JCS to support the INF Treaty.

42. Thus, U.S. efforts to communicate limitations had to be dismissed by the Soviets as a ruse or greeted as a military opportunity. Either way, the result was not promising for those who hoped to avoid a cataclysmic U.S.-Soviet encounter.

43. The Defense Intelligence Agency estimated that the Soviets would store an additional missile for each launcher—yet the Soviets were reporting totals that were hundreds of missiles lower than were obtained by that formula (U.S. Senate 1988c: 69–70, 108).

44. Indeed, U.S. policymakers had feared that the Soviets could add the third stage of that missile, perhaps without flight-testing, to the SS-20 for a quick breakout from the SALT II treaty.

45. Indeed, the Soviets had done so when the United States had effectively reduced the numbers of its warheads with the 1979 (Montebello) deployment decision (see, for example, Senator John McCain in U.S. Senate 1988c: 121).

46. The Senate Committee on Foreign Relations, in its official report on the INF Treaty, noted the discrepancy between the administration's pronouncements that "compliance with past arms control commitments is an essential prerequisite for future arms control agreements" and the administration's willingness to negotiate the INF Treaty without having resolved outstanding Soviet compliance issues (especially the radar at Krasnoyarsk) (U.S. Senate 1988b: 53).

47. On the definition of "effective verification," see Nitze in U.S. Senate (1988a: 1:289). Consequently, Harold Brown remarked, "I don't think there is any operational difference between what the present Administration is talking about and what we meant" (U.S. Senate 1988b: 44).

48. This section draws heavily from Talbott (1985), the definitive work on the internal politics of arms control in the first Reagan term.

49. Michael R. Gordon, Reagan Is Warned by Senator Nunn over ABM Treaty, *New York Times,* February 7, 1987, 1.

50. George de Lama, Study Backs Reagan on Arms, *Chicago Tribune,* May 14, 1987; Norman Kemster, Congress Gets Legal Study of ABM Treaty, *Los Angeles Times,* May 14, 1987.

51. Elaine Sciolino, Schultz Indicates Way to Sidestep ABM Treaty Fight, *New York Times,* December 14, 1987, 1.

52. Within the intelligence community, the CIA (especially its Office of Soviet Analysis) was the least sanguine about Gorbachev's ability to survive the domestic distress that eventually led to the Soviet Union's demise (Berkowitz and Richelson 1995: 37). Compare the judgments pertaining to the impact of the Soviet economy on Soviet strategic prerogatives found in NIE 11-3/8-88, which closely parallels the DIA position, with those produced by the Office of Soviet Analysis (U.S. DI 1988).

53. Perhaps disingenuously, Perle denied, however, that amendments that forced the United States to renegotiate with the Soviet Union would kill the treaty (U.S. Senate 1988a: 3:435).

54. The opponents included Eugene Rostow, who had served under Reagan as director of the U.S. Arms Control and Disarmament Agency, and General Bernard Rogers, who had served as NATO's top military commander throughout much of Reagan's two terms.

55. For a critical view of the evidence supporting this position, see Prados (2011).

56. Simply stated, "without the change in the Soviet leadership, the U.S. strategy of 'peace through strength' would have failed after 1985 as it did before" (Risse-Kappen 1991: 175).

57. For a discussion of Soviet options in the absence of the SALT II constraints, see Sartori (1985/86: 152–155).

58. The administration pushed, for instance, for accelerated Trident II SLBM procurement and the B-1 bomber program, which had been cancelled by Carter.

Chapter 5 • Nuclear Arms Reductions after the Cold War

1. In the fall of 1991, the secretary of defense signaled the end of the Cold War by ordering strategic missiles and bombers off alert.

2. It was named for its two Senate sponsors, Sam Nunn and Richard Lugar.

3. Barton Gellman, Keeping the U.S. First, *Washington Post,* March 11, 1992, A1.

4. Barton Gellman, Pentagon Abandons Goals of Thwarting U.S. Rivals, *Washington Post,* July 24, 1992, A1.

5. For instance, the Bush administration argued that space testing of elements of an ABM system was permitted if the devices were not "components," as defined by their "stand alone" capability (John Pike in U.S. Senate 1991a: 48). Still, the U.S. Congress prohibited the administration from obligating or expending monies for tests, however, that violated the "restrictive" interpretation of the ABM Treaty.

6. The Protocol was accompanied by legally binding commitments—in the form of letters—from the leaders of the Ukraine, Kazakhstan, and Belarus to eliminate nuclear weapons from their territory.

7. A good summary of the treaty and its content is found in U.S. Senate (1992c: 6–11, 103–129), from which this discussion is partly drawn.

8. This refers to the number of warheads to which a given U.S. or Russian weapon system is credited.

9. The alternatives—setting the count to the maximum number that were flight-tested or using a mathematical formula to determine a missile's warhead capacity (the preferred U.S. approach)—produced numbers that exceeded planned deployment levels (Woolf 1992: 268).

10. These include a specified type (for the United States, the Minuteman III; for the Soviet Union, the SS-N-18) and two nonspecified types, for which a 500-warhead download maximum is imposed.

11. On the downloading provisions and limitations on new-types of missiles, see Woolf (1992: 269–271).

12. The uneven numbers can be taken as a Soviet incentive to move toward more stabilizing systems (the "slow flyers") and deference to the relative superiority of the U.S. strategic bomber force.

13. Under the letters, Belarus, Ukraine, and Kazakstan were not obligated to transfer the materials to Russia, though these parties did sign agreements with Russia to that effect and lacked internal means of disposal (U.S. Senate 1995b: 9). On the challenges of negotiating Ukrainian denuclearization in the wake of the Lisbon Protocols, see Garnett (2012).

14. For a detailed discussion of the dangers of deteriorating Russian warning capabilities, see Forden et al. (2000).

15. Nuclear experts generally agreed that Russia would target each U.S. launcher with two warheads to increase the probability of a missile kill but that assigning a larger number of warheads to a target would increase the probability of warhead fratricide, whereby incoming warheads disable or contravene the effects of others.

16. Secretary of Defense Richard Cheney was correct, then, to denigrate their significance: "If they want to waste their resources producing nondeployed missiles, that is certainly their call, but we do not believe that is a militarily significant threat" (U.S. Senate 1992b: 2:123).

17. Indeed, in rewriting the logic of war-fighting, Cheney also appears to rewrite history. In his telling, the rigid insistence on equity in arms control negotiations was a perverse Soviet preoccupation. In his words, Moscow was "absolutely uptight, if you will, about total equity" (U.S. Senate 1992b: 2:140).

18. Risk is a function of the probability and military consequences of cheating.

19. For instance, they sought not to restrict numbers of nondeployed missiles given the larger U.S. stockpiles; they strenuously resisted verifiable limits on sea-launched cruise missiles on which the U.S. military would increasingly depend; and they resisted anytime/anywhere inspections once their potential impact on the U.S. military (and industry) became apparent. Ultimately, the treaty would guarantee only three short-notice inspections a year of "suspect sites" that maintain or produce motors for missiles (see Woolf 1992).

20. For a more extensive discussion of the potentially excessive costs of verification, see McFate and Graybeal (1988).

21. By the end of Clinton's term, the National Target Base purportedly consisted of around 2,500 targets, located overwhelmingly in Russia (McKinzie et al. 2001: 9–10).

22. It was these values that Undersecretary of Defense Walter Slocombe had in mind when he maintained that foreign leaders might "be less risk averse, they may put a very low value on the suffering of their own population and a greater value on the survival of the regime and being able to dominate a region" (U.S. Senate 2000: 25).

23. Even Slocombe conceded, however, that a nuclear strike, regardless of its targets, would produce "very substantial civilian casualties" (U.S. Senate 2000: 20).

24. The treaty was formally called the Treaty Between the United States of America and the Russian Federation of Further Reduction and Limitation of Strategic Offensive Arms.

25. The last U.S. B-52 was produced in 1964, and the last Minuteman III missile was deployed in 1975 (U.S. Senate 1995b: 14).

26. James Lindsay, The Nuclear Agenda: Arms Control and Missile Defense Are Back in the News, Fall 2000. Available at www.brookings.edu/research/articles/2000/09/fall-defense-lindsay, accessed February 24, 2013.

27. In 2001, one rigorous analysis concluded that a 1,300-warhead U.S. strike against Soviet nuclear capabilities would produce around 14 million Soviet casualties, including 10 million deaths, and that a limited countervalue strike would produce casualties in excess of 50 million (McKinzie et al. 2001: x).

28. That these weapons can be hidden inspires concerns about their breakout potential if large numbers are held "off the books" for future use and concerns that their accuracy and prompt delivery, as land-based missiles, might allow their effective application in a first strike on adversary land-based missiles in their hardened silos.

29. To quote Senator John Warner, the chairman of the Senate Armed Services Committee, "The Clinton administration has failed significantly to move the United States away from the lingering effects of mutually assured destruction. The administration continues to characterize the ABM Treaty as 'the cornerstone of strategic stability,' even though it is clear that this treaty fundamentally prevents the United States from confronting new post–Cold War threats" (U.S. Senate 2000: 3). Indeed, some critics—including a member of Senate Armed Services Committee who voted against the START II Treaty—insisted that U.S. concessions to the Russians on missiles defense negated any advantage that the United States could obtain from reducing force sizes under the treaty (see Senator James Inhofe in U.S. Senate 2000: 22).

30. The report was better known as the Rumsfeld report, named after the commission's chairman, Donald Rumsfeld, who would become secretary of defense in the Bush administration. On the report and its political impact, see Garwin (1998) and Gronlund and Wright (1998).

31. On these liabilities of defense, see Lebovic (2007).

32. Michael Wines, After U.S Scraps ABM Treaty, Russia Rejects Curbs of START II, *New York Times*, June 15, 2010, 2; Michael Wines, Facing Pact's End, Putin Decides to Grimace and Bear It, *New York Times*, December 14, 2010, 14.

33. To have referenced the START Treaty as the START I Treaty would have implied the existence of the START II Treaty.

34. David E. Sanger, Nuclear Arms Treaty: The Accord; Bush and Putin to Sign Pact to Cut Nuclear Warheads; Weapons Can Be Stockpiled, *New York Times*, May 14, 2010, 1.

35. This, itself, was not a new position: neither START I nor II required warhead destruction.

36. On facets of the U.S. "commitment trap," see Sagan (2000).

37. On this issue of audience costs, see Fearon (1994, 1997).

38. Button Gaffe Embarrasses Clinton, BBC News, March 7, 2009. Available at http://news.bbc.co.uk/2/hi/europe/7930047.stm, accessed February 4, 2013.

39. Quoted in Chris Baldwin, Putin Says Russia Threatened by "Unipolar World," Reuters, November 4, 2007. Available at www.reuters.com/article/2007/11/04/us-russia-putin-idU.S.L0449803320071104, accessed February 4, 2013. Out of fairness to Putin, it must be said that, with mounting U.S. debt and the downturn in the global economy, he changed his tune. In 2011, he declared that the United States was acting like a "parasite" by "shifting part of the weight of its problems onto the world economy." Quoted in Alena Chechel, Scott Rose and Jack Jordan, Putin Denounces American Parasite while Russia Increases Treasuries 1,600%, Bloomberg, August 19, 2011. Available at www.bloomberg.com/news/2011-08-18/putin-slams-u-s-parasite-after-1-600-jump-in-russia-holdings.html, accessed February 4, 2013.

40. Article VI of the NPT states, "Each of the Parties to the treaty undertakes to pursue negotiations in good faith on effective measures relating to cessation of the nuclear arms race at an early date and to nuclear disarmament, and on a treaty on general and complete disarmament under strict and effective international control."

41. Peter Baker and Mark Landler, Delays on Arms Control Pact Bog Down U.S. Efforts to Reset Relations with Russia, *New York Times,* March 10, 2010, 6; Peter Baker, Twists, Turns, and Anger on Way to Arms Pact with Russia, *New York Times,* March 27, 2010, 4.

42. Thus, Russian totals apparently included no warheads for bombers, whereas U.S. totals included the number of weapons that were stored with a bomber (U.S. Senate 2010: 13).

43. For the arguments, including the minority view of five senators, see U.S. Senate (2010).

44. Peter Baker, Republicans Pose Test for Treaty with Russia, *New York Times,* April 10, 2010, 4.

45. Senator John McCain quoted in Peter Baker, Senate Rejects Amendment Blocking New START Treaty, *New York Times,* December 19, 2010, 35.

46. For instance, hawkish critics of the SALT II Treaty voiced concerns that the temporary limits in the Protocol would eventually become permanent.

47. Peter Baker, Impassioned Senate Debate on Arms Treaty, *New York Times,* December 17, 2010, 8.

48. The issue of the negotiating record was an ongoing concern. It haunted the INF Treaty ratification debate, when the Senate sought payback for the Reagan administration's reluctance to release the negotiating record upon which the broad interpretation of the ABM Treaty was based (Nolan 1991: 380–381). On the negotiating record and New START, see U.S. Senate (2010: 61–65).

49. The parties also had the right to inspect nondeployed systems.

50. Critics also noted that the United States was entitled to the same number of inspections as the Russians despite their larger number of facilities. But one could argue that this was a Russian advantage only if the United States planned to cheat on the treaty.

51. Indeed, supporters argued that the cost of the conversion and elimination requirements under the START Treaty was forcing the United States to keep certain weapons in the active inventory, rather than replace them.

52. Statement by Air Force Lt. Gen. James R. Clapper Jr. George Lardner Jr., Republics' Procurement of Arms Said to Plunge, *Washington Post,* January 23, 1992, A20.

53. Senator Helms's Bargaining Chips, *New York Times,* August 28, 1995, A14.

54. Michael R. Gordon, U.S. Proposes Deeper Cuts in Atom Arms to Russians, *New York Times,* March 9, 1997, 9.

55. Michael Gordon, In a New Era, U.S. and Russia Bicker over an Old Issue, *New York Times,* April 25, 2000, A1.

56. Thomas W. Lippman, Clinton, Yeltsin Agree on Arms Cuts and NATO, *Washington Post,* March 22, 1997, A1.

57. Elizabeth Becker and Eric Schmitt, G.O.P. Senators Tell Clinton They Oppose Him on ABM Treaty and Defense System, *New York Times,* April 22, 2000, A1.

58. The blockage of the test ban treaty stemmed from Republican concerns that the United States would be prevented from conducting tests to ascertain the reliability, or to engage in the modernization, of U.S. warheads when U.S. adversaries were not similarly bound due to inadequate sensors to monitor global compliance.

59. Eric Schmitt, Pentagon Feels Pressure to Cut Out More Warheads, *New York Times,* May 11, 2000, A12.

60. James Dao, U.S.-Russia Atomic Arms Pact Wins Senate Panel's Backing, *New York Times,* February 6, 2003, 13.

61. Mary Beth Sheridan and Walter Pincus, Obama Must Decide Degree to Which U.S. Swears Off Nuclear Weapons, *Washington Post,* March 6, 2010.

62. Peter Baker, Senate Rejects Amendment Blocking New START Treaty, *New York Times,* December 19, 2010, 35; Jennifer Steinhauer, Fate of Arms Treaty Tied to Policy on Gays, *New York Times,* December 17, 2010, A12.

63. Peter Baker, Arms Pact Passes One Test as Senate Acts to Debate It, *New York Times,* December 16, 2010, 10.

64. See Jon Kyl, The New START Treaty: Time for a Careful Look, *Wall Street Journal,* July 8, 2010.

65. On the lineup of opponents and supporters, see Peter Baker, Senate Passes Arms Control Treaty with Russia, 71–26, *New York Times,* December 23, 2010.

66. See John R. Bolton and Paula A. DeSutter, A Cold War Missile Treaty That's Doing Us Harm, *Wall Street Journal,* August 15, 2011.

REFERENCES

Adelman, Kenneth L. 1984. Arms Control with and without Agreements. *Foreign Affairs* 63(2): 240–263.

Alperovitz, Gar. 1965. *Atomic Diplomacy: Hiroshima and Potsdam*. New York: Vintage Books.

Arkin, William M. 2000. The SIOP—Forever Immoral. *Bulletin of the Atomic Scientists* 56(5): 72.

Arms Control Association, 2002. Parsing the Nuclear Posture Review. *Arms Control Today* 32 (March). Available at www.armscontrol.org/act/2002_03/panelmarch02.

Axelrod, Robert. 1984. *The Evolution of Cooperation*. New York: Basic Books.

Ball, Desmond. 1980. *Politics and Force Levels: The Strategic Missile Program of the Kennedy Administration*. Berkeley: University of California Press.

———. 1982/83. U.S. Strategic Forces: How Would They Be Used? *International Security* 7(3): 31–60.

Ball, Desmond, and Robert C. Toth. 1990. Revising the SIOP: Taking War-Fighting to Dangerous Extremes. *International Security* 14(4): 65–92.

Berkowitz, Bruce D., and Jeffrey T. Richelson. 1995. The CIA Vindicated: The Soviet Collapse *Was* Predicted. *National Interest* 41 (Fall): 36–47.

Bernstein, Barton J. 1975. Roosevelt, Truman, and the Atomic Bomb, 1941–1945. *Political Science Quarterly* 90(1): 23–69.

———. 1989. Crossing the Rubicon: A Missed Opportunity to Stop the H-Bomb. *International Security* 14(2): 132–160.

———. 1991. Eclipsed by Hiroshima and Nagasaki: Early Thinking about Tactical Nuclear Weapons. *International Security* 15(4): 149–173.

———. 1995. Understanding the Atomic Bomb and the Japanese Surrender: Missed Opportunities, Little-Known Near Disasters, and Modern Memory. *Diplomatic History* 19(2): 227–272.

Bertram, Christoph. 1981/82. Nuclear Weapons in the 1980s: The Implications of Theater Nuclear Weapons in Europe. *Foreign Affairs* 60(2): 305–326.

Betts, Richard K. 2003. Politicization of Intelligence: Costs and Benefits. In *Paradoxes of Strategic Intelligence*, ed. R. K. Betts and T. G. Mahnken. London: Frank Cass.

Blacker, Coit, D. 1987. *Reluctant Warriors: The United States, Soviet Union, and Arms Control*. New York: W. H. Freeman.

Broscious, S. David. 1999. Longing for International Control, Banking on American Superiority: Harry S. Truman's Approach to Nuclear Weapons. In *Cold War Statesmen Confront the Bomb: Nuclear Diplomacy since 1945*, ed. John Lewis Gaddis, Philip H. Gordon, Ernest R. May, and Jonathan Rosenberg. Oxford, UK: Oxford University Press.

Brosius, Hans-Bernd, and Anke Bathelt. 1994. The Utility of Exemplars in Persuasive Communications. *Communication Research* 21(1): 48–78.

Brown, Harold. 1983. *Thinking about National Security: Defense and Foreign Policy in a Dangerous World*. Boulder, CO: Westview.

Brzezinski, Zbigniew. 2012. *Strategic Vision: America and the Crisis of Global Power*. New York: Basic Books.

Burr, William. 2005. The Nixon Administration, the "Horror Strategy," and the Search for Limited Nuclear Options, 1969–1972. *Journal of Cold War Studies* 7(3): 34–78.

Burr, William, and Jeffrey T. Richelson. 2000/01. Whether to "Strangle the Baby in the Cradle." *International Security* 25(3): 54–99.

Burr, William, and Svetlana Savranskaya, eds. 2009. Previously Classified Interviews with Former Soviet Officials Reveal U.S. Strategic Intelligence Failure over Decades. Available at www.gwu.edu/~nsarchiv/nukevault/ebb285.

Bush, George W. 2002a. *The National Security Strategy of the United States of America*. Available at www.whitehouse.gov/nsc/nss.pdf.

———. 2002b. *National Strategy to Combat Weapons of Mass Destruction*. Available at www.whitehouse.gov/news/releases/2002/12/WMDStrategy.pdf.

———. 2006. *The National Security Strategy of the United States of America*. Available at www.whitehouse.gov/nsc/nss/2006/nss2006.pdf.

Cahn, Anne H. 1998. *Killing Detente: The Right Attacks the CIA*. State College: Pennsylvania State University Press.

Caldwell, Dan. 1991. The SALT II Treaty. In *The Politics of Arms Control Treaty Ratification*, ed. Michael Krepon and Dan Caldwell. New York: St. Martin's Press.

Chayes, Antonia Handler, and Abram Chayes. 1990. From Law Enforcement to Dispute Settlement: A New Approach to Arms Control Verification and Compliance. *International Security* 14(4): 147–164.

Claude, Inis L., Jr. 1984. *Swords into Plowshares: The Problems and Process of International Organization*. New York: McGraw-Hill.

Cote, Owen R., Jr. 2003. *The Third Battle: Innovation in the Navy's Silent Cold War Struggle with Soviet Submarines*. Newport Paper #16. Newport, RI: U.S. Naval War College Press.

Craig, Campbell, and Sergey Radchenko. 2008. *The Atomic Bomb and the Origins of the Cold War*. New Haven: Yale University Press.

Daalder, Ivo H., and I. M. Destler. 2009. *In the Shadow of the Oval Office: Profiles of the National Security Advisers and the Presidents They Served from JFK to George W. Bush*. New York: Simon and Schuster.

Davis, Lynn E. 1975. Limited Nuclear Options: Deterrence and the New American Doctrine. *Adelphi Paper* No. 121. London: International Institute for Strategic Studies.

———. 1988. Lessons of the INF Treaty. *Foreign Affairs* 66(4): 720–734.

DeSutter, Paula A. 2010. Verification and the New START Treaty. *Heritage Lecture* No. 1160. (July 12). Washington, DC: Heritage Foundation.

Divine, Robert A. 1978. *Blowing on the Wind: The Nuclear Test Ban Debate, 1954–1960*. New York: Oxford University Press.

Dower, John W. 2010. *Cultures of War.* New York: W. W. Norton.

Duffy, Gloria. 1988. Conditions that Affect Arms Control Compliance. In *U.S.-Soviet Security Cooperation: Achievements, Failures, Lessons,* ed. Alexander L. George, Philip J. Farley, and Alexander Dallin. New York: Oxford University Press.

Dunn, Lewis A. 1990. Arms Control Verification: Living with Uncertainty. *International Security* 14(4): 165–175.

Earle, Ralph, II. 1989. The Political Environment. In *Defending Deterrence: Managing the ABM Treaty Regime into the 21st Century,* ed. Antonia Handler Chayes and Paul Doty. Washington, DC: Pergamon-Brassey's.

Eden, Lynn. 2004. *Whole World on Fire: Organizations, Knowledge, and Nuclear Weapons Devastation.* Ithaca, NY: Cornell University Press.

Fearon, James D. 1994. Domestic Political Audiences and the Escalation of International Disputes. *American Political Science Review* 88(3): 577–592.

———. 1997. Signaling Foreign Policy Interests: Tying Hands Versus Sinking Costs. *Journal of Conflict Resolution* 41(1): 68–90.

Feiveson, Harold A., and John Duffield. 1984. Stopping the Sea-Based Counterforce Threat. *International Security* 9(1): 285–300.

Finel, Bernard I., and Kristin M. Lord. 1999. The Surprising Logic of Transparency. *International Studies Quarterly* 43(2): 315–339.

Firestone, Bernard J. 1999. Kennedy and the Test Ban: Presidential Leadership and Arms Control. In *John F. Kennedy and Europe,* ed. Douglas Brinkley and Richard T. Griffiths. Baton Rouge: Louisiana State University Press.

Forden, Geoffrey, Pavel Podvig, and Theodore A. Postol. 2000. False Alarm, Nuclear Danger. *IEEE Spectrum* 37(3): 31–39.

Freedman, Lawrence. 1977. *U.S. Intelligence and the Soviet Strategic Threat.* Boulder, CO: Westview.

———. 2004. *Deterrence.* Cambridge, UK: Polity Press.

Friedberg, Aaron L. 1980. A History of the U.S. Strategic "Doctrine"—1945 to 1980. *Journal of Strategic Studies* 3(3): 37–71.

Garnett, Sherman W. 2012. The "Model" of Ukrainian Denuclearization. In *Security Assurances and Nuclear Nonproliferation,* ed. Jeffrey W. Knopf. Stanford, CA: Stanford University Press.

Garthoff, Raymond L. 1978. On Estimating and Imputing Intentions. *International Security* 2(3): 22–32.

———. 1983. The NATO Decision on Theater Nuclear Forces. *Political Science Quarterly* 98(2): 197–214.

———. 1990. *Deterrence and the Revolution in Soviet Military Doctrine.* Washington, DC: Brookings Institution.

Garwin, Richard L. 1998. The Rumsfeld Report: What We Did. *Bulletin of the Atomic Scientists* 54(6): 40–45.

Gates, Robert. 2010. *Nuclear Posture Review Report.* Available at www.defense.gov/npr.

Gavin, Francis. 2012. *Nuclear Stalemate: History and Strategy in America's Atomic Age.* Ithaca, NY: Cornell University Press.

Gelber, Harry G. 1974. Technical Innovation and Arms Control. *World Politics* 26(4): 509–541.

Glaser, Charles, L. 1989. Why Do Strategists Disagree about the Requirements of Strategic Nuclear Deterrence? In *Nuclear Arguments: Understanding the Strategic Nuclear*

Arms and Arms Control Debates, ed. Lynn Eden and Steven E. Miller. Ithaca, NY: Cornell University Press.

———. 1997. The Security Dilemma Revisited. *World Politics* 50(1): 171–201.

———. 2010. *Rational Theory of International Politics: The Logic of Competition and Cooperation*. Princeton, NJ: Princeton University Press.

Glasser, Robert D. 1992. Enduring Misconceptions of Strategic Stability: The Role of Nuclear Missile-Carrying Submarines. *Journal of Peace Research* 29(1): 23–37.

Goldgeier, James M. 1999. *Not Whether But When: The U.S. Decision to Enlarge NATO*. Washington, DC: Brookings Institution.

Gordin, Michael D. 2009. *Red Cloud at Dawn: Truman, Stalin, and the End of the Atomic Monopoly*. New York: Farrar Straus and Giroux.

Gray, Colin S. 1979. Nuclear Strategy: A Case for a Theory of Victory. *International Security* 4(1): 54–87.

Gray, Colin S., and Keith Payne. 1980. Victory Is Possible. *Foreign Policy* 39 (Summer): 14–27.

Greene, Benjamin P. 2003. Eisenhower, Science, and the Nuclear Test Ban Debate, 1953–56. *Journal of Strategic Studies* 26(4): 156–185.

———. 2007. *Eisenhower, Science Advice, and the Nuclear Test-Ban Debate, 1945–1963*. Stanford, CA: Stanford University Press.

Greenwood, Ted. 1975. *Making the MIRV: A Study of Defense Decision Making*. Cambridge, MA: Ballinger.

Gronlund, Lisbeth, and David Wright. 1998. What They Didn't Do. *Bulletin of the Atomic Scientists* 54(6): 46–51.

Grynaviski, Eric. 2010. Necessary Illusions: Misperception, Cooperation, and the Anti-Ballistic Missile Treaty. *Security Studies* 19(3): 376–406.

Guertner, Gary L. 1988. Three Images of Soviet Arms Control Compliance. *Political Science Quarterly* 103(2): 321–346.

Halsted, Thomas A. 1971. Lobbying against the ABM, 1967–1970. *Bulletin of the Atomic Scientists* (April): 23–28.

Hewlett, Richard G., and Jack M. Holl. 1989. *Atoms for Peace and War, 1953–1961: Eisenhower and the Atomic Energy Commission*. Berkeley: University of California Press.

Hixson, Walter L. 2003. *The American Experience in World War II: The Atomic Bomb in History and Memory*. New York: Routledge.

Hoffman, Aaron M. 2006. *Building Trust: Overcoming Suspicion in International Conflict*. Albany: State University of New York Press.

Hoffman, David E. 2009. *The Dead Hand: The Untold Story of the Cold War Arms Race and Its Dangerous Legacy*. New York: Doubleday.

Holdren, John P. 1986. The Dynamics of the Nuclear Arms Race: History, Status, Prospects. In *Nuclear Weapons and the Future of Humanity: The Fundamental Questions*, ed. Avner Cohen and Steven Lee. Totowa, NJ: Rowman and Allanheld.

Holloway, David. 1994. *Stalin and the Bomb: The Soviet Union and Atomic Energy, 1939–56*. New Haven, CT: Yale University Press.

Huntington, Samuel P. 1999. The Lonely Superpower. *Foreign Affairs* 78(2): 35–49.

Jacobson, Harold Karan. 1964. The Test-Ban Negotiations: Implications for the Future. *Annals of the American Academy of Political and Social Science* (351): 92–101.

Jervis, Robert. 1976. *Perception and Misperception in International Politics*. Princeton, NJ: Princeton University Press.

———. 1978. Cooperation under the Security Dilemma. *World Politics* 30(2): 167–214.

———. 1982/83. Deterrence and Perception. *International Security* 7(3): 3–27.

———. 1984. *The Illogic of American Nuclear Strategy*. Ithaca, NY: Cornell University Press.

Jervis, Robert, Richard Ned Lebow, and Janice Gross Stein, eds. 1985. *Psychology and Deterrence*. Baltimore, MD: Johns Hopkins University Press.

Kahneman, Daniel, and Amos Tversky. 1979. Prospect Theory: An Analysis of Decision under Risk. *Econometrica* 47(2): 263–291.

Kaplan, Fred. 1982. Strategic Thinkers. *Bulletin of the Atomic Scientists* 38(10): 51–56.

Katz, Amrom H. 1979. *Verification and SALT: The State of the Art and the Art of the State*. Washington, DC: Heritage Foundation.

Kaysen, Carl. 1999. The Limited Test-Ban Treaty of 1963. In *John F. Kennedy and Europe*, ed. Douglas Brinkley and Richard T. Griffiths. Baton Rouge: Louisiana State University Press.

Keohane, Robert O., and Lisa L. Martin. 1995. The Promise of Institutionalist Theory. *International Security* 20(1): 39–51.

Kirkpatrick, Jeane. 1982. *Dictatorships and Double Standards: Rationalism and Reason in Politics*. New York: Simon and Schuster.

Krass, Allan S. 1985. Verification and Trust in Arms Control. *Journal of Peace Research* 22(4): 285–288.

Kristensen, Hans M. 1997. Targets of Opportunity. *The Bulletin of the Atomic Scientists* 53(5): 22–28.

Kristensen, Hans M., Robert S. Norris, and Matthew G. McKinzie. 2006. *Chinese Nuclear Forces and U.S. Nuclear War Planning*. Federation of American Scientists and the Natural Resources Defense Council. Available at www.nukestrat.com/china/Book-127-172.pdf.

Kydd, Andrew. 2000. Trust, Reassurance, and Cooperation. *International Organization* 54(2): 325–357.

Labrie, Roger P. 1979. The SALT I Agreements: Overview. In *SALT Handbook: Key Documents and Issues, 1972–1979*, ed. Roger P. Labrie. Washington, DC: American Enterprise Institute for Public Policy Research.

Lapp, Ralph E. 1970. *Arms beyond Doubt: The Tyranny of Weapons Technology*. New York: Cowles.

Lebovic, James H. 1990. *Deadly Dilemmas: Deterrence in U.S. Nuclear Strategy*. New York: Columbia University Press.

———. 1996. *Foregone Conclusions: U.S. Weapons Acquisition in the Post–Cold War Transition*. Boulder, CO: Westview.

———. 2007. *Deterring International Terrorism and Rogue States: U.S. National Security Policy after 9/11*. London: Routledge.

Leiber, Keir A., and Daryl G. Press. 2006. The Rise of U.S. Nuclear Primacy. *Foreign Affairs* 85(2): 42–54.

Levi, Barbara G., Frank von Hippel, and William H. Daugherty. 1987/88. Civilian Casualties from "Limited" Nuclear Attacks on the Soviet Union. *International Security* 12(3): 168–189.

Levy, Jack S. 1997. Prospect Theory, Rational Choice, and International Relations. *International Studies Quarterly* 41(1): 87–112.

Licklider, Roy E. 1970. The Missile Gap Controversy. *Political Science Quarterly* 85(4): 600–615.

MacBride, James Hubert. 1967. *The Test Ban Treaty: Military, Technological, and Political Implications*. Chicago: Henry Regnery Company.

Maloney, Sean M. 2007. *Learning to Love the Bomb: Canada's Nuclear Weapons during the Cold War*. Washington, DC: Potomac Books.

March, James G., and Herbert A. Simon. 1993. *Organizations*. Cambridge, MA: Blackwell.

Marquardt, James J. 2007. Transparency and Security Competition: Open Skies and America's Cold War Statecraft, 1948–1960. *Journal of Cold War Studies* 9(1): 55–87.

May, Ernest R. 1999. Introduction. In *Cold War Statesmen Confront the Bomb: Nuclear Diplomacy since 1945*, ed. John Lewis Gaddis, Philip H. Gordon, Ernest R. May, and Jonathan Rosenberg. Oxford, UK: Oxford University Press.

McDermott, Rose. 2001. *Risk-Taking in International Politics: Prospect Theory in American Foreign Policy*. Ann Arbor: University of Michigan Press.

McFate, Patricia Bliss, and Sidney N. Graybeal. 1988. The Price for Effective Verification in an Era of Expanding Arms Control. *Annals of the American Academy of Political and Social Science* 500 (November): 73–90.

McKinzie, Matthew G., Thomas B. Cochran, Robert S. Norris, and William M. Arkin. 2001. *The U.S. Nuclear War Plan: A Time for Change*. National Resources Defense Council.

Mearsheimer, John. 2001. *The Tragedy of Great Power Politics*. New York: Norton.

Meyer, Stephen, M. 1984. Verification and Risk in Arms Control. *International Security* 8(4): 111–126.

Moore, David W. 2005. Majority Supports Use of Atomic Bomb on Japan in WWII. Gallup News Service. Available at www.gallup.com/poll/17677/majority-supports-use-atomic-bomb-japan-wwii.aspx.

Morgan, Patrick M. 2003. *Deterrence Now*. Cambridge, UK: Cambridge University Press.

Morris, Ellis. 1991. SALT I and SALT II (1972, 1979). In *Verification of Current Disarmament and Arms Limitation Agreements: Ways, Means, and Practices*, ed. Serge Sur. United Nations Institute for Disarmament Research. Aldershot, UK: Dartmouth.

National Academy of Sciences (NAS). 1985. *Nuclear Arms Control: Background and Issues*. Washington, DC: National Academy Press.

National Security Archive (NSA). 2012. Jimmy Carter's Controversial Nuclear Targeting Directive PD-59 Declassified. Available at www.gwu.edu/~nsarchiv/nukevault/ebb390.

Neidle, Alan. 1988. Nuclear Test Bans: History and Future Prospects. In *U.S.-Soviet Security Cooperation: Achievements, Failure, and Lessons*, ed. Alexander L. George, Philip J. Farley, and Alexander Dallin. New York: Oxford University Press.

Nevid, Jeffrey S. 2009. *Psychology: Concepts and Applications*, Third Edition. Boston: Houghton Mifflin.

Newhouse, John. 1973. *Cold Dawn: The Story of SALT*. New York: Holt, Rinehart, and Winston.

Nolan, Janne E. 1989. *Guardians of the Arsenal: The Politics of Nuclear Strategy*. New York: Basic Books.

———. 1991. The INF Treaty. In *The Politics of Arms Control Treaty Ratification*, ed. Michael Krepon and Dan Caldwell. New York: St. Martin's.

———. 1999. *An Elusive Consensus: Nuclear Weapons and American Security after the Cold War.* Washington, DC: Brookings Institution.

Oelrich, Ivan. 1990. The Changing Rules of Arms Control Verification: Confidence is Still Possible. *International Security* 14(4): 176–184.

Oliver, Kendrick. 1998. *Kennedy, Macmillan, and the Nuclear Test-Ban Debate, 1961–63.* New York, St. Martin's.

Osgood, Charles. 1962. *An Alternative to War or Surrender.* Urbana: University of Illinois Press.

Pape, Robert A. 1996. *Bombing to Win: Air Power and Coercion in War.* Ithaca, NY: Cornell University Press.

Paul, T. V. 2009. *The Tradition of Non-Use of Nuclear Weapons.* Stanford, CA: Stanford University Press.

Pharo, Per Fredrik Ilsaas. 2000. A Precondition for Peace: Transparency and the Test-Ban Negotiations, 1958–1963. *International History Review* 22(3): 557–582.

Pieragostini, Karl. 1986. Arms Control Verification: Cooperating to Reduce Uncertainty. *Journal of Conflict Resolution* 30(3): 420–444.

Pike, John E., Bruce G. Blair, and Stephen I. Schwartz. 1998. Defending against the Bomb. In *Atomic Audit: The Costs and Consequences of U.S. Nuclear Weapons Since 1940,* ed. Stephen I. Schwartz. Washington, DC: Brookings Institution.

Pipes, Richard. 1977. Why the Soviet Union Thinks It Could Fight and Win a Nuclear War. *Commentary* 64(1): 21–34.

Platt, Alan. 1991. The Anti-Ballistic Missile Treaty. In *The Politics of Arms Control Treaty Ratification,* ed. Michael Krepon and Dan Caldwell. New York: St. Martin's Press.

Podvig, Pavel. 2008. The Window of Vulnerability that Wasn't: Soviet Military Buildup in the 1970s—a Research Note. *International Security* 33(1): 118–138.

Potter, William C. 1978. Coping with MIRV in a MAD World. *Journal of Conflict Resolution* 22(4): 599–626.

Prados, John. 1986. *The Soviet Estimate: U.S. Intelligence Analysis and Soviet Strategic Forces.* Princeton, NJ: Princeton University Press.

———. 1993. Team B: The Trillion-Dollar Experiment. *Bulletin of the Atomic Scientists* 49(3): 23, 27–31.

———. 2011. *How the Cold War Ended: Debating and Doing History.* Washington, DC: Potomac Books.

Quester, George H. 1970. *Nuclear Diplomacy: The First Twenty-Five Years.* New York: Dunellen.

Rice, Mark. 2012. H-Diplo FRUS Review No. 11. Available at www.h-net.org/~diplo/FRUS/.

Richelson, Jeffrey T. 1986. The Dilemmas of Counterpower Targeting. In *Strategic Nuclear Targeting,* ed. Desmond Ball and Jeffrey T. Richelson. Ithaca, NY: Cornell University Press.

Risse-Kappen, Thomas. 1991. Did "Peace through Strength" End the Cold War? Lessons from INF. *International Security* 16(1): 162–188.

Rosch, E., C. B. Mervis, W. D. Gray, D. M. Johnson, and P. Boyes-Braem. 1976. Basic Objects in Natural Categories. *Cognitive Psychology* 8(3): 382–439.

Rose, Gideon. 1998. Neoclassical Realism and Theories of Foreign Policy. *World Politics* 51(1): 144–172.

Rosenberg, David A. 1979. American Atomic Strategy and the Hydrogen Bomb Decision. *Journal of American History* 66(1): 62–87.

———. 1983. The Origins of Overkill: Nuclear Weapons and American Strategy. *International Security* 7(4): 3–71.

Rostow, Eugene V. 1987. Why the Soviets Want an Arms-Control Agreement, and Why They Want It Now. *Commentary* 83(2): 19–26.

Rovner, Joshua. 2011. *Fixing the Facts: National Security and the Politics of Intelligence.* Ithaca, NY: Cornell University Press.

Sagan, Scott D. 1987. SIOP-62: The Nuclear War Plan Briefing to President Kennedy. *International Security* 12(1): 22–51.

———. 1989. *Moving Targets: Nuclear Strategy and Nuclear Security.* Princeton, NJ: Princeton University Press.

———. 2000. The Commitment Trap: Why the United States Should Not Use Nuclear Threats to Deter Biological and Chemical Weapons Attacks. *International Security* 24(4): 85–115.

Sartori, Leo. 1985/86. Will SALT II Survive? *International Security* 10(3): 147–174.

Schear, James A. 1985. Arms Control Treaty Compliance: Buildup to a Breakdown. *International Security* 10(2): 141–182.

Schelling, Thomas C. 1960. *The Strategy of Conflict.* London: Oxford University Press.

———. 1966. *Arms and Influence.* New Haven: Yale University Press.

Schweller, Randall L. 1994. Bandwagoning for Profit: Bringing the Revisionist State Back In. *International Security* 19 (Summer): 72–107.

Seaborg, Glenn T. 1981. *Kennedy, Khrushchev, and the Test Ban.* Berkeley: University of California Press.

Seay, Douglas. 1989. What are the Soviets' Objectives in Their Foreign, Military, and Arms Control Policies? In *Nuclear Arguments: Understanding the Strategic Nuclear Arms and Arms Control Debates,* ed. Lynn Eden and Steven E. Miller. Ithaca, NY: Cornell University Press.

Sigal, Leon V. 1978. Bureaucratic Politics and Tactical Use of Committees: The Interim Committee and the Decision to Drop the Atomic Bomb. *Polity* 10(3): 326–364.

Simpson, John. 2012. The Role of Security Assurances in the Nuclear Nonproliferation Regime. In *Security Assurances and Nuclear Nonproliferation,* ed. Jeffrey W. Knopf. Stanford, CA: Stanford University Press.

Smith, Gerard. 1981. *Doubletalk: The Story of the First Strategic Arms Limitation Talks.* Garden City, NY: Doubleday.

Sokolski, Henry D. 2001. *Best of Intentions: America's Campaign against Strategic Weapons Proliferation.* Westport, CT: Praeger.

Steinbruner, John D. 1974. *The Cybernetic Theory of Decision: New Dimensions of Political Analysis.* Princeton, NJ: Princeton University Press.

Stimson, Henry Lewis. 1947. The Decision to Use the Atomic Bomb. Harper's Magazine. February.

Stockholm International Peace Research Institute (SIPRI). 2007. *Armaments, Disarmament, and International Security.* Stockholm, Sweden: SIPRI.

Talbott, Strobe. 1980. *Endgame: The Inside Story of SALT II.* New York: Harper and Row.

———. 1985. *Deadly Gambits: The Reagan Administration and the Stalemate in Nuclear Arms Control.* New York: Vintage Books.

Tannenwald, Nina. 2007. *The Nuclear Taboo: The United States and the Non-Use of Nuclear Weapons since 1945.* Cambridge, UK: Cambridge University Press.

Terchek, Ronald J. 1970. *The Making of the Test Ban Treaty.* The Hague, Netherlands: Martinus Nijhoff.

Thee, Marek. 1988. The Pursuit of a Comprehensive Nuclear Test Ban. *Journal of Peace Research* 25(1): 5–15.

Trachtenberg, Marc. 1988/89. A "Wasting Asset": American Strategy and the Shifting Nuclear Balance, 1949–1954. *International Security* 13(3): 5–49.

———. 2007. Preventive War and U.S. Foreign Policy. *Security Studies* 16(1): 1–31.

U.S. Congress. 1987. *Soviet Compliance with Arms Control Agreements.* Subcommittee on Arms Control, International Security, and Science of the Committee on Foreign Affairs. Washington, DC: U.S. Government Printing Office.

U.S. Department of Defense. 1975. *Annual Report to the Congress.* Washington, DC: U.S. Government Printing Office.

———. 1982. *Annual Report to the Congress.* Washington, DC: U.S. Government Printing Office.

———. 1989. *Soviet Military Power: Prospects for Change.* Washington, DC: U.S. Government Printing Office.

U.S. Department of State. 2012. *Foreign Relations of the United States, 1969–1976.* Volume 16, Soviet Union, August 1974–December 1976. Washington, DC: U.S. Government Printing Office.

U.S. Director of Central Intelligence (DCI). 1968. (Special) National Intelligence Estimate (NIE): The Soviet Approach to Arms Control, Number 11-16-68. Available at www.foia.cia.gov.

———. 1970. National Intelligence Estimate (NIE): Soviet Forces for Intercontinental Attack, Number 11-8-70. Available at http://nsarchive.chadwyck.com.

———. 1977. National Intelligence Estimate (NIE): Soviet Strategic Objectives, Number 11-4-77. Available at http://nsarchive.chadwyck.com.

———. 1978. National Intelligence Estimate (NIE): Soviet Capabilities for Strategic Nuclear Conflict through the Late 1980s, Number 11-3/8-78. Available at http://nsarchive.chadwyck.com.

———. 1980. National Intelligence Estimate (NIE): Soviet Capabilities for Strategic Nuclear Conflict through 1990, Number 11-3/8-80. Available at http://nsarchive.chadwyck.com.

———. 1981. National Intelligence Estimate (NIE): Soviet Capabilities for Strategic Nuclear Conflict, 1981–91, Number 11-3/8-81. Available at http://nsarchive.chadwyck.com.

———. 1988. National Intelligence Estimate (NIE): Soviet Forces and Capabilities for Strategic Nuclear Conflict through the Late 1990s, Number 11-3/8-88. Available at www.foia.cia.gov.

———. 1989. National Intelligence Estimate (NIE): Soviet Policy toward the West: the Gorbachev Challenge, Number 11-4-89. Available at www.foia.cia.gov.

U.S. Directorate of Intelligence (DI). 1982. Soviet Spending for Defense: Trends since 1951 and Prospects for the 1980s. Available at www.foia.cia.gov.

———. 1988. Soviet National Security Policy: Responses to the Changing Military and Economic Environment. Available at www.foia.cia.gov.

———. 1989. Intelligence Forecasts of Soviet Intercontinental Attack Forces: An Evaluation of the Record. Available at http://nsarchive.chadwyck.com.

U.S. Senate. 1963. *Hearings, Nuclear Test Ban Treaty.* Committee on Foreign Relations. Washington, DC: U.S. Government Printing Office.

———. 1970. *ABM, MIRV, SALT, and the Nuclear Arms Race.* Subcommittee on Arms Control, International Law and Organization of the Committee on Foreign Relations. Washington, DC: U.S. Government Printing Office.

———. 1978. *The National Intelligence Estimates A-B Team Episode concerning Soviet Strategic Capability and Objectives.* Senate Select Committee on Intelligence. Washington, DC: U.S. Government Printing Office.

———. 1979a. *Military Implications of the Treaty on the Limitation of Strategic Offensive Arms and Protocol Thereto (SALT II Treaty).* Parts 1–4. Committee on Armed Services. Washington, DC: U.S. Government Printing Office.

———. 1979b. *The SALT II Treaty.* Parts 1–6. Committee on Foreign Relations. Washington, DC: U.S. Government Printing Office.

———. 1979c. *The SALT II Treaty, Report of the Committee on Foreign Relations.* Committee on Foreign Relations. Washington, DC: U.S. Government Printing Office.

———. 1985. *Strategic Defense Initiative.* Subcommittee on Strategic and Theater Nuclear Forces of the Committee on Armed Services. Washington, DC: U.S. Government Printing Office.

———. 1988a. *The INF Treaty.* Parts 1–6. Committee on Foreign Relations. Washington, DC: U.S. Government Printing Office.

———. 1988b. *The INF Treaty, Report of the Committee on Foreign Relations.* Committee on Foreign Relations. Washington, DC: U.S. Government Printing Office.

———. 1988c. *NATO Defense and the INF Treaty.* Part 1. Committee on Armed Services. Washington, DC: U.S. Government Printing Office.

———. 1991a. *The SDI as It Relates to the ABM Treaty.* Committee on Foreign Relations. Washington, DC: U.S. Government Printing Office.

———. 1991b. *START: Present Status and Prospects.* Committee on Foreign Relations. Washington, DC: U.S. Government Printing Office.

———. 1992a. *Defense of Defense Appropriations for Fiscal Year 1993.* Committee on Appropriations. Washington, DC: U.S. Government Printing Office.

———. 1992b. *The START Treaty.* Parts 1–2. Committee on Foreign Relations. Washington, DC: U.S. Government Printing Office.

———. 1992c. *The START Treaty, Report of the Committee on Foreign Relations.* Committee on Foreign Relations. Washington, DC: U.S. Government Printing Office.

———. 1993. *The Treaty Between U.S. and the Russian Federation on Further Reduction and Limitation of Strategic Offensive Arms (The START II Treaty) Treaty Doc. 103-1.* Committee on Foreign Relations. Washington, DC: U.S. Government Printing Office.

———. 1995a. *Consideration of Ratification of the Treaty Between the U.S. and the Russian Federation on Further Reduction and Limitations of Strategic Offensive Arms (the START Treaty) Treaty Doc. 103-1.* Committee on Foreign Relations. Washington, DC: U.S. Government Printing Office.

———. 1995b. *START II Treaty, Report of the Committee on Foreign Relations.* Committee on Foreign Relations. Washington, DC: U.S. Government Printing Office.

———. 1996. *Capability of the United States to Monitor Compliance with the START II Treaty.* Select Committee on Intelligence. Washington, DC: U.S. Government Printing Office.

———. 1997. *National Missile Defense and the ABM Treaty.* Subcommittee on International Security, Proliferation, and Federal Services, Committee on Governmental Affairs. Washington, DC: U.S. Government Printing Office.

———. 2000. *U.S. Strategic Nuclear Force Requirements.* Committee on Armed Services. Washington, DC: U.S. Government Printing Office.

———. 2009. *The President's Decision on Missile Defense in Europe.* Committee on Armed Services. Washington, DC: U.S. Government Printing Office.

———. 2010. *Treaty with Russia on Measures for Further Reduction and Limitation of Strategic Offensive Arms (The New START Treaty), Report of the Committee on Foreign Relations.* Committee on Foreign Relations. Washington, DC: U.S. Government Printing Office.

U.S. Team "B." 1976. *Intelligence Community Experiment in Competitive Analysis: Soviet Strategic Objectives, An Alternative View.* Available at www.foia.cia.gov.

Vasquez, John A. 1997. The Realist Paradigm and Degenerative Versus Progressive Research Programs: An Appraisal of Neotraditional Research on Waltz's Balancing Proposition. *American Political Science Review* 91(4): 899–912.

Waller, Forrest E., Jr. 2009. New Directions in Strategic Nuclear Arms Control. In *Arms Control and Cooperative Security,* ed. Jeffrey A. Larsen and James J. Wirtz. Boulder, CO: Lynne Rienner.

Walt, Stephen M. 1987. *The Origins of Alliances.* Ithaca, NY: Cornell University Press.

Wells, Samuel F., Jr. 1981. The Origins of Massive Retaliation. *Political Science Quarterly* 96(1): 31–52.

Wenger, Andreas. 1997. *Living with Peril: Eisenhower, Kennedy, and Nuclear Weapons.* Lanham, MD: Rowman and Littlefield.

Wenger, Andreas, and Marcel Gerber. 1999. John F. Kennedy and the Limited Test Ban Treaty: A Case Study of Presidential Leadership. *Presidential Studies Quarterly* 29(2): 460–487.

Wheeler, Nicholas J. 2009. Beyond Waltz's Nuclear World: More Trust May be Better. *International Relations* 23(3): 428–445.

Wohlforth, William C. 1993. *The Elusive Balance: Power and Perceptions during the Cold War.* Ithaca, NY: Cornell University Press.

Wohlstetter, Albert. 1974a. Is There a Strategic Arms Race? *Foreign Policy* 15 (Summer): 3–20.

———. 1974b. Is There a Strategic Arms Race? (II) Rivals but No "Race." *Foreign Policy* 16 (Autumn): 48–92.

Woolf, Amy F. 1992. *START: Evolution of Selected Provisions.* Congressional Research Service. Reprinted in U.S. Senate 1992a, 2:263–285.

———. 2001. *Arms Control after START II: Next Steps on the U.S.-Russian Agenda.* Washington, DC: Congressional Research Service.

———. 2008. *Nuclear Arms Control: The Strategic Offensive Reductions Treaty.* Washington, DC: Congressional Research Service.

———. 2011. *The New START Treaty: Central Limits and Key Provisions.* Washington, DC: Congressional Research Service.

Young, Ken. 2007. U.S. "Atomic Capability" and the British Forward Bases in the Early Cold War. *Journal of Contemporary History* 42(1): 117–136.

Zubok, Vladislav M. 1999. Stalin and the Nuclear Age. In *Cold War Statesmen Confront the Bomb: Nuclear Diplomacy since 1945,* ed. John Lewis Gaddis, Philip H. Gordon, Ernest R. May, and Jonathan Rosenberg. Oxford, UK: Oxford University Press.

Zubok, Vladislav M., and Constantine Pleshakov. 1996. *Inside the Kremlin's Cold War: From Stalin to Khrushchev.* Cambridge, MA: Harvard University Press.

INDEX